WRITING FOR RESULTS

In Business
Government
The Sciences
The Professions

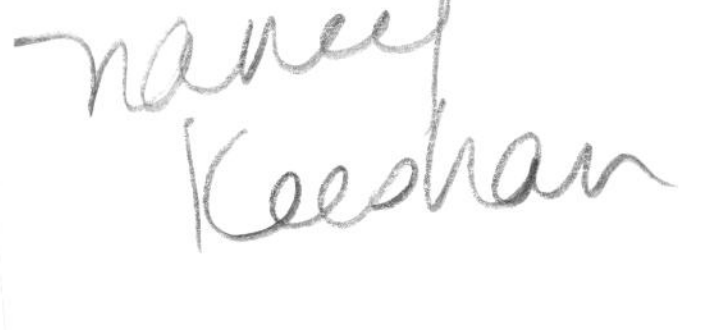

WRITING FOR RESULTS

In Business
Government
The Sciences
The Professions

SECOND EDITION

DAVID W. EWING
Harvard Business Review

JOHN WILEY & SONS
New York Chichester Brisbane Toronto

Library of Congress Cataloging in Publication Data

Ewing, David W

Writing for results in business, government, the sciences, and the professions.

Edition of 1974 published under title: Writing for results in business, government, and the professions.

Includes bibliographical references and index.

1. Commercial correspondence. 2. Government correspondence. I. Title.

HF5721.E9 1979 651.7′5 79-11756

ISBN 0-471-05036-9 (cloth)

ISBN 0-471-82590-5 (paper)

Printed in the United States of America

10 9 8

To Betsy

Preface

Since the first edition of *Writing for Results* appeared in 1974, a great many people have written to me about it with their reactions and suggestions. Many of these comments have come from writing instructors and students. Many others have come from business managers. Many have come from scientists, engineers, lawyers, accountants, consultants. Quite a few reactions have come from government officials, including one whose office was in the White House.

For this new edition the editors at John Wiley & Sons and I have sought to profit from these reactions, to make the present book more useful and interesting. The basic concepts and framework are the same as in the first edition. However, the meat on the bones is often different. More than a hundred cases and problems have been added at the ends of chapters. Two new chapters have been written. Six other chapters have been completely rewritten. The balance of material has been revised, some of it extensively. Many improvements have been made in the format and design of the book. Some sections of the first edition have been dropped.

For writing instructors, these revisions should make the book a more valuable teaching tool. The questions and problems at the ends of chapters can be given as assignments for subsequent classes. The cases—that is, the writing problems described as writer–reader situations—should be especially useful for class discussions where the instructor seeks involvement and controversy. Although sometimes disguised, the cases are drawn from actual situations in business, government, science, and the professions; and, although some ways of handling the case problems are better than others, they lend themselves to no easy "right answers."

The Appendix lists the considerations that might be raised in discussing a case. This analysis is presented to illustrate the range of discussion that should be possible for any of the cases. As the Appendix also suggests, a given case may be useful at several points in the book; that is, it may raise questions discussed in chapters other than the one to which the case is appended.

For the person interested in using this volume to improve his or her writing, the book has several possible values. It contains specific rules and checklists for composition—from a chapter on correct usage to a chapter on analytical and advocacy writing. It contains concepts and philosophies designed to guide one's general approach to writing—from a chapter on psychology and persuasion to a chapter on visual aids. In addition, people studying by themselves will find that a great many problems and questions in the chapter assignments can be used for self-testing.

There seems to be no satisfactory way of teaching writing or learning to write without devoting much attention to detail, putting up with repetition and drudgery, and painstakingly spelling thoughts out on paper. Author Kurt Vonnegut, Jr. once said that writing "is like making wallpaper by hand for the Sistine Chapel." (And then, no matter how carefully you planned, you sometimes find you must scrape some of the wallpaper off and replace it!)

Yet, the aim of this book is to remove one major curse that has plagued writing instruction. This is the curse of litany, dullness, patness, pedestrianism. Good writing—that is, writing that persuades or informs as the writer intends—should be personally challenging. It should be as interesting and even exciting to do as an assignment in marketing or financial analysis or engineering or architecture. Situational analysis, which is the theme of this book, can make it that. If there is one "secret" of the good writer in business, government, science, or the professions, it is—and always has been—an instinct for situational analysis.

I am grateful to many people for their help, but I shall mention only a few of them. Millicent R. Kindle typed the manuscript, handled considerable correspondence, revised the section on expungible words and phrases, and took care of several other problems. Professor Allen J. Rubin of the Graduate School of Business, Pace University, offered a critique of the first edition that I found especially instructive. Valuable suggestions and encouragement also came from Ruth G. Newman. Ruth T. Bennett supplied me with some examples, quotations, and other sources that proved to be quite helpful. Ray Ring contributed two new charts that enhance this volume; he also drew the many charts for the original edition that are retained in this revision. In addition, I wish to express my gratitude to the editor at Wiley, Robert Lawless, who edited this edition and saw it into production, and Peter W. Peirce, who handled some of the questions and arrangements necessary for getting the revision started.

I am greatly indebted to Rebecca L. Ewing for her careful job of indexing.

DAVID W. EWING

Winchester, Massachusetts
February 1979

Contents

PART ONE

INTRODUCTION

Easy writing's vile hard reading.

Richard B. Sheridan

***For we write you nothing
but what you can read
and understand.***

Paul, II Corinthians 1:13

Chapter 1

Improving Our Writing

The media have reported many opinions on the sorry state of writing skills in the United States, but one of the most important causes has escaped attention. Our notions of life in the managerial, professional, and scientific worlds are unrealistic.

Take business and government, for example. Most people picture executives as men or women of action, pounding their desks, exhorting salespeople, dashing for planes, phoning from their cars, negotiating on the golf course, agreeing to major commitments, making big deals. "Neither television nor the movies show [the executive] opening his attache case at home or in the office, sitting down at his desk, and struggling, sometimes for hours, to draft a report or proposal," Michael E. Adelstein observes. "Nor do they show the time and energy that he devotes every day to writing."[1]

[1]Michael E. Adelstein, *Contemporary Business Writing* (New York: Random House, 1971), p. 8.

We picture scientists studying test tubes in laboratories, engineers huddled in front of computer consoles, lawyers advising clients in the corridors outside courtrooms, physicians kneeling by accident victims, accountants detecting mysterious discrepancies in balance sheets. We don't visualize these people, either, drafting reports, rewriting letters, pondering over the rough drafts of memoranda. But they do—and for hours at a time.

If our mental notions were more realistic, we might attach more importance to the art of writing reports, memoranda, and letters. We might allocate more time to writing in planning research projects and investigations. We might not consider writing courses a necessary—or perhaps unnecessary—evil.

And we might save our organizations hundreds of millions of dollars and ourselves endless hours of personal agony, all the inevitable results of mistakes and misunderstandings due to shoddy writing.

For an insurance company a well-written report on a claim investigation often leads to swifter and more appropriate action by management. "Look at this claim report," a manager tells me. "See how clear it is—tells me step by step what I need to know. With this in front of me, I called the person involved and in only ten minutes of conversation saved us several thousand dollars in liability."

For a bank, a well-written memorandum on, say, a credit trend may mean that responsible executives reading it can act at once rather than go hunting around for clarifying materials or interrupt their routines to call the writer and ask for elucidation.

Not without good reason do managers, professionals, and scientists spend so much time writing. As the technical content of their exchanges rises, so does the need for precision. In the old days a chief engineer might instruct his messenger to tell the foreman in charge of earthworks, "Build the dam 10 feet higher and see if that stops the runoff." Oralness was adequate. But today the chief engineer more likely instructs the foreman that, according to the latest computer calculations, a 290-foot-high dam is required to store 71,000 acre-feet of water and control runoff 97% of the time—a message that cannot be entrusted to the telephone, let alone a baffled messenger. A written directive and perhaps a summary of the computer analysis is necessary.

Another reason why managers, professionals, and scientists spend many hours writing and rewriting is the proliferation of colleagues and audiences who should be informed about new findings, developments, and viewpoints. Between 1960 and 1977 the number of managers and administrators rose about one-third—from 7.1 million to 9.3 million, according to the Bureau of Labor Statistics. The number of professional and technical workers came close to doubling—from 7.5 million to 13.7 million. For the average man, woman, group, or team represented by these figures, the number of important linkages and associations is increasing dramatically.

In large organizations, moreover, the number of layers of management and staff work has increased, adding further to the demand for written communications. And it may be essential to communicate in writing with geographically far-flung audiences outside the organization. Thus the American Telephone & Telegraph Company sends quarterly reports and newsletters as well as the annual report to some 3 million stockholders. This one company's financial relations program may send out printed information in greater quantities than all United States corporations did a century ago.

Not too many years ago a sales manager, let us say, sent an important memo on quality to the production chief, with carbons being distributed to the marketing vice-president and the director of purchasing. Including the carbon for his or her own office file, the total distribution was four. Today? "Run off 19 copies," the sales manager tells the secretary. "One for production, one for purchasing, two for marketing, one for consumer affairs, one for quality control, two for planning. . . ."

If one pair of figures tells the astonishing story of the

burgeoning of writing in business, government, science, the professions, and other fields, it is the following: In 1978, according to Dataquest, Inc., an organization located in Menlo Park, California, there were about 2,296,000 copying machines in use in the United States. Dataquest estimated, on the basis of a 250-day work year, that some 420,000,000 images or copies were produced *daily* by these copying machines.

Whether you find these numbers gratifying or horrifying—"Deal with the paper, answer and file it, read it and sign it and send for some more" is the squirrel-cage picture C. Northcote Parkinson conjures up—you must concede that they tell us something significant about the role of writing in work life. Regardless of the cavalier approach to writing that may have been taken by the colleges, graduate schools, and training institutes they have attended, managers, scientists, and professional people are putting a great deal of valuable time into workday writing—and into reading what their counterparts write.

APPROACHING WRITING REALISTICALLY

With this amazing proliferating and burgeoning and spreading and intensifying of written communication going on all about us, it will not do to teach writing by mechanical formulas. The need is for a *situational* approach.

If you are in management, the professions, or science—or studying for any of those fields—writing for results calls for some of the same basic skills you take for granted in other activities. It calls on your ability to relate yourself to an associate, a prospective customer, a colleague, an interested observer in a related field. It calls on your sense of timing and appropriateness in view of the mood, the atmosphere, the "culture" of your organization or discipline. It calls on your awareness of priorities, your capacity to classify, your need to be logical, your desire to be persuasive. It calls on your intuitive senses, your experience in judging and appraising.

In short, effective writing means analyzing and planning as well as doing. It means diagnosing as well as prescribing. You do not order solutions from a Sears Roebuck catalog. You do not follow ten easy steps. Effective writing depends on good strategies and tactics, not just correctly placed adverbs and pronouns. It is playing the Oakland Raiders in the playoffs, not running out for passes in sandlot football. It is multidimensional, not unidimensional. It is brains, flesh, and blood, and a table with people sitting around discussing, not shadows and computers. John Crowe Ransom writes:

> God have mercy on the sinner
> Who must write with no dinner,
> No gravy and no grub,
> No pewter and no pub,
> No belly and no bowels,
> Only consonants and vowels.[2]

Accordingly, when we go to Part II we begin by discussing the question of whether a contemplated report, memorandum, or letter should be written at all. Only with a legitimate purpose and need is there a sound basis for analyzing the other issues.

Next we examine four questions of strategy. How should the document begin? What manner of persuasion, what style of approach to the intended readers meets the need and fits the mood? How can the information and ideas best be organized? If the piece of writing calls for reasoning and judgment, what makes for a sound presentation?

These issues having been considered, we go on, in Part III, to matters of execution and detail—conveying an appropriate tone, developing coherence and clarity, writing

[2]John Crowe Ransom, *Survey of Literature*, quoted in John Bartlett, *Familiar Quotations* (Boston: Little, Brown, 1968), p. 1009.

correctly, and pursuing an effective style. (Some of the chapters in Part III are sequels to chapters in Part II and might be read or taught in parallel—for instance, Chapter 7 on tone in conjunction with Chapter 4 on persuasion strategies, and Chapters 8 and 9 on coherence and clarity in conjunction with Chapter 5 on organization. However, Parts II and III reflect an important difference in emphasis.)

Now, almost every author knows you cannot neatly separate planning from executing. As you begin to write, the document may assume a life of its own. Writing is somewhat like having a baby, in that no matter how carefully you plan and research it in advance, you may learn and experience things from the doing that you never dreamed of in the beginning. Even so, the planning and conceiving must come first. If you begin your letter, memorandum, or report with a strategy, you can learn more about strategy during the doing, and do more to improve both. We must begin with the questions in Part II even though later, while dealing with the questions in Part III, we may see that our beginning notions need revision.

Let me illustrate.

I am looking at a memorandum written by a bright staff assistant in the management information services division of a company. I know from having read the document as well as from the person's eyes that it is a failure. Yet it is an important communication. It bears on a decision involving millions of dollars and the time and efficiency of a great many operating people.

> **Question:** This is terribly wordy. Why don't you say "The computer broke down" instead of "The effectiveness of the computer was believed to be terminated"?
>
> **Answer:** That's not what I mean. You see, the computer itself can still run.
>
> **Question:** Then why not say "The computer became useless"?

Answer: Well, that's not what I mean either. You see, it was useful for the original purpose but the requirements were changed.

Question: In that case why not just write "This computer can't do the job for us anymore"?

Answer: Well, that's what I would like to say, you know, but there are too many people who disagree with me.

Question: We're focusing on the wrong point here, then, aren't we. Why not write instead about the new demands on your computer and just raise questions about its value now?

Answer: Yes. That's what I better do.

Here is a smart and willing person with an important message—not a person who ever could write artfully for *The New Yorker* but one who could write clearly, competently, persuasively for an organization that serves countless customers. However, there is no hope of bringing that clarity and competence out until a sound intention is conceived—sound not only in terms of the facts but also in terms of the politics of the organization. Tactics have to follow strategy.

Now I am talking with a scientist who has studied the growth of trees on windy seacoasts, snowy mountains, and rocky banks. In conversation she is charming and articulate, but the paper she has written is atrocious.

Question: Since you are writing this for lay people, wouldn't it be better to use simpler language at the beginning? For instance, instead of observing that "displacement of the main stem from the vertical is followed by a recovery process from the horizontal or angular in which the original vertical position is regained" why not simply state that after being bent or tilted, trees grow straight again?

Answer: But you don't understand. That is too simple. They don't always grow straight again.

Question: These words say they do, though, don't they? You write: "the original vertical position is regained."

Answer: Yes, but it occurs to me that morphologists will read

> my paper too, and while they will understand if I say it in my way, they won't if I state it baldly, as you suggest.
>
> **Question:** Wouldn't it be possible to say it in such a way that both lay people and the experts will be satisfied?
>
> **Answer:** Yes, but I must change the wording. I must write: "After being bent or tilted, the trees *strive* to go straight again . . ."

Here is another case where unconsidered strategy is foiling any attempt to streamline the sentence, to put some life into it, and, so to speak, to throw out the dead wood. In the back of her mind, the writer is worried about her colleagues in morphology. Although she is writing mainly for lay people, she can't dismiss the possibility that experts may see her document. But rather than correct the picture in her mind, she buries it in an underbrush of jargon. Result: experts may not scoff at her, but no one will read her.

Similarly, disorganization of thought thwarts attempts to write succinct and expressive sentences. The writer who goes from point *A* to point *C*, back to point *A* for a qualifying thought and then to point *B*, then to *C* again for another thought, then to *E* and *D*, and so on back and forth like a crazy Ping-Pong ball—for this writer there is little hope of writing with clean hard nouns and robust verbs. In the wings of the mental stage there is too much disarray. Only *after* the intended audience, plot, purpose, and style are decided on does the writer feel free to use, or feel able to use, plain English.

This time the person sitting opposite me is a graduate student. In conversation he appears to be energetic, sensitive, decisive—a leader. But his paper is full of tired words and phrases—in fact, the sheets even look worn out, like a roller towel in a roadhouse's men's room.

> **Question:** What is your key point here? That is the first problem. You write: "The continuation of inflation appears to be a near certainty. However, it is also a probability that diminution of the rate will occur. However, the continuance of infla-

tion indicates the desirability of continued investment in bonds." You see, both the first and third sentences mention the same point, and there are two distracting "However's" . . .

Answer: The key point is that investors should keep their money in bonds.

Question: Oh. It's not the projected slowdown in the inflation rate?

Answer: Not at all. What I'm doing is making a recommendation.

Question: Then you want to subordinate the first part, don't you? Why not begin by saying something like "Although the inflation rate is diminishing. . . ."

Answer: I'll say "Although the rate of inflation is slowing down, bonds will continue to be a sound investment."

And so I never have to mention the second problem with the paper, which is its verbose, comatose style. Once this writer sees clearly what he wants to emphasize, he makes his point simply and naturally.

In Part IV we see how the situational approach applies to writing for publication and helps amateur writers place articles in professional journals. In Part V we look at what I call the "writer's wheel," which is a way of thinking about the relationships of different needs in writing. Among other things, the writer's wheel shows how matters like correctness, style, and clarity—the tactical details—may affect the accomplishment of a writer's strategy.

EFFICIENT LEARNING

The disadvantage of the situational approach is that it is more involved and takes longer. No claim for "instant learning" can be made; no microwave ovens are available for making a piece of raw writing crisp and tasty in a couple of minutes.

The advantage of the situational approach is that it gets

the results you want to get. It is the *only* approach to writing that works—that can be proved without doubt to work consistently in the real world of the manager, the staff specialist, the professional, the scientist. General B. H. Liddell Hart once observed, "In strategy, the longest way around is often the shortest way home." This is true in writing, too.

From the standpoint of teaching and learning, the situational approach has a further value. It exploits the purposiveness of writing in business, government, science, and the professions. It does the same thing for writing education that it does for the teaching of medicine, law, management, engineering—indeed, of any field in which there is a clear, definable aim and a method of measuring results. It makes objective analysis and comparison of alternatives possible. It does this by enabling us to learn pragmatically what writing efforts have succeeded and what efforts have failed. Without the situational approach—without, that is, a careful look at what the writer wants to accomplish, with what readers, and in what circumstances—we have no benchmark of success. Oh, we can say that this piece of writing fails in correctness, because the nouns and verbs don't agree or because the participles dangle. But perfection in grammar, punctuation, and syntax does not suffice to make the writing succeed in communicating as intended. We can also say that this document has a good measure of clarity and that one doesn't—but, again, clarity by itself doesn't get the job done.

If we can make useful judgments about the effectiveness of a document, we can also make useful judgments about what a teacher has taught and what a learner has learned. For the instructor, the situational approach means that he or she can say, at the end of a course or program, "I helped this class learn how to write effectively," which is a larger accomplishment than, say, "I helped this class learn how to write correctly." The instructor can say, "I helped this class learn how to write *appropriately,*" which is a greater achievement than, say, "I helped this class learn how to write interestingly."

A memorandum on a scientific experiment serves an explicit, measurable purpose no less than does the experiment itself. A report on a financial trend serves as clear an aim as the investigation into that trend. A careful letter explaining a consultant's opinion has as practical a mission as the study and reflection that went into forming the opinion.

Because of this explicitness of purpose, people like my management information specialist, my biologist friend, and my graduate student can respond swiftly and surely to competent instruction. If you have any doubt about this, you can dispel it simply: Before participating in a good writing course, write or revise a letter or memorandum on some assigned topic—especially a challenging or troublesome topic—with pertinent information being given about the situation. Later, after completing all or part of the course, undertake a similar assignment. (If you prefer, you might conduct your "before and after" test using different chapters of this book.) Then ask a capable neutral person to referee the two attempts, or, better still (though it is more difficult), ask a panel of capable neutral people to role-play as readers of the two attempts. In almost all cases the second effort will be found to be superior.

PART TWO

STRATEGY AND SUBSTANCE

The strongest memory
is weaker than the palest ink.

Proverb

A lion roars (one would guess)
because it feels like roaring,
not because it has
any profound thought to express.

C. Northcote Parkinson

Chapter 2

To Write or Not To Write

I once asked a senior executive in a large company, "What is the most important step people in this organization could take to improve their written communications?" Without hesitation he answered, "Not writing them at all!"

He was overstating the case, of course, but a great many people in business, government, and the professions know exactly what he meant and sympathize with him. With written communications, as with almost everything else, there can be too much of a good thing. As a conservative estimate, I believe that at least 20% of the reports, letters, and memoranda going out on a typical day in business and government should not be sent. Some close observers I know would double the size of this estimate.

For managers, professionals, and scientists writing is a means to an end, justifiable only if it is better than or as good as any other means available of accomplishing a desired purpose. The end may be political, such as furthering one's personal interests; it may be social or organizational, such as creating better understanding among a group of employees who work together; it may be economic, such as showing how production costs can be lowered; it may be scientific, such as reporting new meteorological data that may help other scientists understand a problem.

If a piece of writing cannot serve such a purpose, it should not be written. A grade school student once wrote, "Many lives have been saved by the not swallowing of pins." We might change that wry statement to read, "Many hours could be saved by the not writing of letters, memos, and reports." But time is not the only cost, though perhaps the most serious one from the standpoint of productivity. Ill-advised commitments to writing have caused many heads to roll in business and government, have produced countless (and needless) misunderstandings, and have led to much unnecessary anguish and gnashing of teeth.

What is more, writers' motives sometimes come under criticism. Business leader Robert Townsend of *Up the Organization* fame has referred to the incidence of "murder-by-memo" in business. He adds, "A zealous use of the Xerox machine gun can copy down dozens of otherwise productive people."

A few years ago several executives of a New York company collaborated in writing a report to a community agency. The report dealt with a highly controversial social issue, and the executives spent many hours on it. They organized and reorganized the facts and ideas, they massaged the words and phrases so they would sound just right, they procured expert help on matters of style and correctness. They asked every question except the most important one: *Should they have written the document at all?* As a result, when one of the executives was asked about the report later on, he answered, "Did we finish it? I'll say we finished it. We got it typed up on bond paper, bound with handsome covers, and delivered by hand. It was a beautifully executed disaster."

His answer reminded me of a scene in *Zorba the Greek*. When someone asks Zorba if he has a wife, he answers, "A wife, children, a house—the whole catastrophe." We pay careful attention to the appearance and format of our written communications; we work hard on readability, syntax, and sentence structure; we agonize over matters of organization and clarity. But we gloss over the question of when reports, letters, and memoranda *should* be written.

What might we in business, government, and the professions do to end these great wastes of time, energy, and productivity? One good way would be for us to consider more carefully *whether* to write, giving this question at least as much thought as we give to questions of style, clarity, and organization during the act of writing. My observation of wise and skillful writers suggests six questions that should be asked. A "no" answer to any one of them should lead us to banish further thought about putting words on paper.

1. Do I have a clear and practical purpose in writing?

C. Northcote Parkinson and Nigel Rowe tell of the time British Prime Minister Benjamin Disraeli informed Queen Victoria, with obvious emotion, "Your Majesty, I am proud to announce that through a great feat of technology the electric telegraph now links London with the continent of India, and your Majesty's Government is now able to communicate directly and promptly with the peoples of India." Queen Victoria, after pondering this news for a moment, replied, "I dare say, Mr. Prime Minister, but what of relevance does my Government have to say to my subjects in India?"[1]

[1]C. Northcote Parkinson and Nigel Rowe, "Better Communication: Business's Best Defense," *The McKinsey Quarterly*, Winter 1978, p. 19.

It is not enough that our letters or reports vent an emotion or "relieve an itch." There must be one or more persons whom we want to influence; we should have a practical motive for influencing them; and it should be clear to us how we want them to act or think as a result of our communication.

Too often we use writing as a means of catharsis, like the character in an Ernest Hemingway novel who "had gotten rid of many things by writing them." Opening the valve may be momentarily pleasing for us, but what about the harried reader? "Blessed is the man," George Eliot once said, "who, having nothing to say, abstains from giving in words evidence of the fact."

A company once asked for my advice on a proposed report about its activities to control community drug abuse. Several prominent executives in management had spent hundreds of hours and thousands of dollars of company money on behalf of grassroots projects to educate youth on drug abuse, to counsel addicts, and to make the community in general more understanding of the problem. But it soon became clear that the report had no practical purpose. The company had nothing to gain from publicity about its role because the actions it desired were already being performed effectively. In fact, it had something to lose because publicity might create suspicion that its efforts were motivated by public relations considerations, not a genuine desire to help solve a local problem. Management wisely decided not to undertake the report and to keep a "low profile" instead.

In another case the staff of a magazine was wondering how to celebrate the publication's fiftieth anniversary. Suddenly one of the editors had an idea; in John Keats' words, "Sudden a thought came like a full-blown rose, flushing his brow." Why not put out a book describing the magazine's history and impact on readers? Looking into the proposal, the staff learned that a book publisher would be willing to finance the project and hire a good journalist to do the writing. The way was clear! But then the staff began thinking more critically about the idea. To help the writer get his or her material, the editors would have to spend many hundreds of hours of precious time. More important, who would read the book—and what would they get out of it? Might it even seem self-congratulatory to them? If the purpose was to build goodwill for the magazine, couldn't that be done better by putting all available time into the publication itself?

The staff backed off from the proposed project. From the historian's viewpoint, the decision was a mistake; from the editors', it was right.

Parkinson and Rowe compare much of the writing that goes on in organizations with a person making a call in a glass-sided telephone kiosk. The telephoner waves his arm, points a finger, clutches his fist, taps his foot, grins. All this may be good for self-expression but it's useless to the person at the other end of the line. The authors continue:

> Those who sit in head offices may relieve their feelings in letters, telegrams, notices, and memoranda, but these are often as meaningless as the gesture made when we are on the telephone. What people say or write or print often means nothing at all and is not even meant to mean anything. It is merely the bureaucratic equivalent of breaking wind.[2]

2. Am I the right person to be sending this communication?

Sometimes the idea of committing certain thoughts and information to paper is right but the wrong person or group is contemplating doing it. Suppose, for example, that the administration of a college has been at odds with a group of students on campus who feel they are being discriminated against in the classroom and curriculum. As frequently happens in a case like this, one member of the administration, say, an assistant dean, talks at length with the dissidents, gets to know them, learns the facts of their case well, and comes to appreciate the feelings they express. He or she becomes a recognized friend of the minority group, taking its side on all questions. The ad-

[2]*Op. cit.*, p. 25.

ministration decides to issue a statement conceding some of the minority group's claims and announcing its intention to alter its policy.

Should the statement come from the assistant dean? The credit for bringing the change about is mostly his—he would seem to "deserve" the recognition. However, the *dean* is the one who should sign the statement. He, and only he, has the authority to pledge the administration as a whole to make the change; it is his word that the minority group wants most to hear.

Now consider another case. Suppose there has been vandalism on the campus and the dean appoints a fact-finding committee to investigate, with the assistant dean acting as chairman. The committee finds that two of the minority group students are responsible for the damage. In this instance, the assistant dean might indeed be the right person to issue the report. For although he may not possess as much clout as his superiors, he has more credibility because of his understanding and friendship with the dissident group. They cannot claim that *he* was biased.

3. Is this the right time to be writing?

Timing is a critical dimension in all aspects of communication. Just as a joke can fall flat if told at the wrong time or a common observation can turn a whole discussion around if made at just the right moment, so the effectiveness of a piece of writing depends in part on when it is read. Is the reader ready for it, in view of other things that have happened, or is he or she likely to regard it as irrelevant or redundant?

Sometimes the answer requires only a little common sense. If we are preparing a lengthy memorandum on procedures to be used in complying with tax legislation while Congress is debating a change in the law, no one will fault us for delaying the final copy until the solons vote. As another example, once a sales executive of a company showed me a detailed description of some new procedures he had tested for analyzing potential customers' readiness to buy. It was in memorandum form, but only one copy was in existence. "It's a beautiful job," I said. "Why don't you send it around and get some reactions?" He answered, "Not on your life. The vice-president I report to is leaving. A memo on this would kill it in the eyes of my next boss."

In "Case of the Questionable Communiqués," Ruth G. Newman analyzes the dilemma of some plant managers who want to notify employees about the increase in company earnings while making it clear to them it is premature to think about a wage increase. She describes the reaction of a commentator on the case, John S. Fielden, dean of the College of Commerce and business Administration at the University of Alabama:

> Once upon a time a kindergarten teacher had her charges playing with dried navy beans. Suddenly an insane thought rushed through her mind. "For heaven's sake, children! Don't put beans up your nose!" Whereupon half the children started stuffing beans up their noses, wondering why they hadn't thought of the fun themselves.

Mr. Fielden warns that writing to the workers to say, "Things are going well. We are now making a profit. But don't think about a raise" is nothing more than saying "Don't put beans up your nose!"[3]

If the timing does not seem right, we should hold off writing until conditions change, or perhaps discard the idea altogether. If the timing does seem right, we can go on to the next question.

4. Is the written word too risky?

Unlike words spoken in conversation, the written word stays indelibly clear for an indefinite period. And if it is photocopied for hundreds of people to read, it loses none

[3]Ruth G. Newman, "Case of the Questionable Communiqués," *Harvard Business Review*, November–December 1975, p. 36.

of its authenticity, as the spoken word does when repeated from person to person.

Thus writers assume a greater risk of permanency than speakers do—they have to live much longer with their words. They would be fools not to appraise this risk seriously on those many occasions where relationships are delicate, sensitive, or charged in some other way that may lead them to regret their words as soon as someone has read them.

In business negotiations many important agreements are never committed to writing. In such cases the principals know the deals depend more on their intentions than on verbal construction, and they would rather run the risk of forgetfulness or a change of heart than having the secret terms photocopied and leaked to outsiders. But perhaps the best example of literary censorship is organized crime. In the novel *The Godfather* we find no references to file copies of important agreements made by the Corleone family—this was not an oversight on author Mario Puzo's part!

Consider the situation of the federal or state official who wishes to test public reaction to a new idea. If he (or she) is wise, he will send up his trial balloon in comments added to the end of a speech or in a supposedly impromptu press conference—or perhaps, if he is very prominent in the administration, he will arrange for a less important official to toss the idea off in a speech or press conference. If the idea seems to meet with approval, it can be tested further in a more formal communication or through more official channels. If the idea does not take, it can be dropped. For the time being, therefore, it is wise to write nothing.

Personal criticism is another case in point. If we put personal criticism in writing and it turns out that the criticism is based on poor evidence, the communication could haunt us for some time to come. Or, if the words or criticism are taken in a different sense from that intended, they may threaten the subject person or group in a way that our spoken words never could. John Fielden adds:

> One of the perennially difficult problems facing any subordinate is how to tell a superior he is wrong. If the subordinate were the boss, most likely he could call a spade a spade; but since he is not, he has problems. And, in today's business world, bosses themselves spend much time figuring out how to handle problem communications with discretion. Often tender topics are best handled orally rather than in writing.[4]

5. Is a written communication too rigid an approach?

On many occasions it is important that we be able to "feel our way" with our audience. We can do this if we are talking but not if we are writing. For instance, a company executive may have a feeling in his bones that the time is ripe to put "old Peckinpaugh," the vice-president, out to pasture. In a lunch conversation with other executives he might throw the idea off—"By the way, Peckinpaugh is eligible for early retirement now if we want him to leave. . . ." If the proposal is greeted with looks of horror, he can drop it then and there; but if the reaction is, "Hey, how about that?" he can push it further. However, if he adds the thought in a memorandum to the personnel manager on, let us say, retirement benefits, the suggestion cannot be erased if it stirs up a storm.

Many people could offer experiences like the following: Once I was preparing for an important meeting with a group of businessmen in New York. The chairman of the group asked if I would like to outline my presentation in writing so it could be studied in advance of the session. I begged off because there were too many things I did not know about the group's knowledge and opinions regarding the problem to be discussed. If the men were well-informed, I knew I could skip some time-consuming points and focus on the final decision to be made; if they were not, that strategy would be disastrous. If the group had strong biases, those, too, had a crucial bearing on what should be said. Since there was no way in advance

[4]"What Do You Mean I Can't Write?" *Harvard Business Review*, May–June 1964, p. 149.

of testing these uncertainties, I opted to put nothing in writing in advance of the meeting and to "play it by ear."

Nearly four centuries ago Francis Bacon took a more sparing view of written communications than most of us would today, but his observations are as valid as ever:

> It is generally better to deal by speech than by letter; and by the mediation of a third than by a man's self. Letters are good, when a man would draw an answer by letter back again; or when it may serve for a man's justification afterwards to produce his own letter; or where it may be danger to be interrupted, or heard by pieces. To deal in person is good, when a man's face breedeth regard, as commonly with inferiors; or in uncertain cases, where a man's eye upon the countenance of him with whom he speaketh may give him a direction how far to go; and generally, where a man will reserve to himself liberty either to disavow or to expound.[5]

A manager in a retail firm once became incensed about a letter an associate had written to a customer. The manager himself was dealing with the customer, and it appeared to him that his negotiations were fouled up by the associate's letter. So he wrote a memorandum about his grievance and circulated it to all executives at a staff meeting. Tempers flared and lasting ill will was created. "If he had come to me in person," the associate said, "I would have told him I was sorry, explained something that would have relieved him of any anxiety, and the matter would have been forgotten quickly."

6. Can a written presentation meet the need?

The written communication suffers from many inherent limitations. It is impersonal, one-way, undimensional, usually colorless, and unanimated. Frequently, it simply does not possess much-needed qualities possessed by other forms of presentation that may be available such as audiovisual and panel presentations. As a result, the

[5]Quoted by Mary C. Bromage in *Writing for Business* (Ann Arbor, The University of Michigan Press, 1965), pp. 108–109.

shrewd communicator may reject it in favor of other techniques.

Such a decision was made by a friend of mine in the Department of Defense who had the job of persuading defense contractors to adopt a new system for allocating research time, development funds, and other resources. He and his assistants would go from company to company expounding the new approach. Rarely did he count much on written descriptions to put his ideas across—they simply would not have "cut the mustard." Instead, he used audiovisual presentations with frequent opportunities for the audience to ask questions and argue with him. It was vital that he have two-way communication to keep them interested and alert. It was also vital that they be able to *see* certain ideas in slide form as well as observe his own manner of giving emphasis to certain thoughts; and they needed to *hear* the approach explained as well as read about it.

Under its famous golden arches, McDonald's uses audiovisual training machines in more than a thousand hamburger franchise operations to train, efficiently and at minimum cost, employees who turn over fairly rapidly. Manuals and written instructions could not suffice. Again, to explain processes to patients some doctors and dentists use not written explanations but portable audiovisual cassettes that the patient can switch on by himself and operate in the waiting room.

THEY ALSO SERVE WHO ONLY STAND AND DON'T WRITE

For the value of written communications to be high in an organization, there must be a low incidence of communications that never should have been written and circulated. Excessive communications are a form of pollution, and like excessive water or air pollution from an industrial plant, they create all sorts of negative feelings. Early in the 1960s, *The New York Times* did a story on Litton

Industries in which it was reported that "Litton prefers a small staff that is so overworked they have no time to write memos to each other." An organization rarely profits from going to such an extreme, but its motives for doing so are usually understandable. Management is sick of reading "all that garbage"!

Perhaps the first thing a financial executive asks, when presented with a proposal for a new plant or distribution facility, is what the investment will accomplish for the company. Is the facility needed to meet demand? Will it protect the company's market position? Will it contribute to profitability? Similarly, before starting the first line of a written communication we should ask what we hope to accomplish by it. The late C. A. Brown, chairman of the English department of the General Motors Institute, once stated the need as follows:

> We say it as simply as we possibly can, and that is, that a report is a communication from someone who has information to someone who wants to use that information. The report may be elaborately formal, it may be a letter, or in a great many organizations it is simply a memorandum, but it is always planned, *for use*.

Too often business writing is presented and taught as a prepackaged pabulum of instant clarity, miracle readability, and new improved syntax. It is time to realize that this view is oversimplified and inaccurate. Business writing is a far more sophisticated mix than can be formularized in a junior cookbook. It benefits from writing skills—yes. But more important still is an understanding of the writer-reader situation, with all its possible complexities and subtleties, and of what such a situation may imply for written communications.

Some of the best decisions about business writing have been *don't* decisions—don't write it, don't send it now, don't let this person or that send it. We would do well to study more cases of written communications that were never written, rather than focusing exclusively on documents that have been written and delivered. Else we may unconsciously adopt the presumption that all written communications are good, at least if they are readable, correctly phrased, and articulate. A scotch verdict—not proved—should be reached more often in our discussion of the need for proposed reports and memoranda.

"Oh that my words were written!" Job cried out (*The Book of Job* 19:23). "Oh that with an iron pen and lead they were graven in the rock for ever!" Job's cry is echoed in countless offices and studies, for it springs from fairly universal urges and aspirations. But we should take fewer clues from Job and more from *Ecclesiastes*. "For everything there is a season," the preacher wrote, and in his famous list of examples he included "a time to keep silence, and a time to speak."

PROBLEMS AND CASES

1. Describe how the purpose of a memorandum or report differs from the purpose of (a) a short story in a popular magazine; (b) a newspaper reporter's account of wrongdoing at city hall.
2. According to some observers of organizational behavior, many memoranda are written not to communicate information to other people but to record information the writer can use in his or her defense in case something goes wrong. Do you consider this a justifiable purpose for writing a memorandum?
3. You have to fire an employee of your department. Under what circumstances, if any, could you justify communicating with the person only by a telephone call? Under what circumstances, if any, would you convey the bad news only by a letter or memo? When might you use both—and in what order?
4. A well-known consumer activist organization publicly criticizes, in a trade magazine, the safety of a new brake design of a leading automobile. The manufacturer asks for your advice concerning who should answer the criticism in a letter to the magazine. Should the letter be signed by (a) the head of the quality-control department, (b) the vice president in charge of safety engineering, (c) the company president, or (d) another official?

5. A family friend borrows $1000 from you in October, promising to repay it at the rate of $100 per month beginning January 1, with 6% interest added. The first payment still has not arrived as of January 10. Would you get in touch with the person, who lives in another city? By letter or by another method?
6. You are the new director of a hospital that is in financial difficulty. At the annual banquet for trustees and staff members, you are to speak on the goals of the hospital for the next five years, including important changes in policy. Would you have copies of your speech printed for distribution after the banquet and, if so, what manner of distribution (e.g., copies on a table for anyone who wants them, copies mailed out the following day)?
7. Because of an energy crisis, a municipal agency must ask all employees to begin working earlier in the morning. The agency director asks for your advice. How should it communicate the bad news? Give the director your answer and reasons in memorandum form.
8. Of the six criteria described in this chapter for deciding whether to write, which one, in your opinion, is most easily overlooked? Support your answer with an example.
9. In his book, *The Corporate Prince* (Van Nostrand Reinhold, 1971), Qass Aquarius states:

> Suppose an adversary walks into your office with a sudden demand or plan about which you are either uncertain or opposed; one tactic is to ask him to put his request in writing. This gives you time to think about it, makes the adversary think through his position, possibly cools him off or encourages him to modify his demands, and it gets the adversary on paper, which may later prove to be highly advantageous for the document may prove to be his undoing.
>
> As a general rule, having one's adversaries put plans or criticisms in writing is a very sound one. Sometimes merely requesting that a subordinate put something in writing thwarts his entire gambit. This can be either good or bad. It is bad if it stifles initiative or otherwise blocks off sound ideas [page 56].

Write a commentary expressing your agreement or disagreement with the author's viewpoint and reasoning.

10. ***Mrs. Beard's Bombshell:*** While the Republican Party was planning its 1972 national convention for San Diego, International Telephone and Telegraph Corporation (ITT) was involved in antitrust litigation with the U.S. Department of Justice. According to syndicated columnist Jack Anderson, Dita B. Beard, "ITT's high-powered Washington lobbyist," wrote a memorandum discussing the possibility that several hundred thousand dollars in cash and services that ITT was contributing to the support of the San Diego convention would help the company get favorable settlements of its antitrust suits. The text of the purported memo, with the ITT symbol at the top and the words "Personal and Confidential," follows; reprinted from *The Star-Spangled Hustle* by Arthur I. Bloustein and Geoffrey Faus (Garden City, N.Y., Doubleday, 1972) by permission:

DATE: June 25, 1971

TO: W. R. Merriam

FROM: D. B. Beard

SUBJECT: San Diego Convention

I just had a long talk with EJG. I'm so sorry that we got that call from the White House. I thought you and I had agreed very thoroughly that under no circumstances would anyone in this office discuss with anyone our participation in the Convention, including me. Other than permitting John Mitchell, Ed Reinecke, Bob Haldeman and Nixon (besides Wilson, of course) *no one* has known from whom that 400 thousand commitment had come. You can't imagine how many queries I've had from "Friends" about this situation and I have in each and every case denied knowledge of any kind. It would be wise for all of us here to continue to do that, regardless of from whom any questions come; White House or whoever. John Mitchell has certainly kept it on the higher level only, we should be able to do the same.

I was afraid the discussion about the three hundred/four hundred thousand commitment would come up soon. If you remember, I suggested we all stay out of that, other than the fact that I told you I had heard Hal up the original amount.

Now I understand from Ned that both he and you are upset about the decision to make it four hundred in *services*. Believe me, this is not what Hal said. Just after I talked with

> Ned, Wilson called me, to report on his meeting with Hal. Hal at no time told Wilson that our donation would be in services ONLY. In fact, quite the contrary. There would be very little cash involved, but certainly some. I am convinced, because of several conversations with Louie re Mitchell, that our noble committment has gone a long way toward our negotiations on the mergers eventually coming out as Hal wants them. Certainly the President has told Mitchell to see that things are worked out fairly. It is still only McLaren's mickey-mouse we are suffering.
>
> We all know Hal and his big mouth! But this is one time he cannot tell you and Ned one thing and Wilson (and me) another!
>
> I hope, dear Bill, that all of this can be reconciled—between Hal and Wilson—if all of us in this office remain totally ignorant of any committment ITT has made to anyone. If it gets too much publicity, you can believe our negotiations with Justice will wind up shot down. Mitchell is definitely helping us, but cannot let it be known. Please destroy this, huh?

(W. R. Merriam, the addressee, was head of ITT's Washington office; "EJG" and "Ned" both were E. J. Gerrity, head of public relations for ITT; "Mitchell" was Attorney General John Mitchell, later to become a celebrity in the Watergate affair; Reinecke was Lieutenant Governor of California; Haldeman was the well-known assistant to President Richard Nixon; "Wilson" was Robert Wilson, a California Republican; "Hal" was ITT President Harold S. Geneen; "Louie" was Louis R. Nunn, former governor of Kentucky; "McLaren" was Richard W. McLaren, former head of the Antitrust Division in the Justice Department.)

Suppose you are Dita Beard, it is June 25, 1971, and this memorandum, typed but not initiated or sent out, is lying on your desk. Would you mail the memorandum as it is? Would you revise it and then mail it? Would you destroy it and communicate the information in some other way? Would you destroy it and forget the whole thing? Express your views in a short memorandum.

11. ***Disruptive Dissident:*** In 1977 an investigative panel of lawyers and doctors under the chairmanship of Norman

Dorsen, professor of law at New York University, looked into allegations that the Food and Drug Administration in Washington, D.C., had been suppressing honest and well-intentioned dissent from professional employees. One of the leading cases reviewed by the Dorsen panel concerned Dr. Marion Bryant, a physician originally employed in the Cardio-Renal Division of the FDA. Dr. Bryant alleged he had been put under improper pressure to approve drugs that should not have been approved.

According to the Dorsen panel's report, several of Dr. Bryant's superiors felt he was discourteous and disruptive in staff meetings where he disagreed with the views of the division heads. One of these superiors, on October 15, 1973, wrote Dr. Bryant a memorandum entitled "Your Behavior at Rounds and Other Meetings." The memorandum reprinted from *Investigation of Allegations Relating to the Bureau of Drugs, Food and Drug Administration*, April 1977 (U.S. Department of Health, Education, and Welfare), pp. 233–234, read:

> I would like to request that you refrain in the future from disruptive behavior such as snickering loudly at other people's presentations, interrupting without restraint, and heckling colleagues whose views may differ from your own. The common courtesies which educated people extend to each are granted to you, and I would request that you in turn grant them to others.
>
> May I also request that you make every effort to base your opinions on evidence and data. The purpose of Rounds and other scientific meetings is to solve problems through the consideration of evidence, not simply to deal with colorful assertions which attract attention but accomplish little else.
>
> This memorandum is a private communication between the two of us. However, I wish to make clear that failure on your part to correct these problems in the future will result in formal personnel action.

Suppose you are the author of this memorandum, it is October 15, 1973, and the memo is lying in front of you, typed up but not sent out. Would you mail it as is? Revise and then mail it? Destroy it and communicate your displeasure in some other way, or perhaps not at all? Express your views in a memorandum.

If the bugle gives an indistinct sound,
who will get ready for battle?

Paul, I Corinthians 14:8

I don't know where I'm goin'
But I know I'm on the way

American Folk Song

Chapter **3**

Making a Strong Start

If symbols of value were to be attached to the various parts of a report, memorandum, or important letter, the beginning would have to be shown in gold. The opening lines make an enormous difference. Word for word, they deserve more thought by the writer than the middle sections and even the end.

Too many written communications start off with an idea or piece of information that has little to do with the main point as developed at the end. The communications are exercises in thinking for the writers, not efficient transfers of thoughts or facts that readers should know. Many reports, letters, and memoranda actually mislead the reader at the outset. Two prices are paid for such a false start:

Depth of readership. Readers may lose interest and proceed no farther if they do not perceive quickly what the writer wants to say. This reason is perhaps best known to journalists, but it has a nearly universal validity. Certainly few executives, salesmen, accountants, engineers, or lawyers have the time to read to the end of a document to determine what its real message is.

Quality of readership. The communication that opens on the wrong note loses impact. This reason, though rarely cited, is very important to understanding. If our reader does not see what our communication is all about, but gets instead an uncertain, confusing, or misleading notion of the main point to be presented, he or she is likely to miss much of the force of our message. Perhaps the reader will get the idea straight before getting halfway through or reaching the end, but by that time some important facts, observations, or arguments offered will have been blown out the window.

I have seen these failures occur many times in business and government—to the disadvantage of both writers and readers. But you do not have to take my word for it. The principle is easily tested by simple experiment. Prepare two reports with identical facts and arguments, but let one have a garbled beginning and the other a clear preview of the message. Give them to comparable groups of people for reading under time pressure, and test the groups for recall and understanding of the message. The contrasts in understanding should be marked.

Exhibit 3-1 shows the results of a test I once made with about 75 people of comparable age and background. I wrote three beginning sections for a report of about 750 words. The first, which I gave to group *A*, was just a little uncertain and "fuzzy." By the time the readers got to the top of the second page (of three), however, they were following the author; that is, they saw what the report was saying and understood the approach. The second version, which I gave to group *B*, had a poor beginning, one that repeated a few banal observations and suggested a motive different from the writer's real motive before making clear what the writer wanted to say. The readers

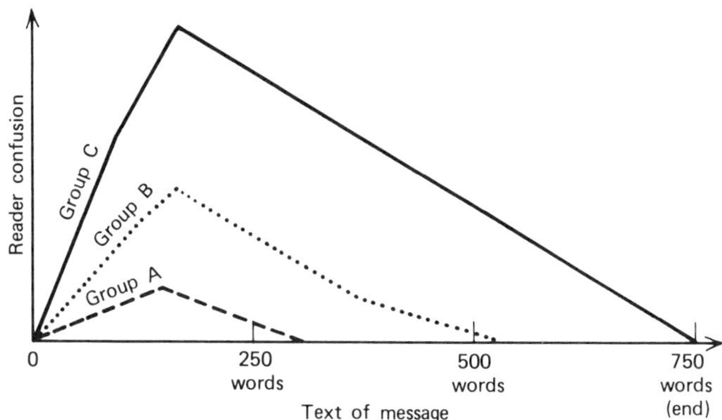

Exhibit 3-I Effect of misunderstanding at the beginning of a message.

in group *B* missed most of the point of the information on the second page and did not "catch up" with the author until the beginning of the third page (500 words into the message). The third version, which I gave to group C, had a very bad beginning, one that raised questions quite different from (though related to) the questions the writer intended to deal with. The readers in this group never did catch up with the author. When they got to the ending, they realized the point was different from what they expected, and so they had to go back and reread the second and third pages in order to understand the actual point.

United States Ambassador to Russia, Charles (Chip) Bohlen, once compared a power struggle in the Kremlin to a wrestling match under the living room rug. The observer can see tremendous heavings of the rug and tell what a formidable struggle is going on. But not until the wrestlers come out from under the rug can he tell who has won or lost. The same analogy is appropriate for the communication that starts out without a clear notion of where it is going. The thoughts struggle and heave in literary obnubilation, but not until the end does the "victor" emerge. "Most of the time I don't really know what the letters are trying to tell me," Albert Schweitzer once complained at his post in Africa. "They wander so, ach!"

In this respect, writing is like many other endeavors, where a common cause of disaster is an initial failure to decide what is to be done. Here are two projects. One of them is recorded by thick, messy files of correspondence, the other by a slim, neat file. Look into the first records of the former and you'll probably find that the project heads weren't sure where they were going and how. Numerous meetings, misunderstandings, and fresh starts were the inevitable result. But check the early records in the file for the second project and you'll probably find a well-defined purpose that led swiftly and naturally into the kinds of action necessary for accomplishment. A poorly started report or memorandum, like a football team that gets off to a poor start, may be saved by heroic efforts at the middle and end, but the issue may be in doubt for an uncomfortably long time.

What illusions often lead managers and professionals to begin in the wrong way? What specific qualities make a good opening? What guidelines will help us to write better beginnings? These are the questions we consider in the remainder of this chapter.

PUTTING THE WRONG FOOT FORWARD (OR IN YOUR MOUTH)

One of the most common misconceptions is that the reader wants a blow-by-blow account of how the writer came to his or her conclusions. When you make this error, you probably do so with the best of intentions. You want to put the reader in your place as much as possible. You have done some research or talked to a series of individuals and groups, and you want to give your reader the feel of what you experienced so that he or she will know just as well as you do why the conclusions are justified. So you lead off with what you saw and heard in the first phase, then you describe what the next series of tests or interviews produced, then you give the highlights of what you learned in the next phase, and sooner or later you come to your conclusions and recommendations.

Business consultant Robert Gunning has put his finger on the fallacy of this approach. "When you read a mystery story, when you go to a movie you hope to be entertained for an evening or for several hours," Gunning notes. "You want suspense. You are paying for it. But when you read for information, quite the opposite is true. In reading for information one resents every moment he has to spend.... Think of that ever-growing pile of reading material on your desk. No one ever has time for it all."[1]

For a specific example, consider the letter that follows (the situation is disguised to protect the identity of the writer). It was sent to a Midwestern magazine publisher by the head of an advertising audit and promotion agency. The firm had been retained by the magazine for about a year. Observe how the writer "snows" the reader with a lengthy recitation of his agency's work before getting to the point.

Dear Bill:

As you may know, this firm rarely sends results of advertising readership surveys through the mail to advertisers and prospective advertisers.

We have been distributing in this manner 75 copies each month in Detroit, 120 in Chicago, 40 in Milwaukee, and over 75 in other cities, as described in our schedule.

In Detroit, the materials are distributed by personnel from this office; in Chicago, by our representative, Winston Walkley; and in Milwaukee and other cities, our affiliate, Vancil & Sons. With the exception of the December period, when the freight strike and other problems entered in, all contact work was completed by the 16th of the month.

Surely you can appreciate that each of these distributions re-

[1]Robert Gunning, *More Effective Writing in Business and Industry* (Boston, Industrial Education Institute, 1962), pp. 3–11.

quires considerable time and effort. To see the key person at such organizations as . . . [the letter continues at some length with names of companies, organizations, and individuals contacted for purposes of distributing the survey copies and findings personally]

To accommodate our growing efforts as described, it would be most helpful to us, if you are agreeable, to increase the supply of survey issues and readership finding summaries as follows: 100 copies to Detroit, 120 to Chicago (same as before), 60 to Milwaukee, 75 to Vancil & Sons for distribution to other cities. Can you instruct your shipping department to make these changes?

Very sincerely yours,

[Signed by the writer]

The publisher who received this letter read it halfway through, decided it was a progress report of some kind, and, because he was very busy, put it aside to look at when he had more time. Not until the writer telephoned several weeks later and asked about the letter did the publisher realize what action was desired. If the request for additional copies had been stated at the beginning, with a short explanation of the reasons, the publisher would have written his okay on the letter and sent it promptly to the shipping department for compliance. Time, money, and bother would have been saved.

A second illusion that gets writers off to the wrong start is the notion they can "think it out as they write it." When you are under this illusion, you begin writing too soon, before it is clear in your mind what you want the reader to think or do. So you flounder around, bit by bit clarifying what it is you want to say—and usually before the end you succeed. But by that time your cause may be lost.

A third illusion is that everything in a truly fine report or brochure is so worth savoring that it makes practically no difference in what order the items appear. In fact, it may even be assumed that the reader's delight will be increased if the many different pieces of information are thoroughly jumbled at the start, like the pieces of a jigsaw puzzle when poured out of a box. This error might seem to be one that is made only by amateurs, but unfortunately that is not the case. This illusion has trapped writers from the most prestigious organizations; some of the worst beginnings to be seen are in documents prepared by well-known media executives and academic officials, who sometimes appear to assume that they should befuddle the reader as much at the start as does a novel by William Faulkner.

A fourth illusion is that a case must be built logically and from the foundation up before the writer is entitled to reach conclusions and make recommendations. So the document begins with a careful description of the purpose and method of data collection, perhaps followed by an elaborate categorization of the material to be disseminated. Care is taken to see that the ending follows logically and satisfyingly from all that goes before.

To the writer of the report, who already knows what the recommendations are, this start seems eminently logical. He must prove his case rationally, must he not? The trouble is that readers, who may be interested only in the possible implications of the report for them (e.g., in case the boss mentions it at the next staff meeting), are likely to see the careful buildup as a kind of exhibitionism—at least until they know what the writer is up to. Or worse, they may never look in the right place for the crucial points.

A fifth illusion is that written communications should follow academically- and research-oriented outlines. In academe the paradigm may call for beginning with a statement of the problem to be solved, then describing the tests, methods, and alternative formulations employed to solve the problem, next documenting the results obtained, and finally presenting the writer's conclusions. (Naturally, the format varies from field to field, depending on the subjectivity of research, amount of quantification, and similar factors.) In a technical or scientific organization the model outline may be (a) statement of problem, situations, and/or need; (b) analysis of how the problem or need developed; (c) alternative solutions; (d) solution recommended by writer; (e) steps in implementation, costs, and/or procedures needed to carry out the preferred solution.

Of all misconceived approaches, this one is most deserving of the anti-Nobel prize. Surely it is important to detail research concepts and background in a technical or scholarly report. But this information hardly seems relevant until readers know what the general conclusions are, and therefore have (1) gained some interest in the methodology, and, more important, (2) acquired a notion of the subject matter so that they know what to look for in evaluating the methodology. For example, if some of the findings seem highly unusual, readers might want to look carefully at the interview methods and respondents; if the findings seem particularized in terms of certain events, they might want to check the dates of the interviews; if the findings seem anomalous or internally inconsistent, they might want to concentrate on other aspects of the approach; if the findings are as predictable as the circumference of a wheel, perhaps they couldn't care less how the findings were made.

I am sitting opposite a scientist whose voluminous and serpentine introduction winds back and forth like a torchlight parade through Harvard Square.

Question: But I say in my introduction that the findings will be reported in Section VII-D. Curious readers can simply jump ahead to that part, can they not?

Answer: Yes, but why not save them the trouble. After all, you are the seller, so to speak, and they are the buyer. It is up to you to make your offering attractive and convenient to read.

But for those who hold the fortress against delusion, life is not simple. In this case, it is complicated by the fact that some well-meaning agencies and organizations re-

quire their employees to follow a structured outline with the conclusions and recommendations deferred to the end. Is all lost in this situation? With a little ingenuity you may still be able to inject a short preview of your conclusions in the statement of problem or need required at the beginning. For instance, I recall a proposal by a government office for a change in requisitions procedure. The writer stated succinctly the problem caused by the procedure, as required for the first section, but immediately added a short paragraph denoting the conclusion: "After consideration of alternatives, it is the opinion of this office that Rule 38 should be revised to read...." Then he proceeded obediently to the sections next required in an official report. Thus he satisfied himself and the government, too.

A sixth illusion is that if the gist of the message is highly controversial or unpopular, the reader should be led to it gently and circuitously to avoid giving offense. The writer feels that, if he or she can somehow put off the unpleasant conclusion and "prepare" the reader ahead of time with sufficient facts and observations, the blow will be softened.

This assumption is troublesome. Readers do not like to be manipulated any more than listeners in a conversation do—and they are as quick as listeners are to sniff out the writer's devious motives. Naturally, it is a good idea to state the gist of the message in a tactful, discreet manner at the onset of the communication. As we shall see shortly, this can almost always be done with a little extra thought. But leave the fun-and-games approach out of writing—at least out of the introductions.

In summary, you need to put yourself in the shoes of your intended readers, when you begin. You have the information and arguments in hand; you see how the points all relate to one another; you see it as a whole. But your readers do not. They will have to see your material in linear sequence, with one idea coming after another. Not until the end can they hope to see the wholeness, the interrelationships and coordinates. This difference in viewpoint is basic to your strategy. The difference is portrayed visually in Exhibit II. As the writer, you want to introduce readers to the "core idea" right at the beginning—in square one—to help them make sense of the rest.

REQUIREMENTS OF A GOOD OPENING

What should the opening paragraph or section of an important report, letter, memorandum, brochure, or other document do? The answer varies, depending principally on the nature of the message, the amount of controversy and surprise involved, and the mood of the intended readers. However, it is possible to generalize on the range of acceptable answers.

At the *very minimum*, opening sentences or paragraphs should clarify the nature of the subject to be discussed and, at least in a general way, point toward the conclusions, recommendations, or findings set forth later. In other words, although you do not offer a succinct rundown or preview of the main ideas you will deal with, you do make your purpose perfectly clear, specify the principal issues or questions you will take up (sometimes these are the same as the purpose), *and* give the reader a general notion of the thrust of the proposals or conclusions you will produce.

When is such an opening adequate? It serves if you do not have ideas or proposals that can be summarized succinctly, if you know that your readers do not happen to need the usual guidance at the beginning, and when your ideas or proposals fly in the face of what readers hope to hear. Here are some specific situations in which a minimum-requirement opening is enough:

- You may simply be reporting on various conversations with suppliers or salespeople whose complaints or concerns vary

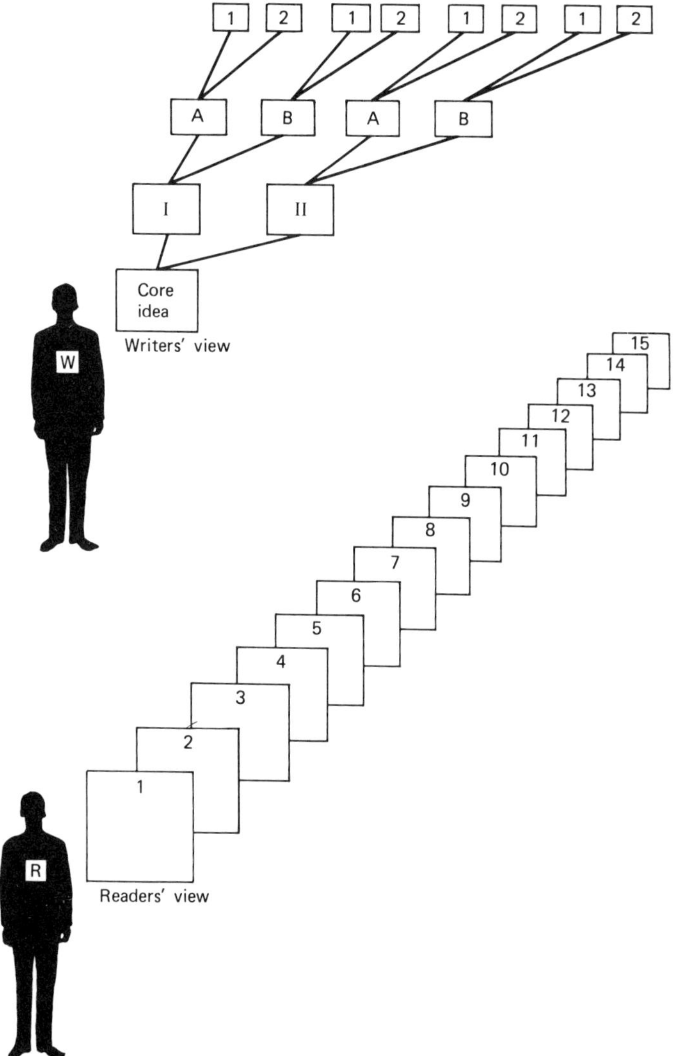

Exhibit 3-II Difference in perception between writer and reader. (Source: James W. Souther and Myron L. White, *Technical Report Writing*. New York: John Wiley & Sons, 1977; p. 41.)

widely and do not affect immediate decisions to be made by the organization. In this case you should make it clear why you are bothering to write the memorandum or report, what kinds of talks you have had, and what the range of opinions is, but it would be silly to try to invent a conclusion or action proposal, because you have none.

- You may only be giving a status report on projects under way, and the prospective success, failure, and problems involved may be far from clear. Here again, you want to clue your readers as to the situation and indicate any important questions that seem to be emerging—and of course you want to clarify your purpose in asking them to read the document now—but it would be premature to try to make a clear picture out of a foggy one.
- In 1964, during a period of a top-management power struggle for control of *The Saturday Evening Post,* one of the editors became greatly concerned that credit was going to the wrong editorial leaders. Getting worked up about the situation, he wrote a letter one day to Walter Fuller, an influential director (and former chief executive) of Curtis Publishing Company. Whether the content of the letter was well advised I do not know, but I think it opened in an appropriate way. The writer was about to offer a long, detailed account of the editorial in-fighting that had been going on, and neither the specific facts nor his general opinions would be welcome news to Mr. Fuller. Remembering the old adage that if you have bad news to report it is wise to keep one foot in the stirrup, he limited the information in the opening as follows: "Dear Mr. Fuller: I write this letter to you—without the knowledge of my superiors—because I share with my fellow senior editors an intense concern. We are afraid that, simply through poor communications, the Board of Directors may be about to make a tragic mistake...."[2] (The editor then began telling about his coming to the *Post* in 1956, the people he had worked with, recent promotions and dismissals that had occurred, confrontations, opinions about the likely course of future events, and so on.)

When is a minimum-requirement opening not enough? It

[2]Otto Friedrich, *Decline and Fall* (New York, Harper & Row, 1969), p. 163.

falls short of the need in most cases when you have findings to report, conclusions to offer, recommendations to make. In such cases, state as fully and succinctly as possible what your main conclusions, findings, and/or recommendations are. Naturally, you cannot be definitive in a short space (at least, if your subject is complex), and, understandably, you may feel nervous about being imprecise, omitting qualifications that are important, and in other ways leaving broad statements open to criticism. But your readers will not worry about these matters as much as you do. They know that more precise, qualified descriptions of the conclusions can be made in the body of the document. In the meantime you have told them what to look for. Now they can read more intelligently and efficiently. They will understand the relevance of any background you proceed to give them next on problems encountered, methods of investigation used, and similar matters.

What does such an opening look like? Let me offer some examples:

- "Compulsory national health insurance would encourage hypochondriacs to monopolize a doctor's time." This opening is cited by James M. McCrimmon as a good one for a thesis of 500 to 1000 words which documents such an argument against health insurance. This lead, McCrimmon points out, is "restricted, unified, and precise." It is far preferable to such an opening as, "There are serious objections to compulsory national health insurance"—which does not specify the objections the author will present.[3]
- "I know of no justification, either economic or political, for any further granting of Lend-Lease aid to Russia, for any agreement on our part that Russia, not being a contributor to UNRRA, should receive any substantial amount of UNRRA aid, or for any extension of U.S. government credit to Russia without equivalent political advantage to our people."[4] This

[3]James M. McCrimmon, *Writing With a Purpose* (Boston, Houghton Mifflin, 1963), p. 40.
[4]George F. Kennan, *Memoirs 1925–1950* (Boston, Little, Brown, 1967) p. 269.

was the way George F. Kennan opened a memorandum to the U.S. State Department in 1945 (Kennan was then serving with the United States embassy in the Soviet Union). In the body of the document he went into various arguments backing up the assertions in the opening paragraph. It is a superb example of an introduction that states precisely the main idea and the grounds of argument to be used.

- "Sir: Some recent work by E. Fermi and L. Szilard, which has been communicated to me in manuscript, leads me to expect that the element uranium may be turned into a new and important source of energy in the immediate future. Certain aspects of the situation seem to call for watchfulness and, if necessary, quick action on the part of the administration. I believe, therefore, that it is my duty to bring to your attention the following facts and recommendations. . . ."[5] Thus begins a document that changed the world—Albert Einstein's letter to President Franklin D. Roosevelt in 1939, informing the President about the practicality of a nuclear bomb and urging him to set up a research project. Leo Szilard, Edward Teller, and Einstein had discussed the letter at some length—over cups of tea—and one of the conclusions they reached was that the letter had to convey simply, in the opening sentences, the heart of the message. They did not succumb to the temptation to let Einstein's name carry too much of the burden; his name would be sufficient to call the President's attention to the letter, they knew, but the text itself must be good enough to gain his interest and create understanding.
- "In my opinion *The Saturday Evening Post* is not in its present form a magazine that is editorially capable of attaining the success we are struggling to achieve. We have done a number of editorial readership studies. We have made comparisons with the *Post* in the 1957–61 period when the *Post* was already on its extended downtrend. The *Post*—to oversimplify—is providing the reader with one, possibly two worthwhile articles in each issue and very little else."[6] This is the opening of the "famous Miller report," submitted

[5]Ronald W. Clark, *Einstein: The Life and Times* (New York, World, 1971), p. 556.
[6]Otto Friedrich, *op. cit.*, pp. 204–205.

by consultant A. Edward Miller to the top management of Curtis Publishing Company in 1965. Although the merits of his findings were hotly disputed, the style of introduction stands as a good example for business and professional writers.

- "Top-level Navy brass, other government officials, and prominent civilians met at the Naval War College in Newport in late March to discuss the Navy's future. More important than the meeting's failure to resolve anything was the sheer scope of disagreement on fundamental issues...."[7] Notice how much information this beginning of a detailed report gives on the subject at hand. In addition to the principal conclusion, which is that no consensus was reached, the opening lines tell us who was at the meetings, where they were held, when, and why they were called.

GUIDELINES FOR GETTING STARTED

Now that we know what a good beginning looks like, let us turn to the practical question: How do you go about writing such a beginning in a letter, memorandum, or report?

Let us assume you have the information all ready to assemble. Some of it is in your mind, some of it in charts or other reports in front of you, some of it in rough notes on a piece of scratch paper. The ideas you want to put across are clear enough to you, but expressing them will take at least a couple of pages—and maybe much more. You have lived with these ideas; you are literally steeped in them. "How in the world," you wonder, "am I to put the gist of them in a short opening paragraph or section? They're not that simple!"

You need to do the same thing that practically every good writer has done since the first cogent stone tablet was written by a caveperson: Step back mentally from the

[7]Deborah Shapley, "Navy Meeting Drifts on a Sea of Unanswered Questions," *Science*, April 21, 1078, p. 282.

details and try to see just the essence of the message. Here are some suggestions that may help.

Imagine a scenario like the following. You meet the reader on a street downtown and can talk with him or her for only a minute before hurrying on. He says, "I hear you're doing a report on customer service. What's up?" You would have to forget that mass of data and notes collected; your mind would leap to a few basic points or recommendations. "Well, we're concerned about rising complaints over delays in shipments of louvered screen," you might say (forgetting your data on when the complaints first began coming in, the rate of increase, the breakdown made of sources by size of customer order, and other background points covered in your notes).

You add: "So we asked the sales department in Toledo to make a study of order processing, shipment procedures, and safety stock levels." (You would leave out the other study possibilities considered but not followed up, and you would not bother your listener with the size of the sample of orders reviewed, the number of interviews held with people in the shipping department, and so on—all items that might go into the *body* of a written report.)You might finish with these words: "It finds that orders are processed faster than ever before, and that shipping procedures are generally okay—but stockouts occur almost twice as often as in any previous year. In fact, the safety stock level hasn't been changed since 1967, even though sales have doubled. We think it should be increased at least 25%." (You would like to say a lot more about how that 25% figure was arrived at, what was learned about stockouts in prior years, and changing customer expectations that affect the safety stock level—again, details for the body of a report—but you are already late for your appointment and must hurry on.)

Here is your opening, made almost to order! You have stated the reason for the communication and described the gist of it. Imagine such a conversation, jot it down, edit it a little, and you should have the right kind of lead for your document.

This kind of mental game playing may also help to solve the case of the report or letter with bad news. Suppose the person you meet on the street is going to be shocked or displeased by the findings of the study. Would you try to talk around the real problem by reciting all the steps, problems, interim findings, and alternatives considered in the course of the study? He (or she) would sense immediately that you are conning him. Besides, you don't have time to offer yourself like a human garage sale. Much better to tell him as tactfully as you can—but frankly—what the outcome was. "The findings come as a surprise," you might say. "The trouble is not order processing or shipping, as many people would have thought, but safety stocks...."

As another example, here is the beginning Robert Gunning suggests for a report on metallurgical tests that contradict the boss's expectation:

> The work requested in January regarding the optimum alloy for the such-and-such part is now complete. The data lead to a conclusion that no one would have predicted in light of your previous experience, namely that a 90 percent aluminum alloy would be the best choice.
>
> We are well aware of failure of aluminum in several previous uses. But many factors not present in this instance were at work there.
>
> In any case, from the viewpoint of wear, fabrication, or cost the 90 percent aluminum alloy proved best of 36 tested. Here are the details....[8]

In terms of amount of disclosure, this beginning does not go far as the ideal, but considering the circumstances, it previews the main idea well enough.

A well-known Episcopal minister had the difficult task of telling his many friends that he was leaving the church. His decision would take a great many words to explain, and he knew it would be interpreted in many ways. In his long and informative letter he began with a

[8]Robert Gunning, op. cit. pp. 3–55.

two-sentence paragraph that might have been nearly identical with what he would have announced orally had he met one of those readers on the street and had just a minute to give the news. He wrote: "After long and careful thought I have had to take a step which will perhaps be most disturbing to many of you, though to others it may come as no surprise. I have come to the conclusion that I cannot remain in either the ministry or the communion of the Episcopal Church."[9]

The chance-meeting scenario is not the only one that will work. There are other ways of visualizing the right opening. One engineer I know imagines that he must send a telegram capsulizing the ideas of his report. Another manager asks herself: "What's all this about?" That question, she reports, helps her to stand back from ideas she has been living with and see them in perspective. Still another businessman tells me, "I ask myself, 'What does the receiver need most to know? If he's interrupted halfway down the first page and may never come back to my report, what is the minimum he should have learned?' "

One of the most helpful steps, especially in the case of reports and letters about complicated technical subjects, is to remind yourself about your purpose in writing. State it as a question which you must answer briefly for the reader before you proceed into the details of methodology, research design, hypotheses, findings, and so forth. Thus, if your purpose is to:

- *Disclose a new approach or concept that may be helpful to the people in a field* . . . mention the idea in a general way and indicate why it is important.
- *Recommend a solution to a certain problem* . . . state in general terms what the problem is and what way you will propose for solving it. . . .
- *Evaluate work or a project previously reported* . . . specify

[9]Alan Watts, *My Own Way* (New York: Pantheon Books, 1972), p. 207.

the work and indicate briefly what you have decided about its significance, feasibility, usefulness, integrity, or relevance.

- *Justify the expense and time of a project or new funds and support for it* . . . mention the project and support required and tell the reader in a few words why the support is justified.
- *Report on the progress of a project or program* . . . mention the highlights of what you have found, that is, the satisfactoriness or unsatisfactoriness of progress in general, and where things seem to be going best and worst.
- *Provide information to support a project, program, product, or service* . . . tell the reader what the project or product is, what kinds of information will follow, and any general appraisal of the information that the reader should keep in mind while reading it.
- *Instruct readers about principles or procedures* . . . specify the subject to be explored, what kinds of instruction will be given, and any general appraisals of them that the reader should keep in mind.
- *Establish your record, reputation, or credibility for work done* . . . summarize this purpose frankly and, if the reason for your concern is not apparent, describe it briefly, too.

CAVEAT FOR THE CONVERT

Although the approach described has been tested and validated countless times, you can be sure that you will be challenged from time to time when you apply it. Sooner or later someone will jump to the defense of a report or memorandum that starts off with only a little more interest and appeal than a railway timetable. "The president himself called up to say how much he likes it," the person will say. Or, "Why, we had more requests for copies of that brochure than anything else we sent out!" Or (perhaps most likely), "Half a dozen people told me how good they thought it was!"

Be not led astray. Friends are not always objective. Associates may have disguised motives for offering a compliment. Some people are as ignorant about good writing as they are about good art. Moreover, some reports and letters are so strong in substance that they succeed *despite* poor beginnings.

One of the sorriest reports I ever saw was also an influential one. Thanks to a combination of fortunate timing and the personal eminence of the author, readers somehow were motivated to dig through a ponderous and meaningless introduction and, with literary gas masks and spades, to attack the soggy middle stratum of the text. In that morass they found gold. In their pleasure and excitement, some of these readers later managed to forget the travail of reading the document. "Good report," they said. "Fine job!"

Such compliments were relatively harmless for the author to hear—he was incapable of writing much better anyway—but they could have been dangerously misleading for anyone who took them uncritically. More than one might-have-been-good writer I know took the wrong road as a result of assuming, during the impressionable years, that the documents people called "good" were also well written.

PROBLEMS AND CASES

1. Thanks to an ingenious new time machine, President Abraham Lincoln, shortly before delivering his Gettysburg Address, is able to ask for your counsel on his speech. The national situation is the same except that newspapers, photocopying, and distribution services exist 1978-style, and Lincoln hopes his speech will be publicized in many newspapers. How, if at all, would you rewrite the first 100 or so words?
2. Before mailing the memorandum shown at the end of Chapter 2, Dita Beard tells you her mind is made up to send it, but she wonders if the beginning should be changed. If you would advise her to revise it, write the new opening you think she should use.

3. Produce an example of a report, memorandum, or article that in your opinion is likely to have received poor *quality* of readership because of a poor beginning.
4. Is it inconsistent to seek both high quantity of readership and high quality of readership in the opening paragraph of a report or memorandum?
5. Prize-winning author James Michener was once asked why the first 100 or so pages of some of his books were so "slow"—so lacking in dramatic quality and eyecatching items for the reader. Michener replied that the reader should be able to plow through a "slow" opening if he or she was serious about reading the whole book. Is Michener's philosophy inconsistent with that described in this chapter?
6. As an editor of an economics journal, you have the unhappy task of writing rejection letters to many a hard-working, well-qualified author. One such letter must be written to Dr. Walkley Talkley, Franklin D. Roosevelt Professor of Economics at Big Ten University, who wrote, in his covering letter with a 6000 word manuscript on "Macroeconomic Miasma," that it "contains such an important message I took my whole Christmas vacation period to write it." Write the opening and middle parts of your rejection letter. Assume that the remainder of the letter can contain (if you deem this appropriate) several specific technical objections to the manuscript.
7. Referring back to question 5 at the end of Chapter 2, assume you decided to write the borrower, having tried in vain to reach him or her by telephone. Write the opening section of your letter.
8. The boss calls you in and says, "I want all of our technical and scientific employees to know about Chapter 3 of *Writing for Results*. I want you to write a 1000-word digest of it for our employee publication." Write the opening paragraphs (up to 150 words) of your condensation. Assume the publisher, John Wiley & Sons, has given you permission to do the digest.
9. Present an example of a report based on (a) an academically-oriented outline; (b) a research-oriented outline.
10. The 1973 Annual Report of Dow Chemical Company begins as follows:

> The year 1973 was another outstanding one, stained only by the deaths of nine Dow people while working for the company. Five of these were employed by Gruppo Lepetit (three in Argentina, one in Brazil, and one in Italy), three by Dowell and one by the Texas division of Dow Chemical, U.S.A. We mourn these losses; we are determined to prevent their repetition. Nothing comes before this in our priorities.

Assume that the year is 1973, this document is in rough-draft stage, and you have been asked to advise management about it. What opinions would you offer?

11. ***The Public-Spirited Power Company:*** Northeast Utilities, a grouping of four Massachusetts and Connecticut utilities, was considering construction of a large hydroelectric plant near the border of western Massachusetts and Connecticut. Its forecasts indicated that a plant capable of producing 2 million kilowatts of power would be required to meet future needs. Northeast's engineers had picked two desirable locations for the new plant.

However, instead of choosing one of these sites and *then* trying to win the approval of residents and public officials—the traditional approach in such situations—management decided to involve the public at the outset. It would make a sum of $180,000 available for the creation of an independent committee of residents to study the two sites and make recommendations as to whether (a) either was desirable, and, if so, (b) which was more desirable.

Northeast printed up and distributed to area residents, public officials, and others copies of a nine-page document entitled, "Report on Preliminary Pumped Storage Hydroelectric Site Examinations at Canaan (Falls Village), Connecticut and Sheffield, Massachusetts." The first page, entitled "Introduction," of the report follows. If this copy had been brought to you while still in rough-draft form, how would you have reacted to it? If you would like to see specific changes made, what would they be? Write your recommendations in a memorandum to Northeast's president.

Northeast Utilities is embarking on a new approach to the problem of siting major electric facilities. We are asking citizens and government agencies to join us in essential studies and to assist in the decision-making process.

We are using this approach for the first time to conduct environmental and engineering studies of two sites in northwestern Connecticut and southwestern Massachusetts as part of a regional effort to develop a large pumped-storage hydroelectric project to help meet electric needs of the late 1970s. To assure that alternatives for providing this power are fully investigated, utilities elsewhere in New England will examine other promising sites so that a final decision can be reached on a regional basis.

We want to stress that our efforts during 1970 will be directed to studies only. No land has been acquired or optioned and we have pledged not to seek property until these first phase studies are completed. If, based on this public examination, one of the locations proves suitable from an environmental, engineering and economic viewpoint, we would then expect that site to be given regional consideration to meet the power needs of New England.

By this process of open public examination, well in advance of any final decision, we hope to avoid a crisis atmosphere which too often has characterized recent siting determinations. Therefore, we are seeking the early participation of private citizens and governmental agencies to assure the representation of all public interests concerned with power supply development within a context of environmental quality.

In addition to our own environmental and engineering studies we have requested the New England River Basins Commission, a regional resource agency, to conduct its own independent review. As a further public process, we have asked the New England Natural Resources Center to organize a citizen evaluation group from among interested environmental organizations in Litchfield County, Connecticut, and Berkshire County, Massachusetts.

The two sites have been designated as Canaan Mountain at Canaan (Falls Village), Connecticut, and Schenob Brook at Sheffield, Massachusetts.

We reiterate that our objective is to seek a new approach to plant siting which will fairly reflect environmental, engineering and economic considerations. In conducting studies of the two sites, we are committed to a completely open evaluation of all the factors which bear on these considerations. We welcome and look forward to an examination undertaken in a spirit of open-mindedness and cooperation to the end that the broad public interest will be well represented and well served.

Lelan F. Sillin, Jr.
President and Chief Executive
Northeast Utilities

12. ***Stoplight for Stockholders:*** The following letter, dated August 30, 1974, was sent out to all stockholders of the Magnavox Company under the president's letterhead:

To Our Shareholders,

In March of this year, when the acquisition of Motorola's consumer electronics business for consideration of approximately book value, by Matsushita Electric Industrial Company, Ltd., was announced, The Magnavox Company publicly stated that if the transaction were consummated, its effect would be a permanent restructuring of the industry which would require the Company to realistically consider its available options.

Subsequently, the Company instituted studies internally and with outside consultants. Inevitably, these studies entailed consideration of possible realignment of businesses which included discussions with North American Philips Corporation.

In light of these discussions, the Company was shocked at the inadequacy of the offer of $8 per share in relationship to a book value in excess of $11.00 and at the fact that the offer was made unilaterally without benefit of negotiation.

The Company's Board of Directors at its meeting on August 29, 1974 therefore decided not to recommend to the shareholders acceptance of the offer as made and has retained the investment bankers of Lazard Freres and Co. and Merrill, Lynch, Pierce, Fenner & Smith to consider alternatives available to the Company and to make appropriate recommendations. The Company has also asked its attorneys to evaluate the matter.

At this time we recommend you defer hasty action which would foreclose the possibility of tendering your shares at a more favorable price.

Very truly yours,

R. H. Platt
President

If this letter had been given to you in rough-draft form, before being mailed, would you have advised revision or rewriting? If so, offer your improved version.

13. ***The Case for Cranes:*** In their fine text, *Designing Technical Reports* (Indianapolis: Bobbs-Merrill, 1976), J. C. Mathes and Dwight D. Stevenson criticize the memorandum that follows on the ground that "the reader cannot tell from the first paragraph where the writer stands on the issue" (pp. 117–118). Suppose this memorandum were written to a senior official whose rank hostility toward installing such cranes is well known to the writer. Would you be able to defend the memorandum in that case? Explain your position pro or con in a brief note to the writer.

There are a number of us that do not want to put container cranes on the V ships unless we absolutely have to; and there are a number of persons who consider the need for cranes absolutely obvious. Without question cranes are costly to install, costly to maintain, have adverse effect on crew size, and reduce the overall container lift capacity. On the other hand, the arguments in favor of cranes may be summarized as follows:

A. Approximately 20% of the projected revenues come from ports that have no cranes.
B. A shipboard crane will supplement port cranes when traffic is heavy and hence reduce the lost time in port. Floating cranes and "jerry-rigged" facilities may work, but not with the efficiency of a shipboard crane.

Our conclusion is that we have given realistic estimates for installing and maintaining the cranes, and that either of the two reasons above appears economically to justify installing the cranes. If they help generate revenue in a tough, competitive situation or reduce port time, the costs of installation and maintenance are more than offset.

14. ***A Student's Soliloquy:*** The paragraphs that follow are the first half of a graduate business school student's paper, written in 1969, on what he hoped to accomplish during the next 15 years. ["Lawrencè Polk," Case No. 4-370-026, Intercollegiate Case Clearing House (Boston, Harvard Business School, 1969), pp. 1–2]. If the student had shown this material to you, with a request that you edit it, including making deletions and additions that seemed desirable to you, how would you have responded?

Before I deliver myself of a weighty tome on the assigned subject, I think that it behooves me to mention an individual ambition that has very little to do with business or society and is not at all limited to the next 15 years. To wit; the next time I am looking out of my apartment on a mild March afternoon, watching the early tulips come up through a somewhat questionable New York atmosphere, I should not like to hear a forecast for a heavy snow warning. Since I have a rather definite intention of remaining within 50 miles of the spot where this is written for the rest of my life, I can only hope that whatever power assigns New York its weather will look kindly on my modest aspiration.

In any case, I shall remove myself from questing after mild weather, and tackle the assigned subject. Actually, from my point of view, the latter subject evolves from the same pattern of thought as does the former, but I certainly hope that it is more reasonable. I think I can best approach this entire area by saying what I don't want and don't expect of the next fifteen years. For one part, I don't care to become an earth shaker in the coming decade and one half, and in general I hope that this earth itself does not radically reorient its society within that time frame. I think that people of my age are generally imbued with the ideas that our society is in trouble and that they have the capacity to alter this situation enormously by their own efforts. By extension, this area of criticism extends to the men and the institutions that currently direct the affairs of this country. I do not believe that the bulk of this criticism is valid, and I believe that I am generally contented with the state and the direction of manners and morals. I do not believe that the frontiers of challenge lie in seeking to redirect and alter the basic nature of our environment, but rather in attempting to soften the divisions and the differences that have arisen; and that this point of view leads me strongly to the course of individual fulfillment, rather than attempting to pursue a career of public service or attempting to bring the principles of "social responsibility" to business. Even in the areas in which I think some kinds of changes would be good, I don't think that my individual efforts would be able to change a thing. In the first place, I have, or am going to have, too many other commitments to have the time or energy to go around being a white knight. Secondly, white knights generally have to hurt some people to help a majority, and that kind of a dilemma usually leads me to looking for ways to ameliorate the status quo without altering it. Finally, I for one have a fair notion that the majority of contemporary leaders are sincere men with humane feelings, and therefore the persistence of many serious problems is a testimony of intractibility of the problems, rather than to the evilness or the ignorance of the leaders.

In ending a series of observations that tend to be almost as negative as they are general and vague, I should point out that I do not have a cynical or grey, hopeless attitude on the nature of our society. While I have spoken of the futility of individual white knightery and the apparent intractibility of problem areas, I do believe that progress toward a just society has been achieved in the last ten years, and that current trends favor a continuation of this process. My real point is that this progress has been achieved in the past, and can best be achieved in the present, without me personally, or businessmen as a class, getting involved in a campaign for moral regeneration that speaks loudly and acts ostentatiously.

After all of that high philosophy, I really think it's time for me to wander back to the heading of this paper and talk about what I would like to accomplish and what I would like to see. Actually, that is really the easiest part of this paper. Individual fulfillment can rationalize a multitude of sins, and here is my catalogue. In the first place I intend to be rich and have already resigned myself to the sacrifices that that goal entails. In fifteen years I should like to be the equivalent of a multi-millionaire with good prospects for increased aggrandizement for the rest of my working life.

> Although it's hard to set a dollar figure, I can set one sort of a goal by saying that I would like to be number one man from my first-year section in terms of net personal worth. My career plans, and my avocation is the corporate finance area of investment banking, but I would not restrict myself, if I saw big opportunities in another area. . . .

15. ***Presidential Preface:*** The 1971 *Annual Report* of The Carborundum Company, Buffalo, N.Y. was published in booklet form—45 pages including about a dozen photos. Company sales for the year were reported at $311.4 million, the highest ever despite poor business conditions, and income was $13.5 million. The first two pages of text of the Annual Report were entitled, "Comments from the President," and signed by William H. Wendel. The first five paragraphs of Mr. Wendel's statement are reproduced below by permission.

> "Point of no return" is a navigational term. It refers to that point in a journey where it is better to go ahead than to turn back. It is a calculation of many variables that have occurred, and that will occur. Neither course, going ahead or turning back, is without obstacles, although one is superior to the other. The option of doing nothing does not exist.
>
> The concept seems to have application in business, even though the variables are more numerous and the equations more complex.
>
> To go back or turn back, that is the question. Ask it every day of every business and of every aspect of business. Knowing where we have been is easy, although we never fully understand the currents that put us there. Knowing where we are going and what will force us off-course, there's the rub. We can only be certain that the forces will be more diverse, numerous, powerful, rapid, and concealed than ever. How else can we account for unpredicted events such as the rebuke of technology in the cancellation of the SST; the leader of the military-industrial complex requiring federal aid; and the complete shift to wage and price controls and devaluation of the almighty dollar?
>
> The number of examples will accelerate, affecting not just businesses, but nations and the relations among them, largely because the forces are so well hidden. The iceberg is an accurate analogy. Only the top tenth is visible. By the

> time we know where the rest is, and what is in it, and how big it is, the damage is done; it may be too late to change course.
>
> To turn back or go ahead? We did both last year. The Tysaman abrasive machine business was liquidated. It was a costly move, but the decision eliminates a drain on earnings. Hindsight says we waited too long. Warehouses were closed down or consolidated. Capital projects were cancelled or postponed. Even management development programs were curtailed.

Suppose Mr. Wendel has just finished the rough draft of these paragraphs and has shown them to you with a request for your reactions in writing. Write a memorandum to him indicating what changes, if any, you think he should make in the opening, and for what reasons.

Devise, wit; write, pen.

William Shakespeare

The difficulty is not to write,
but to write what you mean,
not to affect your reader,
but to affect him precisely as you wish.

Robert Louis Stevenson

Chapter **4**

Strategies of Persuasion

When we review reports, letters, and memoranda that get the intended results, we find a fascinating diversity of approaches. Some are gentle in approach, taking readers by the hand and leading them to a certain finding or recommendation. Others are brisk and abrupt. Some are objective in approach, carefully examining both sides of an idea, like a judge writing a difficult decision—at least until the end. Others burst with impatience to explain one side, and only one side, of a proposal or argument. Some flow swimmingly, others erupt like Mount Vesuvius.

How is it possible that communications taking such different approaches can all be effective? It is not sufficient to answer glibly, "It depends on the situation," or "Communications should mirror the personal style of the communicator." *How* does a written communication depend on the situation? *Which* style of the communicator should be reflected in a given communication? Examine the writing of most business executives, professionals, and public leaders, and you will find not one but *many* styles of exposition.

RULES EVERY PERSUADER SHOULD KNOW

The explanation lies in a set of relationships among the communicator, the reader, the message, and the time-space environment. These relationships work in predictable ways and are an important part of the knowledge of every good business and professional writer. They come into play in the planning stages of writing, when the writer is considering how he or she will proceed, and in the main body of the presentation, to accomplish what he or she has promised in the opening paragraphs. The relationships affect some of the most important decisions a writer makes—the choice of ideas to use, the comparative emphasis to be given various arguments pro and con, the types of reasons and supporting material used, the establishment of credibility, and other matters.

It is convenient but self-defeating to follow fixed prescriptions for persuasion, such as to put your strongest arguments first or last or to identify with the readers. Such nostrums were fine for the age of patent medicines and snake-oil peddlers, but not for the age of diagnostic medicine. What is more, they are belittling. They assume that writers are witless. Good writers vary their approaches in response to their readings of different situations. Just as a good golfer plays an approach to a green differently depending on the wind, so a good writer uses different strategies depending on the crosscurrents of mood and feeling.

How should you choose your approach to a group of readers? What elements of the approach should be tailored to the situation? These are the topics of this chapter.

Let us assume that the substance of the intended message is clear in your mind, and that you have written—or can write at any time—the kind of opening described in the previous chapter. (If, after reading this chapter, you are interested in some further thoughts on persuasion, see Chapter 7.)

1. Consider whether your views will make problems for readers.

J. C. Mathes and Dwight W. Stevenson tell of the student engineer who was asked to evaluate the efficiency of the employer plant's waste-treatment process.[1] He found that by making a simple change, the company could save more than $200,000 a year. Anticipating an enthusiastic response, he wrote up and delivered his report. Although he waited with great expectations, no accolades came. Why? What he hadn't counted on was that now his supervisors would have to explain to their bosses why they had allowed a waste of $200,000 a year. They were far from elated to read his report.

"If you want to make a man your enemy," Henry C. Link once said, "tell him simply, 'You are wrong.' This method works every time." Under the illusion that their sciences are "hard," physicists, biologists, and others may assume that it is necessary only to worry about setting the facts forth accurately. From posterity's standpoint, perhaps yes—but not from the standpoint of writing for current results. As Kenneth Boulding, head of the American Association for the Advancement of Science, has pointed out, the so-called "hard" sciences are in many ways "soft," and vice versa. "You can knock forever on a deaf man's door," said Zorba the Greek, and the deaf man can be a physicist as well as a marketing manager or public official.

[1]J. C. Mathes and Dwight W. Stevenson, *Designing Technical Reports* (Indianapolis: Bobbs-Merrill, 1976), pp. 18–19.

If your views are bad news for readers, you proceed to report them, but with empathy and tact and an effort to put yourself in the reader's shoes. You work as carefully as if you were licking honey off a thorn.

2. Don't offer new ideas, directives, or recommendations for change until your readers are prepared for them.

"Should I state my surprising findings at the very beginning of my memorandum?" a writer asks. "Should I go slow with my heretical proposal and hold the reader's hand?" asks another.

Generally speaking, the answer to all such questions depends on the extent of your audience's resistance to change, the amount of change you are asking for, the uncertainty in readers' minds as to your understanding of their situation, and what psychologists call the "perceived threat" of your communication, that is, how much it seems (to readers) to upset their values and interests. The more change, uncertainty, and/or threat, the slower you should proceed, the more carefully you should prepare your readers.

For instance, if your boss is enthusiastic about a new promotion scheme that he (or she) has paid a consultant $25,000 to devise, naturally you will want to go slow in shooting it down (at least if you want to stay in his good graces). In fact, any written criticism of the scheme is probably out of order until you have had a chance to talk with him and get a feel for the proper timing of any forthcoming criticism. When you do commit yourself to writing, you should probably review the arguments *for* the new scheme as fairly as possible, making it crystal clear to him that you understand them. Only then does it become timely to turn to the facts or conditions that, in your opinion, raise serious questions about the plan.

On the other hand, suppose the faulty promotion scheme is of little personal interest to your boss—it is not his (or her) "baby." Now the situation is different. You can launch right into the shortcomings, throwing your heaviest objections first. The fact is that the boss may not even want to know about the lesser objections, much less the supporting arguments once advanced for the plan; the main things he should know are that (a) the plan is in trouble and (b) the major, most compelling reasons why.

Clearly, this strategy is plain, everyday common sense—what you would normally do in communicating orally instead of in writing. Only in writing you must be more explicit and thorough, because a document lacks the expressiveness and visual advantages of a spoken dialogue.

Now consider another type of situation. Suppose it is your unhappy task to write a department manager that the extra appropriations he (or she) was promised have been cancelled. First of all, how would you handle it if you saw him often and could talk with him personally? As pointed out in Chapter 3, you would not (we hope) pussyfoot around trying to withhold the bad news from him. Also, once you had indicated the main message, you would probably backtrack a little and make it clear that the step is being taken with reluctance.

"Joe, it looks as if we're not going to be able to give you the extra budget we promised," you might say, getting down to business. That is the message in a nutshell—now for the review of common ground. "We know how much you have counted on getting those people and funds. There's no doubt you could manage them well and put them to good use. And we know that the morale of your people is involved in this, too. But the fact is that the sales we counted on are not coming in. We've got to cut somewhere, and, frankly, we feel it's got to be your department because . . ."

If you are communicating by letter or memorandum, the strategy is exactly the same (only "Joe" may now be "Mr. Wyncoop"). After your lead, you review the main needs as he and you understand them, perhaps spelling them out more than you would have in a face-to-face meeting but choosing the same ones. Only then do you turn to the new conditions that make it necessary to do an about-face.

3. Your credibility with readers affects your strategy.

In general, communication research indicates that the chances of opinion change vary with the communicator's authority with his or her readers. In their succinct summary of the field, *Persuasion*, social scientists Marvin Karlins and Herbert I. Abelson point out that credibility itself is a variable; that is, it can be influenced by the words of the communicator.[2] Above all, as psychologists repeatedly emphasize, credibility lies in the eye of the beholder.[3]

In the letter about atomic fission to President Roosevelt (see Chapter 3), scientists Szilard and Teller agreed that Einstein should sign the letter, not only out of personal respect for him but also because of their knowledge that Roosevelt was in awe of him.

In written communications there are two types of credibility. It may be given or it may be acquired. Between the two lies a world of practical difference.

Given credibility may result from your position in an organization. If, let us say, you are the boss writing directions to a subordinate, your credibility is likely to be high. Given credibility also may result from reputation—a well-known chemist has more credibility in communications about polymers than a good industrial engineer has, but the latter would possess more credibility in communications about time-and-motion studies. It may result from the individuals and groups the writer is associated with—if he or she is a member of the same trade union the reader belongs to, a union held in high esteem by both, he or she has more credibility in a memorandum on griev-

[2]Marvin Karlins and Herbert I. Abelson, *Persuasion* (New York, Springer, 1970); see pp. 107–132.

[3]See, for example, Ralph L. Rosnow and Edward J. Robinson, Eds. *Experiments in Persuasion* (New York, Academic, 1967).

ance procedures than a member of the board of directors would have.

Though you may be high in given credibility, you may yet need to remind some readers of the fact. In the case of an obvious credential, such as a position in an important organization, a letterhead may be enough to do the trick. Another device is to insert a few lines of biographical data at the head of a report or brochure. If you have had experience or associations that carry weight with the reader, perhaps you can interject them early in the message. "During a visit I had last week with Zach Jarvis," you might say, knowing that Dr. Zachary P. Jarvis is a magic name with your reader, or, "The Executive Committee of the Aberjona Basin Association asked me to join their meeting on Monday . . ." knowing that group carries a triple-A rating in the mind of the reader.

Of course, you do not want to overplay your hand at such name dropping. A report to a fairly diverse audience by a famous black organization began simply:

> The National Association for the Advancement of Colored People has for many years been dedicated to the task of defending the economic, social and political rights and interests of black Americans. The growing national debate about energy has led us to examine the question to ascertain the implications for black Americans.[4]

Again, an attorney of the American Civil Liberties Union, in a letter to members of the organization soliciting donations, began:

> My dear friend:
>
> I am the ACLU lawyer who went into court last April to defend freedom of speech in Skokie, Illinois, for a handful of people calling themselves "nazis."
>
> The case has had an enormous impact on my life.
>
> It has also gravely injured the ACLU financially. . . .[5]

[4]*The Wall Street Journal*, January 12, 1978.
[5]David Goldberger, letter dated March 20, 1978.

Acquired credibility, on the other hand, is earned by thoughts and facts in the written message. I may not know you from Adam. Yet if you send me a letter or report that carefully, helpfully describes something I am interested in, you gain credibility in my estimation.

Some studies suggest that if you are low in given credibility and seek to acquire it with an audience, a useful technique is to cite ideas or evidence that support the reader's existing views.[6] As Disraeli once said, "My idea of an agreeable person is a person who agrees with me." The very fact that you feel confident and knowledgeable enough to articulate these views is likely to lift you several notches in the reader's estimation.

Still another approach is that old standby of persuaders—identifying yourself, in an early section, with the goals and interests of the audience. Possibly the most famous example of this strategy is the opening of Marc Antony's funeral oration in Shakespeare's *Julius Caesar*: "I come to bury Caesar, not to praise him. . . ."

Finally, you can acquire credibility by citing authorities who rate highly with your intended audience, or by exhibiting documentary evidence that, because of its source, lends prestige and authority to your proposals or ideas.

"For success in negotiation," say C. Northcote Parkinson and Nigel Rowe, "it is vitally important that people will believe what you say and assume that any promise you make will be kept. But it is not good saying: 'Trust me. Rely on my word.' Only politicians say that."[7]

Even if you have prestigious credentials, you cannot take too much for granted. In an age of television sets, radios, cassettes, and record players in every home, credibility—at least with the public—may come quicker for the singer or comedian than for the judge, business executive, or medical researcher. In fact, because of an

[6]Karlins and Abelson, *op. cit.*, pp. 115–119.

[7]C. Northcote Parkinson and Nigel Rowe, "Better Communication: Business's Best Defense," *The McKinsey Quarterly*, Winter 1978, p. 26.

association with an organization or profession, you may be stereotyped as a member of "them" or "the establishment." It may behoove you to establish that you are a person with a name, a personality, certain interests, certain experiences—not just a nameless representative.

4. If your audience disagrees with your ideas or is uncertain about them, present both sides of the argument.

Behavioral scientists generally find that if an audience is friendly to a persuader, or has no contrary views on the topic and will get none in the near future, a one-sided presentation of a controversial question is most effective.[8] For instance, if your point is that sales of product X in the St. Louis territory could be doubled and you are writing to enthusiastic salespeople of product X, your best course is to concentrate on facts and examples showing the enormous potential of product X. There is no shortage of evidence showing that people generally prefer reading material that confirms their beliefs, and that they develop resistance to material that repudiates their beliefs. (As we shall see presently, however, this does not mean you cannot change their minds.)

But suppose your audience has not made up its mind, so far as you know. In this case you would do well to deal with *both* sides of the argument (or all sides, if there are more than two). Follow the same approach if the reader disagrees with you at the outset. For one thing, a two-sided presentation suggests to an uncertain or hostile audience that you possess objectivity. For another, it helps the reader remember your view by putting the pros and cons in relationship to one another. Also, it meets the reader's need to be treated as a mature, informed individual. As Karlins and Abelson point out:

[8]Experiments supporting this conclusion are reported by Carl I. Hovland, Arthur A. Lumsdaine. and F. Sheffield in *Experiments on Mass Communication* (Princeton, Princeton University Press, 1949). Cited by Karlins and Abelson, *op. cit.*, p. 22.

> Conspicuously underlying your presentation is the assumption that the audience would be on your side if they only knew the truth. The other points of view should be presented with the attitude "it would be natural for you to have this idea if you don't know all the facts, but when you know all the facts, you will be convinced."[9]

Karlins and Abelson tested the reactions of audiences in post-war Germany to Voice of America broadcasts. They found that the most persuasive programs were those that included admissions of shortcomings in United States living conditions.[10]

Again, observation of businessmen's reactions to scores of *Harvard Business Review* articles advocating controversial measures convinces me that the most influential articles have been those that have acknowledged the shortcomings, weaknesses, and limitations of their arguments. When an author wants to sell a new idea to a sophisticated audience, he or she should be candid about the soft spots in his argument.

5. Win respect by making your opinion or recommendation clear.

Although strategy may call for a two-sided argument, this does not mean you should be timid in setting forth your conclusions or proposals at the end. We assume here that you have definite views and seek to persuade your audience to adopt them. The two-sided approach is a *means* to that end; it does not imply compromising or obfuscating your conclusions. An official at Armour & Company once criticized many reports from subordinates to bosses on the ground that, after presenting much data, they concluded, in effect, "Here is what I found out and maybe we should do this or maybe we should do that." The typical response of a boss to such a memorandum, he noted, was

[9]Karlins and Abelson, *op. cit.*, p. 26.

[10]See *Factors Affecting Credibility in Psychological Warfare Communications* (Washington, D. C., Human Resources Research Office, George Washington University, 1956).

to do nothing. Hence, the time taken both in writing and reading was wasted.[11]

6. Put your strongest points last if the audience is very interested in the argument, first if it is not so interested.

This question is referred to by social scientists as the "primacy-recency" issue in persuasion. The argument presented first is said to have primacy; the argument presented last, recency. Although studies of the question have produced inconsistent findings and no firm rules can be drawn, it appears that if your audience is deeply concerned with your subject you can afford to lead it along from the weakest points to the strongest. The audience's great interest will keep it reading, and putting the weaker points at the start tends to create rising reader expectations about what is coming. When you end with your strongest punch, therefore, you do not let readers down.

If your audience is not so concerned with the topic, on the other hand, it may be best to use the opposite approach. Now you cannot risk leading readers along a winding path. They may drop out before you reach the end. So grab their attention right at the beginning with your strongest argument or idea.

In any case, put the recommendations, facts, or arguments you most want the reader to *remember* first or last. Although experiments by social scientists on the primacy-recency issue are inconclusive, there is a firm pattern on the question of recall. The ideas you state first or last have a better chance of being remembered than the ideas stated in the middle of your appeal or case.

7. Don't count on changing attitudes by offering information alone.

"People are hostile to big business because they don't know enough facts about it," businesspeople are heard to

[11]John Ball and Cecil B. Williams, *Report Writing* (New York, Ronald, 1955).

say. Or, "If customers knew the truth about our costs, they would not object to our prices." Companies have poured large sums into advertising and public relations campaigns on this assumption; civic organizations have often based their hopes on it.

"The trouble with the assumption," state Karlins and Abelson, "is that it is almost never valid. There is a substantial body of research findings indicating that cognition—knowing something new—increasing information—is effective as an attitude change agent only under very specialized conditions."[12]

Social scientists do concede, however, that presentations of facts alone may strengthen the opinions of people who already agree with the persuader. The information reassures them and helps them defend themselves in discussions with others.

8. "Testimonials" are most likely to be persuasive if drawn from people with whom readers associate.

It is well known that a person's attitudes and opinions are strongly influenced by the groups to which he or she belongs or wants to belong—work units in a company, labor unions, bowling teams, social clubs, church associations, ethnic associations, and so on. To muster third-party support for your proposal or idea, therefore, you would do well to cite the behavior, findings, or beliefs of groups to which your readers belong. In so doing, you allay any feelings of isolation readers might have if tempted to follow your ideas. You suggest that they are not alone with you, that there is group support for the points being made.

As every school child learns, the predominant attitudes of a group toward individuals or regarding standards of behavior, performance, or status influence an individual member's perceptions. For instance, a study of boys at a camp demonstrated that their ratings of various individu-

[12]Karlins and Abelson, *op. cit.*, p. 33.

als' performances at shooting and canoeing were biased by their knowledge of the status of the rated individuals in the camp society. Thus a boy generally regarded as a leader was seen as performing better with the rifle or canoe than was a boy generally regarded as a follower, even though the first boy's performance was not actually superior.[13]

In addition, it seems fair to say that as modern television, radio, records, and cassettes have brought national celebrities into the home and automobile, these people, too, have been stamped with approval or disapproval by millions of groups across the country.

Accordingly, if your readers are young, dissident, or "long hairs," refer to a Richard Dreyfus or a Joan Baez for supporting statements, not to a Gerald Ford or an Arnold Palmer. If your readers are electrical engineers, quote well-regarded scientific sources as your authority, not star salespeople or public relations people. Take into account also that the more deeply attached your readers are to a group, the greater the influence of the group norms on them. For instance, one experiment by social scientists showed that the opinions of Catholic students who took their religion seriously were less influenced by the answers of nonserious Catholics than were the opinions of Catholic students who placed little value on their church membership.[14]

9. Be wary of using extreme or "sensational" claims and facts.

Both research in behavioral science and common sense confirm this rule.[15] Do not be misled by the fact that

[13]*Ibid.*, p. 50.

[14]See H. Kelley, "Salience of Membership and Resistance to Change of Group-Anchored Attitudes," *Human Relations*, August 1955, pp. 255–289. Cited in Karlins and Abelson, *op. cit.*, p. 58.

[15]See, for example, *Building Opposition to the Excess Profits Tax* (Princeton, Opinion Research Corporation, August 1952), and R. Weiss, "Conscious Technique for the Variation of Source Credibility," *Psychological Reports*, Vol. 20, 1969, p. 1159. Both cited in Karlins and Abelson, *op. cit.*, pp. 36–37.

flashy journalists make successful use of extreme and bizarre cases to dramatize a story. The situation in business and professional writing is different from that in journalism.

When you seek the confidence and cooperation of your readers—and typically you do in the kinds of communications we deal with in this book—it is best to write in terms of the real world as you and they perceive it. Observable, believable, realistic statements carry more weight than any other kind. Although you want reader attention, you do not want to shock your audience with outlandish examples or arguments. These may help you to succeed in making the reader sit up—but they will also provoke distrust and suspicion.

Examples are common in the letters sections of newspapers. A writer who identified himself as a former vice-president of a well-known bank opposed a large power company's plan to build a new plant in a rural area near his town. His letter began as follows: "A great many of us . . . are profoundly disturbed by the proposal now being considered to disrupt and destroy the marvelous little valley southwest of [name of town], in order to build bigger and better power plants. This would be a devastating blow to the last unspoiled bit of country left in Connecticut. . . .[16]"

Like a batter who hits the first two pitches foul and quickly gets two strikes against him, this writer managed to distort the first two sentences he wrote. The proposed plant, though a very large one, would not "disrupt and destroy" the valley—only a small section of the valley area would be affected. Moreover, the valley was not "the last unspoiled bit of country" in the state—it was only a small parcel of the state's beautiful countryside. These exaggerations might have drawn cheers from rabid foes of the project, but the writer wasn't interested in appealing to them; he wanted to win uncommitted readers. At the

[16]*Lakeville Journal*, April 2, 1970, p. 11.

very beginning, however, he antagonized them with hyperbole.

10. Tailor your presentation to the reasons for readers' attitudes, if you know them.

Your chances of persuading readers are better if you can plan your appeal or argument to meet the main feelings, prejudices, or reasons for their beliefs. For instance, if reader beliefs are the result of their wanting to go along with certain groups they like or associate with, your best bet (as indicated earlier) is to show the acceptability of your point to these groups. If their attitudes reflect personal biases, such as an old grudge against someone in power, it is best to tailor your presentation to that prejudice. And so on.

Summarizing the implications of several behavioral studies, Karlins and Abelson present the example of three people who say they are against private ownership of industry. How should their reasons for this position influence one's choice of a strategy of persuasion? The authors explain:

> One of them feels that way because he has only been exposed to one side of the story and has nothing else on which to base his opinion. The way to change this man's opinion may be to expose him to facts, take him to visit some factories, meet some workers and supervisors. A second person is against private ownership because that is the prevailing norm or social climate in the circles in which he finds himself. His attitudes are caused by his being a part of a group and conforming to its standards. You cannot change this fellow just by showing him facts. The facts must be presented in an atmosphere which suggests a social reward for changing his opinion. Some kind of status appeal might be a start in that direction. A third person may have negative attitudes toward private industry because by making business the scapegoat for all his troubles, he can unload his pent-up feelings of bitterness and disappointment at the world for not giving him a better break. . . . Trying to change this third person with facts may actually do more harm than good. The more the evidence shows how wrong he is, the more he looks for reasons to support his

beliefs. This kind of person can sometimes be influenced by helping him to understand why he has a particular attitude.[17]

11. Never mention other people without considering their possible effect on the reader.

Other people may, as we saw earlier, be introduced for the sake of "testimonials." More commonly, however, other people's names are mentioned in the course of explaining a situation, narrating an event, or completing the format of a message. This use of names, too, may affect the power of your message.

A reference to the actions of another person—however simple and unobtrusive it may seem to you the writer—may alter your relationship with readers. If readers consider that person a friend or enemy, their natural reaction is to begin thinking of the possible bearing of your communication on their friendship or antagonism. This reaction can have significant implications for your approach.

To illustrate, a doctoral student who had failed to meet his school's program requirements tried to muster faculty opinion in support of his petition for readmission by appearing daily at the entrance to the dining hall and handing out leaflets to faculty members. One such leaflet contained these words: "I am very unhappy about the strain my case has created for Professor [name of the program director]. I am distressed if last Friday's handout . . . created the impression that I was harking on his mistakes. I have told him and I tell you that I could understand his actions and decisions. . . ." The leaflet went on at some length to explain the doctoral student's feelings about the problem.

What this writer did not realize was the impact of the professor's name on his communication strategy. Almost everyone who received the leaflet was a colleague of the professor in question. Therefore the leaflet made it necessary for them to think of their relationship with the professor when they made up their minds about the petition.

[17]Karlins and Abelson, *op. cit.*, p. 92.

And their relationship with the professor was more important to them than their relationship with the doctoral student.

If the doctoral student considered it essential to mention the professor, he could have elected to: (1) try to win readers over while convincing them that their relations with the professor would not be affected, or (2) show that the professor was so far off base that readers were morally bound to risk their relationship with him. In the latter case, the leaflet should have contained ready-to-use arguments that readers could draw on in explaining to the professor why they sympathized with the doctoral student. Since the leaflet did neither of these things, it was a failure in persuasion.

Don't overlook the possible effect of distribution. Letters often go to third parties, with "cc" typed at the bottom followed by the names of those people. A memorandum often contains the names of several addressees in the "To" line at the top. Covering letters with reports may indicate several groups of readers. All this may affect your strategy. The background information that you could omit if writing only to Jones may be quite necessary if Brown, too, is an important reader; and the rather offhand treatment you give to a certain test or episode if writing to Jones and Brown might not be fitting at all if Larabee also is an intended reader. Many times the wise manager or professional rewrites part of a letter or memo after deciding to send a copy of it to an additional person who was not considered when the first draft was made.

Many people have strong feelings about "blind copies," that is, copies sent to persons other than those indicated after the "cc" at the end of a letter or in the "To" line of a memorandum. Some people feel that blind copies never should be sent. Others feel that since a letter or memo is the property of the writer, he or she can distribute it at will. Although the latter view is legally correct, only an obtuse writer will distribute copies thoughtlessly if the content is in any way confidential, personal, or politically sensitive.

SIZING UP YOUR READERS

We have a tendency to abstract written communications from real life, to act as if the customary ground rules of influence and persuasion don't apply to a message that is in writing.We act with a naiveté almost unheard of in our face-to-face relationships. Not seeing readers, we act as if they weren't real people. "If we write the information clearly, accurately, and correctly," we think wishfully to ourselves, "surely that satisfies the requirements of a piece of paper." But Josh Billings' puckish maxim, "As scarce as truth is, the supply has always been in excess of the demand," applies to truth on paper as well as truth in conversation.

Think of your intended readers as the real people they will be when they take your letter or report out of the "in-box." Only then can you decide intelligently what information and ideas to emphasize and in what order to present them. To help you think of readers as three-dimensional people, ask yourself some questions about their situation and relationships with you. Are they:

- Deeply or only mildly interested in the subject of your communication?
- Familiar or unfamiliar with your views, competence, and feelings about them?
- Knowledgeable or ignorant of your authority in the area discussed, your status, and your associations of possible importance to them?
- Committed or uncommitted to a viewpoint, opinion, or course of action other than the one you favor in your letter, report, or other document?
- Likely or unlikely to find your proposal, idea, finding, or conclusion threatening or requiring considerable change in their thought or behavior?
- Inclined or uninclined to think and feel the way they do about the subject because of identifiable reasons, prejudices, or experiences?

- Associated formally or informally with groups or organizations involved in some way with the idea or proposal you deal with?

With answers to questions like these in mind, you will not see your readers as shadows on the wall. They will sit across from you. You can write as if talking *with* them, not talking *to* them.

PROBLEMS AND CASES

1. "I'm not asking you to marry my family, dear, only me," your bride said before the wedding. Her deceitful brother, Caligua, sells you for $2900 a used automobile that he swore was in perfect condition—"driven only now and then by a little old lady." You never had a chance to test-drive the car or look under the hood. On the second day of your honeymoon drive through the Ozarks, the car breaks down. A competent garage mechanic says the engine block is cracked, the valves are badly worn, the connecting rods are broken, and the carburetor "looks bad." You will have to proceed the rest of the way in a rented car. Write Caligua a short letter explaining the situation and requesting that he share the cost with you.
2. Using an example from personal experience, explain the difference between given credibility and earned credibility.
3. Your boss attends a writing program in which the principles of persuasion described in this chapter are recommended. "That psychological stuff is nonsense," he snorts. "Those people who want you to tiptoe around don't know their knees from their elbows." Your peers choose you to write him a short memorandum defending the persuasion principles described here for use in position papers and other reports. Hold the memorandum to 200 words or less.
4. You are in charge of the advertising and promotion for a new brand of peanut brittle. You learn that an endorsement of the product can be obtained from any of the fol-

lowing: a leading nutritionist, a well-known folk singer, a famous athlete. Your budget allows you to buy but one person's testimonial. Which one would you take, and why?

5. In Shakespeare's *Julius Caesar,* Antony delivers the funeral oration to an audience that, sympathetic at first to Brutus and the other conspirators who murdered Caesar, believes Caesar was a tyrant and doesn't want to hear Antony defend him. Antony begins: "Friends, Romans, countrymen, lend me your ears; I come to bury Caesar, not to praise him . . ." (Act III, Scene II). Taking the first 30 lines of the funeral oration (down through "You all did love him once—not without cause"), write your appraisal of their persuasion value as if the oration had been written for public distribution.
6. "Techniques of persuasion based on psychology are a dubious method of manipulating reader opinion," asserts one critic, "because the reader is not always aware how his feelings are being changed." Explain your agreement or disagreement in a brief memorandum, supporting your position with an actual or fictional example.
7. Comment in writing on the following statement: "No one is wrong. At most someone is uninformed. If I think a man is wrong, either I am unaware of something or he is. So unless I want to play a superiority game I had best find out what he is looking at. 'You're wrong' means 'I don't understand you'—I'm not seeing what you're seeing. But there is nothing wrong with you, you are simply not me and that's not wrong." [From Hugh Prather, *Notes to Myself* (New York: Bantam, 1976).]
8. Write a short critique of the following statement:

> Be sure that you know what your correspondent is asking before you begin to answer him. Study his letter carefully. If he is obscure, spare no trouble in trying to get at his meaning. If you conclude that he means something different from what he says (as he well may), address yourself to his meaning, not to his words, and do not be clever at his expense.
>
> Get into his skin, and adapt the atmosphere of your letter to suit that of his. If he is troubled, be sympathetic. If he is

rude, be specially courteous. If he is muddle-headed, be specially lucid. If he is pigheaded, be patient. If he is helpful, be appreciative. If he convicts you of a mistake, acknowledge it freely and even with gratitude. But never let a flavour of the patronising creep in. (Sir Ernest Gowers)

9. ***The Chafing Chairman:*** (The names and many details described have been fictionalized.) To stimulate knowledge and interest in government among its 3500 employees, QRS Industries, Inc., created a voluntary employee organization called the Political Involvement Council. The brainchild of the company's vice-president for urban affairs, the council was instructed to avoid partisan leanings of any kind and, so far as possible, develop a balance of Republicans, Democrats, and local political affiliations in its membership.

   Alfred Adams agreed to serve as chairman of the council. An assistant counsel in the company's legal department and 27 years old, he was a "political activist" who had energetically organized earlier volunteer employee groups to work on municipal improvement, environmental, and drug control projects. He had worked for three years at QRS Industries.

   Adams accepted the task with some reluctance because most of the work would have to be done during evenings and weekends, which meant giving up other extracurricular activities in which he was involved. But both the president of the company and the vice-president for urban affairs stressed the importance of the council "if we really mean what we say about QRS's role as a corporate citizen and our interest in involving young employees." They assured him of their complete support.

   During the first nine months of work, Adams experienced a series of frustrations in his efforts to make the council a strong force in the company. Several hundred employees—mostly young people—enrolled as members, but attendance at meetings was only fair, and few members seemed willing to spend much time on council projects, such as creating audiovisual instruction materials, putting up posters, and arranging for guest speakers to address employee meetings. The excuse commonly given was "conflict with work."

One Sunday evening at home, after a series of telephone conversations with various members of the council, Adams marched to his desk and wrote the following memorandum to the vice-president for urban affairs:

> I would like to call your attention to an incident that is a key symptom of the malaise that is upon employees in this company. I say malaise because—aside from intangibles—membership in Political Involvement Council is disappointing, attendance and involvement leave much to be desired, and our output is poor; this, in spite of the fact that more employees than ever are in the company, and there are more young people who indicate interest in civic activities. We would probably have a healthier situation if you and other policy makers would exert more effort to identify and encourage interest, competence, and willingness to work among these new resources.
>
> Last year I was asked to act as Chairman of the Council. After careful consideration I decided to make a serious commitment and even declined some other activities so I wouldn't be "spread too thin." My wife has spent many weekends helping me. I have just heard second-hand, and had confirmed, that two meetings directly concerned with company involvement in political programs were held last month. Not only was I never advised beforehand of the meetings but I never received *any* results of the meetings from *any* of the participants.
>
> The present ebb should be no surprise if this is at all typical of the recognition and encouragement given "new blood."

Suppose you are a close friend of Adams and he held up sending the memo out until you read it and advised him. Would you urge him to revise it, and, if so, what specific revisions would you suggest? Would you advise him to mail it as is?

10. ***An Anxious Ally:*** The text of the following cablegram, sent on June 3, 1965 by Prime Minister Harold Wilson of Great Britain to President Lyndon B. Johnson, is taken from pp. 448–449 of *The Pentagon Papers* (Bantam, 1971):

> I was most grateful to you for asking Bob McNamara [Secretary of Defense under President Johnson] to arrange the

> very full briefing about the two oil targets near Hanoi and Haiphong that Col. Rogers gave me yesterday.
>
> I know you will not feel that I am either unsympathetic or uncomprehending of the dilemma that this problem presents for you. In particular, I wholly understand the deep concern you must feel at the need to do anything possible to reduce the losses of young Americans in and over Vietnam; and Col. Rogers made it clear to us what care has been taken to plan this operation so as to keep civilian casualties to the minimum.
>
> However, I am bound to say that, as seen from here, the possible military benefits that may result from this bombing do not appear to outweigh the political disadvantages that would seem the inevitable consequence. If you and the South Vietnamese Government were conducting a declared war in the conventional pattern, this operation would clearly be necessary and right. But since you have made it abundantly clear—and you know how much we have welcomed and supported this—that your purpose is to achieve a negotiated settlement, and that you are not striving for total military victory in the field, I remain convinced that the bombing of these targets, without producing decisive military advantage, may only increase the difficulty of reaching an eventual settlement.
>
> The last thing I wish is to add to your difficulties, but, as I warned you in my previous message, if this action is taken we shall have to disassociate ourselves from it.

Do you think this is a persuasive message? Give your reasons. What principles of written persuasion does the cablegram illustrate or fail to embody?

11. ***The Air-Cooled Car:*** In 1921 General Motors was trying to develop an air-cooled car for the market. Charles F. Kettering, GM's research chief, was in charge of the project, which had received a high priority in top management's thinking. When unexpected problems arose during the tests of the new mechanism, the engineers got into many arguments, and Kettering himself became discouraged. The executive committee of management then canceled the project. Worried about Kettering's morale, the executive committee sent him the following letter of confidence, dated November 30, 1921:

Dear Kettering:—

It is most important in our opinion that your mind be kept free from worries foreign to the development of the air cooled car and other laboratory work.

In the development and introduction of anything so radically different from standard practice as the air cooled car is from the regular water cooled job, it is quite natural that there should be a lot of "wiseacres" and "know-it-alls" standing around knocking the development.

In order that your mind may be completely relieved as to the position of the undersigned with respect to the air cooled development, we beg to advise as follows:—

1st. We are absolutely confident in your ability to whip all problems in connection with the development of our proposed air cooled cars.

2nd. We will continue to have this degree of confidence and faith in you and your ability to accomplish this task until such time as we come to you and frankly state that we have doubts as to the possibility or feasibility of turning the trick and you will be the first one to whom we will come.

We are endeavoring in this letter to use language such as will result in complete elimination of worry on your part with respect to our faith in you and this work and if this language fails to create this result, then won't you kindly write quite frankly advising in what respect we have failed?

Due to the fact that criticisms are bound to continue until the air cooled cars are in active production and use, would it not be well for you to agree with us that at any time you have occasion to pause and wonder about our faith and confidence in you and this development, that you will pull this letter out of your desk and read it again, after which you will write to us in consideration of our frankly stating that we will write to you first in case of any doubt?

Do you think this letter serves its purpose? What principles of written persuasion does it embody or neglect? Would you have suggested changes in it, had you been a member of the executive committee in November, 1921? Put your thoughts in memorandum form to Alfred P. Sloan, Jr., then chief executive and chairman of the committee.

12. ***Apprehending an Assassin:*** In Frederick Forsyth's thriller, *The Day of the Jackal* [New York: Bantam, 1872], the first clues about a plot to assassinate French President Charles de Gaulle come from the confessions of a suspect named Kowalski. Colonel Rolland, in charge of the investigation (and later to become the hunter of "Jackal"), proceeds as follows (pp. 210–211):

> Finally he sat down to write a report, which had only one listed recipient and was headed "for your eyes only."
>
> He wrote carefully in longhand, describing briefly the operation which he had personally mounted of his own initiative to capture Kowalski; relating the return of the ex-legionnaire to Marseilles, lured by the ruse of a false belief that someone close to him was ill in hospital, the capture by Action Service agents, a brief mention for the record that the man had been interrogated by agents of the Service and had made a garbled confession. He felt bound to include a bald statement that in resisting arrest the ex-legionnaire had crippled two agents but had also done himself sufficient damage in an attempt at suicide that by the time he was overcome the only possible recourse was to hospitalize him. It was here, from his sick bed, that he had made his confession.
>
> The rest of the report, which was the bulk, concerned the confession itself and Rolland's interpretation of it. When he had finished this he paused for a moment, scanning the roof-tops now gilded by the morning sun streaming in from the east. Rolland had a reputation, as he was well aware, for never overstating his case or exaggerating an issue. He composed his final paragraph with care.
>
> "Enquiries with the intention of establishing corroborative evidence for the existence of this plot are still under way at the hour of writing. However, in the event that these enquiries should indicate the above is the truth, the plot described above constitutes in my view the most dangerous single conception that the terrorists could possibly have devised to endanger the life of the President of France. If the plot exists as described, and if the foreign-born assassin known only by the code-name of the Jackal has been engaged for this attempt on the life of the President, and is even now preparing his plans to execute the deed, it is my duty to inform you that in my opinion we face a national emergency."

> Most unusually for him, Colonel Rolland typed the final copy of the report himself, sealed it in an envelope with his personal seal, addressed it, and stamped it with the highest security classification in the Secret Service. Finally he burned the sheets of foolscap on which he had written in longhand and washed the ashes down the plug of the small hand basin in a cabinet in the corner of his office.

Write a short critique of Rolland's understanding of the art of persuasive written communications.

13. Write a short critique of the following statement by economist John Kenneth Galbraith, in an article in the *Atlantic Monthly*, March 1978, p. 105.

> In the case of economics there are no important propositions that cannot be stated in plain language. Qualifications and refinements are numerous and of great technical complexity. These are important for separating the good students from the dolts. But in economics the refinements rarely, if ever, modify the essential and practical point. . . .
>
> Complexity and obscurity have professional value—they are the academic equivalents of apprenticeship rules in the building trades. They exclude the outsiders, keep down the competition, preserve the image of a privileged or priestly class. The man who makes things clear is a scab. He is criticized less for his clarity than for his treachery.
>
> Additionally, and especially in the social sciences, much unclear writing is based on unclear or incomplete thought. It is possible with safety to be technically obscure about something you haven't thought out. It is impossible to be wholly clear on something you do not understand. Clarity thus exposes flaws in the thought. The person who undertakes to make difficult matters clear is infringing on the sovereign right of numerous economists, sociologists and political scientists to make bad writing the disguise for sloppy, imprecise or incomplete thought. One can understand the resulting anger.

14. ***Signals to the Secretary of State:*** If you had been William R. Merriam, public relations head and a vice-president of International Telephone & Telegraph Company in the fall of 1970, and wished to persuade Secretary of State Henry A. Kissinger to help protect the company's business interests in Latin America, would you have sent the following memorandum? Assuming there were com-

pelling reasons to write, would you have written it in this form? If not, show your revisions. (The memorandum was written on ITT's Washington office letterhead. The paper referred to at the end was fairly long and detailed.)

TO: Dr. Henry A. Kissinger

FROM: William R. Merriam

DATE: October 23, 1970

CONFIDENTIAL

Dear Dr. Kissinger: As a result of recent events in Latin America, foreign private enterprise in that area is facing its most serious exposure.

President Nixon, one year ago, in his speech before the Inter-American Press Association said, "We will not encourage private investment where it is not wanted, or where local political conditions face it with unwarranted risks."

ITT does not wish to go where it is not wanted, but we, too, have President Nixon's "strong belief that properly motivated private enterprise has a vital role to play in social as well as economic development."

Our company knows the peoples of the Americas deserve a better way of life and we believe we have a substantial interest in diminishing their problems. The countries themselves are unable to furnish necessary development funds, the U.S. taxpayers cannot, and U.S. private enterprise can provide only that part which a proper climate affords. Everyone agrees the job will have to be done on a coordinated basis.

ITT has given serious consideration to circumstances now facing Hemisphere development. We are convinced the present moment is a most expedient time to reappraise and strengthen U.S. policy in Latin America.

I attach a paper containing our estimations plus specific reference to the Chilean situation. This is respectfully submitted; I would appreciate your comments.

Sincerely,

William R. Merriam,

Vice President

See first that the design
is wise and just; that ascertained,
pursue it resolutely.

William Shakespeare

To drift is to be in hell,
to be in heaven is to steer.

George Bernard Shaw

Chapter 5

Organizing Facts and Ideas

Over the years many businesspeople, lawyers, teachers, and others have taken a kind of sadistic delight in showing me bad examples of writing they have had to read. "This is the kind of stuff I mean," one will say, pulling a report off a pile on his desk. "It's practically unreadable." Another will say, "See this? It's a mess!" Still another will tell me, "Only an idiot could understand this one. It goes all over the place."

One difficulty with these tedious reports and letters is that they are cluttered with jargon, abstract words, repetitious phrases, and unwieldy sentences—the faults usually alleged to be the cause of unreadability. But often the problem goes farther. If the shortcomings in style were corrected, the communications would still be painful to read. Why? The parts do not fit together. There is no "flow" of ideas. The reader loses his or her way and finds the prose meaningless.

Whether in a one-page memorandum or a 40-page report, organization plays an extremely significant role in readability and comprehension. For it is by organizing facts and ideas properly that the writer establishes meaningful relationships, and it is by seeing such relationships that the reader understands the material. "If a man can group his ideas," Robert Louis Stevenson said, "he is a good writer."

John Ball and Cecil B. Williams put it this way:

> If I encounter a new concept, I try to find its internal relationship (the way it hangs together) and to find something I already understand that it can be related to. If I can't establish such relationships for the new concept I just won't understand it at all. What do I mean, relationships? Well, a brother and sister are related, and so are two events that happened the same time or place, two ideas based on the same premises, two answers to the same question, two books by the same author, two ways of doing the same job. Causes are related to effects: the muddy track is related to the thunderstorm. Heat is related to friction. Physical laws are related to each other, and to some laws that haven't been codified yet. What we know is always related to something we don't know, and with luck what we don't know is related to something we already have in our experience.[1]

Indeed, it is impossible to read a written communication with comprehension *unless* one fact is tied to another, one idea is associated with another, one suggestion is related to another experience. As Duncan E. Littlefair points out, "Thought is itself an awareness of interrelationships . . . it is impossible for a person to be conscious of disconnected events. Consciousness *means* that events are seen as possessing some degree of relationship."[2]

[1]John Ball and Cecil B. Williams, *Report Writing* (New York, Ronald. 1955), p. 65.

[2]Duncan E. Littlefair, *The Glory within You: Modern Man and the Spirit* (Philadelphia, Westminster, 1973), p. 47.

Littlefair also makes the interesting observation that among people troubled by a sense of emptiness and futility, the central problem typically centers about lack of awareness of how activities, people, and things relate to one another.

In short, both theory and everyday experience demonstrate the key role played by organization in good writing. In unusual circumstances a sloppily organized letter or report will convey its message to the reader despite its structural faults. Most of the time, however, disorganization is as devastating to a written communication as it is to an army or a retail store.

In this chapter we deal with what Dartmouth's David Lambuth used to call "organization of the whole," that is, the structure of the main points, groups of facts, and ideas in a letter, report, memorandum, or other communication. We do not now consider the organization of sentences within a paragraph or short set of paragraphs. The latter topic, which in this book is called "coherence" for the sake of a different label, is analyzed in Chapter 8. (Actually, both words, "organization" and "coherence," are appropriate for referring both to the structure of the whole and the train of thought within paragraphs, so our distinction is an arbitrary one. A perfectionist might prefer such terms as "macro-" and "microorganization" or "macro-" and "microcoherence.")

In addition, bear in mind that our subject in this chapter is closely related to the subjects of the two previous chapters. For purposes of the discussion to follow, we must assume that:

1. Your report, memorandum, or letter has (or will be given) a good beginning, as described in Chapter 3.
2. The principles of persuasion, as described in Chapter 4, have been considered. If you are dealing with controversial or sensitive questions in your document, those principles come first. Only after they are met should you worry about the logical, rational organization of your material, as dis-

cussed in this chapter. For example, if sound strategy calls for putting your strongest points last, because of the psychology of the situation (see rule # 6), put them last even if, from the standpoint of pure reason, it might seem more logical to put them first or in the middle.

THE BASIC APPROACH

Let us suppose that you know what specific message you want to put across and also have considered the strategy of approaching your reader effectively. In your mind and perhaps in a sheaf of notes and computations you have considerable material to use. How do you go about deciding *what* facts, figures, and ideas to use and *how* to put them together on paper?

Naturally, different people approach this important task in different ways. Some work intuitively, and some work systematically; some work by trial and error, and some work logically; some work fast and intensely, and some work slowly. Our cognitive processes vary so much that it is futile to generalize about personal style. But at the same time it must be recognized that there are some relatively fixed requirements of *readers* and *readership* to meet. Your thinking and writing styles may be different from mine, but in the end you must satisfy some of the exact same needs of the reader that I do. We are like commuters to Boston from my home town of Winchester. They take a variety of roads and modes of transportation, and most of these people are quite fixed in their ways, but when all is said and done they accomplish the same net change in distance and elevation.

Not surprisingly, therefore, good communicators in business and the professions find it possible to help and criticize one another's writing in valid ways, despite their differences in style, ability, and experience. Given a series of written communications on the same topic to grade, they will mark them consistently. And given the same writing problem, they will agree on the value of certain steps in organizing the material effectively.

First, almost all good business and professional writers I know would agree that, whatever your personal style, you cannot communicate with the reader unless you impart a sense of direction or movement to your facts and ideas. Organizing an important letter, report, or memorandum is more like making a movie than taking a photograph. Another analogy has been suggested by Dartmouth's famous writing teacher:

> Think of a piece of writing as a trip from a definite starting point to a definite destination. At the very start we look for a signpost pointing the way and naming the place we are headed for. At every fork of the road we need directions—legible and understandable directions. From time to time we glance back over the road we have already come, in order to remind ourselves of our position and direction. At the end we want to know that we have arrived at the point we set out for. Reminders of this sort are just as necessary in writing as they are in posting a road.[3]

Second, good business and professional writers generally would agree, I think, that all but the most unusual men and women need to make notes on paper in planning an important, nonroutine communication. Mental notes are not enough. Your notes need not be voluminous, nor do they need to be neat outline-type entries on an 8½ × 11 inch sheet of paper or on index cards—scrawlings on the back of a drugstore bill suffice for some people. But you must jot them down *before* you start writing—the big points and, if some of them are complicated, some of the key backup points, too.

If you do not do this, you may forget the ideas later on. How often I have seen that mistake made—by myself as well as others. At the outset, with the main reason for writing and the reader's needs fresh in mind, you think you cannot possibly forget them. But then you become

[3]David Lambuth and others, *The Golden Book of Writing* (New York, Viking, 1964), pp. 6–7.

absorbed in the details and fine points of the writing. Next, interruptions occur, and you are diverted by other tasks. Alas, before you know it, you have lost one or two of those key ideas somewhere in the magnetic tapes and drums of your "upstairs computer."

Third, you need to follow some procedure that forces you to sort the material you plan to put on paper. What should that procedure be? No one can tell you, for the reasons given earlier, but whatever it is, it must make you compare pieces of information and arrange them. For instance, Ball and Williams suggest thinking of the pieces as if they were a pile of cards to put in order.[4] If you were given a shuffled deck of cards to put in order, you would divide the main pile into four piles, with all the clubs in this group, the spades in that group, the hearts in that one, and the diamonds in that one. Next you would tackle each group, putting the cards in order of ace, king, queen, jack, and so on down. Similarly in writing, you first arrange your pieces of information in categories, and then put the items in each category in logical order.

An analogy I find helpful is the shopping list. Suppose the people in your family have jotted down on a list, as the items have come to mind over a period of days or weeks, all the things to take on a camping trip to upper Michigan. Bread, butter, eggs, matches, sunburn cream, apples, 27-inch shoelaces, briquettes, aspirin, flashlight batteries—30 or 40 items, perhaps, in different people's handwriting, in no logical order at all, and sometimes the same item listed more than once. Now comes the time to do the shopping, and you want to make the best use of your time. So you start at the top. You jot down "supermarket" as one heading and under it list the first four items. But sunburn cream means a trip to the drugstore, so you write "drugstore" as another heading and list the fifth item under it; when you come to the ninth item, you

[4]Ball and Williams, *op. cit.*, pp. 38–39.

put that under "drugstore," too. The shoelaces mean a third heading, "shoestore"—and so on.

This is the way to go about arranging the many information pieces for your report, memorandum, or letter. Your first item may pertain, let us say, to the *need* for safety measures while preparing solvent tanks for welding and repairs, so you make that the first category. Other items suggest such categories as "recommended new procedure," "failure of existing measures," "who should act," "technical problems that may be encountered," and so on. Don't worry about the order of categories yet. Just identify the main topics and bunch appropriate items under each.

After this is done you begin thinking about what order the main categories should be in (just as you would decide which stores to go to first and last in the case of the shopping list). Do not try to combine the two steps. Like the outfielder in baseball who tries to catch a fly ball and throw it to an infielder at the same time, thus dropping the ball and failing to put either man out, you may muff both steps at once.

Let us take a specific example. Suppose you are putting together a report on changes to consider in your company's manufacturing policies. As you have talked with senior managers, supervisors, staff people, and consultants and have gone through files of memoranda and letters, you have taken notes and marked certain passages on a wide variety of topics. Also, you have many mental notes. Going over this information one item at a time and deciding what it means, you make the following list of possibilities:

1. Locate plants near markets or near sources of materials.
2. Closer or looser control of production.
3. Pioneer in new processes or use only those proved out by a competitor.
4. Take more risks in design or minimize risks by waiting for more market information.

5. Increase or decrease the size of the industrial engineering staff.
6. Allocate more executive time, or less of it, to production planning and cost control.
7. Freeze new designs earlier or delay until last possible moment to accommodate engineering change orders.
8. Increase or decrease supervision of assembly workers.
9. Increase or decrease the ratio of technically trained operators to nontechnically trained workers.
10. Increase or decrease inventory stocks.
11. Concentrate manufacturing in one large plant or spread it among several smaller ones.
12. Develop tighter quality controls or relax them somewhat.
13. Instruct engineering to release designs only when completely packaged or "design as they go."
14. Functional organization pattern, geographical responsibility, or product-focused pattern.
15. Buy more or fewer components.
16. Many customer specials, few specials, or none at all.

Looking this list over and pondering it, you realize that many of these 16 items are closely related. You jot down the following major categories (again, noting them as you identify them, not worrying yet about the order of presentation):

Plant and equipment (items 1, 11, 15)
Production planning and control (items 2, 10, 12)
Product design and engineering (items 3, 7, 13, 16)
Organization and management (items 4, 6, 14)
Staffing and labor (items 5, 8, 9)

Now turn to the question of order. Perhaps the logical order would be that shown above. However, knowing the "politics" of the situation (see Chapter 4), you decide it would be best to begin with categories about which there is already some agreement—say, product design and production planning. You leave until last the two topics your seniors are quite sensitive about, facilities and organization.

CLASSIFYING DATA

"Okay," the novice says. "I hear you, and it doesn't sound too hard." But then comes the actual doing, and the tune changes. When he or she starts jotting down a long list of disjointed facts and ideas on a subject to be discussed in a report to top management or a letter to an important client, the question of organization may suddenly become quite perplexing. Now the writer may ask despairingly, "How do I know what clusters of points *to look for*? My subject isn't like other subjects!"

A surprisingly high percentage of business and professional communications break down into a finite list of categories, despite a nearly infinite range of subject matter. This is because of the emphasis on analysis, logical differentiation, priorities, evidence, interpretation, and recommendation. If you were to take a fair sampling of business, scientific, and professional communications, you would find no end of variety in the precise, specific descriptions of these categories. But time and again you would find a report by, say, a geologist breaking into the same basic *kinds* of divisions as a memorandum by an air force logistics specialist, let us say, or a brochure by a market research firm.

In most managerial and professional communications, judging from many samples I have studied, the main topics fall into one or more of the following categories:

- New findings, conclusions, or questions (e.g., "Involvement of Central Catecholamines in Clinical Hypertension," section heading in a report on antihypertensive drugs)
- Recommendations and proposals (e.g., "Needed Changes in Personnel Files," section heading in a memorandum on privacy)

- Alternative plans, programs, sequences of steps (e.g., "Other Methods of Purchase," section heading in a memo on procurement)
- Problems and limitations (e.g., "Problems in Using Discounted Cash Flow" in a financial analysis)
- Methods, processes, techniques employed (e.g., "Exponential Smoothing" in a brochure on forecasting)
- Descriptions of other research, experiments, or studies that may be relevant (e.g., "Studies of Leaching in Unpolluted Regions" in a report on leaching in a region)
- Trends, changes, variations (e.g., "Effect of Enrichment in Polyaromatic Hydrocarbons" in a report on crankcase oils)
- Background on problems, recapitulation, historical reviews (e.g., "Precedents for Tort Liability" in a legal brief)
- Discussions of special aspects, considerations, dimensions (e.g., "Possibility of West German Withdrawal" in political study)
- Stages of time, action, process (e.g., "Seasonal Variations" in a retailing analysis)
- Places under investigation, analysis, or consideration (e.g., "Diving Observations Off Santa Barbara" in a report on Pacific electric rays)
- Levels, functions, topics of concern (e.g., "Implications for Middle Management" in a report on reorganization)
- Degrees of significance (e.g., "Secondary Needs" in a military request for appropriations)
- Definitions of terms (e.g., "Sociological Terms Used" in a paper on population behavior)
- Arguments pro and con, conditions favorable and unfavorable (e.g., "Problems in Kinetic Proofreading" in a paper on protein synthesis)
- Topics explored, sections of analysis, divisions of study (e.g., "Summary of Results" in a report on testing)

If you keep such possibilities in mind as you go over the items of information and opinion you want to put in your written communication, you should have no trouble in developing a good list of categories. Do not worry at first about whether actually to use section headings in the writing, or, if you do, what kinds of headings. That is a "finishing detail."

IS IT WORTH THE EFFORT?

"But this will take a lot of time," you protest, "and I'm very busy." Of course you are. And so is your reader! If you take a stream-of-consciousness approach, putting thoughts down as they come into your head, like rogue elephants running wild in the forest, you may finish the communication faster, but at the price of (a) your reader's time, (b) comprehension on the part of your reader, and (c) further clarification in your own mind of the relationships among the issues. The last point should not be underestimated. As people have been finding out for centuries, writing is an excellent discipline for developing a rational, consistent viewpoint on a subject.

Remembering how busy General Maxwell Taylor must have been as chairman of the Joint Chiefs of Staff in 1963, how would you have liked to have been in his swivel chair when he received the following cablegram, dated October 31, 1963, from General Paul Harkins, United States commander in Vietnam?

> Your JCS 4188-63 arrived as I was in the process of drafting one for you along the same lines. I share your concern. I have not as yet seen Saigon 788. I sent to the Embassy for a copy at 0830 this morning—as of now 1100—the Embassy has not released it. Also CINCPAC 0-300040Z infor JCS came as a surprise to me as I am unaware of any change in local situation which indicates necessity for actions directed. Perhaps I'll find the answer in Saigon 768. Or perhaps actions directed in CINCPAC 300040Z are precautionary in light of Gen. Don's statement reported in CAS 1925 that a coup would take place in any case not later than 2 November. It might be noted Don also is supposed to have said CAS Saigon 1956—that though the coup committee would not release the details, the Ambassador would receive the complete plan for study two days prior to the scheduled times for the coup.

> I have not been informed by the Ambassador that he has received any such plan. I talked to him yesterday on my return from Bangkok and he offered no additional information. He has agreed to keep me completely informed if anything new turns up.
>
> Incidentally he leaves for Washington tomorrow (31st) afternoon. If the coup [one word illegible] to happen before the second he's hardly going to get two days notice.
>
> One thing I have found out, Don is either lying or playing both ends against the middle. What he told me is diametrically opposed to what he told Col. Conein. He [word illegible] Conein the coup will be before November 2nd. He told me he was not planning a coup. I sat with Don and Big Minh for 2 hours during the parade last Saturday. No one mentioned coups. To go on:
>
> Both CAS Saigon 1896 and 1925 were sent first and delivered to me after dispatch. My 1991 was discussed with the Ambassador prior to dispatch. My 1993 was not, basically because I had not seen CAS Saigon 1925 before dispatch and I just wanted to get the record straight from my side and where my name was involved.
>
> The Ambassador and I are currently in touch with each other but whether the communications between us are effective is something else. I will say Cabot's methods of operations are entirely different from Amb Nolting's as far as reporting . . . is concerned.
>
> Fritz would always clear messages concerning the military with me or my staff. . . .[5]

On and on for more than 600 words goes this morass of muddied thoughts and tangled recommendations, covering various individuals' communication procedures, differences between his (Harkins') viewpoint and Ambassador Lodge's, information about General Diem, the likelihood of the war effort's changing for the better, Diem again, back to Ambassador Lodge's assessments,

[5] *The Pentagon Papers* (New York, Bantam, 1971), pp. 219–221. As for background, "JCS," "CINCPAC," and other such abbreviations refer to numbered organizational communications. General Don—Tran Van Don—was Chief of Staff of the South Vietnamese armed forces. "Big Minh" was South Vietnamese general Duong Van Minh. The coup referred to was the planned overthrow of the Ngo brothers, of whom Ngo Dinh Diem was President of South Vietnam. The coup succeeded, and the brothers were murdered on November 2. The Ambassador referred to was Henry Cabot Lodge, United States Ambassador to South Vietnam during 1963 and 1964.

once again to the future of the war and United States military philosophy, again the idea of getting rid of Diem!

Yet this is what all of us are likely to write unless we take simple preliminary steps to list our facts and ideas, group them, and put the groups in order. General Harkins was an intelligent man. The mistakes in his writing are typical of the stream-of-consciousness approach. Note how individual *words* accidentally trigger thought changes in Harkins' mind, throwing him off the track of *ideas* he had in the back of his mind when he began the lengthy cablegram. For example:

- The mention of "plan" in the final sentence of the first paragraph reminds him of Ambassador Henry Cabot Lodge, who had talked to him about a plan. So now the ambassador becomes the subject for two paragraphs.
- In the sixth paragraph he happens to mention Ambassador Nolting. This name derails his thought again; the next paragraph is about Nolting and a man whom Nolting's name brings to mind.

Looking at the cablegram as a whole, I suspect that Harkins wants to convey three important messages. First, there is some treachery going on regarding a coup. Second, a coup is not in the interests of the United States because (a) things will get better in South Vietnam, (b) Diem is strongly anti-Communist, and (c) it is unfair to throw him out after eight years of nurturing him. Third, because communications are fouled up, Harkins is getting the blame for things he should not be blamed for. How much simpler General Taylor's task as reader would have been if all words had been grouped around these points!

Because Harkins doesn't take a few minutes to organize his thoughts, he reminds us of the old storyteller Mark Twain used to describe. The old man started many stories but never got to the end of one because always somewhere along the way a word or name would remind him of *another* story to tell.

PRETESTING A WRITING PLAN

If your communication is a very important one, it pays to go a step further and systematically outline the key ideas. Whether this is done on the back of a manila envelope or on a fresh sheet of paper makes no difference, so long as you make the points clearly and in enough detail to reveal gaps in the thought, illogical sequences, inconsistencies, and needless repetitions. An outline has the further value of enabling you to remember quickly what your train of thought was and to start with a minimum of "mental retooling" after you have been interrupted in the writing and diverted to a different task. In short, outlining is a proven tool of efficiency and time management. For instance, H. J. Tichy observes:

> I have seen executives study their jottings, divide them into two memorandums, and then direct them to different readers. Their readers responded better when they did not have to wade through what did not concern them to find what did. I have also seen an executive examine his outline of a letter, telephone to discuss three possibilities, and wire a confirmation of the action selected. That saved the energy and time involved in a long letter and a long reply. The most common improvement is the removal of unnecessary material. Apparently writers tend to expand a short work when they first think of the contents, and if they do not examine and plan, they dictate much more material than a reader needs. Outlining helps them to keep short works to proper length.[6]

Of course, outlines are not like blueprints that must be followed meticulously. After beginning your report or letter you may find it wise to deviate from your outline, perhaps dropping one part and adding another. This is easily done when you have a plan to begin with.

Suppose you are preparing a memorandum for a client or for employees of your company on the threat of organized crime. After you have sorted your facts and

[6]H.J. Tichy, *Effective Writing* (New York, Wiley, 1966), pp. 95–96.

thoughts and worked out a tentative order for them, you produce the following "skeleton" (which is similar to one used by a manager in a New Jersey company):

September 16, 1972

TO: All employees

FROM: Alvin Ames

SUBJECT: How to defend against infiltration by organized crime

I. History of organized crime in our city
   A. From 1960 to 1970
   B. Since Mayor Wing's administration, 1970—
II. The threat of the Mafia
   A. Gambling
   B. Narcotics
   C. Embezzlement
III. How the Mafia could make inroads into a company in our industry
   A. Work through agents in the company to sell narcotics, start gambling, etc.
   B. Loans to employees followed by pressure
   C. Becoming a supplier to company, using contracts to organize gambling, dope rings
   D. Purchasing stock in company
IV. Defense against the Mafia
   A. Prohibition of any and all gambling on premises
   B. Surveillance of drug users before apprehending them—who supplies them?
   C. Inform police and FBI of any suspicious behavior
   D. Rigorous screening of suppliers
   E. Employee education
      1. Nature of threat
      2. How to alert management without incurring reprisal from agents or sympathizers
      3. Security measures
         a. In data-processing department
         b. Plant guards
         c. Locking doors and files
         d. Surveillance of weekend work

Now look your outline over critically. Forget the details. Concentrate only on the flow and sense of it. Is anything out of order? Indeed, several weaknesses seem apparent.

First, if your statement of the subject is accurate—if the purpose is really to show employees *how* to keep organized crime out—then topics I, II, and III are irrelevant. They are informative and pertinent, but they do not show the reader what action to take. To handle this problem, you could sharply condense those topics into a short introduction—or, perhaps better, needle the facts into explanations of the steps to take. (Of course, another possibility is that your statement of subject is too narrow, that what you should write instead is "Subject: The threat of organized crime and how to counter it.")

Second, topic IV of the outline and the subject statement deal with the same point; IV is not part of the outline but the whole of it. If your subject statement is right as it stands, should you begin with point A under IV?

Third, topic III is repetitious of topic II. Why discuss the gambling and drug threats in II, and then start explaining them all over again in III-A, B, and C?

Fourth, if embezzlement is named as a major threat in point II-C, why is it omitted from the discussion of inroads under topic III?

Fifth, computer security is not mentioned until point IV-E-3-a. Is this reasonable? In a great many companies, computer security is such a crucial part of the picture that it shares top billing in prevention. Is your company different in that respect? If not, this aspect probably should be mentioned earlier in the outline.

How you resolve these questions depends, of course, on your knowledge of the situation and your assignment. But it should be evident that the outline technique—a comparatively simple and quick method at this stage—has shown you how to make some major improvements in the cogency, cohesiveness, and readability of your memorandum *before* you start writing things out.

James M. McCrimmon urges students to subdivide topics as much as they can at the outline stage. Failing to take such a step, the student writer *may* be able to subdivide and organize adequately when he starts to write out the section, McCrimmon says, "but that requires him to do better planning while writing than he did when he was concerned only with planning. *In practice, students almost never correct the deficiencies of an outline during the composition of an essay.* Flaws in the outline are almost certain to be preserved."[7] The observation is as valid for business and professional writers in general, in my opinion, as it is for students.

HOW TO CURE THAT TIRESOME GROUPING

Some reports and memoranda make readers feel as if they have aged and gone stale, and for good reason. The writer has made no effort to organize, streamline, or boil down the thoughts in different sections. The sections are left like the untended playroom of a child who never sorts things out and never throws useless things away.

Here, from a consultant's report to a retailer, is an example of a tiresome grouping:

> Great Lakes Stores have recently lost market share to Galaxy Stores because of the following factors:
>
> - Galaxy's colorful and efficient advertising approach, while Great Lakes changed from a previously successful strategy to an ineffective one.
> - Galaxy remodeled its stores in such a way as to attract new customers.
> - Galaxy increased its media expenditures by over 10%.
> - Great Lakes' competitive ability is hindered by a poor system of control over inventories, purchasing, and sales promotion.

[7]James M. McCrimmon, *Writing with a Purpose* (Boston, Houghton Mifflin, 1963), p. 62.

- Withdrawal of advertising support for Great Lakes leading to decline in patronage and amount of sales volume.

One reason this grouping is tiresome is that the author fails to draw any conclusion, apparently believing that to be the reader's job. In fact, the listing doesn't allow the reader to reach a conclusion—at least, at first—because classifying the actions as "factors" isn't specific enough to guide the mind to a conclusion. Also, the points are jumbled and sometimes overlap one another.

To begin sorting out this tiresome list, first classify the actions by subject:

Great Lakes

Poor control over inventories, purchasing, and sales promotion
Reduction in advertising leading to decline in patronage and sales

Galaxy

Colorful and efficient advertising
Remodeling of stores to attract more customers
Increase in media expenditures

Next, inspect the revised list for elements of likeness. All three of Galaxy's actions involve marketing; so does one of Great Lakes' actions. Therefore, these can be grouped to contrast Galaxy with Great Lakes. However, the control weakness at Great Lakes (first item in the column) must be set apart.

In addition, the first and third items in the Galaxy list logically go one after the other, because they involve advertising and promotion.

It is now possible to revise the statement so that it is livelier and communicates more effectively:

Great Lakes Stores have been losing market share to Galaxy Stores for two reasons. First, because of poor control over inventories, purchasing, and sales promotion, Great Lakes' competitive ability has suffered. Second, Galaxy follows a more effective marketing strategy. While Great Lakes has reduced its advertising and has experienced declines in patronage and sales volume, Galaxy has:

- Increased its media expenditures by more than 10%.
- Advertised in colorful and efficient ways.
- Remodeled its stores to attract more customers.

HEADINGS AND NUMBERS

Many written communications do not need headings. For example, most letters you write do not need them. Yet it is fair to say that business and professional writing would be better in general if headings were used more often. It is better to err on the side of too many headings than too few or none.

Actually, there is only one danger you run when you employ headings: that you will put a fact or recommendation under the wrong rubric and thus obscure it from the reader, just as a document may be lost because it is put in the wrong drawer in a desk. But I think this risk can be exaggerated. Your reader mentally improvises headings as he or she goes along, and there is a greater danger that he or she will invent an incorrect heading for a section than that you will misplace items of information.

Basically, there are two types of headings—topical and instructive. The first type includes headings like "Cost trends," "Operations 1972–1974," and "How to Reduce Employee Turnover." Such headings identify a subject but do not clue the reader as to the main theme or idea of the material following. Instructive headings, by contrast, convey the gist of the information following. They are like headlines. Examples of instructive headings are "Lubrication Systems Preserve Parts" and "Need for 10% Increase in Salespeople's Salaries."

Both topical and instructive headings, in turn, can be

classified as "lazy" or "helpful." A lazy heading is one that pops into mind because it is so obvious—one like "Problem" or "Materials" or "Selective Plugging." A helpful heading is one devised after a minute of additional thought in an effort to guide the reader more. For instance, "Problem" becomes "Lower Recovery Because of Plugging"; "Materials" becomes "Types of Cores Used in Testing"; and "Selective Plugging" becomes "10% Increase in Oil Recovery Produced by Selective Plugging."

Obviously, an instructive heading is more helpful to the reader than a topical heading. You may have seen documents a reader could thumb through and learn from simply by glancing at the instructive headings—and how often it happens that at least one heading challenges the reader to stop and go through the section paragraph by paragraph. But instructive headings may be difficult to devise and are not always wise. If you must strain too hard to create them, you may produce ludicrous or misleading captions.

As for the format of headings, you can take your choice of various possibilities. To mention the best-known ones:

No tier. Headings can be capitalized and inserted at the beginning of the first line of a new section, as in the paragraph series you are now reading. If the headings follow in logical sequence, you may want to enumerate or alphabetize them.

Single tier. If you want the headings to stand out more, place them on separate lines before the first lines of text in sections. Frequent examples of this pattern can be seen elsewhere in this book.

Double tier. If you divide your message into several main parts, and one or more of these parts contains subparts that you want to stand out, use headings and subheadings. Thus:

EMPLOYMENT

Scope of Procurement

Commercial aircraft manufacturing is primarily a Pacific Coast industry, in the sense that that is where the major manufacturing companies assemble their airplanes. The Boeing Company's Washington State operations, and McDonnell Douglas and Lockheed with major commercial facilities. . . . [this section continues for several paragraphs]

Manufacturing Payrolls

Total U.S. commercial aircraft manufacturing payrolls in 1970 amounted to more than $3.5 billion. This money, . . . [section continues with a long paragraph and map]

Jobs

When payrolls are related to individual jobs, we see that there were nearly 260,000 people directly employed in the manufacture of commercial aircraft in 1970. . . . [section continues through one more paragraph, followed by two other sections][8]

Of course, the style can vary widely; for example, the main headings can be centered instead of capitalized, and the subheadings can be run into the paragraph (as in the no-tier approach). But be sure to make the two types of headings *different* in appearance.

Digital style. A pattern often followed by engineers makes use of a decimal system, with the first digit specifying the main section, the second digit specifying the subsection, and sometimes a third digit specifying a sub-subsection. (Sometimes the second digit is replaced by a letter of the alphabet.) For instance:

3.1.2 Equipment installations—There are 11 friction hoists installed in Canada, with the first unit purchase in 1955. Haulage systems, incorporating our battery and trolley locomotives, track switches, and power rectifiers have been supplied to various mines...

[8]*Commercial Aircraft Exports: A Survey of National Benefits* (Aerospace Industries Association of America, 1971), 19 pp.

STANDARDIZED ORGANIZATION PLANS

Sometimes your organization scheme already has been worked out for you. For example, salesmen's call reports are likely to be requested on printed forms indicating the date of call, person called on, type of account, and result of call. Again, you may be directed to use colored sheets for different sections, with white for "Synopsis," blue for "Recommendations," and so on. These schemes may be convenient for those who must use the information or put it on a computer. For those reporting information, too, they may be convenient—but not if the forms are too detailed. One is reminded of the old farmer in Lyndonville, Maine who sat down one evening by the lamp to fill out a government form that was almost overdue. Like many of us in similar circumstances, the numerous imperatives of the form did not put him in a good mood. There, staring him in the face from a box at the top right-hand corner of the form were the words in bold type: "Do Not Write In This Space." Before proceeding further, he took his pen and wrote in that space, in equally bold letters, "I Write Where I Goddam Please."

Students and graduate students, too, may be expected to follow fixed outlines when writing papers. One common outline is the following:

Abstract

A. Purpose of paper

B. Brief summary of results or conclusions

C. Summary statement of significance and applications of work

I. *Introduction*

A. Statement of problem

B. Summary of previous work and publications on problem

C. Purpose of paper
D. Method of attacking problem and accomplishing purpose
E. Explanation of novel or original features of work
F. Statement of organization of main body

II. *Body of Paper*

This part is left to the discretion of the writer, except that the arrangement of information is expected to follow the plan indicated in part I, section F above.

III. *Conclusions*

A. Statement of how the original objectives were met
B. Summary of work done
C. Evaluation of work done and statement of limitations
D. Contribution to knowledge, i.e., what the work has done that is new or different
E. Discussion of applications and significance of work or results

FINAL REVIEW

When you finish your draft and review it before final typing and sending, it is useful to have a mental checklist of questions concerning the coverage and arrangement of topics. Every good business and professional writer I know has such a checklist and uses it without fail, even though he or she may have outlined the communication carefully before drafting it.

Here are some candidate questions for your checklist. They will help you avoid putting your reader in the position of the person described by William J. Gallagher who ordered a television set so that he could view a program in which he was vitally interested, but received instead a crate filled with tubes, wires, resistors, and a multitude of other electronic components.[9]

1. **Are all the points suggested in the introduction developed in the body of the write-up?**

If the introduction mentions points A, B, and C, but only A and C come in for attention later in the document, either you should add a discussion of B or leave that point out of the introduction. (If you want to mention it without covering it in any detail, leave it until the end.) Also, cover the points *in the same order* they are mentioned in the introduction. Otherwise your readers may become confused, wondering, as they go from A to C, "Has he already covered B only I missed it?"

2. **Are the sequence and development of points complete?**

Although this is the kind of question that organization planning is supposed to anticipate, it needs to be asked again in the final review. What often happens is that we add, change, extend, or condense our original thinking on a point when we begin writing it out. We end up casting a situation or reason in a light different from that envisaged at the beginning. Or we raise whole new questions and issues that become unclouded in our minds as we explain our thoughts in detail. And so we need to ask this question all over again when the draft is done. We are like the home boat builder I knew who carefully designed the beam of his boat to be two inches less than the width of the basement doorway. He held his boat to that dimension all right, but while constructing it he found to his delight that he could make it more than a foot longer than planned. When he tried to take the finished hull out of the

[9]William J. Gallagher, *Report Writing for Management* (Reading, Mass., Addison-Wesley, 1969), p. 3.

basement, he found it was three inches too long to make the turn at the top of the stairs.

If you thought of a new alternative in writing a section on courses of action, is its cost included in the discussion along with the costs of other alternatives? If you thought of a new objection to some viewpoint as you wrote the ending and set it forth strongly and convincingly, should you plant the seed of it in the early sections, so that the reader is prepared for it? If your report includes both conclusions and recommendations, are the former as clear and distinct from the latter as you had expected to make them when you began writing?

3. Are there ideas, proposals, or sections that should be combined?

Look for items that seem to say about the same thing or that are closely related. The distinctions may be real to you. But from your reader's standpoint would they appear to be duplicate ideas? If so, by combining them you can save the reader time, as well as improve readability.

Exhibit I shows the topic sentences of the first half of a report to top management by a marketing manager in an appliance company. The year was 1971, and he wanted his company to pay more attention to "consumerism" in its marketing and manufacturing programs. (I add the outline style here in order to identify the sentences.)

Exhibit I. Topic Sentences of Part of a Report to Top Management

I. Our competitors approach consumerism dishonestly. . . .
   A. Too many companies in our industry subscribe to "cosmetic consumerism," an attempt to mollify critics, not solve problems. . . .
   B. Their brand of consumerism is gingerbread, added for effect, not substance. . . .

   C. Band wagonism is rife. Companies hop aboard the consumerism movement because:
      1. They are afraid not to have a consumerism program. . . .
      2. They think it is a good marketing gimmick. . . .
   D. They create consumerism positions for show—a respectable place to put worn-out executives who have many years of service and shouldn't be booted out. . . .
   E. Management may not understand the full implications of consumerism. . . .

II. Our company must take an honest approach. . . .
   A. Consumerism is a valid movement. . . .
      1. It is a mainstay of our competitive enterprise system. . . .
      2. It focuses on customer satisfaction, which is the true nexus of business. A company can't profit and endure without making its customers better off than before. . . .
   B. "Cosmetic consumerism" is doomed to fail. . . .
      1. Eventually it will be exposed as a gimmick and reveal a company's low regard for consumers. . . .
      2. When a company puts itself on the line to produce for the consumer, it becomes a vulnerable target when it fails to produce. . . .
      3. The cosmetic brand of consumerism contributes to growing distrust of the competitive market system. . . .

III. Consumerism could produce important bonuses for our company. . . .
   A. Real benefits can be reaped from true consumerism. . . .
      1. It leads to increased sales and profits because consumers are satisfied. . . .
      2. Public attitudes toward our company would improve. . . .
      3. We would get an unexpected bonus—an end to the isolated executive (the executive who is not on consumer's wave length). . . .
   B. A consumerism program would get our marketing people out of the office. . . .
      1. It would mean they would visit customers at their homes. . . .

2. The distance between management and customers would evaporate. . . .

C. The evils of management isolation would be avoided. . . .

1. It allows an executive to lose sight of the company position in the total scheme of the market. . . .
2. It creates a chasm between worker and consumer. . . .
3. It robs the worker of "pride of authorship"—he doesn't see his product in use. . . .

D. Important operational benefits would materialize, too. . . .

1. With the company-customer gap closed, there should be a reduction of the time lag between feedback on customer complaints and corrective action in the research department, manufacturing, etc. . . .
2. There should be a reduction of management reaction time to consumer responses to products. . . .
3. Consumer relations ought to improve. . . .

Now, when this memorandum was outlined, the arrangement of ideas made good sense to the writer. But as the draft was being written, some of the distinctions and patterns became blurred. They might still seem defensible to the writer, but the reader would sense overlap, repetition, and misarrangement of sections. For instance:

- Point II-A deals with two advantages of consumerism in order to demonstrate the validity of the movement. Yet point III asserts that "bonuses and 'real benefits' can be reaped from consumerism." Since both points deal with benefits, why not put them together? This would produce a stronger, more persuasive case that important advantages could be gained.
- Point II-B, on the failure of cosmetic consumerism, seems to be out of place. The logical place for it seems to be after points I-A, -B, and -C, which mention the dishonesty of most approaches. Also, point III-C refers to management isolation, yet points 2 and 3 under it refer to worker isolation.
- Point III-A-3 says that an unexpected bonus of the new approach would be putting an end to the "isolated executive."

Points III-B and III-C also deal with executive isolation; in addition, point III-D-2 concerns the problem of management isolation from the marketplace, and point III-D-1, the problem of research isolation. Why not put all these aspects of company isolation together? A single united point would be stronger and more efficient than several partial points.

Part I of the memorandum would then state that competitors are approaching consumerism dishonestly, would specify how they are doing that, and assert that failure lies ahead of them. Part II would assert that "cosmetic consumerism" is doomed to fail for three reasons (those given in II-B of Exhibit I). And Part III would look as follows in skeleton form:

III. Consumerism could produce important bonuses for our company. . . .
- A. It would make for long-run strength in competition. . . .
  1. Customer satisfaction would lead to increased sales and profits. . . .
  2. Public attitudes toward our company would improve. . . .
- B. It would lead to better marketing operations. . . .
  1. Executive isolation from the consumer would be ended—managers would visit customers in their homes. . . .
  2. The company research and manufacturing departments would be able to respond faster to customer complaints. . . .
- C. Employee satisfactions would grow. . . .
  1. As the chasm between workers and consumers decreases, workers would gain more "pride of authorship." . . .

4. Is there a clear relationship between the facts and ideas?

It should be readily apparent to your reader how each part of a major point reinforces that point. If there is any doubt about such relationships, either the wording is at fault and should be revised, or the organization needs to be revised. Remember that unless your reader sees the relationships, he or she cannot understand the ideas.

To help those relationships become apparent, each subsection should "point back" to the statement in the main section. "Pointing back" is a phrase borrowed from James McCrimmon, who uses it to describe how amplifying or supporting ideas should tie in with the main thought—both in sense and in wording. For example, if you state that there are three advantages of a value-added tax, your section on that point should contain nothing but advantages, no more or no less than three, and each topic sentence pointing to one of them should use the word "advantage" or a close synonym like "benefit" or "gain." Then not only does the thought "point back," but the words also remind the reader of the tie-in with the lead statement.

5. Are the main points clearly distinguished from supporting points?

As stated earlier, if main headings and subheadings are used, the former should have more space and prominence (e.g., a separate line) than the latter do; also, main heads can be distinguished from subheads by means of a numbering system. Here, for instance, is an excerpt from a bulletin of the U.S. Bureau of the Budget on the so-called planning-programming-budgeting system:

> 4. *Program structure.* The program structure should group agency activities in a way that facilitates. . . .
>   a. *Program categories.* The categories in a program structure should. . . .
>   b. *Program subcategories.* Subcategories should provide a meaningful. . . .
>   c. *Program elements.* A program element covers agency activities. . . .[10]

[10]Bulletin No. 68-9, Executive Office of the President, April 12, 1968.

6. Are the ideas, parts, and/or sections arranged in logical order?

If you are describing priorities, are the most important ones first and the least important ones last? If you are describing the time stages of a process, do the first ones come first and the last ones last? If at the beginning you identified six questions to be considered, are they considered in that order in the body of the communication? If you are calling for changes in a way of doing things, have you first made clear the *need* for change before describing the ability of your proposals to meet that need and their practicality in terms of costs, contractual commitments, and so on? If your company must solve several problems, are the most urgent ones dealt with first?

The excerpt above from the PPB bulletin is a good example of logical progression. The largest classification, "program categories," is explained first; then the next largest classification, "program subcategories," is described; and then the smallest group, "program elements" (which make up the subcategories as defined) is covered.

7. Is there sufficient elaboration or detail for each question, issue problem, or topic dealt with in the document?

For example, if your memorandum mentions seven stages in the establishment of a proposed incentive system for sales representatives, do not discuss five or six in depth and leave the remainder undescribed. If the others are unimportant, leave them out of your scheme or mention them only incidentally in a closing paragraph.

This is not to say that all stages or topics mentioned in introducing a discussion have to be given equal space or emphasis; that is wholly unnecessary. The point is simply that if you set the reader up to expect information on a certain number or sequence of ideas, you leave him or her confused if you do not follow through on that plan.

"What about the fourth item?" the reader thinks. "Is it supposed to be covered somewhere that I didn't notice?"

8. Is there an appropriate ending?

By the time you have finished the body of a detailed report, it may be tempting to stop. Not only are you tired, but all the facts and recommendations seem as familiar to you as the back of your hand. For the reader, however, matters are not so obvious, especially if the document is complicated and technical. The following observations come from J.C. Mathes and Dwight W. Stevenson:

> Too many report writers, apparently feeling some misdirected urge to "let the facts speak for themselves," or feeling that the summary in the opening component is conclusion enough, omit any kind of conclusion from the discussion. They just stop. Yet, if the discussion is to stand on its own it must be ended. To leave out the report's ending is to obscure the detailed conclusions some readers seek. You are expecting them to add up the discussion for themselves, and to do it correctly. If you are lucky, your readers may be both willing to do that and capable of doing it well. More likely, however, you will find they resent having to do it and that they are not able to do it as well as you would like. The solution, therefore, is obvious; to complete the discussion and complement the purpose stated in the beginning, you must always include an ending.[12]

For the content of a conclusion or summary, you can reintroduce the problem and restate the objectives and findings of your study, or you can distil the highlights of the information you have described, or you can digest the main arguments you have set forth. Sometimes, after a brief mention of the principal ideas, you can think ahead about the implications for the future or for the reader or perhaps for the reader's organization.

[12]J.C. Mathes and Dwight W. Stevenson, *Designing Technical Reports* (Indianapolis: Bobbs-Merrill, 1976), p. 95.

PROBLEMS AND CASES

1. "Thought is itself an awareness of interrelationships," stated one authority. List some simple ways by which a writer conveys to the reader his or her "awareness of interrelationships" between the facts and ideas described.
2. Present an example, real or imagined, of the conflict between the rules of persuasion described in Chapter 4 and the rules of good organization described in this chapter.
3. Take a short report or document that you have found troublesome to read and (a) outline it, and (b) describe any improvements in the report that might have been made had a careful outline been written in advance by the writer.
4. Take a report or document that has few or no headings, make three photocopies of it, and (a) insert a series of "lazy" topical headings on one photocopy, (b) insert a series of "helpful" topical headings on the second photocopy, (c) insert a series of instructive headings on the third photocopy.
5. Suppose a friend of yours looks at versions (a) and (c) in the previous question and says, "Frankly, I doubt (c) is more readily understood than (a)." Devise and describe a simple test of comparative readership of the two versions to prove he or she is wrong.
6. Following the suggestions offered in the text, reoutline parts I and II of the memorandum described in Exhibit I. (Follow the style used in the text for showing an improved outline of part III.)
7. Write a commentary on the following statement, using short examples to illustrate both the taxi ride and the horseback ride mentioned.

   > There should be two main objects in ordinary prose writing: to convey a message, and to include in it nothing that will distract the reader's attention or check his habitual pace of reading—he should feel that he is seated at ease in a taxi, not riding a temperamental horse through traffic. (Robert Graves and Alan Hodge)

8. ***Controlling Computer Error:*** An executive task force of a

large corporation studied its management information system and computer hardware, investigated alternative kinds of equipment, and recommended, in its report to top management, that a "mass storage system"—an advanced form of computer equipment—be installed. The following passage, reproduced by permission, is taken verbatim from the task force's written report. Do not worry if you don't know what kinds of equipment some of the terms refer to (e.g., "disk data sets," "scratch tapes"). Read the passage enough times so that you can pick up the sense of it, then (a) decide if the passage could be improved (b) if your answer is "yes," write an improved version. Assume that the intended readers include some top officials who are not experts in computer hardware but can, if they wish, get an explanation quickly of any technicality that concerns them.

By enabling a data center to put its data on line by means of the mass storage system, there will be a significant reduction or elimination of the need for human intervention to make data available for processing. Today a customer with normal tape and disk data sets is required to have extensive external cataloging procedures and manual controls over his tape library. To respond to requests for use of the data, he must be able to locate and issue the proper volumes, maintain external labels for active, backup, and scratch tapes as the data set migrates through its useful life, transport the requested data sets from the library to the machine room, provide temporary storage in the machine room or hallways pending usage, modify the run sheets to reflect the appropriate serial number, respond to mount request with the proper reel and the proper drive, demount the used reel at job end, provide temporary storage in the machine room for the used reels pending return to the library, transport the reels back to the library, log in the reels reflecting their changed status, and file the reels in proper storage slots. All of this must be done without human error. Even the best run computer operations in the larger establishments often cannot provide reels for reuse within a single shift once they enter the cycle described above. The opportunity for error in the existing procedure is overwhelming. This causes system and thruput delay which, though not always quantified in dollars cost, is significant.

9. ***A Review of Requirements:*** Troubled by conflicting forecasts of equipment costs and confusion in technological planning, the management of a southwestern company assigned 10 executives to a task force to review computer ("hardware") problems and research needs. After several months of study, the chairman of the task force drafted the following "interim report" for the company president (the names, dates, and places are disguised):

FROM: Midge Bomont

TO: Dave Howard

DATE: May 19, 1972

A hardware planning effort is currently underway to determine the long-term (five years) equipment needs of the users of the Houston Research Center. In analyzing where we are at this time, I have drawn several conclusions:

(1) The departmental requirements for the next four years are not well defined. The requirements we can foresee for the major Houston Center users project the needs for 1973 and 1974. The needs that result from the Dallas division plan will not be available until February or March, the needs of the El Paso unit for 1978 and 1980 have not been sized and this work cannot be started until after the current election. Several of the production division plans are still to be developed. Since these divisions have a major impact on the Houston Center operation, we cannot make a long-term decision without a better understanding of their requirements.

(2) There is a need to increase the capacity in 1973 to meet division projections. This required about a 15% increase in 1973 with a similar increase in 1974. In addition, a commitment has been made to headquarters to provide a bio-medical capability and they are developing a major system using this capability. We must,

therefore, provide this facility. The sizing of this requirement has not been completed.

(3) The El Paso division is acquiring a company that has a sizable research center performing services similar to the El Paso Center.

(4) There is a desire to provide additional services to divisions that will permit them to increase the productivity of research and provide non-scientific personnel with easy access to the labs to perform a variety of analytical and special studies.

Based on these conclusions, I recommend that we proceed as follows:

(1) Firm up requirements in the next six weeks to the extent possible.

(2) Select a research program that will satisfy requirements of 1973 and 1974 and form a basis for moving ahead.

(3) Expand the El Paso Center to handle bio-medical research and to provide the basis for a second, larger research center if we decide to take the multi-research center route some time in the near future.

(4) We need a thorough understanding of the future requirements and a clear definition of our long-term objectives.

With this approach I believe we can satisfy both the desire to move to new technology and the need to continuously review our requirements and remain flexible enough to change as requirements change.

Before sending the report, Midge Bomont asked for editorial suggestions from other members of the task force. If you had been one of them, would you have suggested changes? If so, write the report as you think it should be sent.

10. ***The Metallurgical Measurer:*** The following report is reproduced by permission of Armco Steel Corporation, Middletown, Ohio. It is reprinted from John Ball and Cecil B. Williams, *Report Writing* (New York: Ronald, 1955), pp. 116–117. Write an improved version of it.

TO: Mr. R.H. Heyer, Supervising Metallurgist
Research Laboratories

FROM: James C. Wilkins

SUBJECT: A Method for Measuring Grain Size:
Report on Trip to Butler
to Demonstrate This Method

On November 22 and 24, 1950, the Metallurgical Laboratories at the Butler Plant were visited for the purpose of showing the Metallurgical personnel the method of grain size determinations used by the Research Laboratories.

The standard grain size charts for low carbon steel, austenitic stainless steel, wheel steel, and stabilized steel were shown to the Laboratory personnel. The grain size measuring instrument was demonstrated on both the Bausch & Lomb ILS metallograph in the General Metallurgy Laboratory and the B&L research metallograph in the Wheel Works Laboratory. No changes would have to be made in the present design of the grain size measuring instrument for use with the ILS metallograph. The only problem would be the darkening of the room in the area of the metallograph by a sliding curtain or by some other means. Mr. Hindman indicated that this problem would be worked out in some way.

The Wheel Works Laboratory has the metallograph located in a room which can be darkened. It was found that it is a very simple matter to remove the binocular eyepiece from the B&L research metallograph and to insert the single tube eyepiece with the projection prism attached to it. However, the bracket for holding the disks would have to be somewhat different from the present instrument used in the Research Laboratories. It would be a very simple operation to adapt the grain size measuring instrument to this model metallograph.

Considerable interest was expressed by the Butler personnel in adopting this method of grain size measurement. At the present time they are measuring grain size by observing their micros through the eyepiece and using the A.S.T.M. Standards as a comparison. This method is far from being as accurate and convenient as the projection method using Armco materials as a standard. The metallographic section of the Research Laboratories has found this method to be very satisfactory. Therefore, it is believed that this method should be made available to Armco Metallurgical Laboratories.

11. ***DOD's Diagnosis:*** In February 1975 James R. Schlesinger, Secretary of the Department of Defense, submitted his regular budget report to the Congress. Part II of the report was entitled "Strategic Forces." The following is the first half of the second section of Part II.

B. SIGNIFICANT DEVELOPMENTS IN FOREIGN STRATEGIC CAPABILITIES

The strategic forces of the Soviet Union constitute by far the major external strategic capability which the forces of the United States must be designed to counterbalance. The strategic forces of the People's Republic of China, while growing slowly in size, are still significant only in a regional context. Hence, the following discussion deals principally with the Soviet forces.

1. The Soviet Union

Last year I reported to the Congress that the Soviet Union was in the midst of an ICBM development program which was unprecedented in its breadth and depth. Four new ICBMs—the "light" solid fuel SS-X-16, the "medium" liquid fuel SS-17, the "medium" liquid fuel SS-19 and the "heavy" liquid fuel SS-18—were being flight tested simultaneously. But of far greater importance with regard to the strategic balance, all four of those missiles employed a post boost vehicle (PBV), i.e., a bus type dispensing system, and all except the SS-X-16 were being flight tested with MIRVs. Now, a year later, I must report to the Congress that this most impressive development program is nearing completion and that we have evidence that all four of these new ICBMs have started, or soon will start, operational deployment. What remains to be ascertained at this time is simply the extent, composition and pace of that deployment.

Of the four new ICBMs being flight tested, the SS-19 is clearly the most successful. This new missile's throw-weight is about three to four times greater than the SS-11.

In contrast to the SS-17 and the SS-18, the SS-19 has been flight tested solely with MIRVed payloads and probably will be deployed with six RVs.

CEPs are difficult to estimate with any degree of precision, especially when they are relatively small. We are convinced, nonetheless, that the SS-19 is clearly intended to achieve high accuracy; the Soviet designers have done everything right to attain that goal. The SS-19 missile itself probably has started deployment.

The SS-18, which is comparable in volume to the SS-9, is being flight tested in both a single RV and a MIRV mode. The single RV version has been designated the Mod 1, and the MIRVed version the Mod 2. The SS-18 Mod 1 has a computer aboard and is believed to be more accurate than the SS-9. With its large warhead yield, this missile would have a good hard target capability.

The SS-18 Mod 2 can carry as many as eight RVs or alternative MIRV payloads. Like the SS-19, it has several features which indicate that accuracy is a prime objective. We can assume that the accuracy of this system could also be improved in time by a series of refinements in the current guidance system.

Flight testing of the SS-18 Mod 1 is further advanced than that of the Mod 2. Consequently, we believe the Mod 1 is now operational, and will be followed later by the Mod 2.

The SS-18, like the SS-17, is designed to be cold-launched, i.e., the missile is boosted out of its silo by a gas generator before the main booster motors are ignited. The other two new ICBMs (the SS-X-16 and the SS-19) are hot-launched in the conventional manner, i.e., their main booster motors are ignited in the silos as in the case of the earlier Soviet ICBMs and all of the current U.S. ICBMs. The SS-18 will be deployed in the new type silos.

The SS-17 has certain features that are technologically more advanced than the SS-19, but high accuracy does not appear to be a prime objective at present. The SS-17 is not much larger in volume than the SS-11, but it carries four times the payload of the SS-11 Mod 1. We believe that the SS-17 will be deployed with four RVs. This missile would not have as good a hard target capability as the SS-19.

The SS-X-16 may be slightly smaller in volume than the SS-13, but it carries about twice the throw-weight over about the same range. Although equipped with a bus, the

> SS-X-16 has thus far been tested only with a single RV. However, we cannot preclude the possibility that the SS-X-16 will be deployed in a MIRV, as well as a single RV, mode.
>
> A land-mobile version of the SS-X-16 may be under development. Although the Interim Agreement itself does not restrict the development of land-mobile systems by either side, the U.S. Government has unilaterally declared that it would consider the deployment of such missiles, during the period of the Interim Agreement, inconsistent with the objectives of the Agreement. Under a new SALT agreement, based on the Vladivostok summit meeting, any mobile ICBMs would be counted against the aggregate limits. In any event, we believe the SS-X-16 would be deployed first in silos, and only thereafter in a land-mobile mode.

Bearing in mind the audience to which this material is addressed, make any revisions you think might improve the organization and readability of Secretary Schlesinger's exposition. Incidentally, though the definition is nowhere to be found in the report, MIRV stands for "Multiple Independently Targetable Reentry Vehicle." ICBM stands for "Intercontinental Ballistics Missile."

Come now, let us reason together.

Isaiah 1:18

The information we have is not what we want;
the information we want is not what we need;
and the information we need is not available.

Finagle's Law

Chapter 6

Making A Written Analysis Convincing

Written communications that analyze a problem or situation have become very important in business, government, science, and the professions. This development is receiving nowhere near the amount of attention it deserves. We still act as if negotiations, descriptive reports, accounts of transactions, and sales literature made up most of the writing done by business and professional people.

Not so. For one thing, scientists, with their penchant for testing and evaluation, are becoming ever more numerous and influential in organizations. In a government agency like the Department of Transportation, or in a corporation like General Electric, Texas Instruments, or Monsanto, scarcely a day goes by that analytical reports are not being requested from physicists, geologists, biologists, ecologists, and many others. The steadily rising influence of engineers is another important influence—they fill the mails with reasoned proposals for undertaking complex tasks and programs, assessments of technical performance, evaluations of safety and environmental hazards, and other analytical documents.

In addition, business schools have been pouring into business, government, and the professions hundreds of thousands of managers trained to analyze management problems instead of decide them by "gut feel." Whether business education succeeds in "professionalizing" its graduates is a moot question, but surely it succeeds in encouraging them to diagnose a problem in a methodical way, search for its causes, look for different ways of solving it, and decide what is the best way. Much emphasis may be placed on bringing to bear the documented experience of companies that have faced similar problems.

If it is important for professionals and managers to practice approaching many problems analytically in oral discussions, why is it not important to do so in written communications? If we insist on reducing all written communications to problems of sentence style, clarity, grammar, and punctuation, we are like a golfer playing with only a couple of clubs or a football team playing with only a couple of plays.

To be sure, the written analysis cannot compete in numbers and frequency with the sales letter, the credit letter, the directive, the activity report, and the memorandum conveying a piece of information. But when it does come into play, it may affect the most important kinds of decisions that can be made. This is why John S. Fielden, dean of the College of Commerce and Business Administration at the University of Alabama, has predicted:

> In tomorrow's world of scientific management it may be the methodical, painstaking, research-oriented executive who will inherit the earth. This executive will be more afraid of having a subordinate who can write beautiful reports but who has no respect for evidence than he will of having a lumbering subordinate whose reports exhaustively separate facts from opinions, and axes being ground from impartial rendering of objective information.[1]

One executive I know described his feelings after attending a writing program that emphasized "shirt-sleeves English." He reported that in discussing sample letters and reports, no matter what subject they dealt with or to whom addressed, all sentences were chopped to 14 words or less, preferably words averaging no more than two syllables, and the evidence for a proposition was chopped down to two or three facts and statements. According to the instructor, this streamlining and face-lifting was necessary to make a piece of writing "readable" and "persuasive."

Unfortunately, this rigorous discipline also made it impossible to analyze many types of problems in a professional manner, to fortify a proposition with evidence, or to qualify a statement in a manner that would make it acceptable to the kinds of readers my friend usually communicated with. "I felt stripped of the language tools I need to use," he said. "They wanted me to write for high school kids!" His frustration brought to mind George Jean Nathan's acid comment on a playwright who talked down to his audience: "He writes his plays for the ages—the ages between five and twelve."

In this chapter we concentrate on some practical tests and steps for writers of analytical reports and memoranda. Let us begin with some negative injunctions, since they have the broadest possible application.

[1]John S. Fielden, "Keeping Informed: For Better Business Writing," *Harvard Business Review*, January–February 1965, p. 169.

I. THOU SHALT NOT PREJUDGE BY USING "LOADED" WORDS

An egregious error of many written analyses is that they beg their own conclusions; that is, words and expressions are used that refer not to the fact of a thing, person, event, or relationship but to the writer's own conclusion about that thing. When you are diagnosing and reasoning, you must limit yourself to objective, analytical words, else your argument is not an analysis. Only at the beginning and end of the document (or of its main sections) are evaluations appropriate.

For example, if you wish to make the case that departmental morale is poor, backing up your contention with data, you should present that information in the body of the message with objective facts and numbers. Here you stick to the factual evidence: turnover is high, complaints are more numerous than average, attitudes are poor compared to attitudes in other departments, and so on. In presenting this evidence, do not inject such modifiers as "apathetic" attitudes, "alienated" workers, and "chronically poor" morale. When you use terms like these, you describe your conclusions rather than reasons and evidence. Only near the end of the report, when you present your conclusions, are you justified in using value-laden terms.

Consider an historical example. Shortly before World War II, Eleanor Roosevelt, the President's wife, parted ways with the American Youth Congress. She had been on friendly terms with the organization until Communist sympathizers began to control it; when that happened and she refused to support the organization further, she became a target of its scorn. Among other things, Youth Congress propagandists sought to make the public believe that her endorsement of youth work camps was part of a plot to create Nazi-type forced labor. The *Young Communist Review* declared (the italics are added for the sake of easy reference):

> At secret conferences in Washington offices, behind locked doors of incorporated "youth" organizations, in private conversations in Park Avenue living rooms, at expensive dinners in swanky socialite clubs, they are *scheming* to put all young non-conscripted men and all young women into *forced labor camps* on the *Hitler model*. . . . "They" are Franklin D. Roosevelt, President of the United States; Eleanor Roosevelt; a host of officials. . . .[2]

Now, what the Communist organ wanted to prove to the public was the very thing indicated in the italicized phrases. The reasons and evidence cited *were* the conclusions. Therefore, we would have to rate this passage poor as part of a written analysis. The argument has as many faults as the geology of California.

Now consider Mrs. Roosevelt's reply to the Youth Congress. In a letter to Youth Congress leaders in December 1940 she reasoned:

> I have been thinking a great deal about my own position in all this lately, because while I believe in the complete sincerity of you, and while I respect the way in which you work for your convictions, and therefore feel no differently personally toward you than I ever have, still I find myself in complete disagreement with your political philosophy, and therefore with the leadership which you at present represent in the youth movement. I do not think that you represent the majority of youth, but I do think you have a right to try to further your ideas and to express your opinions and you should be heard in every gathering. However, when I do not agree with you, I also have an obligation not to help you and not to appear to agree with you.[3]

Note the absence of value-laden words and prejudgments in this excerpt. She does not brand the Youth Congress leaders as "neo-Fascist," "antidemocratic," or "un-American." She does not call their political philosophy "dangerous" or "irresponsible." She states objectively the fact of her disagreement with them and concludes

[2]See Joseph P. Lash, *Eleanor Roosevelt: A Friend's Memoir* (New York, Doubleday, 1964), p. 230.
[3]*Ibid*, p. 228.

that this makes it necessary for her to withdraw her support.

II. THOU SHALT NOT BEAR CONCEALED ASSUMPTIONS

In practically every written analysis you have to make assumptions. There is nothing new about this—you have been making them in oral and written discussions for years. Unlike people who listen when you argue a point, however, people who read your argument can stop and ponder the exact phrasing and reasoning you use. Therefore you should take care to point out all important assumptions you make.

When do you make assumptions? Whenever you take *probable* relationships, qualities, or results for granted. If, for example, you state in your report that a reduction in the cost of a product will lead to greater sales, you make an assumption. Cost reductions do not lead in every instance to greater buying (in the case of some kinds of products, in fact, just the opposite may be true), but you assume that the common experience will repeat itself. Again, suppose that you have found a way to streamline a procedure for taking physical inventory. Perhaps a seemingly unpleasant step has been eliminated. Naturally, you assume, in presenting your conclusions, that employees in certain departments will be pleased. Chances are that you are perfectly right, but since there is no iron law that such an effect follows such a step, you could be wrong. Hence you must consider this relationship an assumption, not a fact.

The trouble with assumptions is they are too easy to make. Often we use them when, with a little extra effort, we could get facts instead. For example, it may be unnecessary to assume that a 10% price increase will decrease sales. A price test in an area or with a sample of prospective customers may provide you with a fairly good factual test of the price-buyer relationship. (You would still have to assume that buyers at large would react as the buyers in your test did, but that is a less dangerous assumption.)

When you make assumptions, how should you point them out? The means are simple. You can use phrases such as, "assuming such-and-such to be true," "if this pattern holds," and "it therefore seems likely to me . . ." For instance:

- A paper in front of me argues: "A social system built on a pyramid of alienation is necessarily distortive of human need, imperialistic, violent, nasty, brutish, and, one hopes, short-lived." The writer's assertions run wild, like rogue elephants in the forest. He has made no definitive study of the effects of such an egregious social system—indeed, perhaps no one has. At the very least, he should preface his sweeping statement with some such qualifier as "In every case I know of . . ."
- A consultant wrote to the top executives of a corporation about a difficult conflict between competing divisions in the company. An important piece of evidence was a letter that, unfortunately, was not crystal clear. In commenting on a key passage in that letter, the consultant prefaced his statement as follows: "If I read correctly between the lines of Mr. Masterson's letter of April 19 . . ." Thus he alerted readers to an important assumption he had to make.
- In the letter quoted earlier, Eleanor Roosevelt wrote to the American Youth Congress leaders (italics added for emphasis): "*I do not think* that you represent the majority of youth." It was an assumption she had to make, and, since it was important, she pointed it out.

Related to assumptions is what composition instructors call *inferences*. An inference is a conclusion deduced from evidence and, strictly speaking, should be distinguished from an assumption, which is not necessarily based on evidence. For all intents and purposes here, however, we can consider inferences to be much the same thing as assumptions. Certainly, your obligation to the reader is the same in the case of inferences as in the case of assumptions; that is, you should point them out so the reader will not confuse them with facts. In the words of Robert D. Shurter and J. Peter Williamson:

> It is especially important to label your assumptions. Be honest enough with the reader of your reports to tell him when you have no data and are relying on assumption or when you are not certain of the validity of an inference but will assume it is valid for purposes of further discussion. Your reader may disagree with your assumptions: He may feel his experience and general knowledge are a better guide than yours. At the same time, he may respect your inferences as being based on a familiarity with the data greater than his own.[4]

Now for a word of caution. Ralph Waldo Emerson once said that the good rain, like a bad preacher, doesn't know when to leave off; similarly, those who become fastidious in pointing out assumptions may go much farther than any reader requires. For instance, it is not necessary to point out that we *assume* the sun will rise tomorrow because it has every day in the past. J. H. Menning and C. W. Wilkinson make the point nicely with an anecdote about the skeptical farmer who was asked to look at a black sheep in the pasture. He remarked, "At least it is black on this side."[5] (A sequel is the case of the city slicker who bought a cattle farm. "How many head of cattle do you have?" a friend asked. He replied, "I couldn't count because I was looking at them from the rear.")

III. THOU SHALT NOT COMMIT LAPSES IN LOGIC

William G. Gallagher describes the role of logic:

> Logic is essential to evaluation. When data are abundant, logic supplies structure and interpretation. When data are unavailable,

[4]Robert D. Shurter and J. Peter Williamson, *Written Communications in Business* (New York: McGraw-Hill, 1964), p. 107.
[5]J. H. Menning and C.W. Wilkinson, *Communicating through Letters and Reports*, 4th ed. (Homewood, Ill., Richard D. Irwin, 1967), p. 668.

> logic supplies experience. When data are inconsistent or unreliable, logic supplies meaning beyond the reality of the data. And when data and reality part company, logic helps to identify and explain the separation. Thus, logic is the pathway by which the analyst reaches conclusions.[6]

You cannot hope to do much writing without falling into some traps of logic, but with a little care you should be able to improve vastly on the performance of numerous writers. The following comes from a widely distributed corporate promotion piece: "Because our salesmen are the most energetic and hard-working in the industry—our incentive systems see to that—an increase in our share of the market seems inevitable. . . ." In terms of logic, this statement looks as follows:

Major premise: Our salesmen are the most energetic and hard-working in the industry.
Minor premise: The most energetic, hard-working salesmen make the most sales.
Conclusion: Therefore our share of the market will inevitably increase.

Few marketing managers would defend the minor premise in the above syllogism, for they know that the "marketing mix" is the important thing. Many energetic, hard-working salesmen fail to sell because their products are inferior or their training is poor.

Here are other logic traps to watch out for:

Begging the question. A lawyer wrote her client: "I urge you to settle out of court because that is the wisest course in a case like this . . ." Since any prudent client wants to take the wisest course, the reason given is no reason at all; it is simply the objective sought.

Uncritical use of averages. For many purposes of analysis and recommendation, an average may be one of the *least* meaningful figures that can be obtained. Like the

[6]William G. Gallagher, *Report Writing for Management* (Reading, Mass., Addison-Wesley, 1969), p.48

man who had his head in the refrigerator and his feet in the oven and who, on the average, felt pretty good, many people and things described by averages are unreal. A government agency executive recently became disturbed, it is reported, because his annual report on fleet vehicles showed a rise in average cost per mile—this despite all the efforts and admonitions he had given employees to curb costs. What had happened was that the cars had been driven less, because of the pressure to reduce costs. Although charges for gas and driver time were thus reduced (and overall costs were reduced), the average per mile rose because depreciation and insurance costs stayed the same.

False inferences from correlations. Any form of circumstantial evidence may be misleading, and correlations are one of the most deceitful forms of all. A health research group issued a report stating that people who drink three or more ounces of alcohol a day develop heart disease earlier than nondrinkers do, from which facts it is deduced that staying "on the wagon" is the route around the heart infirmary. Likewise, a report stating that people who exercise regularly experience fewer serious emotional problems than do people who shun sports and calisthenics suggests that jogging or tennis is the way to stay away from the local "shrink." Such nonsense. How many other characteristics of the three-ounce drinkers (e.g. insecurity, nervousness, physical discomfort) may account for the higher incidence of heart disease among them? How many other aspects of the psyches of nonexercisers (e.g., fear of injury) may account for the extra visits they pay to psychiatrists? Robert Frost once pointed out the stupidity of a popular generalization in his wry comment, "The reason worry kills more people than work is that more people worry than work."

The moral of all this is not that you should avoid correlations in proving a point—they may be the best evidence you have. The moral is you should point to the frailties of such correlations—let the reader know you are not oblivious to the possible weakness in your case.

Murder by example. "Every American is in danger of being murdered," states one student paper. "For example, in Cambridge on the night of March 19 . . ." The gory and bizarre example given dramatizes that murder can happen to anyone, but it doesn't support the lead statement. In fact, the odds against it are something like a half-million to one, even in the area mentioned.

When we draw conclusions from examples, incidents, and observations, we infer. This reasoning process is called induction to contrast it with deduction (an example of which was given in the syllogism about energetic salesmen). The more supporting examples or observations we have from a variety of times and places, and the fewer the exceptions, the more likely that our conclusion is a valid one.

Examples are the first thought of the troubled innocent and the last appeal of the unmitigated scoundrel. Editors and journalists know this. If you have oceans of evidence to support a statement that your audience seems to question, your first thought is to cite a typical example of the evidence. And if you have only one example to support an absurd or preposterous statement that your audience questions, you throw it in brazenly, as if there were plenty more like it.

Ideally, every letter, memorandum, brochure, and report that cites one incident to support a point would have an exhibit or appendix attached containing all the incidents of that sort known to the author. Since this is out of the question, how can you indicate to your readers that your example, instance, or illustration is not the only cherry that could be plucked from the cake? Here are some of the possibilities: (a) A general statement that the example is typical, such as "In alleging graft in the state highway department, Mrs. Jones' accusations were typical of those made by all 150 respondents in our study . . ." (b) Pair the example with a second or third one from a different place or circumstance, indicating the range of possible examples, such as "Air pollution indexes higher than 0.2 were found in cities from Los Angeles to Newark

. . ." (c) A footnote to a source where further evidence can be obtained. (d) An invitation to readers to request substantiating examples and evidence.

Nonplusing by non sequitur. "Nobody goes to that restaurant any more," Yogi Berra reportedly once said of a well-known eating place in New York, "it's too crowded." In a similar category, despite their earnestness and expensive printing, are such statements as these from brochures and leaflets: "Justice would be better served by giving the criminal six 20-year terms . . ." (will 120 years in jail really teach this 50-year-old culprit more than 50 or 60 years would?); "Call it dissent, protest, whistle-blowing, or by whatever other term you prefer, such questioning of corporate management amounts to disloyalty" (even if it's the boss who is guilty of lying and cheating?); "Either taxation must be reduced or the American business system will collapse" (even if taxes which help business are reduced, such as taxes for better roads, postal service, and law enforcement?).

IV. THOU SHALT NOT COVET EXPERT KNOWLEDGE OF UNCERTAIN VALUE

When you use the testimony of an expert, the results of a study, or the experience of another organization to shore up your reasoning, be sure you can fairly state that the expert is a qualified one for this point; that the study was adequate in sample size, questioning technique, and other respects; and/or that the organization's experience was not distorted by unusual circumstances. One of the more exasperating experiences suffered by readers of analytical reports is that names of supposed experts and authoritative studies are thrown at them page after page, without any indication whether the experts and studies can truly be taken at their face value for the argument at hand—or worse, no indication that the writer ever thought to question his or her sources.

If you cite the opinion or finding of an authority, give his or her name and position; do not say, "According to one expert . . . ," or "Leading cost accountants believe. . . ." Also be sure that he or she is *currently* regarded as an authority by people in the field, that the opinion used is in one of his or her *areas of special competence*, and that he or she is *not biased* concerning the issue. For example, you would not want to rely on an opinion from Muhammed Ali that he could have knocked out Jack Dempsey or Joe Louis in seven rounds, nor on the judgment of a veteran steel company executive as to what is wrong in university administration, nor on the opinion of a company's public relations agency for an objective assessment of the company's growth prospects.

If you cite a study or expert opinion to support a point, is it the only one available? If there are other studies on the same question or other expert opinions, do they confirm or conflict with the conclusion you cite? This matter, too, should be clarified in your analysis. Of course, if there is a conflict of expert opinion, you should be able to defend your choice.

V. THOU SHALT NOT INCLUDE IRRELEVANT INFORMATION

As H. R. Clauser, one-time editor of *Materials Engineering*, pointed out, one of the unkindest tricks you can play on readers is suddenly to present them with an isolated, irrelevant fact. As an example he gave the following paragraph. The last sentence (italicized for our purposes) had no connection with anything else in the article from which it was taken. Moreover, because "hardenability," the irrelevancy, might be related to the subject of "carbide content," readers could be doubly confused.

> A further control of carbide content can be obtained by composition variations. The carbide content is increased by the addition of chromium or by lowering the carbon equivalent, and it is de-

> creased by the addition of copper or nickel. *Hardenability is significantly increased by the addition of molybdenum or chromium and is moderately increased by the addition of copper or nickel.*[7] [Italics added]

Clauser considered such irrelevancies common in technical writing. My editor friends in scientific, legal, medical, and business publications would regard them as common in their fields, too. The trouble, as Clauser noted, is that "most of us do some thinking as we write and sometimes even write in order to think," with the result that unwanted associations generated by our thinking "drop unnoticed into our paragraphs." The only sure cure is to seek out such irrelevancies when we review and revise, and to urge any friends who review our writing to do likewise.

VI. THOU SHALT NOT LET A POINT STARVE OR BE GLUTTED WITH EVIDENCE

Not quite as disconcerting as the irrelevant fact or paragraph, but still befuddling, is the pouring out of supporting facts and data on an obvious or minor point, while a controversial or crucial point is left starved for evidence. "The best strategy is always to be very strong, first generally, then at the decisive point," said Karl von Clausewitz. This goes for analytical writing as well as warfare. It's tempting to bury readers with the data we have rather than the data that should be marshaled, and, like Oscar Wilde, we can resist anything except temptation.

The best self-discipline to ensure watchfulness of this commandment is outlining. When you are outlining you are still flexible, you still have time to find or devise

[7] H.R. Clauser, "Writing Is for Readers," *STWP Review* January 1961, pp. 12–17; reprinted in *The Practical Craft*, W. Keats Sparrow and Donald H. Cunningham, Eds. (Boston: Houghton Mifflin, 1978) p. 151.

evidence to shore up a weak point. Like von Clausewitz's military planner, get your troops and reinforcements positioned then, rather than waiting until the battle of drafting the memo or report against a deadline is under way.

VII. THOU SHALT NOT COMMIT OCCULTERY

One of the most common analytical failings in reports—especially reports from operations specialists to generalists, from young people to senior people, and from "insiders" to "outsiders"—is that one or more steps in the reasoning are left out. To go along with the writer's occult reasoning, therefore, the reader must possess extrasensory preception or a blind faith in the author's integrity.

"Half the reports I get from operations research people and behavioral scientists," one leading executive complains to me, "sound like stuff from witch doctors." He may be informed, for instance, that because statistical deviation is greater than a certain number, a certain test cannot be accepted. He confesses that although the cause and effect may be clear to the operations researcher, "it is clear as mud to me." By simply explaining the deviation point—the test results fluctuated so much that many of them could be accounted for by chance—the writer could avoid the "witch doctor" taint.

Here are some other forms of "occultery" you should strive to avoid in written analyses:

Combining studies employing inconsistent concepts, definitions, methodologies, and so on. A report on managerial behavior links together dozens of behavioral science studies in an attempt to prove some unusual points about managerial attitudes and action patterns. But some of the studies include supervisors and foremen under the rubric of "manager"; others, only executives at the department-head level and up; others, staff specialists as well as operating people. Again, a recent report on multinational companies relies on studies by various experts to prove its thesis. But some of the studies are based solely on interviews and observations of actual performance, some on performance data alone. From an analytical standpoint, both reports are like a broken basket of snakes, with some getting out through the sides and bottom though the top is on tight.

Putting coffee cans in the tea cupboard. Another good way to annoy careful readers is to put sections of information under the wrong rubric. For instance, a report on changing legal trends discusses changes in: (a) property rights, (b) employer prerogatives, (c) invasion of privacy, (d) rules of evidence, and (e) public values. Now, that last item may well be relevant to the conclusions of the report, but it certainly does not fit under the heading of *legal* trends.

SOME STEPS IN ANALYZING CURRENT PROBLEMS

Although the promotion literature of training institutes may make it sound as if there were a universal prescription for problem solving, in actuality there are various approaches that seem to work well. In a careful written discussion of an operating problem, the steps that follow may not be the only ones you should include in your report. It is a pretty good bet, however, that each of these steps should be recognized somewhere in your analysis.

For convenience I shall use examples from business, but these steps apply to other areas as well.

1. Define the key problem—the most important one to solve now, as you see the situation.

A careful observer of analytical writing once pointed out that "written reports always are clearer if the problem under investigation is fully and precisely stated at the outset. A cardinal weakness of many business communications is the writer's failure to . . . tell what problem he is addressing and why he believes it is a problem worth discussing."[8]

[8]Richard L. Larson, "How to Define Administrative Problems," *Harvard Business Review*, January–February 1962, p. 76.

There are three tricks to doing this step right. First, you must keep problems separate from causes and decisions—not always an easy thing to do when you are immersed in a situation. A well-known exercise in problem analysis concerns a plant that manufactured parts for the automobile industry.[9] A sudden and dangerous rise in the number of panels that had to be rejected worried managers so much they were practically climbing the walls. In their debates they tended to say, for instance, "Our real problem is the need to train supervisors," or "Discipline in the shop is the main problem." But those were not the problems to be solved; the first explanation was a *decision* that might be made to solve the problem, while the second was a possible *cause* of the problem.

What is a problem? The question seems rudimentary, yet it is surprising how many written analyses go off the track at this juncture. A problem can be defined as a situation or condition that is unwanted and different from what is normal, expected, and intended. As one manager in the rejected panels case says: "The simplest way to solve a problem is to think of it as something that's wrong, that's out of kilter, something we want to fix."

Second, you must put your finger on the *key* problem. The trouble with problem situations is that usually there are many difficulties. A problem in quality control may be related to a problem in marketing strategy, and that in turn may be related to a problem in finance. Unless you want to write a book instead of a memorandum or report, you must settle for defining the one problem that, if not solved, will cause more trouble more quickly than any other problem not solved. Thus, in the case cited, rejected panels was defined as the key problem because, as one executive put it, "If we don't correct this reject problem and produce what's required by Detroit, we may not be around to worry about *any* problems."

[9]See Perrin Stryker, "Can You Analyze This Problem?" and "How to Analyze That Problem," *Harvard Business Review*, May–June 1965, p. 73, and July–August 1965, p. 99

Third, define the problem concretely and as precisely as you can, not abstractly or generally. For example, a problem defined as "reducing the reject rate on side-door panels to 0.5%" is far preferable to "improving quality control" or "finding a way to meet customer requirements."

2. **Describe the main dimensions of the key problem, as you see them.**

What is often referred to as the "Kepner–Tregoe method" is valuable here.[10] You may not want or need to follow it "to a T," but it indicates clearly the *kind* of problem description that separates a good written analysis from a mediocre or poor one.

The dimensions of the problem are (a) what, (b) where, (c) when, and (d) extent. For added clarity, it often helps to specify what is *not* involved in these dimensions along with what is involved. Thus in the rejected-panels case some of the dimensions specified were rough spots and "burrs" on a certain type of panel under the "what" dimension but not on certain other types of panels; production lines 1, 2, and 4 under the "where" dimension but not line 3; the exact times the excessive rejects began showing up under the "when" dimension; and the varying percentages of rejects on the different projection lines, under the "extent" dimension.

When you are trying to diagnose a problem alone or in group discussion, the approach described can be very helpful. But whether you use the Kepner–Tregoe method, your own patented method, or some other, you should indicate the dimensions of the problem early and clearly. Only in rare cases can you assume that the reader sees the problem as you do. If the reader does not, and if you do not specify clearly the what, where, when, and extent of the problem as you see it, the rest of your

[10]See Perrin Stryker, "How to Analyze That Problem" *op, cit.*, pp. 101–110.

analysis may be discounted, misinterpreted, or rejected because of misunderstanding.

3. Specify the cause or causes of the problem.

Having specified the nature of the problem exactly, the causes you describe should account precisely for the difficulties. If, following the Kepner–Tregoe method, you think of the cause as a change of one sort or another that makes performance fall short of standard, then that change must explain what is wrong, where it is wrong, when it went wrong, and the extent to which it is wrong. Moreover, if you have the right cause, it will apply to what is wrong but not to what is not wrong. For example, in the rejected-panels case, a change in materials or method that would have affected production line 3 (where no rejects were experienced) as well as lines 1, 2, and 4 (where rejects were happening) would have to be ruled out as a cause.

In one case cited by Richard L. Larson, a wholesale distributor of women's clothing is troubled by declining sales.[11] According to the case report, the president blames the problem on inability to sell to chain apparel stores and suburban branches of downtown stores. Accordingly, his solution is to increase the pressure on buyers of those stores. But the solution does not work. What is wrong? If the president were to define the problem more precisely, he would see that the cause must lie elsewhere. No change is noticeable in buyer-seller relations that can account for sales falling off when they did and to the extent they did. However, it appears there may be changes in the efficiency of deliveries from company warehouses and in the quality of competitors' goods—changes that tie in fairly closely with the what, where, when, and the extent of the company problem.

If you were making a written analysis of such a prob-

[11]See Larson, *op. cit.*, pp. 69 and 75.

lem, therefore, you should focus on those possible explanations. If they hold up, it would be important to point out their cause-and-effect relationship to the declining sales problem. And if, let us say, the problem is limited to certain lines of apparel or certain customer areas, you should be able to show that the causes have affected those lines and areas only, not other areas where no problems are in evidence.

4. Describe alternative ways of coping with the causes of the problem.

A key word in this step is "describe." In a good written analysis you do not at this stage evaluate alternative solutions. You indicate the major possibilities, as you see them—objectively, reportorially, factually. The most common error is to set up false choices or rule out certain alternatives because of judgments about what is desirable.

For example, suppose the problem is that profits are zero and your company is in severe competition, just breaking even at the present sales volume. The cause you have identified is increasing price competition. Alternative solutions? Your hunch from the beginning has been that cost reduction is the answer—and you can't wait to prove it on paper! So quite unwittingly you set up a false dichotomy: The alternatives are to raise prices or lower costs. Of course, the former is out of the question, because of stringent price competition, so you have set the stage for proving the latter. But what have you done? In your anxiety to promote the cost reduction answer you have put blinders on and failed to describe the alternatives fairly. For example, what about increasing sales volume? In your view it may not be an answer, but your reader may think differently about that, and in any case part of your obligation in a written analysis is to show the reasonable possibilities before arguing for the one you like best.

5. Outline the course of action you consider best.

First, you should explain why and how the course of action you recommend copes with the causes of the problem better than alternative courses of action do. Also, you should show that the action is practical. Anticipate relevant problems or objections readers may think of. Can the work be carried out by the people and groups who would have the job of implementation? Might it be too expensive or time-consuming? Is the course of action overly risky in terms of legal, competitive, or other constraints? Does it run counter to contracts or agreements the company may have entered into? Is it consistent with labor relations, public relations, and other policies of the organization? Is it salable to buyers, customers, and/or other powerful groups in the marketing process?

Finally, you should indicate what individuals or agencies need to take what action and in what order, if those matters are not obvious. Often action on a project or decision must be undertaken at different levels in the organization, and there may be compelling reasons that this person or group should have the responsibility rather than that person or group. And it may be important to tackle certain problems first, leaving other problems for handling later on.

Unfortunately, this last step tends to be low man on the totem pole in the esteem of many good "idea people." Their inclination is to pass on to others the responsibility for getting a desirable job done. Since business and the professions are institutions that emphasize getting things done, there is not much room for creative analyses that do not get down to brass tacks about implementation. Theodore Levitt writes:

> The trouble with much creativity today, in my observation, is that many of the people with the ideas have the peculiar notion that their jobs are finished when they suggest them; that it is up to somebody else to work out the dirty details and then implement the proposals. . . .

> It may seem splendid to a subordinate to supply his boss with a lot of brilliant new ideas to help him in his job. But advocates of creativity must once and for all understand the pressing facts of the executive's life: every time an idea is submitted to him, it creates more problems for him—and he already has enough.[12]

Levitt urges close attention to implementation and follow-up. He points out that the amount of detail that is appropriate depends on four factors: (1) the position or rank of the idea originator (e.g., is he or she a powerful boss, a new subordinate, or an outsider?), (2) the complexity of the idea or solution proposed, (3) the nature of the problem area (is it a change in copy in an advertisement, which can be done simply by working on words, or a change in a complicated price structure, which involves much study and analysis?), and (4) the attitude and job of the person to whom the idea or proposal is submitted. Do these factors remind you of the kinds of points described in Chapter 4, in our discussion of persuasion?

Perhaps an aging anecdote will help to put the point across. During World War II a man came to the U.S. War Department and said he had a way to destroy all the Nazi submarines in the Atlantic Ocean. They asked how, and he replied, "Simple. Boil the ocean." But how could that be done? He replied, "That's your problem."

In the best of all possible worlds, the bright "idea person," having described a wonderful idea in writing and delivered it to the right officials, would go off and join the ghosts of Edward Lear "under a lotus tree eating of ice creams and pelican pie, with our feet in an azure coloured stream with the birds and beasts of Paradise a–sporting around us." But organizations don't pick up good ideas and run with them, like someone returning a kickoff in football. Only individuals in organizations do—individuals who have an incentive to do so.

Not until this reality is understood can one master the

[12]Theodore Levitt, "Creativity Is Not Enough," *Harvard Business Review*, May–June 1963, pp. 74 and 78.

transition from student to practitioner in a company, scientific firm, government agency, or other organization. What J. C. Mathes and Dwight W. Stevenson tell engineering students is applicable to many other students:

> In college, students write for an audience of one person—a professor; in industry, they must learn to write for a large, diverse audience in an organization. In college they write for a reader who knows the field and probably knows more about their technical material than the writer does; in industry, they must learn to write to people who perhaps do not know the field or who almost certainly know less about the material than the writer. In college, they write for pedagogical purposes—to demonstrate to a professor their mastery of concepts, processes, and information; in industry, their mastery is assumed, and they must learn to write for instrumental purposes—to help people in an organization make judgments and act upon the results they present.[13]

PROPOSING NEW PLANS AND PROGRAMS

Because of the nature of their work, managers, professionals, and scientists spend a great deal of time considering future needs and courses of action. An ecologist analyzes the impact of a proposed project or operation on the local environment and urges a different course of action. A company department head sends a written request to top management for new equipment and more personnel—why they are needed, how much, the cost, how he will use them, and so forth. The vice-president for planning of a university outlines in writing for the president and trustees his convictions that a new type of educational program should be launched.

In some ways these reports and memoranda are like written analyses of current problems; for instance, you must pay just as careful attention to evidence that your proposal for action is practical and feasible. But there are distinct and important differences in emphasis. For one

[13]J. C. Mathes and Dwight W. Stevenson, *Designing Technical Reports* (Indianapolis: Bobbs-Merrill, 1976), p. xv.

thing, you deal not so much with something that has gone wrong as with something that needs to be done to satisfy future needs and demands. For another, the implications for readers are different. According to Frank F. Gilmore:

> Executives are recognizing that to seek to convince someone to abandon his position and to accept theirs is to challenge much that has been learned about human relations. To advocate a proposition is to deny listeners the privilege of participation. Moreover, by advocating proposals, executives are arguing for change which is often perceived as a threat to the established order of things. And they are beginning to realize that it is all too easy to have their cherished preconceived ideas, prejudices, biases, and misconceptions creep into their argument in the place of logical conclusions based on carefully analyzed pertinent data.[14]

Let us consider the most important questions to ask about a written proposal for a new project, program, or method of handling a need. These questions should be asked both in preparing and reviewing such a proposal.

1. Is the need for action clear?

Even though there may have been oral discussions clarifying the need for a new approach, be sure not to take too much for granted. The need may not be nearly so clear to your readers as it is to you. Remember former budget director Bert Lance's oft-quoted statement that "You don't fix it unless it is broke." If there is likely to be any feeling of this sort regarding the need for change, it should be dealt with clearly in your report, letter, or memorandum.

2. Is it clear what objectives are sought and why they are important?

If readers are to feel sympathy with your solutions, they need to share your concerns about goals and objectives.

[14]Frank F. Gilmore, "Overcoming the Perils of Advocacy in Corporate Planning," *California Management Review*, Spring 1973, p. 127.

3. Is the proposed action or program described adequately?

In the body of your communication, describe the important features of the new plan. Depending on the nature of your communication, earlier talks, subsequent conversations planned, and other documents available, you may also need to provide details, illustrations, charts, and/or exhibits.

4. Is it clear that the proposed action will accomplish the objectives—and that its possible shortcomings have been considered?

There is an ancient Chinese proverb: "To prophesy is extremely difficult, especially with respect to the future." If forecasts of performance are relevant, break them out carefully—your prophecy may still be wrong, but readers will be reassured you have analyzed the outlook, not taken someone else's word for it. If, let us say, your prediction is that oil tanker spills will decrease, look at the important dimensions of the problem—types of tankers, types of accidents, accidents as a cause versus structural failure as a cause, age of ships, maintenance trends, and so forth. Whether you treat such matters briefly or in detail depends on what your readers already know, but don't for a paragraph let them think you have failed to turn the problem inside out. And make it equally clear that, so far as analysis can show, your proposed action meets the need.

Increasingly, good forecasters and planners estimate the *probabilities* of expected events, in their opinion. As a result, readers are becoming more critical and sophisticated about projections. To make a convincing analysis, you may need to make the best estimates you can that sales will exceed this figure or that, or that certain segments of public opinion will change by this amount or that, or that a technical experiment will be completely successful, moderately successful, or unsuccessful. You may end up with a line like this: "We estimate a 60%

probability of complete success, a 25% probability of qualified success, and a 15% probability of failure."

As in a good problem-solving analysis you should also assure your reader that you have weighed the possible limitations and shortcomings of your proposal. For instance, will it be acceptable to the people involved? Will it create legal problems? Is it consistent with contracts and agreements with unions, suppliers, joint venture partners, and/or other interests? What effect will it have on other programs and activities readers are concerned about?

5. **Who should be made responsible for taking action? What arrangements must be made? What tasks should be undertaken first?**

The need for exploring these questions in a planning-type report is as great as for a problem-solving report. The change you are asking for may call for exhausting hours of implementation; it may complicate already strained relationships with associates or create risks for the reader's "track record" of performance. Be sensitive to such possibilities. On the brighter side, a careful look at the "who, how, and when" of implementing your idea may help to convince readers that it is practical and well worth doing.

In his famous letter to President Franklin D. Roosevelt (see Chapter 4), Albert Einstein, for all of his prestige, did not neglect the grubby details of getting atomic fission research started. After setting forth the prospect that nuclear bombs could be developed, and mentioning the far-reaching military consequences, Einstein wrote:

> In view of this situation you may think it desirable to have some permanent contact maintained between the administration and the group of physicists working on chain reaction in America. One possible way of achieving this might be for you to entrust with this task a person who has your confidence and who could perhaps serve in an unofficial capacity. His task might comprise the following:
>
> (a) To approach government departments, keep them informed of

further developments, and put forward recommendations for government action, giving particular attention to the problem of securing a supply of uranium ore for the United States.

(b) To speed up the experimental work which is at present being carried on within the limits of the budgets of the university laboratories. . . .[15]

PROBLEMS AND CASES

1. Think of the periodicals you read—newspapers, magazines, bulletins, periodic reports, and the like. Which one would you give the highest marks to for analytical writing? Using photocopies, reprints, or tear sheets of the first one or two pages of an article in that publication, discuss how it meets the first two criteria described in this chapter (avoidance of loaded words and hidden assumptions).
2. If, by waving a magic wand, you could cure writers in your field or profession of just one of the various common lapses in logic described, which lapse would it be? Present two written examples of the kind of lapse that bothers you the most, pointing out the pitfalls in each example.
3. Taking an annual or semi-annual report of a corporation or other organization, present an example of a lapse in logic, an error in reasoning, or a failure to use expert opinion properly.
4. Comment on the Kepner–Tregoe method described. Do you agree or disagree with its approach for purposes of written analysis? Does it compare favorably or unfavorably with other methods you know about? Is it consistent with the so-called "scientific method"?
5. "We are not won by arguments that we can analyze," said the English novelist Samuel Butler about a century ago, "but by tone and temper, by the manner which is the man himself." Comment on this observation in the light of what you have learned about written analysis. To what extent, if any, does Butler's statement conflict with or limit the role of analytical qualities in writing?

[15]Ronald W. Clark, *Einstein: The Life and Times* (New York, World Publishing, 1971), p.557.

6. ***Letter to a Lieutenant:*** Early in 1863 the fortunes of the Union in the Civil War were coming to low ebb. The Confederacy was winning battles, and there was dissension in the Union armies. As if that were not enough, from President Abraham Lincoln's standpoint, rumors came to him that his own military lieutenants were plotting against him. On January 26, he wrote the following letter to Major General Joseph Hooker [From John D. Glover and Ralph M. Hower, *The Administrator* (Homewood, Ill., Richard D. Irwin, 1957), p. 256. Reprinted by permission. The original letter is owned by Mrs. Aldred Whital Stern of Chicago, Ill.]:

> I have placed you at the head of the Army of the Potomac. Of course, I have done this upon what appear to me to be sufficient reasons. And yet I think it best for you to know that there are some things in regard to which, I am not quite satisfied with you.
>
> I believe you to be a brave and skillful soldier, which, of course, I like. I also believe you do not mix politics with your profession, in which you are right. You have confidence in yourself, which is a valuable, if not an indispensable quality. You are ambitious, which, within reasonable bounds, does good rather than harm. But I think that during Gen. Burnside's command of the Army, you have taken counsel of your ambition, and thwarted him as much as you could, in which you did a great wrong to the country, and to a most meritorious and honorable brother officer. I have heard, in such a way as to believe it, of your recently saying that both the Army and the Government needed a Dictator. Of course, it was not *for* this, but in spite of it, that I have given you the command. Only those generals who gain successes, can set up dictators. What I now ask of you is military success, and I will risk the dictatorship. The government will support you to the utmost of its ability, which is neither more nor less than it has done and will do for all commanders. I much fear that the spirit which you have aided to infuse into the Army, of criticizing their Commander, and withholding confidence from him, will now turn upon you. I shall assist you as far as I can, to put it down. Neither you, nor Napoleon, if he were alive again, could get any good out of an army, while such a spirit prevails on it.
>
> And now, beware of rashness. Beware of rashness, but

with energy, and sleepless vigilance, go forward, and give us victories.

Yours very truly,

A LINCOLN

Because your neighbor, an inventive genius, accidentally beamed his time machine ray on you while testing it, you find yourself as Lincoln's editorial consultant on January 26, 1863. He asks for your advice on the rough draft he has just written.

7. ***Epistle to the President:*** In the fall of 1941 the United Mine Workers (UMW), headed by John L. Lewis, went on strike. After tense negotiations with the mine owners and government representatives, Lewis called a 30-day truce, and production resumed. Near the end of the period, Lewis, dissatisfied with the owners' response to UMW demands, threatened to call the miners out again. President Franklin D. Roosevelt was upset. World War II was going badly in Europe, and in Japan there were ominous signs of militarism (to culminate soon in the attack on Pearl Harbor). On October 26 Roosevelt wrote Lewis asking him to reconsider his decision. Coal production was necessary to produce steel, a basic material of the defense effort. Roosevelt concluded: "I am, therefore, as President of the United States, asking you and your associated officers of the United Mine Workers of America, as loyal citizens, to come now to the aid of your country." Enraged, Lewis replied the next day in the following letter reprinted from Irving Bernstein, *Turbulent Years* (Boston, Houghton Mifflin, 1970), pp. 759–760:

Sir:

Your letter at hand.

I have no wish to betray those whom I represent. There is yet no question of patriotism or national security involved in this dispute.

For four months, the steel companies have been whetting their knives and preparing for this struggle. They have increased coal storage and marshalled all their resources.

Defense output is not impaired, and will not be impaired for an indefinite period. This fight is only between a labor union and a ruthless corporation—the United States Steel Corporation.

Lest we forget, I reassert the loyalty of the members of the United Mine Workers of America as citizens of our republic. This Union gave seventy thousand of its members to the armed forces of the United States in the last World War. The per capita purchases of war securities by its members during that period exceeded those of any other segment of our national population. They are willing, when required, to make equal or greater sacrifices in the future to preserve the nation and its free institutions.

If you would use the power of the State to restrain me, as an agent of labor, then, Sir, I submit that you should use the same power to restrain my adversary in this issue, who is an agent of capital. My adversary is a rich man named Morgan, who lives in New York.

You are aware that twice on Saturday I talked on the telephone with Mr. Taylor in New York; that I urged he meet me on Sunday, so that the mines could work Monday; that Mr. Taylor refused to meet me on Sunday, on Monday, or Tuesday, suggesting a meeting Wednesday; that Mr. Taylor's reason was that the Board of Directors of the United States Steel Corporation would meet Tuesday in New York; that this Board of Directors would determine whether or not Mr. Taylor, in behalf of the Corporation, would accept or reject the Appalachian Agreement when he and I meet on Wednesday.

There are sixteen members of the Board of Directors of the United States Steel Corporation. Mr. J.P. Morgan is a member of the Board. Mr. Morgan determines who else shall sit on the Board. Mr. Morgan dominates the Board. Mr. Morgan will decide what Mr. Taylor will do when he meets me Wednesday. Mr. Morgan's great wealth is increasing from his profits on defense orders. Mr. Morgan has a responsibility at least equal to my own. Mr. Morgan should be asked to make a contribution. I submit, Mr. President, that it is not unreasonable to ask Mr. Morgan's companies to accept the wage agreement approved by the National Defense Mediation Board, and accepted and signed by other captive and commercial coal companies in the nation.

You know, Sir, that I am to meet Mr. Myron C. Taylor at 10:00 o'clock Wednesday morning. This is the hour and

> the date fixed by him. If Mr. Morgan will permit Mr. Taylor to accept the Appalachian Agreement like all other coal operators, then the business can be disposed of in ten minutes and coal production resumed on Thursday. No impairment of defense production will have taken place; but if the country needs additional coal by reason of such brief stoppage, I will recommend to the Mine Workers that they make up the lost production by working additional days each week, until the lost production is regained.
>
> In the interest of settlement, I would be glad, Mr. President, if you concur, to meet with you and my adversary, Mr. J.P. Morgan, for a forthright discussion of the equities of this problem.

Write a critique of the analytical qualities of John L. Lewis' letter.

8. ***The Aggressive Applicant:*** The following memorandum was written in 1917 by a junior officer in the U.S. Army and forwarded with the proper endorsement to the Commander-in-Chief of the American Expeditionary Forces in Europe. [From Martin Blumenson, *The Patton Papers, 1885–1940* (Boston, Houghton Mifflin, 1972), p. 427. Reprinted by permission.] At the time, tanks were an innovation in warfare, and United States development units were still experimenting with basic models. The subject line of the memo read: "Command in the Tank Service."

> I understand that there is to be a new service of "Tanks" organized and request that my name be considered for a command in that service. I think myself qualified for this service for the following reasons. The duty of "tanks" and more especially of "Light Tanks" is analogous to the duty performed by cavalry in normal wars. I am a cavalryman. I have commanded a Machine Gun Troop and know something of the mechanism of machine guns. I have always had a Troop which shot well so think that I am a good instructor in fire. It is stated that accurate fire is very necessary to good use of tanks. I have run Gas Engines since 1917 and have used and repaired Gas Automobiles since 1905. I speak and read French better than 95% of American officers so could get information from the French Direct. I have also been to school in France and have always gotten on well with frenchmen. I believe that I have quick judgment and that I am willing to take chances. Also I have

> always believed in getting close to the enemy and have taught this for two years at the Mounted Service School where I had success in arousing the aggressive spirit in the students. I believe that I am the only American who has ever made an attack in a motor vehicle. This request is not made because I dislike my present duty or am desirous of evading it but because I believe when we get "Tanks" I would be able to do good service in them.

Would you have changed the analytical qualities of this letter if you had written it? Don't feel cowed by the fact that the author later became a famous World War II general.

9. Do you think the junior officer's letter is persuasive? Were his efforts to be persuasive in conflict with the requirements of analytical writing?

10. ***The Peeved Publisher:*** In the heady competition of popular magazines in the 1970's, editors and advertising space salespeople sometimes took to criticizing and baiting their rivals. In the community of magazine publishers, it was no secret in 1978 that the staffs of *New York* magazine and *Cue* lost no love over one another. Incensed by the poisoned arrows coming from *New York* magazine, the chief executive of *Cue* wrote a letter of complaint to the head of the American Society of Magazine Editors, an association representing hundreds of magazines. He sent copies of the letter to the editors of numerous magazines, in and out of the field occupied by his publication and *Cue*. The copy that follows was received by the *Harvard Business Review* in the summer of 1978. The text appeared under *Cue*'s letterhead and was undated.

> Mr. Dennis Flanagan, President
> American Society of Magazine Editors
> c/o Scientific American
> 415 Madison Avenue
> New York, New New York 10017
>
> Dear Mr. Flanagan:
>
> At the risk of being told I am overreacting, I'd like to call your attention to a deliberate editorial slur on the part of New York Magazine. In a recent issue, their editors stated that CUE is "The loneliest magazine in town."

Considering that this is their third editorial attack against us, since we merged with North American Publishing Company, I am beginning to feel these snide slurs are part of a well defined game plan on the part of New York Magazine.

Competition is the life's blood of this industry. And it is the constant challenge of facing competition that has made my 44 years at CUE a joy. In all of that time, CUE's publishers have never allowed a single editor to take a cheap shot at the competition. We have always preferred to let the publication succeed or fail on the strength of its own merits.

Our industry is experiencing an unprecedented prosperity. I can only draw the conclusion that New York Magazine must blame the dramatic improvements in our magazine for their first subscription arrearage on their ABC statement [the Audit Bureau of Circulation's subscriber count], their drop in newsstand sales and the decrease in their ad pages.

Even in these so called, "sophisticated times," when appearing "cool" is more in vogue than showing emotion, it is my gut feeling that a publication should and must work within ethical guidelines. Editors *must be protected from being forced to attack competitive publications on their editorial pages.*

I've sent copies of this letter to other editors and publishers in the hope that while I am now near four score, I will live to see the establishing of an "ethics committee." It would be an honor to participate at the first meeting.

Sincerely,

Mort Glankoff

Founder and Chairman of the Board

Suppose you had been Mr. Glankoff's trusted editorial adviser and he had showed you a rough draft of this letter before having it printed up and mailed to a list of magazines. If you would have suggested revisions, write the version you would have offered him. Assume he was determined to send the letter and wanted only your suggestions, if any, for giving it a stronger appeal.

11. Now suppose Mr. Glankoff shows you the rough draft but wants your counsel also as to whether it should be sent at all, or perhaps in different form. What would you have told him in a brief memorandum?

12. ***The Penitent President:*** President Dwight D. Eisenhower and Henry Luce, the founder and long-time head of *Time*, were old friends. In the last year of Eisenhower's presidency, Luce wrote an editorial that contained both praise and criticism of Eisenhower as the country's chief executive. Eisenhower responded by writing Luce a letter dated August 8, 1960 and marked "Personal and Confidential" at the top. Luce called the letter "surely one of the most interesting that any President ever wrote." The text follows, reprinted from Robert T. Elson, *The World of Time Inc.*, Vol. II (New York: Atheneum, 1973), pp. 468–469. (Luce was known as "Harry" to many of his friends, hence the salutation used by Eisenhower.)

> Dear Harry: . . .
>
> I plead guilty to the general charge that many people have felt I have been too easy a boss. Respecting this there are one or two things that you might like to think over. (I do not mean to defend, merely to explain.)
>
> Except for my first two years as President, during which I enjoyed the benefit of a very skimpy majority in the Congress, I have had to deal with a Congress controlled by the opposition and whose partisan antagonism to the Executive Branch has often been blatantly displayed. The hope of doing something constructive for the nation, in spite of this kind of opposition, has required the use of methods calculated to attract cooperation, even though a natural impulse would have been to lash out at partisan charges and publicity-seeking demagogues.
>
> Another point—the government of the United States has become too big, too complex, and too pervasive in its influence on all our lives for one individual to pretend to direct the details of its important and critical programming. Competent assistants are mandatory; without them the Executive Branch would bog down. To command the loyalties and dedication and best efforts of capable and outstanding individuals requires patience, understanding, a readiness to delegate, and an acceptance of responsibility for any honest errors—real or apparent—those associates and subordinates might make. Such loyalty from such

people cannot be won by shifting responsibility, whining, scolding or demagoguery. Principal subordinates must have confidence that they and their positions are widely respected, and the chief must do his part in assuring that this is so.

Of course I could have been more assertive in making and announcing decisions and initiating programs. I can only say that I adopted and used those methods and manners that seemed to me most effective. (I should add that one of my problems has been to control my temper—a temper that I have had to battle all my life!)

Finally, there is the matter of maintaining a respectable image of American life before the world! Among the qualities that the American government must exhibit is dignity. In turn the principal governmental spokesman must strive to display it. In war and in peace I've had no respect for the desk-pounder, and have despised the loud and slick talker. If my own ideas and practices in this matter have sprung from weakness, I do not know. But they were and are deliberate or, rather, natural to me. They are not accidental.

As ever,

Ike

Write a commentary on President Eisenhower's defense of his style in the White House, noting specifically the lines and phrases that support your point of view and offering an improved version if you think changes are called for.

13. Write a short commentary of agreement, disagreement, and/or interpretation of the following statement by George Doriot, a well-known professor (now emeritus), entrepreneur, and corporate head. Assume he is thinking of written reports.

> Analysis, criticism are of no interest to me unless they are a path to constructive, action-bent thinking. Critical type of intelligence is boring and destructive and only satisfactory to those who indulge in it. Most new projects—I can even say every one of them—can be analyzed to destruction.

PART THREE

READABILITY AND EFFECT

Honeyed words like bees,
Gilded and sticky, with a little sting

Elinor Hoyt Wylie

Apt words have power to suage
The tumors of a troubled mind.

John Milton

Chapter 7

Making the Tone Right

Some public officials I know were once discussing a letter that had come to their organization from another agency executive. The letter dealt with a sensitive question of procedure, and it made everyone in the group feel irritated. Yet it contained no threatening ideas, it was phrased correctly, and it was organized clearly. Why did it get under everyone's skin so much? "The trouble with this guy," one of the officials finally said, "is that he's tone-deaf."

At first it seemed like a strange explanation—after all, writing is not heard, only seen—but everyone appreciated the insight. Several generations ago children, too, were "to be seen, not heard" at the dinner table. But that did not mean they could not communicate. They did it quite well, I understand, by their smiles or grimaces, attentiveness or inattentiveness, and table manners. Their parents "heard" them loud and clear. Similarly, the words of a report, memorandum, or letter are heard by the reader. They may sound comforting or abrasive, harmonious or dissonant, happy or unhappy—just as clearly as a piece of music.

And just as the style of a piece of music may irritate people so much they cannot listen to it, so the words and phrases of a piece of writing may be such a turnoff that readers cannot comprehend it. "I could never get to the merits of that report," a business executive once told me, "because of the writing style." He referred not to errors like wordiness and jargon but to the poor tone of the writing. He may have felt like Mark Twain, who remarked, after hearing some music by Richard Wagner, "It *can't* be as bad as it sounds."

If the tone of your letter, memorandum, or report is inappropriate, your missive may misfire disastrously. Between such phrases as "you allege" and "you say," "this is to inform you" and "you will be glad (or sad) to learn," "I assert" and "it seems to me," there is often a world of difference in readers' minds, however innocuous the difference may seem in your mind or in the dictionary. It is the difference between C and C-sharp on the piano, between B and B-flat on a harp. One by one, such phrases help to form and reinforce impressions in readers' minds. You cannot eliminate the connotations of these words; you can only anticipate them.

The agency executive mentioned did not intend to irritate his readers as he did (though in his heart he may have felt unkind toward them). Without meaning to, he injected words and phrases that subtly conveyed impatience and disdain. It probably never occurred to him he was doing that—and to this day he may not know why he received such a cool, uncooperative response to his letter.

"What is often transmitted most accurately between

people is how they feel rather than what they say, " according to William Schutz. "Thus, if the boss really feels his research scientist is not very important, that feeling will be communicated to the scientist much more readily than any words that pass between them."[1] In everyday conversations we learn this truth faster than in writing, for when we talk with someone, we can watch the listener's face and reactions, gaining clues in real-time, as the computer people say, concerning whether we are going too fast, being tactless, or confusing the listener. On the other hand, in writing we may get no feedback for days or weeks—and sometimes none at all. We have fewer opportunities to see how our written words affect readers.

How do you go about putting the right tone in your writing? In this chapter we deal with ways to do that—the main steps in the process and the possibilities for each step. There is an important and natural connection between this chapter and Chapter 4 on presentation strategy, in that both deal with the psychology of persuasion. But there is a major difference in level of emphasis. In Chapter 4 we concerned ourselves with sequences of thought, the arrangement of claims and facts, the choice of ideas and arguments. Here we are concerned more with the specific words and phrases used in sentences. Just as a battle is won by strategy *and* tactics, so your readers are won by structure *and* tone. In effective writing these two qualities fit together, interlock, and reinforce each other; they act like synergists.

1. Determine the desired relationship.

The first and most basic step in developing an appropriate tone is to decide what relationship you want to maintain or establish with your reader. Are you writing as a

[1]William Schutz, "The Interpersonal Underworld," *Harvard Business Review*, July–August 1958, p.36.

friend and confidant, letting your hair down on a subject and trusting him or her to keep your thoughts confidential? Are you writing as an expert who knows to laypersons who don't know? Are you writing as a salesperson of a product, service, or idea, seeking to retain your reader's goodwill in the future? Are you perhaps writing as an analyst and adviser, wishing to impress on your reader how objectively and thoroughly you have studied a question before deciding on recommendations for his or her action?

Some business and professional people like to think of this step as the *attitudes* one seeks to instill in the reader. "My usual purpose," an investment advisor once said in discussing her letters to clients, "is to keep their trust." Again, a veteran politician once told me, "The purpose of *every* letter I write—even my Christmas cards—is to sell the Republican Party." And once in a seminar a participant, a fund raiser for a church, defended a memorandum he had written to a prospective donor. "I *wanted* to make that man angry," he insisted. "He wasn't giving. I wanted to get his dander up so he could see how much more he could do for us."

If you are like many writers, more than once you will experience difficult conflicts at this early and crucial stage of tone setting. In an unpublished paper written for a class he used to teach at the Harvard Business School, John S. Fielden stated the problem:

> It is frequently necessary for a writer to decide whether he will let his writing reflect his real feelings toward what he is discussing, or whether in the interests of more important business goals he will adopt a tone more appropriate to his present or desired relationship with the prospective reader. The reconciliation of conflicting influences on the tone of the writing is, sometimes, one of the most difficult tasks for a conscientious writer.

I know of no pat rules for resolving such conflicts. As professor Charles Gragg of the Harvard Business School used to say, "Wisdom can't be told."

2. Appraise the reader and situation.

Having determined the desired relationship or reader attitude, you should next consider the situation in which your communication will be read. Does it come to the reader as "just another report," or is it a report he or she has been waiting for with consuming interest? Does it convey good news or bad news? How controversial is it—how likely to be misunderstood because emotions are running high? Is your reader likely to try to read unexpected thoughts into it because of what other people are writing or saying? Does your reader have the kind of training and background that will facilitate or hinder proper understanding of the information you offer?

You must put yourself in the reader's shoes as much as you can. Even then you will fail sometimes, because unforeseeable factors may enter the picture—rumors, unexpected news, or even a sudden case of indigestion on the part of your reader. But your prospects of creating the right tone should improve considerably.

Effective business and professional writers generally tell me they try to visualize their readers before dictating or drafting an important letter or report. Mary C. Bromage makes this suggestion: "Try reading aloud what you have written. Would you be saying it that way if you were actually looking at the person whom you are addressing? And what can you hear him saying in reply?"[2] As the eighteenth century novelist Laurence Sterne observed, "Writing, when properly managed (as you can be sure I think mine is), is but a different name for conversation."

A little imagination can be helpful at this stage. Visualize the people you wish to influence. Ask yourself what they already know, what they believe (perhaps incorrectly), what their chief interests are, what magazines and newspapers they read (*Harvard Business Review* or

[2]Mary C. Bromage, *Writing for Business* (Ann Arbor, The University of Michigan Press, 1965), p. 128.

Penthouse? The Chicago Tribune or Lubbock, Texas *Avalanche-Journal?)* and where they are likely to read your memo or report (on a jolting commuter train or at a quiet lodge in Oregon?). This may seem like such an obvious step that it scarcely needs to be mentioned, but if so, it is too easily forgotten and, like the need for keeping your head down in golf, is worth repeated mentioning.

As an illustration, unseasoned editors are likely to discuss the failings of a manuscript in different ways when (a) writing to an author and (b) talking with an author person to person. Though their decision may be the same in either case, their words are more likely to be blunt and unfeeling in the first case because they write without visualizing the person. But in the second case, confronting the disappointed author face to face, they are inclined to present their reactions in more adroit ways, ranging from conspicuous attempts to point out the "pluses" before mentioning the "minuses" to the use of softened phrases and more gently worded criticisms. In the second case, in other words, seeing or visualizing the author makes them more sensitive to the person's anxieties and feelings of dependence on them for a tactful, helpful critique. Thus they are more aware of the *situation* in which they are communicating.

It stands to reason, of course, that the more delicate the situation, the more care you should take in analyzing it and reviewing the most appropriate ways to respond to it. What are the most important points to check? The lists in Exhibit I may be helpful. The idea for them has been borrowed from George L. Morrisey of North American Rockwell Corporation, who has developed an "Audience Analysis Audit" for use in planning technical briefings.[3] Although the points in Exhibit I differ from Morrisey's in many ways, because our purpose and medium are different, the approach is similar, and I recommend his audit

[3]George L. Morrisey, *Effective Business and Technical Presentations* (Reading, Mass., Addison-Wesley, 1968), pp. 20–21 and back of the book.

whenever a formal oral or written presentation of a technical proposal is planned.

Since tone bears a close relationship to strategy, as discussed in Chapter 4, the checklist in Exhibit I may also be helpful in planning the types and arrangements of facts and ideas to present.

Exhibit I. Checklist for Analyzing the Reader-Writer Situation
(Check the most descriptive terms)

A. Reader's position vis-a-vis writer

Boss____ Subordinate____ Peer, partner, co-worker____ Client or customer____ Supplier____ Consultant____ General public____ Interested member of another organization or cause____ Competitor____

Length of relationship, if any
New____ Less than two years____ More than two years____

B. Reader's preparation for the communication

Requested it____ Expecting it because of prior communications or normal routine____ Not expecting it____

Knowledge of subject
Thorough____ Limited____ None____ Unknown____

Vocabulary level in subject area
High____ Medium____ Low____ Unknown____

Open-mindedness on topic
Willing to change____ Slightly resistant to change____ Committed not to change____ Unknown____

C. Reader's attitude toward writer

Friendly____ Hostile____ Neutral____ Un-

known_____
If known, is attitude firm_____, superficial_____, or variable_____?

D. Reader's concern with subject

Very interested_____ Mildly interested_____ Neutral or indifferent_____ Unknown _____

E. Reader's probable feelings about proposal, findings, or viewpoint of communication

Agreement_____ Disagreement_____ Neutral_____ Unknown_____
If disagreement, is reader likely to take exception because of methodology_____, reasoning_____, findings or conclusions_____, or other (specify)_____?

If disagreement, is reader likely to feel personally threatened (e.g., loss of job, status, or income)_____, or opposed only on grounds of convenience, technique, conflicting policies, and so on_____?

F. Reader's biases, if known

Likes_____ or dislikes_____ flamboyance, cuteness.
Prefers conciseness and meticulous attention to detail_____
Likes_____ or dislikes_____ "hard sell" tactics
Is very particular about letterhead, format, type size, binding, spacing, chart arrangements, and/or related aspects_____
Other (specify) ____________________________

3. Choose words that will be "heard" in the intended way.

Having decided on the tone you want to convey and having reviewed the possible effect of the situation on your communication, your next step is to choose appropriate words for your message. "A word spoken in due season, how good is it!" counsels the biblical author in Proverbs (15:23); inappropriate wording, on the other hand, can overcome the wisest strategy and produce a nonmeeting of the minds.

Judy Johnson and Ruth Newman, teachers of writing, make the following observations:

> Tone . . . communicates an attitude toward subject and audience. For example, by adopting a serious tone you can indicate the importance of the subject or the urgency of the problem. In contrast, by adopting an informal tone you can indicate that a problem is less serious or pressing. Similarly, your tone conveys your attitude toward the audience. You can sound sympathetic to your readers' problems or you can attempt to achieve your goals through a "hard line" approach. . . . A carefully chosen tone can do much to make your argument persuasive.[4]

Semantics rears its head at this stage. If you use the word *liberal*, does it mean the same thing to your readers that it means to you? If you use a phrase like *Pavlovian science* to indicate spurious science, does it have a similar connotation to your readers? If you use the word *justice* in the controversial sense, might it mean *just us* instead to readers from minority groups?

Let us turn now to examine some of the most commonly desired tones in written communications and see how they are created.

Friendliness, warmth, graciousness. In perhaps the majority of your letters and memoranda, you will want your reader to "hear" a friendly tone. But as some possible answers in Exhibit I suggest, the situation may be such that you cannot count on that effect unless you go out of your way to reinforce it. For instance, your reader may be an associate or client who has not yet made up his or her mind about your intentions, or who may even be

[4]Judy Johnson and Ruth Newman, "Written and Oral Communication, " unpublished note; assigned for the course in "Written and Oral Communications," Harvard Business School, 1977.

somewhat suspicious of you; or a touchy state of affairs may exist, so that the reader may overreact negatively to a "cold" tone that slips in anywhere.

To convey a friendly tone, use words such as *glad, pleased, delighted, happy, benefit, pleasure, fine, privilege, grateful, welcome, successful, progressive, generous*, and *rewarding*. "A gentle tongue is a tree of life." (Proverbs (15:4))

Again, do not write, "Pursuant to your application of May 17 to the Zoning Board for a building permit, this is to inform you that said application has been granted." Instead say, "I'm happy to tell you that your request for a building permit has been approved by the Zoning Board." Do not tell a delinquent account, "It has been brought to my attention that your payments due on January 6 and February 6 have not been sent, and are due immediately." Instead tell the recipient, "This is a friendly reminder that your payment due January 6 has not reached us. The February 6 payment is also due. Everyone is apt to overlook such things now and then, and if it has slipped your mind, please let us have your payment by return mail."

In an article in the *Harvard Business Review*,[5] a teacher at the General Motors Institute gives an example of a memorandum well calculated to create hostility and resentment, and shows how to turn it into a memorandum better designed to enlist cooperation. Bugged by indiscriminate use of the office copy machines, an irate manager dictates:

TO: All Employees

FROM: Samuel Edwards, General Manager

SUBJECT: Abuse of copiers

It has recently been brought to my attention that the people who are employed by this company have taken advantage of their

[5]Marvin H. Swift, "Clear Writing Means Clear Thinking Means . . .," *Harvard Business Review*, January–February 1973, p. 59.

positions by availing themselves of the copiers. More specifically, these machines are being used for other than company business.

Obviously, such practice is contrary to company policy and must cease and desist immediately. I wish therefore to inform all concerned—those who have abused policy or will be abusing it—that their behavior cannot and will not be tolerated. Accordingly, anyone in the future who is unable to control himself will have his employment terminated.

If there are any questions about company policy, please feel free to contact this office.

Fortunately, the manager has second thoughts about the memorandum after it has been typed up and placed on his desk. He doesn't want to treat these people like criminals; he seeks their help! So he rewrites the memo:

TO: All Employees

FROM: Samuel Edwards, General Manager

SUBJECT: Use of copiers

We are revamping our policy on the use of the copiers for personal matters. In the past we have not encouraged personnel to use them for such purposes because of the costs involved. But we also recognize, perhaps belatedly, that we can solve the problem if each of us pays for what he takes.

We are therefore putting these copiers on a pay-as-you-go basis. The details are simple enough. . . .

Respect for authority or status. If you are a subordinate writing to your boss or another senior person, bear in mind that your reader probably has a sensitive, well-attuned ear for expressions of deference. He or she is likely to "hear" better than you can imagine (at least, if you have not held similar positions yourself) the most subtle connotations of respect or disrespect for authority. Use words and phrases indicating your awareness that the reader, not you, has the responsibility to decide, that anything you know or suggest is of advisory value only. For instance, if you are arguing for locating a new office in Natick instead of Framingham, sum up with a sentence

such as, "It seems to me, therefore, that the advantages of Natick are more important to us than those of Framingham...," instead of, "Obviously, therefore, we should decide on the Natick location instead of Framingham...."
..."

Make clear what your opinions and recommendations are, but point much more often to facts than to your opinions (your boss will "hear" your opinions more often than you may think). If you must refer to a mistake or shortcoming of your firm or some group in it, begin with a phrase like, "As you know . . . ," instead of the more presumptuous, "I want to call to your attention...," or "Let me remind you...."

At the same time, guard against sounding like a munchkin in a land of giants. Few people respect obsequiousness or excessive deference. Most scientists, other professionals, and managers in senior positions are allergic to the supplicant who "spreads it on too thick" and the mendicant who sounds so awestruck and fearful in writing that he cannot venture an opinion.

What about the tone of a communication from the boss to a subordinate? Now the shoe is on the other foot. It may be important to use a tone reminding the reader of your relationship, especially if you are using your authority to request action. For instance, "listen" to Defense Secretary Robert S. McNamara in a memorandum to the Joint Chiefs of Staff in August 1966:

> . . . I desire and expect a detailed, line-by-line analysis of these requirements to determine that each is truly essential. . . . In the course of your review of the validity of the requirements, I would like you to consider. . . . I expect that you will want to query CINCPAC about these and other units for which you desire clarification. . . .[6]

Some czars with large egos are afraid they will sound like "czardines" if they do not use harsh words or if they fail to remind subordinates of their stupidity. This is non-

[6]*The Pentagon Papers* (New York, Bantam, 1971), pp. 500–501.

sense. The very act of requiring a certain thing done by a certain time, together with the senior person's name, is enough to ensure the so-called "tremble factor" in a directive.

Awareness of delicate situations. Now suppose it is important to keep the readers' goodwill, but for one reason or another you must stick your neck out and deal with a problem about which they feel defensive or take a step which may seem to be out of line or in some other way risk upsetting your relationship. Such situations are indicated in parts of Sections B, C, and E of Exhibit I. When compounded, as they often are, by the fact that your readers are valued clients, seniors, or cherished colleagues, your message may call for more careful thought than almost any other type of writing.

Two working rules should be helpful. First, in your wording err on the side of clarity in showing your sensitivity to the problem. Second, be explicit about your motives and expectations in raising the issue. If your readers get the feeling that you are Dr. Jekyll with something to Hyde, you are going to have trouble getting across to them. Let us look at two examples illustrating these rules.

In the military services there is often considerable jockeying for power and promotion, yet protocol demands that the ploys and plays be carried on in a genteel, behind-the-curtains manner. Several years before World War II broke out, Lieutenant Colonel George S. Patton was asked by one aspiring officer to serve as intermediary in a backstage maneuver. The situation was difficult for Patton, because he himself aspired to please his seniors, and the general to whom he must write was a friend. After beginning with some personal news in his letter to General John J. Pershing, he wrote:

> Now I have to bother you with a personal problem. Gen. Drum has always been more than kind to me and took me to Hawaii on his staff. As you know he is most anxious to follow Gen. Craig as Chief of Staff. So far as I can see the choice lays between him and Gen. DeWitt. Yesterday Gen. Drum wrote me and asked if I could

> find out from you how you felt toward him in respect to his ambition. My loyalty to Gen. Drum makes it incumbent on me to ask you this question but since you are the center of all my loyalty I do not wish to place you in a position which might prove inconvenient to you. If you care to write me some statement which I could quote to Gen. Drum it would be helpful to me in my relations with him. If however you do not feel disposed to say any thing I shall understand your position and will simply have to say to Gen. Drum that I did not feel able to ask you such a question. I trust you will forgive me being this frank and assure you that what ever action you will take will be perfectly satisfactory to me.[7]

If you were reading this letter in Pershing's shoes, "listening" as he no doubt did to the writer's regard for their relationship, could you entertain any doubts about Patton's good intentions?

For a second example, let us take a passage from a confidential report submitted by a consultant to his client early in the 1960s. The consultant, a young man, had been asked to appraise a subsidiary of a parent corporation. The subsidiary had not been doing well, and the consultant's study convinced him that part of the difficulties could be laid at the doorstep of the parent corporation. Coming to the section of his report where this impression should be reported, he had to worry about his status with an important client, about his youth and inexperience, about the probable defensiveness of the executive in top management to whom he was writing if he wrote tactlessly, and about the probability that his opinions would become known sooner or later to the head of the subsidiary, whose friendship he valued because the man had given him much time and cooperation to do his study. He wrote as follows (for background, Newark is the location of headquarters, Okehampton is the location of the subsidiary, "DECL" is the name of the subsidiary, "Masterson" is the head of it, and the reader is president of the parent company).

[7]Martin Blumenson, *The Patton Papers, 1885–1940* (Boston, Houghton Mifflin, 1972), p. 919. As it turned out, Blumenson reports, Pershing chose to make no response to the letter.

> Here we come to most of the problems which I think were bothering you when I was in Newark and also those aspects of the Okehampton situation which you felt required an outsider's point of view. For the most part, such comments as I have will concern Mr. Masterson directly or indirectly. Despite his relationship to you, I have decided that to be less than perfectly frank with regard to my own opinions would do you a disservice. Moreover, I believe that is in keeping with the spirit of my assignment from you.
>
> It was unfortunate that the relationship between you and Mr. Masterson was such that he was the natural and obvious man to start up DECL. For Mr. Masterson—as he would now probably admit—is quite unsuited both by training and by temperament to doing the jobs that have been required of him over the last year. I know nothing at all about the decision to form DECL or what was said at that time. . . .
>
> This is perhaps a somewhat brutal commentary on a decision which must have had far more personal and subtle undertones than I could appreciate. But I am concerned to emphasize that the initial, and almost inevitable, liaison with Mr. Masterson was for this purpose very unfortunate. . . ."[8]

The consultant pulls no punches in this letter, both at the points indicated by ellipses and after he details his impressions forthrightly. But by making his motives explicit, by recognizing the attitude he hopes his reader will take, and by writing with humility—notice, for instance, the ending of the sentence opening the third paragraph—he takes the curse off.

Desire to maintain goodwill. In writing to clients, customers, and prospective buyers of services, products, and ideas you are promoting, use words that emphasize the readers' interests and viewpoint as well as your own desire to serve them. You want them to know that, any current difficulties notwithstanding, you value their goodwill and seek to retain it in the future.

This is relatively easy to do if your readers are satisfied

[8]See "Devonian Electronic Components Ltd. (A)," copyright 1963 by l'Institut pour l'Etude des Methodes de Direction de l'Enterprise, Lausanne, Switzerland; in George Albert Smith, Jr., C. Roland Christensen, Norman A. Berg, and Malcolm S. Salter, *Policy Formulation and Administration*, 6th ed. (Homewood, Ill., Richard D. Irwin, 1972), pp. 664–665.

with the current state of affairs. It is not easy if they are dissatisfied. For instance, in the case of a complaint about a product failure, you are likely to have a reader who is expecting to hear from you but has limited knowledge of your product or idea and a low or medium vocabulary in the subject area (see Section B of Exhibit I); a neutral or possibly hostile attitude toward you but, one hopes, a variable one (see Section C); a real interest in the product or idea (see Section D); and neutral feelings about any suggestions you make—that is, an "I'll see if it works" attitude (see Section E). In responding to him or her, keep these characteristics of the situation uppermost in mind.

For an illustration, let us suppose you are the sales-manager of a sunscreen manufacturer. You are answering a buyer whose letter or phone call states that the newly purchased screen has become loose and "wavy" in the frame. You might respond:

> Dear Customer:
>
> You are correct in saying that your new sunscreen should stay tighter and straighter in the frame than it has. Please call your nearest dealer [give the dealer's name, address, and telephone number] and he will be glad to repair or replace your installation free of charge.
>
> You'll be happy to know this problem rarely happens and is not likely to happen again. Our sunscreen is reputed to perform far beyond the guarantees we make. You should find it gives satisfactory service for many years after the current problem is corrected.
>
> Cordially yours . . .

The simple wording of this letter does not make your reader feel ignorant (though you probably would have preferred to use more concise, technical terms). Moreover, you indicate awareness of the customer's dissatisfaction but assume his or her feelings can be changed—an important point. Finally, such expressions as, "You are correct in saying" (instead of an expression like, "Your letter of June 14 complains . . ."), "Your nearest dealer . . . will be glad," and "you'll be happy" should help the reader to "hear" you as you want to be heard—desirous of serving, confident he or she will think better of you in the future, and proud of your product.

For other examples of good writing to valued customers and prospective buyers, see *Communicating through Letters and Reports*[9] and *Effective Letters: A Program for Self-Instruction.*[10]

Empathy. In almost all cases indicated in Exhibit I—indeed, in almost any case in which you seek to influence a reader's thinking—you should repeatedly express your awareness of and sensitivity to the reader's viewpoint. One of the best ways to do this is the so-called "you attitude." In its most obvious form the "you attitude" simply means choosing the words *you* and *your* wherever possible instead of *I*, *me*, and *mine* or impersonal words. But the "you attitude" should go deeper. It should mean stating the advantages, disadvantages, and implications of an idea or fact in terms of your reader's interest rather than your own. It also should mean being honest with the reader and truly considering his or her viewpoint as faithfully as you can.

But—and this is important—the method does *not* imply altering your opinions for the sake of consensus, nor does it mean subjugating your interests to the reader's. Accordingly, a more accurate label for this attitude is *empathy*, which implies awareness of the relationship between your desires and your reader's, but not self-subordination. Let us consider two contrasting examples.

In the 1960s, during the declining years of *The Saturday Evening Post*, its new president, Martin Ackerman,

[9]J.H. Menning and C.W. Wilkinson, *Communicating through Letters and Reports*, 4th ed. (Homewood, Ill., Richard D. Irwin, 1967) pp. 62–63 and other sections.

[10]James M. Reid, Jr., and Robert M. Wendlinger (in collaboration with New York Life Insurance Company), *Effective Letters: A Program for Self-Instruction* (New York: McGraw-Hill, 1978).

wanted to make a statement to readers about the future of the magazine. In the first draft written by a staff writer, the statement began:

> On a fair June day exactly half my lifetime ago I graduated from high school—not just any high school but Benjamin Franklin High School. . . . Today I find myself the chief executive officer of the company that publishes Franklin's magazine. That heritage alone compels dedication, demands that I pledge to you, its millions of mid-20th century readers, that the fundamental resolve of this management is to perpetuate *The Saturday Evening Post*. . . .[11]

In this communication there is zero empathy. The circumstances that made the magazine interesting to its chief executive—power, prestige, money—were of little concern to the reader, who had quite different motives in opening it.

Now let us take another example. While Harry S. Truman was Vice-President-Elect under Franklin D. Roosevelt, in November of 1944, the Director of the William L. Clements Library of the University of Michigan wrote him:[12]

> My dear Vice-President-Elect:
>
> If you are going to be associated with our mutual friend Franklin D. Roosevelt, you are going to have to get used to this kind of thing.
>
> The President's real joy in life is his library at Hyde Park. He made me do a lot of work in organizing it.
>
> Now we, at the University of Michigan, have a comparable library of rarities. In our collections are autographs of prominent Americans, from Christopher Columbus to the present time.
>
> We want yours for our collection.
>
> If there is any truth in that story about your playing Paderewski's Minuet at the Muehlebach while everyone else was jittery about the election returns, what more appropriate than that you give us your autograph on the enclosed?

[11]Otto Friedrich, *Decline and Fall* (New York, Harper & Row, 1970), p. 347.
[12]Bromage, op. cit., p. 53.

> If your secretary tries to ditch this, I'm going after Bob Hannegan; if he fails, I'm going to ask the President to intercede for me—and I know you would not want to have us take up the President's time, now, would you?
>
> Very truly yours,
>
> Randolph G. Adams
>
> Director

(A copy of Paderewski's Minuet accompanied the letter.)

Notice the prominence of the *you's* and *your's* in this letter, beginning with the second word of text. Note, too, the citing of arguments of particular importance *to the reader*—the mention of the name of the reader's boss (Roosevelt) in the first paragraph, the mention of the boss's interest in libraries in the second paragraph, as well as the writer's earlier connection with Roosevelt, the recognition of the reader's prominence, and the general threat in the last paragraph to go over the reader's head to the boss, if necessary. It should be no surprise that the Clements Library got the autograph as requested.

In an interesting discussion of a business school case, "Cooper Fabrics, Inc.," Ruth G. Newman describes a company that has been in hard times but now is experiencing a little prosperity. Ralph Hampton, the general manager, asks his lieutenants for proposed drafts of letters to send employees. Hampton himself also writes a suggested draft. Hampton's letter is attacked by various experts whose opinions Newman solicits. For instance, they jump on the draft because of its I-tone and patronizing sound. One expert (John S. Fielden) says:

> Hampton's letter creates the impression of "I am the big boss." Four of the five paragraphs begin with a reference to "I": "As general manager of this mill I am . . ."; "I would like to add . . ."; "I know . . ."; and "In closing I want. . . ." Even the references to "you" in his letter seem patronizing—"You employees"; "I am sure that you can understand"; and "I want to extend to you on behalf of the whole management and administration team here"—a classic case of little you and big me. Furthermore, read-

> ers are prone to resent statements such as "I am sure you can understand the necessity of holding a line on all costs," because what the writer is doing is airily assuming the problem away. His readers may very well neither understand nor agree.[13]

The examples noted briefly are enough to make the point. Hampton's "little you and big me" is a raw contrast with the "big you and big me" tone of other messages we have looked at, such as the Clements and sunscreen letters in this chapter and the Einstein letter in Chapter 3. The difference in warmth is like January compared to June.

Dependence on the reader's open-mindedness and goodwill. As part of Exhibit I indicates, an important fact of the reader-writer situation may be the reader's superior power and clout. The writer is in the position of having to appeal to the reader for understanding. What kinds of words and thoughts are appropriate in a situation like this?

A fine example is a statement by John T. Thielke, a vice-president of Economics Laboratory, Inc., before the Committee on Public Works of the U.S. House of Representatives in September 1971.[14] The committee was sponsoring an investigation of products polluting streams, lakes, and water supplies. Thielke's company, which manufactured detergents and cleaners and was also doing research and development on nonphosphate, nonpolluting products, was fearful about possible recommendations the committee might decide to adopt. Thielke appeared before the committee and left with it a written copy of his plea.

The statement begins with a series of sentences describing the company's business and its vital stake in the product field under investigation. Then Thielke states: "We are puzzled as to what we should use in place of

[13]Ruth G. Newman, "Case of the Questionable Communiques," *Harvard Business Review*, November–December 1975, p. 26.
[14]Reprinted in *Corporate News*, Economics Laboratory, Inc., White Plains, N.Y., September 14, 1971, p. 1.

phosphate and in which way to turn because of the many state and city laws with 'sanitation conflicts,' and the many confusing and inconsistent stories of the consumer advocates, environmentalists, and ecologists."

There is no suggestion of arrogance or threat-making in the above, no intimation (as often appears in such statements) that the writer's company knows what the country should do. Next Thielke adds: "We need some understanding, your help, and certainly some Federal guidance. . . ."

Now he makes it more explicit than ever how much he values the committee's direction and understanding. A few sentences later he states: "Our company's interest is to provide our customers with products of the highest quality . . . that are safe to use. . . ."

In other words, Mr. and Ms. Legislator, you will not look bad if you hear us out and decide that our cause has some merit. (Several pages of fact and elaboration follow the material described.)

Anger and accusation. Instructors of business and professional writing generally assume that communications should never downgrade the audience. But this oversimplifies life. Rightly or wrongly, intelligent men and women sometimes decide that their purposes are best accomplished by putting down the reader. They do this by expressing coldness, aloofness, anger, or contempt.

If you purposely seek to treat your reader as an errant child, wrongdoer, or traitor, combine "I-words" with words of condescension and deprecation. A master of this combination (because he used it purposively) was the great labor leader, John L. Lewis. In 1936, when his union, the Congress of Industrial Organizations, was expelled from the American Federation of Labor (AFL), he wrote to AFL head William Green, deliberately seeking to humiliate him in the hope of forcing a change of mind. "I overlook the inane ineptitude of your statement published today," Lewis began. "Perchance you were agitated and distraught." Displaying increased sarcasm and contempt as he went on, Lewis added such lines as "I cannot yet believe you would be a party to such a Brutus blow" and "Why not . . . return home to the union that suckled you . . .?"[15]

If you seek to accuse your reader, it is hard to beat the repetition of you-did-wrong phrases if you want your message to sting. Here is a good example, from the beginning of a book author's letter to a critic of the book:

> Dear Professor French:
>
> I was disturbed and a bit angered by your letter regarding the supposed "sexist bias" in my new management text. Frankly, your criticism is unfair and ill-founded.
>
> You completely ignore the long and flattering biography of "Ruth Shuman" that begins Part 5. You ignore the central position of Vice-President "Judith Greene" in Trustworthy Company case, and that a major issue in that case is response to ambitious, capable MBA females. Ms. Greene has visited with my classes when discussing this case. You ignore that Regina Neal, Director in the case of Northside Child Health Care Center, is a female MD. You ignore that the administrators in the case of Open or Closed in the Operating Room are females. You dismiss that fact that all the strong characters in City Community College are women and the weak ones are men and that the case illustrates the fallacy of placing a male in charge just because he is a male. You ignore the unflattering portrayal of Howard Andresen and his response to women's interest. You ignore that this is one of the very first management books to systematically include references to "him and her," "she and he," "his and hers." An experienced female editor worked with me on this and we were very conscious of these points. . . .[16]

Readers more easily forgive you for exaggerating your feelings than for disturbing their positions or actions. Ernest Hemingway once said of someone that "He had gotten rid of many things by writing them." And a character

[15]Irving Bernstein, *Turbulent Years* (Boston, Houghton Mifflin, 1970), p. 415.
[16]David R. Hampton, Charles E. Summer, and Ross A. Webber, *Organizational Behavior and the Practice of Management* (Glenview, Ill.: Scott, Foresman, 1978), p. 180.

in Shakespeare's *Othello* remarks, "I observe a fury in your words, /But not the words."

Familiarity and cuteness. If you want to stress a close, informal relationship with your reader, and your reader knows something about your personal manner, it may be appropriate in a letter or memo to use words that "sound" like your style in easy conversation. Bantering expressions such as "How about that?" and "Bill's got to be kidding!" may be suitable if they are natural for you to use in talk. Injecting first names, as you might in conversation, also may be appropriate—for instance, "The point to emphasize, Alice, is that you stand to lose the interest on this loan unless. . . ." Allusions to "in-house" anecdotes, puns, and cute remarks may have their place, too.

On rare occasions it may be appropriate to use flipness in arm's-length relationships. The ending of Randolph Adams' letter to Vice-President Truman, quoted earlier, is an example. In this case the saucy closing paragraph is in keeping because the request itself deals with an offbeat incident, that is, Truman's playing a piece of classical music.

The appropriateness of familiarity and cleverness depends more than most questions do on the "culture" of reader and writer, local practice, the mood of the times, and the subject. You need to make much the same judgments about these things that you do in conversation with a person. The guiding rule is simple: *Sound like yourself!* Joseph Wilson, the great head of Xerox Corporation, once began a very important memorandum to 13 top executives of the company in this manner: "Never have I made a suggestion which was so unanimously frowned upon by you, my beloved associates, as this one. . . ."[16] I once asked a Xerox executive about this choice of words. "That," he said, "sounds just like Joe Wilson."

Technical level. As Exhibit I suggests, the reader may have an expert understanding of and deep concern for the

[16]John H. Dessauer, *My Years with Xerox* (New York, Doubleday, 1971), p. 110.

subject you are writing about. If you also are an expert, it is appropriate to employ technical terms, allusions, and jargon. In fact, contrary to what journalists usually advise, it may be a mistake *not* to write in that manner. For instance, a newsletter to users of an organization's computer services contained many sentences like:

> IERR is an error return variable, which will be set to some specified non-zero value if an error occurs in attempting to open the specified file for I/O. If an error occurs in attempting to access the file specified and IERR is not supplied, then the FORTRAN Run-Time package will print its own error message and exit to the monitor.

This passage, which would horrify journalists, is perfectly appropriate for the intended readers. To change it in the usual patented ways of editors and rewrite people—reducing the repetition of the word "error," for example, or changing "non-zero value" to "value other than zero," or changing "access" to "gain access to" (which technically would be correct, since "access" is not a verb)—would be to make it less appropriate in tone, not more so. For the expressions used are accepted communication jargon in that community of readers.

But when an expert is writing to nonexperts, a colleague-to-colleague relationship is out of the question. Now the writer must put the information in the reader's terms or else fail to communicate. However, this simple principle appears to be unknown to many insurance companies. For instance:

> If there is other automobile medical payments insurance against a loss under coverage D of this policy the company shall not be liable under this policy for a greater proportion of such loss than the applicable limit of liability stated in the declaration bears to the total applicable limit of liability of all valid and collectible automobile medical payments insurance; provided, however, the insurance with respect to any motor vehicle other than a motor vehicle for which a specific automobile medical payments premium has been charged under this policy shall be excess insur-

> ance over any other valid and collectible automobile medical payments insurance.[17]

Few automobile owners can decipher this complicated prose, yet it characterizes an entire policy which is the only written understanding given the insured by the company. The company or agency might be forgiven if it said, in effect, "Due to circumstances beyond our control, our contract with you, Mr. Automobile Owner, must be couched in legal phraseology, and you will find a copy of it attached for your files. But since it is difficult for anyone but an insurance specialist to read, we are also providing you with a statement in plain English of the policy you have just bought from us. . . ."

How ironic that so few consumerists have seized on policies written in this way for lay people. Such policies are ripoffs, far greater threats to the consumer's pocketbook and well-being than exaggerated claims for electric irons, mouthwashes, chewing gum, and similar items, which to date have taken so much of the consumer movement's time and energy.

Here, for the sake of contrast, is the first paragraph of a memorandum on eczema, written by a dermatologist for his lay clients:

> Eczema is an itchy rash on the face, neck and folds of elbows and knees, often beginning in the third month of life or at various times throughout childhood or adult life. The skin may be moist and crusted just after scratching, or dry and scaly as it heals. It may be thickened and leathery after repeated rubbing and scratching.[18]

Printed on one sheet of photocopy paper, the memorandum proceeds to describe in equally simple terms the

[17]Great American Insurance Company, Massachusetts Vehicle Policy Combination Form, Section 12, Part I.

[18]Robert D. Griesemer, M.D., Winchester, Mass., memorandum on "Eczema" (undated).

causes of eczema, ways to treat it, and special problems. No part of it is beyond the understanding of the average adult in the doctor's clientele. Yet he *could* have described his subject in dense technical jargon, as in the insurance policy quoted. Indeed, he probably would have found it easier to do that.

4. Express ideas that convey the intended relationship.

Good writers in business, government, and the professions often go a step farther than the one just described. In addition to choosing carefully the kinds of words that convey the desired attitude, they state ideas and thoughts that show explicitly what kind of relationship they want with the reader. Such statements can do a great deal to create the right tone in a written communication on a touchy, sensitive subject. It is puzzling that they are not added more often.

In June 1965 British Prime Minister Harold Wilson deplored the bombing of targets around Hanoi in North Vietnam and frankly expressed his objections in a cablegram sent to President Lyndon B. Johnson. Carefully, Wilson chose words having a factual, nonincriminating ring. But he did not want to rely only on the tone of these words to indicate he was not damning the Johnson Administration; to avoid such a connotation, he knew he must make his attitude explicit. Therefore, before listing his objections to the bombing, he wrote:

> I know you will not feel that I am unsympathetic or uncomprehending of the dilemma that this problem [i,e., the bombing of oil targets near Hanoi and Haiphong] presents for you. In particular, I wholly understand the deep concern you must feel at the need to do anything possible to reduce the losses of young Americans. . . .[19]

At the end of the cablegram, to eliminate any doubt at all about his relationship with Johnson, Wilson added:

[19] *The Pentagon Papers as Published by The New York Times* (New York, Bantam, 1971), pp. 448–449.

I want to repeat . . . that our reservations about this operation will not affect our continuing support for your policy over Vietnam, as you and your people have made it clear from your Baltimore speech onwards. . . ."

5. Use an appropriate amount of detail.

Texts on business and professional writing are full of injunctions to "Keep it short!" Detail is all right in school, we are told, but not in memoranda to busy executives or reports to clients, prospective customers, project associates.

Nonsense! Often it is as inappropriate to skimp on detail as it is to state only the main points. A memorandum, letter, or report is not necessarily a Procrustean bed in which not only are the writer's legs trimmed off but everything else except the head and heart. Naturally, wordiness should be avoided—only in a ceremonial document now and then is it appropriate. But in numerous writings we can succeed in developing the right tone *only* if we elaborate, define, qualify, document, and illustrate our points and ideas. "For it is precept upon precept, precept upon precept,/line upon line, line upon line,/here a little, there a little." [Isaiah 28:10]

This is true even for sales letters, the most jealously guarded bastion of the keep-it-short school. Here is some sound counsel from *Advertising Age:*

Prospects will read almost any number of words if they give information and value to the reader. Thus, if you are just trying for an inquiry, you may be able to use a short letter. But if you are answering an inquiry and trying for an order, the reader will accept any amount of copy if you make it interesting.

It is estimated that the salesman talks about 18 minutes in the average sales interview. That represents 6 or 7 typed pages.

Your letter has the same purpose—to capture attention, inform, prove, and persuade to action. So don't quibble over 2, 3 or 4 pages.[20]

It is difficult to formularize decisions about length. The

[20]Reprinted in *Sales and Marketing in Australia*, February–March 1972, p. 24.

need is to respond to the situation, using your natural antennae to pick up all the signals as to what is appropriate and inappropriate. Generally speaking, length is likely to be more appropriate when (a) the quality of your analysis is important to the reader; (b) the reader is intensely interested in the subject; (c) the data you possess are significant; and/or (d) your communication has a vicarious purpose, that is, it must convey the facts or observations you have made as a substitute for readers having made them.

Turning now to the other side of the ledger, when is brevity appropriate? The eager writer, like the good rain and the bad preacher, often doesn't know when to stop. Brevity is called for in situations in which:

The aim is to emphasize a simple but vital point. Especially if you want to register just one feeling, conviction, or opinion in the reader's mind, there may be no more elegant way to do so than by brevity. Rudolph Flesch gives the following before-and-after example for an overly long letter reduced to the appropriate length:

Before:

Gentlemen:

In reference to the above collection item, which you instructed us to hold at the disposal of the beneficiary, we wish to advise that Mr. Ling has not called on us, nor have we received any inquiries on his behalf.

The above information is provided to you in the event you wish to give us any further instructions in the matter.

After:

Gentlemen:

Mr. Ling hasn't called on us, nor have we had any inquiries on his behalf. Do you have any further instructions?[21]

[21].Rudolph Flesch. "Write the Way You Talk," *Reader's Digest,* August 1973. p. 121.

The reader knows the subject or can figure out the idea better, perhaps, than you can. For example, a doctoral candidate who had failed his examinations sought reinstatement in the program by sending written arguments to the faculty members concerned. Some of these communications contained lengthy observations on the rule of law, the role of authority in society, freedom, and similar matters. Such material made for a poor tone in the documents, because his readers could have expressed these thoughts better than he could.

The reader cares only about the conclusion or outcome. Of course, numerous written communications fall in this category—for example, a report on a scientific finding to administrative officials in a public agency, a doctor's report to a client on tests for tuberculosis, or a memo to a sales executive on a quality correction in a product. What do you do if some readers are interested in detail and some are not? One solution is to divide the communication into two parts, one giving the highlights in a general way (and ordinarily appearing at the beginning), and one repeating the main points in a technical, precise way and then amplifying the what, where, who, how, and why aspects in the body of the communication. (For more discussion of this approach, see Chapters 4 and 5).

The subject is pedestrian. In this category fall all sorts of memoranda and letters, such as requests to turn off lights when leaving the building, directives to observe safety regulations, information on holidays to be observed, and so forth. Sometimes we lose our sense of perspective when writing such communications and make them so tedious, overblown, and pompous that the results are more laughable than useful. In his cogent satire on bureaucracy, *The Kidner Report,* John Kidner reproduces this memorandum, attributed to Western Electric Company in North Andover, Massachusetts:

To All Department Chiefs

On November 18, 1969 the Company will observe its 100th anniversary. In honor of this occasion the first rest period for each shift will be extended to twenty minutes.

Prior to the first rest period each department will send one person, for each twenty-five employees in the department, to a pre-assigned cafeteria to pick up cake which will distributed at rest period.

The plant will be divided in half, starting at the main lobby entrance and running straight down the rear of the plant. Departments on the Lawrence side of this dividing line will pick up cake in the south cafeteria; those on the Haverhill side will pick up at the north cafeteria.

During the period from November 12, 1969, through November 17, 1969, departments will pick up tickets at the Public Relations Office for their employees. There will be two types of tickets: pink tickets for 25 pieces of cake and a yellow ticket for odd numbers.

Example: If a department has 80 employees (including supervisors) they will pick up three pink and one yellow ticket. The yellow will be marked five employees and signed by individual department chief. . . .[22]

(The directive continues with information on "cake pick-up times," shifts, and other matters.)

Parts of the invasion plan for Iwo Jima were successfully communicated with less detail than that!

6. Don't underestimate appearances.

Too often business and professional people overlook the role of physical properties in creating the right tone for a written communication. Again and again a message is distorted, in the reader's perception, by hard-to-read typing, the quality or shape of the paper, the symbols or "glyphs" on the letterhead, the color of the paper, margins and spacing, and inappropriate binding (in the case of a long report). These qualities can be just as influential

[22]John Kidner, *The Kidner Report* (Washington, D.C., Acropolis Books, 1972), pp. 57–58.

in a written communication as in the design and packaging of foods, apparel, games, hardware, and other merchandise.

Before readers look at the first sentence of your letter, memo, or report, they may get a variety of impressions about the writer. From an overly "busy" letterhead, they may get the feeling that you are egotistical or vain; from a letterhead design and symbols that have a 1920-like vintage, the feeling that you are out of step with the times; from stingy margins and cramped spacing, the feeling that you are "pushy" or difficult to deal with; from the color, weight, or shape of paper employed, the feeling that you are eccentric; from the poor quality of typing, crudeness of corrections, or hard-to-read photocopies, the feeling that you are careless or thoughtless. The style of charts and tables may convey similar impressions.

Because such feelings are rarely reported by readers, they are easy to overlook. Thoughtful writers do not make this mistake. They know that the appearance of a document is a kind of surrogate for the writer, like a stand-in for a high official at a public ceremony. The wise governor who can't appear personally at a banquet makes sure that his emissary is dignified and personable.

TURNING ON AND TURNING OFF

"Talking is a hydrant in the yard and writing is a faucet upstairs in the house," Robert Frost once said. When writing, you are distant from your reader, out of view—upstairs rather than out in the yard. You must do with fewer words. Your direction and aim are more controlled. Your words are doing double-duty. Perhaps Samuel Butler overstated the need when he wrote, several centuries ago, "We are not won by arguments that we can analyze, but by tone and temper, by the manner which is the man himself." But the truth he was onto is an important one.

Effective writers in science, business, government, and the professions are masters of tone as well as substance. They decide carefully on what they want to say, but they don't stop there. They also choose words, phrases, and formats that effectively convey the intent of the ideas. They see writing as a multidimensional process, as a combinational task. The difference between their writing and the writing of ineffective communicators is the difference between teamwork in a police car and a famous clown act played in a Ringling Brothers circus—four frantic characters drove a car, one pressing on the gas pedal, another on the brake, the third clutching the steering wheel, and the fourth blowing the horn. Nobody needs to be told how the drive ended. When we do not think through our intent in a written communication, we do little better than the clowns did.

As John R. Tremble points out, as a writer you do not, for all practical purposes, exist without the assent of your intended readers. They have the power to shut you off whenever they wish. You are, so to speak, in *their* debt—not the other way around.[23] As a reader, you know this perfectly well. Have there not been many times when you started to read a document, thinking it had something useful for you to know, but tossed it aside after a few paragraphs because you found yourself bored, irritated, or turned off in some other way?

Whether you think of making the tone right as a job of salesmanship, empathy, or "good politics," it is one of the most interesting and rewarding parts of writing. As Tremble says: "The reader's needs, not your own, will dominate your thinking. And it will give you pleasure; you'll quickly learn to enjoy the sense of communion, the fellow-feeling it brings, for, as in a friendship, you'll be in warm, imaginative touch with another human being."[24]

[23]John R. Tremble, *Writing with Style* (Englewood Cliffs, N.J.: Prentice-Hall, 1975), pp. 16–19.
[24]*Ibid.*, p. 19.

PROBLEMS AND CASES

1. In the case of John L. Lewis' sarcastic letter to William Green, what do you think would have been the effect of the words on members of Lewis's union when the letter was printed in a newspaper?
2. Do you think the "Dear Professor French" letter was written for an audience of colleagues as well as for Professor French? If so, what do you think of the writer's strategy?
3. Describe briefly four examples of articles, monographs, or papers you know about that are justifiably long, each for a different reason.
4. Present two examples of memoranda, monographs, letters, reports, directives, or other documents whose physical appearance creates a negative reaction in the reader. Present one example of a document whose physical appearance creates a positive impression.
5. Rewrite Randolph Adams' letter to Harry Truman in a more formal, matter-of-fact, and solicitous tone.
6. Rewrite the "Dear Professor French" letter as Randolph Adams might have written it, that is, in a breezier, warmer, more light-hearted tone.
7. Rewrite John L. Lewis' letter at the end of Chapter 6 in a tone of greater deference to President Roosevelt, conveying a desire to appear cooperative and to stay in the President's good graces.
8. Write a paragraph of 30 words or less typifying Elinor Hoyt Wylie's phrase, "Honeyed words like bees, gilded and sticky, with a little sting."
9. In the August 1973 issue of *Reader's Digest* the well-known writing instructor Rudolf Flesch wrote: "Use contractions freely. There's nothing more important for improving your writing style. Use of *don't* and *it's* and *haven't* and *there's* is the No. 1 style device of modern professional writing." Do you think this rule should be applied to all written communications in a company, professional firm, or public agency? Explain your agreement or disagreement with short examples.
10. In October 1975 an owner of a large tract of land in West

Virginia sent the following eviction notice to 32 families in the town of Hutchinson:

> This area has been leased to a major coal producer for the installation of a coal processing plant, and all houses in this area will have to be removed. Please be advised to look for other housing facilities. This is very urgent. We are giving you 30 days to move.

Comment on the landowner's reason for writing in this manner. Do you think this person was justified? Would you have advised different wording? If so, write the notice as you think it should have been written.

11. In 1977 the top management of a leading newspaper reportedly sent the following memorandum to department heads:

> Department heads will submit to the Managing Editor lists of staffers who have not been properly recognized for superior performance. Lists of staffers who are non-producers also will be submitted as well as the names of those staffers who are disloyal to the [name of newspaper] and who are trouble-makers.

Comment on the tone of this memorandum. What does it tell you about the writer's attitudes? Under what circumstances would it probably succeed or fail in accomplishing its purpose?

12. Authorities on transactional analysis feel that various kinds of behavior, including communication, are affected by one's "life position" or attitude toward others. The four life positions and some of their effects are shown in the table on page 205; adapted from Charles Albano and Thomasine Rendero, *Transactional Analysis on the Job and Communicating with Subordinates* (New York: AMACOM, a division of American Management Association, 1974), p. 29.

Do you think this scheme explains the variations in tone seen in many written communications in business, science, the professions, and government? Write a short memorandum applying this scheme to written communi-

Life Position	**I'M OK— YOU'RE OK**	**#2 I'M NOT OK— YOU'RE OK**	**#3 I'M OK— YOU'RE NOT OK**	**#4 I'M NOT OK— YOU'RE NOT OK**
Communicates	Openly	Defensively Self-deprecatingly	Defensively Aggressively	Hostilely Abruptly
Handles Disagreement By	Seeking clarification and mutual resolution	Perceiving difference in opinion as evidence of his inadequacy	Placing blame on others	Escalating the conflict Involving a third party
Solves Problems By	Consulting others, trusting himself	Relying almost completely on others	Unilaterally rejecting others' ideas	Succumbing to problems
Spends Time	Taking necessary action and producing	Brooding or over-compensating in constant activity	Boasting Provoking others Playing persecutor	Withdrawing Playing a variety of games
Is Moved to Act	On assignment or initiative	By praise or admonition	When forced, may demand official instructions	By reprimands or threats

cations, giving a brief example for each life position to illustrate how it affects the tone of writing. Draw your examples from the different "Problems and Cases" sections of this book.

13. ***The Unhappy Utility:*** Early in 1978 Boston Edison sent the following notice to all its domestic customers:

> To Our Customers:
>
> The Massachusetts Department of Public Utilities has granted Boston Edison its first general rate increase in 14 years. The new rates, now in effect, are indicated on the back of this card.
>
> The rates could be temporary in nature since the Company does not feel that the increase allowed (only 43 percent of our original request) is sufficient to provide a high level of service.
>
> Such an inadequate increase in rates will, in the long run, result in higher costs to the consumer.
>
> Consequently, we have filed with the Supreme Judicial Court of Massachusetts an appeal of the DPU verdict in order to meet our public service responsibilities as an efficient reliable company for the benefit of Company, community and customer alike.
>
> BOSTON EDISON

On the back of the 3 X 6 card appeared the rate schedules granted by the state agency.

If you had been the public relations director at Boston Edison, would you have okayed this text when offered to you for your approval? If you would have changed it, indicate your changes.

14. ***The Sit-Downers Speak Up:*** In January 1937 John L. Lewis' United Auto Workers in Flint, Michigan, went on their famous "sit-down" strike at General Motors. Lewis, Michigan Governor Robert Murphy, and the top management of General Motors were on the verge of reaching an agreement to evacuate the plants when Lewis became convinced the company was trying to double-cross him. He ordered the men to stay in the plants and broke off negotiations with General Motors. On January 21, the day

after President Franklin D. Roosevelt's inauguration for his second term, Lewis gave the following written statement, reprinted from Irving Bernstein, *Turbulent Years* (Boston: Houghton Mifflin, 1970), pp. 535–536, to the press:

> This strike is going to be fought to a successful conclusion. No half-baked compromise is going to allow General Motors to doublecross us again. We are willing to hold immediate conferences with both sides holding their arms—that is, with the men remaining in the plants. . . . We have advised the Administration that the economic royalists of General Motors—the du Ponts and Sloans and others—contributed their money and used their energy to drive the President of the United States out of the White House. The Administration asked labor to help it repeal this attack. Labor gave its help. The same economic royalists now have their fangs in labor, and the workers expect the Administration in every reasonable and legal way to support the auto workers in their fight with the same rapacious enemy.

Presumably Lewis had at least four publics or audiences in mind when he drafted this statement—the United Auto Workers, General Motors negotiators, the White House, and the general public. Analyze how the tone of the statement would have affected each of those audiences.

15. ***The Troublesome Tenor:*** "One of the most erratic artists with whom I had to work at the Metropolitan Opera," states Rudolf Bing, the Met's famous general manager during the 1950s and 1960s, "was also one of the most gloriously talented: Giuseppe Di Stefano." During the fall of 1952 misunderstandings developed between Bing and Di Stefano when the latter asked to be allowed to miss two weeks of rehearsals for the new production of *Bohème* that Bing was getting ready to produce. On October 13 Bing wrote the tenor as follows; reprinted by permission from Rudolf Bing, *5,000 Nights at the Opera* (Garden City, N.Y.: Doubleday, 1972), pp. 192–193:

> My dear DiStefano,
>
> I am afraid your letter of October 7th is extremely depressing to me because in spite of all our conversations it

shows clearly that you still have no conception of what I mean when I talk of "new productions and a new approach to the dramatic aspects of opera." I had hoped that you, as one of the best young tenors, would wish to take part in a new development of American opera but it seems that you are perfectly happy with the ridiculous antics that usually pass on our stage for acting.

I told you that this year "Bohème" will be done in a new production for which I have engaged one of the outstanding film directors of our day. The fact that you have done "Bohème" so often makes the situation much worse because if this production is to be a good one I do not believe that anything of what you have done so far in the way of acting will be acceptable. Of course, this does not apply to you only but to practically the whole cast. Therefore, you will have to unlearn what you have done and to learn new ways of moving and acting on the stage. I had hoped that you would be interested in such possibilities, which could lift you from being a very good singer to becoming a very good artist, but apparently you are only thinking of making a few extra dollars at the Scala and trying to cut rehearsals. You know that I have promised you a substantial extra payment for your being available on the agreed date—I did not do that just to please you; I did that because the minimum of rehearsals which would thereby be made possible is the minimum that you will need to be integrated into the new "Bohème" production. I am awfully sorry I cannot under any circumstances agree to your arriving later and I must warn you that the consequences will be serious.

Now, as to next season your letter does not give me a clear answer. Again, I can only use you for a new production of "Faust" if you are ready and willing to forget completely what has so far happened on the Metropolitan stage which made me blush every time the curtain went up on "Faust." In spite of your exceedingly beautiful singing, what went on on that stage during a "Faust" performance was about the worst I have ever seen anywhere in the world and it will have to be changed from top to bottom. Do you want to be part of that or not? If yes, you will have to work hard. If not, say so frankly . . .

Please let me know clearly and unmistakably: a) that you will arrive ready and available for rehearsals on December 22 as agreed; b) whether or not you would accept an offer for the season 1953–54 . . .

> I hope you realize that this whole letter, although it may displease you in certain aspects, is really a great compliment because if I did not think so highly of you I would not take the trouble to write so fully. Also, you are so much younger than I am I feel that I have not only a right but almost an obligation to try to put you on the right way—believe me, you are not quite on the right way yet. I know that you are an excellent singer, I know that you are a successful singer and I know that you earn a great deal of money—but this is not all. You could be a great artist and in the long run make an even greater career and earn even more money . . .

If you had been in Rudolf Bing's shoes, would you have signed the letter as it stands or would you have redrafted parts of it? If the latter, show the revisions.

He drawеth out the thread of his verbosity finer than the staple of his argument.

William Shakespeare

Why is this thus?
What is the reason of this thusness?

Charles Farrar Browne
(Artemus Ward)

Chapter 8

Practical Guides to Coherence

A sentence or paragraph is said to be coherent when the reader can readily grasp the relationship between the thoughts expressed. When the words in a sentence, the sentences in a paragraph, or the paragraphs in a section do not clearly show the relationships of the points and ideas expressed, the sentence, paragraph or section is said to be incoherent. Some of the thoughts in it appear out of place, distracting, disoriented, "like wormes in the entrayles of a naturall man," to use Thomas Hobbes' phrase. An incoherent paragraph is barking dogs, lunatics, three jukeboxes blaring in a restaurant.

In principle, therefore, the subject of this chapter is much like that of Chapter 5 on the organization of facts and ideas. We deal again with the clarity of relationships, only on a smaller canvas this time. In Chapter 5 we dealt with the molecules that hold the brick together; here we deal with the atoms that hold the molecules together.

There is a similarity between achieving coherence and running a new play in football practice. After first studying the play diagram, the players get in position, the ball is snapped, and everyone runs his assignment. The players return to the starting point, the coaches show them what was not done right, and they run the pattern again, hoping to do it better. Now, the blocking, running, and ball-handling assignments are run at full speed and as naturally and instinctively as possible. For example, if the play is a pass, the quarterback does not think, as he rolls out, about how best to cock his arm, use a blocker, or compute the differences in relative speed of the pass receivers and defenders. If he did, he would never get the ball in the air. He might even suffer the fate of the centipede who, when asked how he coordinated the action of his legs, fell over and died in the effort of trying to explain.

Similarly, if you stop to think analytically about the numerous elements and techniques of coherence, as you try to write or dictate a paragraph, you might become so self-conscious and unbuttoned that you would do a miserable job. What you must do, as a writer, is think about what you want to say and then let it flow in your usual way. Afterwards you will need to go over it and do some fixing—but, just as with the football play, that will not be hard if there are the right makings to begin with.

A friend of mine, a young instructor writing his first book, had the salubrious habit of pouring his thoughts out, throwing them on paper like a bucket of water. Naturally, his first drafts were always full of minor inconsistences, redundancies, misspellings, and sloppy phrasing. Many of his friends shook their heads. How could he stand producing such uneven quality, however much he determined to revise it? A senior professor interrupted. "If only I had learned to do that!" he said. He explained that because he had gotten into the habit, early in life, of trying to make each paragraph near-perfect as he wrote it, his literary production had been severely limited. As if to prove that the old man was right, my young friend went on to become one of the best-known and most prolific writers in his field.

David Lambuth knew from thousands of hours of teaching how hopeless it is to try to write with one half of the brain trying to remember rules of rhetoric. He used this analogy:

> When you have found your idea . . . write it down as nearly as possible as you would express it in speech; swiftly, un-selfconsciously, without stopping to think about the form of it. Revise it afterwards—but only afterwards. To stop to think about form in mid-career, while the idea is in motion, is like throwing out your clutch half-way up a hill and having to start in low again. You never get back your old momentum.[1]

IMPROVING THE FLOW

Let us suppose you have decided on your idea for a paragraph or page or section, shut the door for privacy, and put the idea down as Lambuth says you should do, "swiftly, un-selfconsciously." That creative act completed, you look back at your "baby" and wonder how to improve the coherence. The following tests and guidelines should help you with that task. (You will also doctor your material for clarity, correctness, and style at this stage, but these matters are the subjects of later chapters.)

1. The first or second sentence of a paragraph or series of paragraphs should indicate plainly what the main topic is.

For apprentice writers this should be a golden rule for all documents; for practiced writers it should be a working

[1]David Lambuth and others, *The Golden Book on Writing* (New York, Viking, 1964), p. 4.

rule which is honored most of the time. The so-called topic sentence *can* appear later in the paragraph, but it is almost always appropriate in the first sentence, and that is the safest place for it from the standpoint of clarity as well as coherence. The next safest place is the second sentence (after an introductory or transitional sentence leading up to it).

With your topic sentence at the beginning, continue on that topic until you are finished with it. That may happen in another sentence or two, or perhaps not until several paragraphs have been written. Actually, there is no need to worry about paragraphing in the first draft. Put the material down and review it for that purpose later.

A paragraph that drifts away from the topic sentence and ends up on another subject is called a "broken-backed" paragraph.[2] Reading it is like giving a back rub to a boa constrictor. For instance, a report from an authority on factory automation starts out:

> Technological advances and expanding markets have produced striking reductions in computer costs.

Seeing this first sentence, would you not expect the paragraph to continue with facts about the price reductions that have taken place? Yet the paragraph actually continues:

> The costs of peripheral equipment, systems engineering, and programming have not yet changed dramatically. Therefore, reductions in the total costs of computer-based automation systems are not fully proportionate to the reductions in hardware costs. But the reductions in computer costs have opened up new applications in small processing units and presently allow larger systems to be installed without a commensurately higher investment.

Thus we end up on an idea different from the one we started with. Instead of amplifying the first sentence, the

[2]James M. McCrimmon, *Writing with a Purpose* (Boston, Houghton-Mifflin, 1963), p. 75.

rest of the paragraph drifts to a different topic—indeed, the drift seems to contradict the opening thought. The reader is confused, momentarily paralyzed, like an auto driver approaching two lights side by side, one green and one red. Which should he obey?

Ruth G. Newman makes these observations:

> Each paragraph represents a group of closely related sentences that have been "packaged" for manageability—they all radiate from or support a main idea. . . . Think of the topic sentence as more than a mere label for the package; it should guarantee the contents. It makes a firm commitment to the reader, "This is what you will find within."
>
> Even if every sentence in a particular paragraph gravitates firmly to the main idea, you cannot feel assured that the paragraph is coherent. Within a paragraph, sentences must be ordered so that each grows logically from that which precedes and leads naturally to that which follows. The pieces of the whole must meld together.[3]

Suppose you need more than one paragraph to cover a topic. How should you begin the second, third, and other paragraphs in the series? One useful tool is the transitional sentence, that is, a sentence that links the second (or later) paragraph to the preceding one and keeps the thought going. For example, here is an excerpt from another part of the factory automation report mentioned:

> Considerable risks are entailed in building a computer system around instrumentation that is not already invented, manufactured, and well tested. Much of the grief that has been experienced to date has come from situations in which management decided to install a system that required the use of new types of devices that were "almost ready" for use—only to find that "almost" could be a long time in coming.
>
> In addition, there is the risk that even the best new instruments are subject to random variations. . . .

Here the phrase "in addition" and the repetition of the

[3]Ruth G. Newman, "Building Unity and Coherence into a Written Report," Intercollegiate Clearing House No. 1-378-046 (Harvard Business School 1977), p. 2.

key word, "risk," at the beginning of the second paragraph, signal the reader that the next group of sentences is an addition to the idea in the preceding paragraph.

The principle of coherence for sentences within a paragraph applies to coherence in a series of closely related paragraphs introduced by a "topic paragraph." A topic paragraph performs the same function for the paragraphs that follow as a topic sentence does for the sentences that follow. When a topic paragraph is left dangling by its successors, the reader feels as if he or she had been left dangling, too, like a mountain climber hanging over a precipice.

2. If your paragraph or paragraphs focus on someone or something, keep the viewpoint of that person or object paramount by using pronouns and demonstrative adjectives.

When the paragraph tells what a person said or did or describes the operation of a machine, process, or organization, you ordinarily mention the person or thing in the first sentence or two. In the sentences that follow, keep him, her, or it the subject of attention by using (a) such pronouns as *he, she, it, him, her, they, them, you, I, we, us, some, others,* and *each,* and (b) such demonstrative adjectives as *his, her, your, these, those, this, whose,* and *that.*

A good illustration is a letter of recommendation written by Dr. Thomas Francis, a bacteriologist, to an official of the National Foundation for Infantile Paralysis. Written in 1941, the letter concerned a young medic who was to go on to develop the first widely used polio vaccine. The pronouns and demonstrative adjectives referring to the medic are italicized for the sake of emphasis.

> Dr. Jonas Salk worked with me as an interval fellow between the end of *his* medical school course in July 1939 until March 1940, when *he* began *his* internship at Mt. Sinai Hospital, New York. During that time I found *him* extremely able and interested in

virus problems. *His* internship will end in March and *he* wishes to come to Michigan to work with me again or to continue *his* work. *He* has just come to Ann Arbor to discuss the possibility with me. *His* desire is to work on problems related to cellular factors which are involved in immunity to virus infections. *He* has suggested . . . [the letter of recommendation continues in the same vein, ending with a request that the official talk with Salk and help him].[4]

Simple and natural as this technique is, it is neglected in numerous written communications, creating incoherence and causing loss of time and understanding on the part of readers. Consider the following excerpt from a report to top management on one company's planning system:

> While most executives do not appear to devote much attention to the planning system, managers giving such attention seem to be able to shorten the gestation period of the system significantly. If goals, objectives, and forecasts are used early in the life of the planning system, the development of functional operation is faster. In addition, the personality and work history of involved personnel is important. To the extent that there is past experience with formal planning systems, a background of top-level authority, and respect on the part of other personnel, the development of the planning system will proceed more rapidly.

Now, the writer of the above paragraph is describing the behavior of but one important group of people: executives involved in planning. Yet the paragraph sounds at first blush as if it were dealing with a whole variety of main subjects—goals, functional operation, personality factors, prior experience, and other people's attitudes, as well as the behavior of the planners. Because of its incoherence, the sentences in the paragraph appear to blur and fight with one another. The paragraph is a smouldering cloud of meaning, like a pile of damp leaves in the autumn that can't burst into flame.

See how much better the paragraph is when rewritten from the viewpoint of the planning managers, using pro-

[4]Richard Carter, *Breakthrough: The Saga of Jonas Salk* (New York, Trident, 1966), p. 43.

nouns and demonstrative adjectives to maintain their viewpoint and their concern with the planning system (the words in question are italicized):

> While most executives do not appear to devote much attention to the planning system, *those who* do seem to be able to shorten *its* gestation period significantly. If *they* use goals, objectives, and economic forecasts early in the life of the system, *they* can make *it* develop faster. *Their* personalities and work histories also are important. If *they* have had earlier experience with formal planning systems, held top-level positions, and earned the respect of other people, *they* can develop the system more rapidly.

Demonstrative adjectives have similar value, as the following excerpt, from a paper on anthropology, shows:

> Angiosperms in which the flowers produce large quantities of nectar can be cross-pollinated effectively only by animal visitors with high energetic requirements. *Such* angiosperms evolved only after the appearance of small, nectar-feeding birds, bats, and nonflying mammals. *These* creatures fed at least seasonally on nectar and pollen. . . .

3. If your paragraph deals with the relationships between people, things, and/or ideas, clarify the relationships by using conjunctions and transitions.

The sentences in a paragraph are like the stepping stones across a creek. Readers make their way by going from one sentence to the next. If the sentences lead into one another directly and easily, readers negotiate the paragraph quickly and efficiently; but if the sentences run a crooked course and are poorly spaced, readers will have to halt and think in order to find their way, and then they may not make it at all.

Conjunctions and transitions are like convenient little stepping stones between big ones. They make it unnecessary to stop and figure out how to make the leap from one key sentence to another. They enable the reader's mind to move swiftly, like a person hopping fluidly from one stone to another without pause or hesitation.

The word "conjunction" comes from a Latin verb meaning to join together; "transition" is from a Latin verb meaning to go across. Conjunctions and transitions can be single words or phrases. Some people prefer to call them "directional words." Here are some that are commonly used in business and professional writing:

Purpose: *for this purpose, with this objective, to this end*

Cause and effect: *consequently, thus, therefore, accordingly, as a result, because, hence, since, so*

Comparison and contrast: *similarly, likewise, by, but, however, yet, nevertheless, on the other hand, whereas, in other words, although*

Addition and elaboration: *in addition, moreover, furthermore, besides, again, that is, of course, after all, and, first, second, third. . . . , finally*

Emphasis: *in fact, most important, indeed, above all*

Exemplification: *for example, for instance, in this case*

Time: *meanwhile, in the meantime, at the same time, immediately, subsequently, next, then, at length, formerly*

Place: *here, near, opposite to, adjacent to, to the left (right)*

Conclusion: *to conclude, in conclusion, to sum up, lastly, finally, at last.*

Conjunctions and transitions have no magical effect on the logic of a series of sentences; if suitable relationships among the thoughts do not exist, all the transitions in the dictionary will not put them there. But if there is a logical sequence, transitions can make the going easier for the reader. Consider their value in the following excerpt from a report (conjunctions and transitions are italicized for the sake of emphasis):

> We conclude that the proportion of debt in the capital structure of [the company] can be increased from 25% to 30%. We are unimpressed by objections to such a change. It is said, *first,* that the change will harm the company's ability to borrow at prevailing interest rates. We find no evidence to support this fear. It is said,

> *secondly,* that stockholders will demand a higher rate of return. *Again,* we find no evidence to support the claim. The product base is too stable and profitable to put the company in the category of a speculative firm.
>
> It is true, *of course,* that earnings have fluctuated significantly in the past. *Moreover,* dividends have been cut occasionally despite a corporate policy of maintaining a quarterly rate. *On the other hand,* at no time has the price-earnings ratio dropped below 15. . . .

Just as transitions can help the reader glide from sentence to sentence within a paragraph, so they can help him or her step easily from paragraph to paragraph. In the usual case, transitions come at the beginning of the paragraph, referring to the thought in the preceding passage and connecting it with the group of sentences to follow. But transitions between paragraphs are usually stronger and longer than transitions and conjunctions between sentences. For one thing, a paragraph presents a new idea or aspect of an idea. For another, it takes the reader longer to find out for himself or herself whether the relationship is one of contrast, amplification, emphasis, or some other nature (whereas in the case of sentences, if there is any doubt, a flick of the eye is all that is needed).

This is why some transitions between paragraphs take the form of whole sentences. For instance, a paragraph of amplification following a paragraph describing Pre-Cambrian ore deposits might begin: "But not all the ore is found in Pre-Cambrian formations." Thus it links the former paragraph, which explains that most ore is found in such formations, with the new one, which points to other places where ore is also found.

Often the families of thought are clearly related, like brothers, sisters, cousins, and second cousins who all have the same striking facial characteristic. In this case, few or no transitions are needed, and it is a shame to insert them out of habit or a mistaken belief that they should appear regularly no matter what. When the reader can go naturally from one sentence or paragraph to the next, a transition—even the right one—serves only to clutter the page. "I came, I saw, I conquered," said Julius Caesar, not "I came. In addition, I saw. Finally, moreover, I conquered."

4. Use parallel constructions to emphasize important themes or patterns of facts, if your material lends itself to this approach.

The repetition of sentence patterns is a powerful device, adding both impact and clarity to the ideas and information conveyed. Moreover, once you decide on a parallel construction for a series of sentences, you can let the ideas or facts in your mind flow into that mold—for a satisfying moment or two, questions of form and style will be "automated" for you.

Probably the most famous user of parallel constructions was the apostle Paul. His letters to the various peoples he sought to educate and persuade contain many examples of his genius in the use of parallelism. For instance:

> If I speak in the tongues of men and of angels, but have not love, I am a noisy gong or a clanging cymbal. And if I have prophetic powers, and understand so as to remove mountains, but have not love, I am nothing. If I give away all I have, and if I deliver my body to be burned, but have not love, I gain nothing.
>
> Love is patient and kind; love is not jealous or boastful; it is not arrogant or rude. Love does not insist on its own way; it is not irritable or resentful; it does not rejoice at wrong, but rejoices in the right. Love bears all things, believes all things, hopes all things, endures all things.[5]

In the first paragraph there is a repetition of the "If I . . ." beginnings and the "have not love" phrases; in the second paragraph, a repetition of "love" as the subject and of the verb patterns.

Where facts and figures are numerous, you can some-

[5]The First Letter of Paul to the Corinthians, 13:1–7.

times put sentences or clauses in parallel constructions and itemize them. This gives your pattern greater visibility and helps the reader to separate the parts and mentally "package" the idea. Here is a portion of a report on an investigation of corporate stock ownership:

> In a study of 76 companies listed on the New York Stock Exchange, we find that:
>
> - 16 companies have 50,000 or more stockholders owning 25 or fewer shares.
> - 40 companies have 25,000 or more stockholders owning 25 or fewer shares.
> - 56 firms have 10,000 or more stockholders with 25 or fewer shares.

Not only do the authors of this report make the figures more easy to assimilate by using parallel constructions, but they also make it easier for the reader to see two important contrasts: the *rising* number of *companies* in the categories, and the *falling* numbers of *stockholders*.

Here is a famous example of the use of parallelism to show similarity, progression, and contrast:

> As Caesar loved me, I weep for him;
> As he was fortunate, I rejoice at it;
> As he was valiant, I honour him;
> But as he was ambitious, I slew him.[6]

As with many techniques of expression, parallelism should be used in moderation. "A pattern of gradually lengthening parallel sentences is pleasing, parallel sentences in order of climax are interesting, and parallel sentences in logical or chronological plans are easy to understand," states H. J. Tichy. "But a writer should not be

[6]William Shakespeare, *Julius Caesar*, III, ii.

tempted to contort ideas or structure to make sentences parallel, and he should not place unequal ideas in balanced construction."[7]

5. Use "echo words" to tie together and emphasize a theme or impression that should be dominant.

So-called "echo words" serve to remind the reader of the key thought in a series of sentences. They can be simply synonyms. Or they can be words and phrases that convey a similar meaning. For example, if you are writing about General Electric Company, you might use such echo words as *G. E.*, *company*, *corporation*, *firm*, *organization*, and *manufacturer*; if you are writing about an electrostatic precipitator, you might use such echo words as *equipment*, *machine*, *device*, and *system*.

Echo words serve the same function as do threads of a certain color in a sweater or suit. They show continuity and relationship. In certain kinds of exposition, moreover, well-chosen echo words have a kind of occult power to create feeling, mood, and belief. For instance, in 1966 the Student Nonviolent Coordinating Committee (SNCC), a civil rights organization, was incensed over a series of acts of violence against blacks and over what it considered to be a shameful United States posture with respect to violence. The theme of the fourth, fifth, and sixth paragraphs of a statement issued by SNCC was violent death. It was dramatized by echo words (italicized in the quotation following):

> We ourselves have often been *victims* of violence and confinement *executed* by United States government officials. We recall the numerous persons who have been *murdered* in the South because of their efforts to secure their civil and human rights, and whose *murderers* have been allowed to escape penalty for their *crimes*.
>
> The *murder* of Samuel Younge in Tuskegee, Ala., is no different

[7]H. J. Tichy, *Effective Writing* (New York, Wiley, 1966), p. 277.

> from the *murder* of peasants in Vietnam, for both Younge and the Vietnamese sought, and are seeking, to secure the rights guaranteed them by law. In each case, the United States government bears a great part of the responsibility for these *deaths*.
>
> Samuel Younge was *murdered* because United States law is not being enforced. Vietnamese are *murdered* because the United States is pursuing an aggressive policy in violation of international law. . . .[8]

6. To show that two ideas, things, or events are of equal importance, make them the subjects of (a) separate sentences or (b) different clauses in a sentence connected by a coordinating conjunction or semicolon. But if one idea, thing, or event is of lesser importance, put it in a dependent clause, participle, phrase, or adjective.

Suppose you are the author of the following statement, taken from a report on drug abuse: "The opiate most frequently used by American narcotic addicts is heroin, which can be taken by sniffing through the nose." By making the second half of the sentence a dependent clause (i.e., one that cannot stand alone even though it has its own subject and verb), you have made it less important than the first part. This could have been your intention. But suppose you want to emphasize that heroin can be taken by sniffing? Then you could write the sentence this way: "The opiate most frequently used by American narcotic addicts is heroin, and it can be taken by sniffing through the nose." Or perhaps better still, put the second thought in a fresh sentence: "The opiate most frequently used by American narcotic addicts is heroin. It can be taken by sniffing." (A variation would be to substitute a semicolon for the period and not capitalize "it.")

Of course, there are other ways of deemphasizing one part or another of the idea just quoted, if you want to. For instance, you might write: "An inhalable opiate, heroin,

[8]James Forman, *The Making of Black Revolutionaries* (New York, MacMillan, 1972), pp. 445–446. © 1972 by James Forman.

is the one most frequently used by American narcotic addicts." Or you might write: "Capable of being taken by sniffing, as well as by injection, opium is the narcotic addicts use most." The first of these sentences deemphasizes the inhalability of the narcotic and emphasizes the frequency of use; the second also emphasizes frequency of use.

In short, sentence construction is a useful tool for expressing the relationships of facts, events, and ideas. When your readers see these relationships in the intended way, they will be better able to appreciate the facts and substance of your message.

THE "MAGIC" OF READABILITY

A manager, public official, engineer, scientist, lawyer, or other professional person who "speaks well" always speaks coherently. That is, as the audience listens, it is able to sense the main points the speaker is driving at. It feels and understands that some things are more important than others, that some conditions are caused by others, that some problems are connected with certain other ones, and so forth.

When a manager, public official, engineer, scientist, lawyer, or other professional "writes well," coherence is again a major factor. On paper, coherence is a more demanding quality than it is in speech, because the writer is without the advantages of facial expression, intonation, and other visible or audible circumstances. But its function is exactly the same.

And so is its achievement. You learned to speak coherently when you were a child, not by memorizing rules for coherence but by understanding how to put thoughts together. Similarly, as a business or professional person you do not learn to write coherently by learning rules. You do it by mulling over what you want to say, and then letting it flow as you have long since learned to let thoughts flow.

Then why bother with the six guidelines described—because coherence is rarely good enough the first time through. The *makings* of good coherence should be there, but in reviewing your notes or draft you can almost always find some ways to ham-and-egg it better. The guides should help you with this task.

Coherence is a hand guiding your reader through the dark; it is the color marks on a trail through the woods; it is the lights on an airport runway. Coherence is togetherness, relatedness, compactness, form instead of chaos. It has an enormous influence on readability. Ironically, it generally is omitted from the popular readability formulas. As a result, they often miss the mark. As John S. Fielden puts it:

> Some utterly unreadable (if not incomprehensive) prose can "formula out" to a remarkably high score. In fact, if most of us were to apply *any* of these formulas to the meandering prose immortalized in our Aunt Bessie's letters from home, we would find that the old dear, thanks to having a small vocabulary composed of familiar and personal words, plus a penchant for short (if ungrammatical) sentences, is a master of readable writing.[9]

PROBLEMS AND CASES

1. Improve the following sentences by using parallel structures:
   a. He gave instructions first for checking the computer program thoroughly and then to re-arrange it.
   b. This new machine offers several advantages—durability, ease of operation, and is economical.
   c. She likes reading and to watch opera on TV, although baseball also appeals greatly to her.
   d. Roast beef and shrimp are my favorite foods, and I also love escargot.

[9]John S. Fielden, "Achieving Coherence," Intercollegiate Clearing House No. 9–362–042 (Harvard Business School, 1962), p. 26.

e. Simpson won a Nobel prize for his experiments, but during the same time Simpson's tests became a failure.

2. The following section completes a four-page report from a consultant to the management of an expanding retail food chain, "Fast Stop Foods" (fictional name):

> *Conclusion*
>
> In conclusion, it is recommended that management should pursue the following steps:
>
> 1. Provide a staffing plan
> 2. Contacts with wholesale suppliers for the grocery business in the South Boston area need to be investigated.
> 3. Is the name "Fast Stop Foods" the same as or similar to the name of any other store in area?
> 4. Review control and monitoring system.
> 5. There may be a possibility of leasing a nearby parking lot for Fast Stop customers.
> 6. Hire and train clerks;
> 7. Advertising plan
> 8. Check adequacy of shelf stocks control as used in other Boston stores.

Write an improved version of this section of the report.

3. Improve the following passage from a paper on anthropology:

> Dr. Morton's finagling with his data took the form of inconsistencies and shifting criteria. The inclusion or deletion of large subsamples in order to match grand means with a priori expectations was one favorite tool of the scientist. He included Inca Peruvians to reduce the Indian mean, and raising of the Caucasian mean was accomplished by excluding Hindus. Claiming (falsely) that subsamples with small crania dominated his total collection, Morton later declined to calculate a Caucasian mean at all. His choice of whether to present or not to calculate subsample means depended on what results were desired by him. Subsample means were presented for Caucasians, but subsample means were never calculated for Indians though the means for Indians had equally high values. He presented them for Caucasians to demonstrate the superiority of Teutons and also that Anglo-Saxons were superior.

4. Improve the following passage from a scientific report:

> The only practical basis for a timely warning is seismological data, when the threatened coastline is located close to the location of an undersea earthquake. But these necessarily numerous warnings can reduce public confidence in the warning system. In the last ten years no significant tsunamis were generated.
>
> However, the Alaska Warning Center issued three warnings during that decade. For example, a warning, not a watch, will be issued by the Alaska Regional Tsunami Warning System.
>
> Any Alaskan coastal quake of magnitude 7.0 or greater, rather than the usual 7.5, if it is forecasted within several hundred miles of the coast, will be warned. Many researchers believe that an improvement in the reliability of tsunami predictions could result from the use of specially designed seismographs.

5. Redraft the following passage (the company name is fictional):

> Your Pension Review Committee reaches the conclusion that major and beneficial improvements could be instituted at this time in the Employees Pension Program of "All American Corporation." Having performed an analysis of actual versus potential benefits 1955–1973, it was found that maximum potential benefits achievable had risen as of 1972–1973 to the proximity of $24,727,310 per annum, as compared with actual benefits paid in 1972–1973 of approximately $18,498,400, with an excessive cost-benefit ratio in administrative expenses. Additionally, such findings of the Committee are in contradiction with statements that pension benefits in the company are "the most generous to be found in the industry."

6. ***Discourse on Dress:*** Suppose you had been employed by the U. S. Department of Health, Education, and Welfare in 1970 when the following memorandum—labeled Personnel Management Letter No. 70–3—was drafted. It is reprinted from Arthur I. Blaustein and Geoffrey Faux, *The Star Spangled Hustle* (Garden City, N.Y., Doubleday, 1972), p. 107. If asked to okay or revise it, what would you have done?

> We are frequently asked what the Office of the Secretary policy is with regard to proper dress. Because styles and attitudes about clothing have been changing so rapidly in the past several years, there is often doubt as to what is proper and acceptable dress for the office. We believe that some not-too-rigid guidelines in this area would be helpful to all employees.
>
> It would be impractical to attempt to establish a definitive list of all acceptable and unacceptable items of clothing for office wear. Certain items would clearly fall within one group or the other, but there are many which are not so easily categorized. Often, the nature of the work being performed, where it is being performed, and the season of the year will greatly influence dress.
>
> As a general policy, employees should exercise good judgment and good taste in their dress. They should be groomed in a manner fitting to the surroundings into which their assignments take them. In any event, it is prudent to avoid extremes in both fashion and style.
>
> When questions arise, it is the responsibility of each Division head to give guidance to his employees on matters of appropriate dress.

7. ***The Reappraising Revolutionary:*** In 1967 James Forman, executive secretary of the Student Nonviolent Coordinating Committee (SNCC), wrote a detailed analysis reappraising the policies of that organization. (SNCC was concerned principally with civil rights. It had worked for that cause through protest movements, black voter registration drives, political organizations, and related projects.) In the introduction to the paper, which was written for fellow SNCC members, he was highly self-critical because, as he remarked later, "I still hoped this would help develop the organizational habit of criticism and self-criticism that we needed to move ahead on the revolutionary road."

   Forman had served as the SNCC's executive secretary since 1961. (Later he was to serve for six months as minister of education for the Black Panther Party, and in 1969 he was to write the Black Manifesto delivered to white churches.)

   The first four paragraphs of the introduction, reprinted from James Forman, *The Making of Black Revolutionaries* (New York: MacMillan, 1972), p. 478, follow:

Throughout my history with the Student Nonviolent Coordinating Committee, there have been various discussions about the importance of an education program for the members of the organization. At some time or another, this person or that one has assumed the responsibility for working on this program or aspects of it. It goes without saying that each day we work, we engage in various forms of political education. However, there still has not been a systematic attempt to educate ourselves; to train new members; to instill a sense of the history of the organization, its objectives, success and failures; to discuss and analyze many events occurring in the world.

I assume some responsibility for the failure to implement this internal education program. It was a mistake always to give in to the demands of the moment and not insist in a more active manner that we create and implement a program for the intellectual and political development of our staff. My present evaluation stems from observing and participating in the effects of the failure to do this, from my own development, and from accepting the criticism of many who have been crippled by the lack of an internal education program. Without question, every time we allowed a new member to join our staff without undergoing some indoctrination program, we were contributing to misunderstanding, suspicion, ill-will, wasted effort and time lost. . . .

Today, 1967, six years after the student movement started in February, 1960, we are at Rock Bottom. There is nowhere to go but up or under. We have finally emerged, from my point of view, from many obstacles and can realistically assess what in fact has been true for more than two years: namely, that the massive attack on public accommodations and voter registration has been successful and we have played no small part in that success. With the passage of the 1965 Civil Rights Bill, the entire character of this organization changed. Some of us saw this, but we were unable to convince the organization of this shift and of the absolute need to revamp our programs. One of the reasons for this failure stemmed from the lack of an internal education program. As has been true throughout our history, we have been backed up against many walls, and changes have been forced upon us.

Today, we must face the reality that we have been successful, no matter what may have been all the shortcomings, and we must quickly revamp our entire style of operation—or there is no other way for us to go but out, nothing to do but destroy our effectiveness through lack of direction, lack of confidence in the future, a sense of failure, fatigue, despair, frustration and bad health. These conditions in turn lead to internal bickering, feuding, factional fighting, inertia, inability to work, loss of morale, hanging-on, resignation, walking-out. . . .

Show how the coherence of these opening paragraphs could be improved.

8. ***Kudos for King's Grant:*** In 1972 a public relations firm in Philadelphia wrote a memorandum describing a new community to be developed in New Jersey. Comprising six pages of double-spaced, typewritten copy, the memorandum was sent to various groups of people who might be interested, including editors of publications. About half of the memorandum, mostly descriptions of location, access, and economic aspects, is omitted here.

What is believed to be the largest privately-financed planned unit land development in the United States is taking form in Evesham Township, Burlington County, New Jersey, only 16 miles from Philadelphia.

It is "King's Grant," a new town of 2,500 acres on the western edge of the unique Pine Barrens of mid-Jersey. The Pine Barrens' geologic, botanical and biological features have no exact counterpart in the United States, yet is within an area with over 6 million population.

King's Grant takes its name from the fact that King James II of England made the grants to ensure English settlement almost 300 years ago and ownership of the tracts have come down directly in these years. Most of it is low-lying and even swampy; it is virtually virgin forest and undergrowth.

To William Seltzer, president of Evesham Corporation, the fact that much of the land has lain fallow all these years, because of its non-commercial nature, is its greatest asset as well as a challenge.

Seltzer is an "environmentalist" venturing into land development and has vowed to change the trends.

He is concerned about "suburban sprawl"' of unregulated developments which has "fragmented" suburban society (Residents of housing developments have to go outside their community to reach many of the amenities and there is little community cohesiveness).

The entire concept of King's Grant of Planned Unit Development (PUD) is that of open space, yet one in which every dwelling is directly connected to its environment.

Use of a "lagoon system" of lot layout places each lot or apartment site in companionship to the green open space, the golf course and the 16 lakes. No lot in the entire community backs up on another lot.

This open space, under deed restrictions, must be kept inviolate in perpetuity, and residents are expected to cherish it as "their own."

There will be a complete recreational system, of which much is already being developed. These facilities include an 18-hole championship golf course; tennis courts, swimming pools and 16 lakes to provide boating, fishing and ice-skating.

Equestrian stables, riding rings and 21 miles of bridle paths are being provided. Bicycle and jogging trails are being carved out of the forest.

There will be four village "neighborhood centers". . . .

A system of 16 lakes is combined into four major lake systems. The first 65 acre lake, dredged out of what once was a cranberry bog, has already been completed. The lake will be stocked with fish for angling; sailing and boating will also be one of the water sport attractions. Surface drainage will not go into these lakes, but will form ponds for aeration and purification and then go back to recharge the soil.

One of the most exciting features of King's Grant is its accessibility to major population centers. . . .

To ensure that the ecology will remain as unspoiled as possible, in this famous natural preserve there is a King's Grant staff ecologist. There are over 1500 varieties of plants and trees; home owners will be directed to leave natural lawns avoiding costly upkeep.

Where the necessary bulldozing is going on, the ecologist marks specimens carefully and these are moved to other spots, such as on the four islands in the 65-acre lake in protected natural environments.

The swamp oaks and pitch pines native to the area, some of which are over 200 years old, are being kept along "Brook

> Park" and along the walks and trails. A $10,000 experiment in planting of trees not indigenous to the former bog land—dogwoods, magnolia, willows and others—have already burst into leaf and spring bloom.
>
> It is still a common sight to see tags attached by the ecologist to sheep laurel, pixie moss, soldier moss, bracken ferns, teaberry, turkey beard, sand myrtle or stagger bush, which must not be molested.
>
> Even some insects are being protected and the flora needed to retain them is carefully preserved. There are several deer herds and many other species of wildlife, which, hopefully, will grow accustomed to humans, and remain, to the delight of the children and even the elders.
>
> They will find that the scrub pines and underbush which they now ignore can be very exciting discoveries of Nature's handiwork up close to their own properties.

If you had been asked to try your hand at revising this memorandum, what would you have written?

Clear writers, like fountains,
do not seem so deep as they are;
the turbid look the most profound.

Walter S. Landor

"When I use a word," Humpty Dumpty said,
in rather a scornful tone,
"it means just what I choose it to mean
—neither more nor less."

Lewis Carroll

Chapter 9

How To Make Yourself Clear

It is said that Voltaire used to read everything he wrote to his cook. If she could not understand it, he used to rewrite it. Perhaps a scientist shouldn't be expected to test a report on cultures of rheumatoid synovial cells by reading it to the cook, nor a production control specialist preparing a letter for a customer on quality defects—besides, who is able to afford a cook these days? But there is a moral here for almost all of us who use written communications to convey important information and viewpoints to readers who, we hope, will act on that information. We're not testing our writing often enough for clarity and intelligibility. Clarity is the literary equivalent of a valid credit card, and too many important letters and reports are getting rejected like bad credit cards.

John A. Walter of the University of Texas once queried executives of 200 companies about the principal weaknesses observed in employee writing. Lack of clarity was singled out by 91% of the respondents—more than for any other fault.[1] According to William J. Gallagher, analysts estimate that between 15 and 30% of all letters and memoranda prepared in industry and government either seek clarification of earlier written communications or are themselves answers to such requests.[2] Whether the writer's strategy in such cases is known as the scrambled syntax, what the Japanese call a "black mist," a smokescreen, or an inky cloud, it compares closely with the defense mechanism of a fleeing squid.

In one company with which I am familiar, confusion over the meaning of a research report led to a serious delay in organizing a top management meeting on an urgent problem. In another a muddled report was largely responsible for a poorly timed purchase of vital equipment. In one government agency action on a cause of serious public complaint was delayed because of a confusing report. Instances of this sort are common in business, the professions, and public organizations. But perhaps the largest cost of all is lost time—the thousands and thousands of hours lost every day because of letters, memoranda, and reports that are misread due to no fault of the reader or understood so inadequately that subsequent communications and sometimes meetings must be held to clarify the intended meaning.

At another company some communications specialists rated the readability of various reports and memoranda from top management to employees. A very important memorandum concerning productivity was so wordy and abstract that it fell in a range where even graduate students and scientists often fear to tread. Only a manage-

[1]John A. Walter, *Proceedings, Society of Technical Writers and Publishers*, 1969, pp. 5–60.

[2]William J. Gallagher, *Report Writing for Management* (Reading, Mass., Addison-Wesley, 1969), p. 109.

ment memorandum wishing all employees a happy new year fell in a range that most people can comprehend.

In a meeting on business writing, Ruth Newman once offered the following passage from *The Analects*, Book XIII, by Confucius:

> Tzu-lu said, "If the prince of Wei were waiting for you to come and administer his country for him, what would be your first measure?" The Master said, "It would certainly be to correct language." Tzu-lu said, "Can I have heard you aright? Surely what you say has nothing to do with the matter. Why should language be corrected?"
>
> The Master said, "Yu! How boorish you are! A gentleman, when things he does not understand are mentioned, should maintain an attitude of reserve. If language is incorrect, then what is said does not concord with what was meant; and if what is said does not concord with what was meant, what is to be done cannot be effected. If what is to be done cannot be effected, then rites and music will not flourish. If rites and music do not flourish, then mutilations and lesser punishments will go astray. And if mutilations and lesser punishments go astray, then the people have nowhere to put hand or foot.
>
> "Therefore the gentleman uses only such language as is proper for speech, and only speaks of what it would be proper to carry into effect. The gentleman, in what he says, leaves nothing to mere chance."

Demands for clarity are coming from consumers and users. Early in 1973 the U. S. Labor Department began requiring pension plan administrators to provide participants with easily understood descriptions of the benefits and rules of pension plans. A spokesman for the department described the new regulations as an effort "to let a guy know what he has in simple language."[3]

Buyers of home-improvement materials, games, and products requiring assembly at home are becoming increasingly impatient with instructions that are confusing, overly long, or incomplete. Consumers also are more aware than ever that they should not have to put up with confusing statements and labels on food packages, un-

[3] *The Wall Street Journal*, February 20, 1973.

readable warranties for appliances, and garbled information in owners' manuals.

Insurance policies are an especially egregious example. Using standards of readability developed by Rudolph Flesch and other authorities, Herbert S. Denenberg, an erstwhile insurance commissioner of Pennsylvania, rated life insurance policies in comparison with other writings. On a scale of 100, with the top representing "easily understood," he found that a current book on baseball rated 80, a revised version of the Bible 67, a version of Einstein's theory of relativity 18, and various insurance contracts from 10 to minus 2. "They have been written by and for the insurance industry," said Denenberg, "and have been administered by and for the insurance industry."[4]

As for the automobile insurance policies with which I am familiar, their ambiguity does not unfold, it piles up like garbage. They might be understood by Mongolian idiots or think-tank geniuses, but by none of us in between. They are a generous source of examples of almost every error of clarity. When I tried vainly once again to understand the policy my agent gave me—to gain at least some faint idea of what I was paying about $550 for—I tried to imagine what the authors of that policy must have thought when they completed it. The analogy that came to mind was the Duke of Wellington, who is reputed to have said, as he surveyed his troops before the battle of Waterloo, "I don't know how they look to the enemy, but by God, they terrify me."

In November 1978, in response to popular pressure, a revolutionary law went into effect in New York state requiring apartment leases and other consumer contracts to be written in simple English. The law ran afoul of many practical difficulties, but the pressures behind it continue unabated.

In 1975 Citibank (New York) took the lead in omitting

[4]Jeffrey O'Connell, "Living with Life Insurance," *The New York Times Magazine*, May 19, 1974, pp. 34, 99.

"legalese" from its consumer-loan agreements and sought to rewrite them in understandable English. Many other companies since have been experimenting with the same approach, and some of these, reveling in the self-righteousness of the reformed, now urge plain English on their competitors. Must the language of the law remain fixed and incomprehensible? Is it really true that if you eliminate the boiler plate you reopen the loopholes? Are only lawyers entitled to understand promissory notes, security agreements, stock prospectuses, warranties, and scores of other forms—not lay people?

Reviewing its written communications, Crocker National Bank (San Francisco) came to the standard phrase, "joint and several," used to fix liability in certain contracts. Do most people know what it means? The bank changed the line to read, "both of you are responsible (for payment) and each of you is liable (in case of nonpayment)." Does this use of plain language open any loopholes not present in the old language? It is hard to see that it might.

UNDERSTANDING UNDERSTANDING

Behind much of the muddy, cryptic, abstruse, jargony writing that issues from our offices and studies is a fundamental misconception of how understanding takes place.

Dr. Charles Boelkins, Department of Nutrition, Harvard School of Public Health, offers the following example in a recent letter to me:

> I have a postdoctoral student in my laboratory who is trying to write several papers based on his two years of research. He hasn't published before and his dissertation is his magnum opus. His style . . . is dense, impenetrable, forbidding. To my marginal query, "I don't understand," he responds, "Read it again." He believes the burden of understanding lies with the reader not the writer.

In my view, it would make only a little more sense to say that the burden of making a door-to-door sale lies with the resident prospect, not with the Fuller Brush salesman or the Avon lady. It is the writer who knocks on the door of understanding, not the reader.

Ruth Bennett, an instructor in communications and administrator at Curry College, reminds us that any communication, written or oral, is a kind of transaction. A transaction, in turn, is a unit of social intercourse which consists of a stimulus by one person and a response by another, with the response in turn becoming a stimulus for the first person to respond to.[5] The transactional view of communicating holds that meanings are in people not in words. On the basis of a leading text in the field,[6] Bennett summarizes the implications of this view as follows:

If meanings are in words, then:	*But if meanings are in people, then:*
1. The challenge is to write a message; reading it is easy.	1. Reading a message may be harder than writing it.
2. Your message means the same to your readers as it does to you.	2. Frequently your readers will give your message a different interpretation.
3. It is unnecessary to get feedback from your readers.	3. You should try to get feedback from your readers.
4. If readers misinterpret your message, usually they are to blame.	4. If your message is misinterpreted, you may be as much at fault as your readers are, or more so.
5. If your message fails to get across as intended, someone is to blame.	5. No one may be at fault for a failure in written communication.

If meanings are in people not words, then the faults that we call "jargon," "abstruseness," and "unreadability" are

[5]For an elaboration of this concept, see Eric Berne, *Games People Play* (New York: Grove, 1964).
[6]Sherod Miller, Elam W. Nunnally, Daniel Wackman, *Alive and Aware* (Minneapolis: Interpersonal Communication Programs, Inc., 1975), pp. 153–154.

relative. And if they are relative, it is sheer arrogance for any writer to sit in his office and say, as the writers of those insurance policies and other unreadable forms do—and as, of course, we all do from time to time, however innocent our intentions—that "This is it, this is the way it has got to be." I am indebted further to Bennett for the following passage:

> "I don't know what you mean by 'glory,' " Alice said.
>
> Humpty Dumpty smiled contemptuously. "Of course you don't—till I tell you. I meant, 'There's a nice knock-down argument for you!' "
>
> "But 'glory' doesn't mean 'a nice knock-down argument,' " Alice objected.
>
> "When I use a word," Humpty Dumpty said, in rather a scornful tone, "it means just what I choose it to mean—neither more nor less."
>
> "The question is," said Alice, "whether you can make words mean so many different things."
>
> "The question is," said Humpty Dumpty, "which is to be master—that's all."[7]

In this chapter we deal with two quite different ways of achieving important gains in clarity. The first way is mechanical, the second is artful. The two together are a powerful combination. Of course, this chapter does not stand alone, because clarity is a function not simply of word referents, sentence construction, transitions, and format, but also of coherence and tone, as discussed in previous chapters.

FIRST, SOME EASY FORMAT DEVICES

In many written presentations you can produce an almost magical improvement in the clarity of a document by two devices which, though they resemble packaging more

[7]Lewis Carroll, *Through the Looking Glass* (Chicago: Rand McNally, 1916), p. 186.

than substance, are by no means superficial or secondary in importance. A bonus value of these devices is that they help you and your readers get off to the right start, to avoid the problem that C. Northcote Parkinson warns about—"Go wrong at the beginning and nothing afterwards will go right."

Enumeration

The first device is one you probably are familiar with: the use of numerals and letters to serialize several facts, ideas, instructions, or questions. It is an extraordinarily effective device in reports, memoranda, and letters. Not only does it clarify a series of points and set them in sequential relationship with one another; it also gives them more visibility, hence impact on the reader's mind, especially if the items are set off on separate lines. Here, for example, is an excerpt from a memorandum that played a part in the development of the first vaccine for polio:

> It is impossible at this stage of development to predict the degree of efficacy, on the one hand, and the degree of safety, on the other, of the poliomyelitis vaccine that has been developed. These questions can only be determined after injecting relatively large numbers of human beings.
>
> There is no question of the fact that, with additional research:
>
> 1. A still more effective poliomyelitis vaccine could be produced;
> 2. We would be better informed as to the kind and frequency of untoward effects that might result from the use of the vaccine; and
> 3. We would be better informed with respect to the best route of inoculation and the best time for administration of the vaccine to obtain maximal protection against paralytic disease, etc.
>
> If such research is carried out, a very considerable amount of time will elapse before a poliomyelitis vaccine is made available for widespread use. . . .[8]

[8]Richard Carter, *Breakthrough: The Saga of Jonas Salk* (New York, Trident, 1966), pp. 147–148.

If you are like the great majority of readers of this passage, the three values of additional research that are cited will stand out in your mind. If you remember nothing else, you will remember the writer cited three reasons for further study. And this, of course, was exactly what the author, Dr. Harry Weaver, intended; although he was urging early field trials of the Salk vaccine, he wanted to impress on his audience (health authorities, doctors, and officials of the National Foundation of Poliomyelitis Research) that he was fully aware of the potential benefits of delaying the trials until more research had been done.

Now let us consider an example of unclear writing, and see what a person with Weaver's skill might have done to make it clearer. The U.S. Department of Defense issued an instruction sheet on how to report reimbursable transactions. Part II of this memorandum deals with the reporting of sources; an important section of it is:

> C. The term "automatic" applies to those reimbursements subject to automatic apportionment authority; "other" applies to those reimbursements subject to specific apportionment and all reimbursements in accounts which are not apportioned. The term "intrafund" applies to those reimbursements which occur within the same appropriation account. Reimbursements from non-Federal sources include: reimbursements from sales of meals and commissary items to civilians, military personnel, etc.; and all reimbursements to general fund accounts that are received from trust fund accounts, and from deposit fund accounts established for proceeds from sales of scrap or salvage materiel. Other stub entries are self-explanatory.[9]

Now, this memorandum is in small print. If you put yourself in the position of the clerk or officer reading the instructions under the pressure of deadlines and distractions, would you not find that you would have to read it over—not once but several times—to know what to do? It has been said that prose should include "nothing that will distract the reader's attention or check his habitual pace of reading—he should feel that he is seated at ease in

[9]U.S. Department of Defense Instruction No. 7232.2, June 1, 1966.

a taxi, not riding a temperamental horse through traffic."[10] There is no illusion of riding "at ease in a taxi" in the directive quoted; it is like riding a drunken mule through traffic.

Consider how much better the paragraph would look with the benefit of enumeration (but left exactly the same in all other respects):

> C. The term "automatic" applies to those reimbursements subject to automatic apportionment authority; "other" applies to those reimbursements subject to specific apportionment and all reimbursements in accounts which are not apportioned. The term "intrafund" applies to those reimbursements which occur within the same appropriation account. Reimbursements from non-Federal sources include reimbursements:
>
> 1. From sales of meals and commissary items to civilians, military personnel, etc.; and
> 2. To general fund accounts that are received from (a) trust fund accounts and (b) deposit fund accounts established for proceeds from sales of scrap or salvage materiel.
>
> Other stub entries are self-explanatory.

Even a casual glance now reveals an organization that is not apparent in the original version until after minutes of study.

It does not matter whether you use numerals, letters, or both to serialize items. However, if you use both you should be sure that one is always used for items that are subordinate to the other (as in the example just given). If one is used for both main items and subitems, the reader may be left wondering which numbers (or letters) go with which.

When you use enumeration, use parallel constructions for the items. If one item begins with a verb, all should begin with verbs; if one starts with a noun, all should. The advantages of such parallelism are better emphasis

[10]Robert Graves and Alan Hodge, quoted in James M. Reid, Jr., and Robert M. Wendlinger, *Effective Letters* (New York, McGraw Hill, 1973), p. 23.

and contrast. (For other examples of parallelism, see Chapter 8.)

Finally, don't fall in love with enumeration. Like a suitor with only one good line, it can get awfully tiresome. Here, from *The Pentagon Papers*, is an example of the horrors of enumerative overkill:

> 9. Analysis of OPTION C
>
> (a) Military actions. Present policy, in addition to providing for reprisals in DRV for DRV actions against the U.S., envisions (1) 34A Airops and Marops, (2) deSoto patrols, for intelligence purposes, (3) South Vietnamese shallow ground actions in Laos when practicable, and (4) T28 strikes against infiltration-associated targets in Laos. Additional actions should be:
>
> PHASE ONE (in addition to reprisals in DRV for VC 'spectaculars' in South Vietnam): (5) U.S. strikes against infiltration-associated targets in Laos.
>
> PHASE TWO (in addition to reprisals in DRV against broader range of VC actions): (6) Low-level reconnaissance in southern DRV, (7) U.S./VNAF strikes against infiltration-associated targets in southern DRV.
>
> PHASE THREE: Either continue only the above actions or add one more of the following, making timely deployment of U.S. forces: (8) Aerial mining of DRV ports, (9) Naval quarantine of DRV, and (10) U.S./VNAF, in "crescendo," strike additional targets on "94 target list."
>
> South Vietnamese forces should play a role in any action taken against the DRV.
>
> (b) Political actions. Establish immediately a channel for bilateral U.S.-DRV communication. . . .
>
> (1) Stop training and sending personnel to wage war in SVN and Laos.
>
> (2) Stop sending arms and supplies to SVN and Laos. . . .[11]

When a memorandum of any length (the above went on for several thousand words) is done in this fashion, the

[11]Second draft of a paper, "Action for South Vietnam," Assistant Secretary of Defense John McNaughton, Nov. 6, 1964; *The Pentagon Papers as Published by The New York Times* (New York, Bantam, 1971) pp. 366–367.

reader can easily become bug-eyed. "And it will be sheer terror to understand the message." (Isaiah 28:19)

Headings and Subheadings

As mentioned in Chapter 5, headings and subheadings can be extremely helpful in clarifying the organizational scheme of your memorandum, report, or a long letter. They highlight the topics considered. They help your readers see which ideas are subordinate to others. They give readers a psychological lift—a feeling of accomplishment for having completed the discussion of one topic so that they can move on to the next. Last but not least, headings and subheadings help you as the writer keep your thoughts organized efficiently while drafting and reviewing the document.

Here is an example of the helpful use of headings, from a letter to a prospect interested in attending a summer training program:

> Dear. Mr. McDowell:
>
> You will be glad to know that applications for our summer program this year will be accepted until May 15. Please allow us about two weeks to process and answer an application.
>
> You asked about the costs of the program this year as compared to 1968, when you last attended. As you might expect, expenses have been rising as a result of increased outlays for food, equipment, labor, teachers' fees, travel, and supplies—but not as much as you might expect. Thanks to the understanding of the town fathers in the beautiful little New Hampshire community where we are located, we have secured important concessions in tax rates, utility costs, and other fees. The schedule of expenses is as follows:
>
> FIXED EXPENSES
>
> *Tuition:* The tuition for the basic courses this summer is $950.
> *Board:* The charge for 20 meals per week for the complete term is $390.
> *Room:* All rooms are the same price this summer (a change from previous years)—$235 for the term.

VARIABLE EXPENSES

Trips: Expeditions to Cannon Mountain, "The Old Man," The Caves, and similar sights range from $12 to $35, depending on the length of travel, fees for admission, etc. Judging from experience in recent years, a typical outlay for special trips during the term is in the neighborhood of $60.
Golf: If you wish playing privileges at the Green Idyll Golf Club, the fee is $25. . . .

In the above example, you could have conveyed the same information to the prospect in somewhat less space by omitting the headings—and the prospect could have learned just as much by spending extra time on the document. But the addition of headings makes the letter read faster, even though in fact it is longer. Also, there is less chance for confusion and misunderstanding. Finally, clarity often adds sales appeal. "If they make this effort to help me now," the reader says to himself, "they may be just as helpful later on."

Some Important Little Points

Never forget to identify yourself as the author or sender of a document. Never fail to indicate to whom the document is addressed. Never omit the date. As Robert Townsend notes:

> Memos and all other documents should always bear dates and initials. One of my colleagues once spent a twelve-hour night working on an undated document which turned out not to be the current draft. Why he was not convicted of mayhem remains a mystery.[12]

If copies of a memorandum or letter are being sent to other persons, always indicate their names (unless you are sending the copies surreptitiously). This is done at the end of a letter by putting the letters "cc" before the names; in a memorandum it can be done either on the "To" line or in a note at the end; in the case of a report

[12]Robert Townsend, *Up The Organization* (New York, Knopf, 1970), p. 110.

there may, of course, be recipients who are not known at the time of writing, but the primary audience always should be denoted in the preface, covering letter, or mailing instructions.

When you want to assure the addressee that your communication has *not* been photocopied or carboned for someone else, tell him or her of that fact. "It is an unhappy situation, and the final decision in the circumstances must be yours," Rudolf Bing wrote a conductor with whom he was having difficult negotiations. "No copies of this letter have been sent to anyone else. . . ."[13]

Then there is the matter of abbreviations. Too often writers assume that everyone knows what two or three capital letters stand for when it is not known at all. It may be perfectly clear at Massachusetts Investors Trust that "MIT" stands for that firm, but to many other people in the world the abbreviation stands for Massachusetts Institute of Technology. It may be perfectly clear at Borg-Warner Corporation that "BW" represents that company, but to many other people "BW" stands for *Business Week* magazine. One could go on with many other such examples. Abbreviations become particularly confusing in the case of government agencies and military organizations, where there scarcely seems to be a two- or three-letter combination that is not in use by someone.

The abbreviation problem is easy to solve: Simply spell out the name the first time and put the abbreviation in parentheses after it. From that point on, use the abbreviation as frequently as you want without fear of creating needless confusion.

NEXT, SOME RULES FOR CLEARING UP MUDDY WRITING

Once you've got a clear and coherent format for your report, memorandum, or letter, you can turn to the clarity of

[13]Sir Rudolf Bing, *5,000 Nights at the Opera* (Garden City, N.Y., Doubleday Company, 1972), p. 341.

the text itself. You may be pleasantly surprised at the way the second need shapes up after the first one is taken care of.

It is true that reviewing rough drafts for clarity is not America's favorite indoor sport. Plodding sentence by sentence through an important piece of writing for ambiguities and confusions is rarely fun, however rewarding it may be. In fact, it may be downright appalling to review the words that, an hour or day ago, you put down with such confidence and conviction. If so, the following quotations will serve to remind you that (a) you are in excellent company and (b) if you persevere, you may be well-rewarded for your efforts:

- "No tears in the writer, no tears in the reader." (Robert Frost)
- "What is written without effort is in general read without pleasure." (Samuel Johnson)
- "If what you write is not clear, the reader will not know what you want him to do. If you are confused or wordy, the reader will waste time figuring out what you mean or will have to go back to ask you for a clarification. Improving your writing can enhance your reputation as a thinker and as a leader." (*Writing Guide for Naval Officers,* United States Navy)

Fight Ambiguity and Abstractness

If there were to be a literary Sermon on the Mount, this rule would go at the start. You can rarely achieve complete success in this effort, for words mean so many different things to different people, but you can win most of the battle much of the time.

On the first day of 1976, reported the editors of *The Washington Post* in an editorial, they learned a new word: "thruput." The word was part of the U.S. State Department's explanation of the newly created job of consumer affairs coordinator, which had been given to Joan R. Braden. According to the Federal Register, the coordinator would be expected to "review existing mechanisms of consumer input, thruput and output."

Although the *Post* editors said they enjoyed such adventures of the mind, which the State Department was so good at providing, they confessed that they didn't think the phrase was enlightening. In fact, after going over the complete job description, they concluded that the whole thing was "an output." They ran into such other mind-bogglers as "utilization of professional opinion analysts to input consumer attitudes through the Department." They summed up their reactions by urging: "We think the State Department people who thought all this up should reconsider. They should backput it to the drawing board."[14]

Late in 1977 one of the top executives of a prestigious company, addressing a large audience of managers in the advertising business and the media, wrote: "The data base will grow as an information source through the expansion of the selective dissemination concept of knowledge exchange." Presumably he was thinking of what the experts have come to call distributed processing, but only a mind reader could tell for sure. One is reminded of the poet Alexander Pope's lines:

> Words are like leaves; and where they most abound
> Much fruit of sense beneath is rarely found.

Don't Hide Behind Foot-and-a-half-long Words

Dr. R. Charles Boelkins has supplied me with this anecdote:

> Harry Harlow . . . was the editor of the *Journal of Comparative and Physiological Psychology* during the six years I was one of his graduate students. He had a way with words rare among those who mostly write psychology journal articles, and he tried to teach his way to his students, determined that their papers should reflect his parentage. I recall a seminar paper I wrote for him: I had labored long and mightily over it, yet it came back to me looking like a flayed back of a man who had been whipped. With his red pencil he'd taken the paper apart, reassembled it, and

[14]Reported in *The Christian Science Monitor*, January 17, 1976.

showed me some of the craft of the wordsmith. His last page comment was: "If you really understand something you can explain it to an intelligent 10-year-old. To hide behind big words is only to hide your ignorance."

Erma Bombeck gives me this example of advice from a doctor to a patient:

> You have obviously had an exposure to ivy dermatitis which has created a blisterlike eruption on an inflamed base. Spreading it to other parts of the body occurs by direct transfer of the oily substance. It is recommended that extreme caution be exercised to restrain from distribution of the oily substance to the unaffected areas.

In other words, says Bombeck, "Don't scratch!" (But the doctor should learn to scratch some of the words he or she uses.)

Columnist Thomas H. Middleton received a letter from the parent of a high school student. The parent quoted one of the assignments given to the child:

> Re: *The Catcher in the Rye.* HOMEWORK—One-page composition: It is quite obvious that Holden Caulfield is a distinctive protagonist. Explain the intrinsic ramification of Holden's mass appeal and identification to adolescent and young adult readers.

Middleton called the teacher "Groby" and commented as follows on the assignment:

> I've asked a few friends what they thought Groby meant. The consensus is that he probably meant "Explain Holden Caulfield's mass appeal to young readers" but he garbled it.
>
> I have a strong feeling that Groby is a young man—probably under thirty-five—that he really cares, and that he has a master's degree from one of those schools of education where great value is placed on the number of words and where the meaning conveyed by those long words in a sentence and long sentences is about as important as the collar size and sleeve length of the writer.[15]

[15]Thomas H. Middleton, "Light Refractions," *Saturday Review*, April 29, 1978.

As often as possible, use a word that, as C. Northcote Parkinson calls it, is a hammer blow rather than a handful of cotton wool. As often as possible, avoid what the Roman poet Horace called "foot-and-a-half-long words."

The impact of these two rules on a sentence or paragraph may seem alarming (and conceivably this is one reason wordiness is not corrected—the writer's dismay at the brevity of the clear, uncomplicated paragraph). The result brings to mind Mark Twain's story of the man who came to the dentist to have a tooth pulled. But the tooth was connected to the man's jawbone, the jawbone to the neck bone, the neck bone to the spine, and so on all the way down to the man's big toe. And so when the dentist pulled at the tooth, all the other bones came with it, and the dentist sent the patient home in a pillowcase.

Kill those Euphemisms!

Like viruses, euphemisms are contagious, and like viruses, they also can be quite dangerous. Anxious to please President Richard M. Nixon in 1970, Central Intelligence Agency director Richard Helms later testified that he did not want to embarrass the new president by sitting around an official table talking about killing and murdering. The Interim Report of the U.S. Senate Intelligence Committee found the CIA's circumlocution and Aesopian language reprehensible. The report noted: "Failing to call dirty business by its rightful name may have increased the risk of dirty business being done."[16]

"That wasn't a bombing raid!" Peanuts told his Vietnamese captor in a cartoon serial back in the 1960s. "It was a protective reaction strike!" The U.S. Agriculture Department invented a new term for poor people a few years ago—"limited-resource family." About the same time the superintendent of Dallas schools designated school buses as "motorized attendance modules." The Pentagon, according to *The Wall Street Journal*, awarded

[16]Anthony Lewis, *The New York Times*, November 23, 1975.

a contract for "interior intrusion detection systems"—better known as burglar alarms. The Portland *Oregonian* reported that the state's executive department used the phrase "acoustical attenuation for ball activity area" instead of the normal phrasing, "soundproofing the gym." U.S. Navy officers at a War College meeting in 1978, reports Deborah Shapley, talked about carriers capable of "projecting power" instead of launching major attacks.

Euphemisms are dangerous because they conceal and distort reality. Gertrude Stein once looked at a place she didn't like and exclaimed, "There is no there there." Her observation might also be applied to sentences with euphemisms. Fortunately, this is one error that is well within our everyday power to get rid of.

Check the Logic of Your Sentences

In one of the Marx Brothers movies, Groucho is going down a corridor in a hotel when, inside one of the rooms, a gun shot rings out. Tails flapping, Groucho runs in, crouches down beside a man spread-eagled on the floor, feels for the victim's pulse in the manner of a physician, stares at his watch, and announces, "Either this man is dead or my watch has stopped." I have yet to figure that one out, but of one thing I am quite sure: Groucho Marx's spirit is alive and well today, ghost-writing for many professionals, scientists, and managers.

Inane combinations of words (the words themselves may be simple enough) probably result more often from haste, distraction, or carelessness than from conscious disrespect for the reader. Here are some everyday examples, with the errant phrases and lines italicized for later reference:

> Three major associations of property-liability insurance companies are poised to strike out *in opposite directions*. . . . [From the lead sentence of a report on business insurance.][17]

[17]Quoted by Emery Hutchison in "Things My Mother Never Taught Me about Writing," *Journal of Organizational Communications*, Winter 1972, p. 20.

> The nature and interests of Federal Grand Juries, Federal congressional committees, as well as agencies, departments, or commissions of the Federal government *do not, within the safeguards of strict judicial processes, make a threshold determination* that probable cause legally exists that a crime has been committed. . . . [From a preliminary draft of a bill on news media protection, proposed by U.S. Senator Lowell Weicker, Jr.]

Now, simply apply the test of common sense to these passages. In the first, does the writer really mean that three companies are ready to move in opposite directions? Conceivably, yes (that is, two could be moving in one direction, one in the opposite)—but in all probability he means they are poised to strike in different directions.

As for the Weicker bill provision, the nature and interests of grand juries, agencies, and other organizations cannot make a threshold determination of the existence of probable cause or anything else; only people can do that. What the senator meant was that *members of* grand juries, agencies, and so forth, *should not* make a threshold determination of probable cause, for such people are biased by their jobs and interests.

If you are willing to assume that the reader is patient and has time to spare, then you need not worry so much about problems like these—the reader can figure them out. However, not many government officials, scientists, engineers, clients, and business people these days read in an unhurried atmosphere, with their feet up and crackling fires in the fireplace. Irritation and wasted time are not the only risks you run. There is also the danger that, pressed for time and needing to get on with it, your reader will jump to the wrong interpretation of the muddied words and misconstrue the passage in question.

Avoid Cop-out Phrases

A cop-out phrase or construction is one that enables you to get the key words together into a sentence but in an imprecise, poorly constructed manner. Cop-out phrases are the symptom of tired blood in writers.

For instance, Part III of a several-thousand-word-long automobile insurance policy pays particular attention to the definition of "uninsured automobile," since that is a key term in the contract with the customer. It is not enlightening to learn that such a vehicle is:

> An automobile *with respect to* the ownership, maintenance and use of which there is no bodily injury liability bond or insurance policy applicable at the time of the accident *with respect to* any person or organization legally responsible for the use of such automobile, or *with respect to* which there is a bodily injury liability bond or insurance policy applicable at the time of accident but the company writing the same denies coverage thereunder or is or becomes insolvent; or. . . . [italics added]

What do all these *with respect to*'s mean? Does the first one mean that the car has the disadvantages mentioned? But then what does the second one mean? Perhaps the second *with respect to* simply means *to*. If so, what about the third *with respect to*? On the surface, it seems to have the same meaning as the first. But then again, perhaps it doesn't, because there is no reference this time to ownership, maintenance, and use, and presumably the intent is to maintain some parallelism of thought in the paragraph.

Surely, by taking a little more time and effort, the writer of this passage could have stated the meaning more precisely. For instance, it might have begun: "If the person who owns, maintains, or uses an automobile is not covered by a bodily injury bond or insurance policy at the time of an accident. . . ."

Don't Mummify Your Thoughts

Sometimes we wrap a thought around and around with so much word dressing that the real body of it is almost unrecognizable. If several thoughts in a row are mummified, they may look mostly alike. Consider the following paragraph, the official foreword to a pamphlet of instructions for volunteers on how to record historical sites:

> Historic preservation has been given a new dimension by the

> development of hitherto ignored ways of thinking. The first is the expansion of the meaning of "historical resource" from consideration as a single significant site used, more often than not, as a museum, to economically viable areas which preserve the character of an earlier time. In a community these resources constitute its historical environment. The second is the recognition that our total environment includes this historical environment, and that, therefore, its conservation, like the conservation of our natural resources, is urgently needed.[18]

This paragraph is so muddy that a mudhen would have trouble in it. The trouble is not that the author lacks specific thoughts to express, for he does—and rather profound ones at that. The trouble is that he has not bothered to arrange varied ideas in a manner the reader can assimilate; it is as if he has taken notes made to himself, which *he* can understand, and given them, unrefined, to novices. Historical preservation has taken on new meaning in the spatial sense, he means to say. No longer is it confined to artifacts in a museum; now it can mean a whole area of historical significance. Moreover, it is now seen as a dimension of the *environment* to be respected and conserved. And no longer does environmental protection refer just to the here and now. It also extends to the "what was."

Keep Explanatory Material on Target

Some passages remind us of an explorer's compass on a journey to the North Pole. The letter or report starts off in a certain direction, but as the writer puts the words down he or she thinks of new thoughts and angles, which also must be mentioned. Soon the once-steady aim of the passage wavers, and then spins wildly out of control—or so it seems to the hapless reader.

One might think at first that this mistake would be typical mostly of addled or uncertain minds, but such is

[18]John F.X. Davoren, foreword to *Guide to Inventory Techniques* (Boston, Massachusetts Historical Commission, 1970).

not the case. In fact, some of the most egregious examples are to be found in the written communications of brilliant people. Possibly, the explanation is that acute thinkers get too far ahead of themselves as they grind out a letter or report. Second thoughts, additional angles, further possibilities, and qualifications start popping into their minds, and unless they are careful, they start mentioning these discursions before the main point is clear to the reader.

An example is a letter Dr. Jonas Salk wrote to the Medical Director of the National Foundation for Infantile Paralysis in 1941. While pioneering in the development of a polio vaccine, Salk had been introduced to the official by a mutual friend, Dr. Thomas Francis. Hoping to enlist the support of the official for the research he contemplated, Salk wrote him:

> My dear Dr. Gudakunst,
>
> I have just received a copy of a letter from Dr. Goodpasture to Dr. Francis. . . .
>
> Since seeing you last, I have spoken with Dr. Homer Smith. His advice about arranging the necessary funds for work with Dr. Goodpasture was to get the assurance of the National Foundation that such help will be forthcoming, and to state this fact in applying to the National Research Council. Then, if a fellowship were granted, the National Research Council would make the necessary arrangements for an extension of such a fellowship with the funds so provided. Since I hope to be able to work with Dr. Francis at Ann Arbor, on some other basis, if I am not fortunate enough to be granted the fellowship, I hope the National Foundation will find it possible to permit me to spend the contemplated period with Dr. Goodpasture, independently of a National Research Council fellowship. . . .[19]

Even after briefing yourself on the situation mentioned, you may not be able to read this paragraph without acquiring a feeling of disorientation, going in circles, coming unbuttoned, and developing Arctic madness.

[19]Richard Carter, *Breakthrough: the Saga of Jonas Salk* (New York, Trident, 1966), p. 44.

Don't Let the Subject and Verb Get Too Far Apart

One sure way to confuse and irritate your reader is to string a dozen or more words between the subject and verb of a sentence. For example:

> The unseasonable winter of 1972–1973 was due to the fact that both the polar and tropical jet streams, rivers of rapidly moving air which are hundreds of miles wide and four miles deep, whirling westward around the earth at altitudes of four to seven miles and controlling, as they move, the pattern and direction of hemispheric storm tracks, moved north of their usual channels.

An easy way to correct such a sentence is to break it up, putting the main fact in a short first sentence and the amplifying information in a second sentence:

> The unseasonable winter of 1972–1973 was the result of the polar and tropical jet streams moving north of their usual channels. These streams consist of rapidly moving air masses hundreds of miles wide and. . . .

Keep the Length of Your Sentences Reasonable

Up to a point, long sentences are a matter of personal style and preference. In terms of word count, some sentences can be very long indeed without causing confusion. However, all good things must come to an end sometime, and sooner or later there comes a point when, because of shifts in thought and other factors, even the most beautiful sentence should be completed. Mark Twain once compared excessively long sentences with torchlight parades that snake down the street and wind out of sight in the gloom of night.

Consider the following sentence from a letter Eleanor Roosevelt wrote to a member of the American Youth Congress in May 1940:

> I realize that there will be not only young communists, but many other people and groups who may not like condemning Stalin or the Soviet Union by name, but I think that at the present time,

with the Nazi pact a fact, Finland invaded and Germany proceeding to invade one country after another under a thinly veiled excuse of protecting neutrals, the people of the U.S. have become convinced that the infiltration of alien ideas is bad in any country and they will not support an organization that will not clearly go on record as to where it stands.[20]

The interesting thing about this statement, I have learned from a series of tests on readers, is that its murkiness is almost completely the result of its excessive length. Almost all readers have to go back and read it again—and sometimes still again. You can eliminate the trouble simply by breaking up the sentence:

I realize that there will be not only young communists, but many other people and groups who may not like condemning Stalin or the Soviet Union by name. But I think that at the present time with the Nazi pact a fact, Finland invaded and Germany proceeding to invade one country after another under a thinly veiled excuse of protecting neutrals, the people of the U.S. have become convinced that the infiltration of alien ideas is bad in any country. They will not support an organization that will not clearly go on record as to where it stands.

Go Easy on Combinations of Negatives

Although double negatives often can be justified (such as the last sentence of Eleanor Roosevelt's letter, just quoted), combinations of three or more *not*'s, words with suffixes like *un-*, *non-*, or *dis-*, and words and phrases with negative meanings (such as *with the exception of* or *prohibit*) rarely can be justified. For instance, suppose Eleanor Roosevelt had ended her thought with this sentence: "They will not disapprove of supporting an organization that will not clearly go on record as to where it stands." Now the two *not's* in combination with the negative word *disapprove* cause turmoil in the reader's mind. Similar bewilderment is caused by these sentences:

[20]Joseph P. Lash, *Eleanor Roosevelt: A Friend's Memoirs* (New York: Doubleday, 1964), pp. 117–118.

- He did not, as it turned out, mean that research for new products would not be carried on anyway for reasons other than mercenary ones. [From a memorandum on a research meeting]
- It is unclear how a cluster of excited molecules can fail to cause noncondensation in other molecules. [From a letter on some laboratory tests]

For many people it would be easier to figure out how that centipede walks than to unravel the intent of the writer in sentences like these.

Guard Against Two-faced Conjunctions and "I like you more than Mary" Constructions.

The anonymous person who said to a reader, "I know you believe you understand what you think I wrote, but I am not sure you realize that what you read is not what I meant," may have been aware of another pitfall: conjunctions with two possible and plausible meanings. The most troublesome such conjunctions are *while* and *since*. To illustrate:

- While she sought to relax, she kept in touch with the accountants. (Does the writer mean "Although she sought to relax, she kept . . ." or "During the time that she sought to relax, she kept . . ."?)
- Since the failure rate has been fluctuating, the treasurer has insisted on more caution. (The writer may mean, "Because the failure rate has been fluctuating, . . ." Just possibly, however, he or she means, "Since the time fluctuations began occurring in the failure rate, . . .")

The sentence "I like you more than Mary" was scrawled in a child's hand on a telephone pole by a bus stop. Standing there in the morning, commuters would debate whether the author meant that he or she liked "you" more than he or she liked Mary, or whether the author meant that he or she liked "you" more than Mary liked "you."

Technically, the first meaning is the correct one; in reality, the second meaning is what the authors of many such sentences intend. As a result, "I like you more than Mary" sentences are a frequent source of confusion in the writing of business and professional people. Examples like the following are all too common: "Corporate management fears union power more than the government." Does the writer mean "Corporate management fears union power more than it fears the government," or "Corporate management fears union power more than the government does"?

Don't Allow Ambiguous Antecedents

Another form of murkiness is the pronoun or other word with uncertain antecedents. Regard a word with uncertain antecendents as dubiously as a Boston Brahman considers a social climber with uncertain ancestors. For instance:

- The actions of the finance ministers were based on the need for more orderly markets. These are due to be examined at the forthcoming talks in Brussels. (Does *these* refer to *actions* or *markets*? Strictly speaking, it refers to *markets*, that being the nearest antecedent preceding, but the writer may not have been aware of this rule.)
- The operations research group told the marketing staff it would have to analyze the data again. (Does *it* refer to *operations research group* or *marketing staff?*)

In cases like these, slight revisions are usually sufficient to rectify the confusion:

- The actions of the finance ministers were based on the need for more orderly markets. These actions. . . .
- The operations research group said the marketing staff would have to. . . .

Look Askance at Muddling and Squinting Modifiers

When adjectives, adverbs, and modifying phrases have uncertain relationships in a sentence, they can louse it up—even though grammatically the sentence may be passable. Consider the following:

- My client requested relief in varying ways. (Does the writer mean, "My client made various requests for relief" or "My client requested relief of varying types"? The first is grammatically correct, but the second could be what was intended, or at least what readers think was intended.)
- She pleaded with the hostile Republicans and Democrats to save the bill. (Does the writer mean "She pleaded with hostile legislators on both the Republican and Democratic sides . . ." or "She pleaded with Democrats and hostile Republicans . . ."?)

A related troublemaker is what John B. Bennett calls the "squinting modifier."[21] One example he gives is: "The electrician said Wednesday he would repair the stove." To avoid confusion, Bennett points out, the sentence should read: "Wednesday the electrician said he would repair the stove," or "The electrician said he would repair the stove on Wednesday."

NEXT, THOUGHTS ABOUT WRITING REGULATIONS AND DIRECTIONS

Some people call if "officialese." Some, like writer Thomas Ehrlich, call it "legal pollution." Others call it "gobbledegook." I like to refer to it as "pathological professionalism." It, of course, is the regulation or law that is as dense and full of snakes as the Brazilian jungle. Governor Edmund G. Brown, Jr., of California prefers a metaphor in a marine setting. Bureaucratic regulation-writing, he once said, "demonstrates the squid process—

[21]John B. Bennett, *Editing for Engineers* (New York, Wiley, 1970), p. 86.

spreading ink across the page in wordlike patterns, primarily to protect an organism from attack from the outside."

Why do the perpetrators of these verbal monstrosities, knowing the material must be read and understood by innocent people, proceed with such sinister dedication? They rejoice in the difficulty of their trade. They find psychic rewards in producing esoteric and abstruse word combinations. They revel in the fact that only a small group, an elite counterculture, knows what in hell they are trying to say. Hence the term pathological professionalism, suggested above.

One of the greatest and most discerning judges of the twentieth century, Learned Hand, once wrote:

> Words of such an act as the Income Tax, for example, merely dance before my eyes in a meaningless procession: cross-reference to cross-reference, exception upon exception—couched in abstract terms that offer no handle to seize hold of—leave in my mind only a confused sense of some vitally important, but successfully concealed purport, which is my duty to extract, but which is within my power, if at all, only after the most inordinate expenditure of time.[22]

In 1977 a week-long workshop to teach clearer drafting of regulations was sponsored by the Federal Register. The 30 students who attended came from a variety of well-known government agencies. James Minor, an erstwhile regulation writer himself, now a law school professor and consultant, joined with Fred Emery, director of the Federal Register, in teaching a more humane approach. The two men offer these broad guides:[23]

- Find out what the policymakers have in mind. "This is a lot harder than it sounds," Mr. Minor says, "because most policymakers aren't that sure of what they're trying to do."

[22]See Thomas Ehrlich, "Legal Pollution," *The New York Times Magazine*, February 8, 1976, p. 21.
[23]Alan L. Otten, "Politics & People," *The Wall Street Journal*, February 10, 1977.

- Don't just grab a pencil and start writing. "Think about the fundamental questions that need to be asked," Mr. Emery advises, "and until you've gotten some answers, don't start writing." Counsels Mr. Minor: "Make an outline, and you'll spot things they forgot to tell you. After you've written a first draft, let it sit a few days before you begin rewriting it."
- Be consistent. Don't use different words or phrases to denote the same thing. People affected by the regulation will wonder why the words are different, and courts may cite the differences as grounds to throw the regulation out. "If you use 'dog' in one place," Mr. Minor says, "use it all the way through. Don't suddenly change to 'animal of the canine species.' "
- Keep each regulation as short as possible—but if you have to choose between brevity and clarity, use the extra words you need to be clear. Use short paragraphs and short sentences. Use simple words; longer words aren't necessarily better or more legal.
- Use the active voice wherever possible. Use live words: People should "apply" rather than "make application" and should "decide" rather than "make a determination." Avoid pairs of words having the same effect—"each and every," or "full and complete." Avoid jargon.
- "Don't be wordy and don't be ambiguous," Mr. Minor sums up. "Try to say what you mean, and say it as exactly and economically as possible. Use words in their ordinary sense. We don't write regulations to sound impressive. We write them to be understood."

AND, FINALLY, "SIGNPOSTS" FOR READERS

"The worm not only turns, he often does it without making the proper signal," D.O. Flynn once said. Especially in the case of longer reports, memoranda, and letters, it is often helpful to stop and tell your reader what you have done and what you intend to do next. Typically, such an explanation takes only a few sentences. Simple to insert, it can be an enormous boon to the reader, who, not knowing the line of thought as intimately as you do, sometimes needs to be told in plain terms what is going on. "We all find signs along a highway helpful; they are there to prepare us for what's coming," says John A. Walter, an authority on technical writing. "The same is true of technical presentations. Let the reader know where he is from time to time; put in a sentence—a paragraph if need be—to let him know explicitly where he is and why he is going where he is going."[24]

This need is closely connected with the need for topic sentences and topic paragraphs—as discussed in the previous chapter, coherence and clarity are very closely related. A clear signpost paragraph may serve to clarify the route of thought for the reader, as well as show him the connections between two thoughts or ideas.

Two related devices that help to make a communication clear are (a) an introduction that previews the main theme to follow, and (b) a short summary at the end. The first device is described in Chapter 3. As for the summary, it is most effective when the following ground rules are followed:

- Introduce no new findings or conclusions requiring fresh evidence, arguments, or interpretations. However, it is appropriate to introduce new reflections on the ideas described or new thoughts about their implications.
- Use the same kinds of terms as used in the body of the report or memorandum. New words or levels of technicality are likely to confuse the reader.
- If a rundown of the principal points made is in order, restate them in approximately the same order as their explanation in the body of the communication.
- Enumerate or itemize the main ideas being summarized if there are many of them and if this technique has not been overused in previous parts of the document. Numbers, letters, ornaments (dots, dashes, and so forth, before each new

[24]John A. Walter, "Industrial Communications," *Proceedings, Society of Technical Writers and Publishers*, 1969, pp. 5–59.

item), and enumerative words (first, second, third, and so on) are all appropriate for this purpose.

PROBLEMS AND CASES

1. Put the five ideas of transactional communication ("If meanings are in words . . .") in terms of a dialogue between Humpty Dumpty and Alice, between a thesis writer and his or her professor, or between an insurance policy writer and his or her spouse.
2. Take a section of a memorandum, paper, or report that is hard to read and make it more readable by inserting format devices.
3. Rewrite the definition of "uninsured automobile" quoted from an insurance policy.
4. At the risk of developing Arctic madness, rewrite Salk's letter to Gudakunst.
5. Comment on Walter Landor's statement quoted on the title page of this chapter; use an example to make your point.
6. It has been said that "Words don't mean; people mean." Discuss this statement.
7. The following paragraph ends an article entitled "Speed of Speech and Persuasion" that appeared in 1976 in the *Journal of Personality and Social Psychology:*

> If the impact of speaking rate on attitude change were mediated by either comprehension effects or counterargument disruption, then a highly rationalistic view of the persuasion process would have been supported. However, [our findings] are consistent with a less rationalistic view of the persuasion process. Indeed, to put it somewhat sardonically, it may be irrational to rationally scrutinize the plethora of counterattitudinal messages received daily. To the extent that one possesses only a limited amount of information-processing time and capacity, such scrutiny would disengage the thought processes from the exigencies of daily life.

See how much you can clarify the paragraph in a rewrite.

Indicate which rules described in this chapter you used in your rewrite.

8. Improve the following sentences:

a. In relation to certain criteria, the members of Seward Investments, Inc. must carefully appraise the various plans regardless of their personal inclinations.

b. Add to this mosaic of conflicts the techniques now made possible by computers which could not even have existed previously.

c. This is a report on a study the primary purpose of which was to test the interrelationship between the degree of centralization in corporations' organizational structures and the degree of formalization of their formal planning.

d. Whereas, therefore, the American medical profession was surprised and put in a difficult situation, so far as public relations were concerned, in recent months when a national health organization, without any official consultation with any qualified council or group of the American Medical Association, launched a nationwide comprehensive program for the use of a new vaccine which gives great theoretical promise of success in combating a dread disease and yet which admittedly had been used a few months, without sufficient time to evaluate the safety as well as the efficacy of the vaccine, and with practically no published data in the scientific literature on the use of the vaccine. Earnest attempts of a few medical societies to secure advance information on the proposal, so as to be ready for it, were fruitless until, practically overnight, the national group requested local medical societies to approve and be responsible for the administration of the new vaccine. [From a resolution passed by the American Medical Association in 1955 to censure Dr. Jonas Salk's tests of a new antipolio vaccine.]

9. ***Notes on Nutrition:*** A pharmaceutical concern puts out "as a service to doctors and patients" a five-page leaflet, *New Horizons in Nutrition*. Most of the text is given to an essay by a biochemist who is described as a pioneer in nutrition and the recipient of numerous awards. The first ten paragraphs of the essay follow.

Some may see nutrition as a well tilled field of orthodoxy where established concepts, facts and figures abound and where interlopers and disturbers of the peace must not be allowed to enter.

Within my memory, physics was once looked upon as a well-ordered and relatively complete science with the basic principles already established. But physics "came alive," developed a thousand uncertainties and has extended its horizons in a way never conceived of in the "good old days."

There is excellent prospect that nutrition will likewise "come alive," forget its deadly complacency and reach out to entirely new conquests.

A new horizon in nutrition will be seen by all thoroughgoing environmentalists because they will be compelled to recognize that our bodies need to get from our environment a large number of essential chemicals in addition to the oxygen and water we all take for granted.

This general recognition will come rapidly under one condition—when elementary education awakens to the vital reality that schools should teach youngsters *what they need to know in order to live healthy lives.*

Our bodies, like plants, need lime, potash, phosphate, manganese, zinc, etc., but they also need from the environment many other chemicals that green plants can make for themselves—valine, leucine, phenylalanine, tryptophan, etc.—in addition to a number of vitamins and other nutrients, the number of which is not precisely known.

These facts of life should be common knowledge. They should be known by each youngster long before he or she goes to college. They should also be aware that just as the health and vigor of a plant depends on its getting a good supply of the chemicals plants need, so the health and vitality of their bodies depends on their external food supply of their essential body chemicals. These facts should *all* be regarded as elementary, and not at all revolutionary or astounding.

Nutritional science will awaken to learn how crucial the internal environment of our body cells and tissues is, and that the external nutrition we receive in our food may shape and build our entire lives. Nutritional science will awaken to the probability that all kinds of malformations in bodies and brains (of which we are only vaguely aware) have their roots in the poor internal environment furnished prenatally by prospective mothers. By careful study and proper adjustments it is probable that malformations and mental retardation can be largely obliterated.

These possibilities cease to sound extravagant when the undeniable fact becomes clear that all internal environments as we encounter them in nature are assuredly suboptimal and open to improvement—that is, if we knew our stuff in the field of nutritional science.

The suboptimal nature and improbability of environments is a universal principle of life, applicable not only to our nutritional environment but also to every phase of our environment; climatic environment, the social milieu, the educational environment, the moral environment, the aesthetic environment, etc.

Suppose you had been asked to consult on the presentation of this material. What changes would you have suggested? Redraft the paragraphs above with your changes incorporated.

10. ***Pronouncement on Profit Sharing:*** Rewrite the following note, which appeared in a utility company's profit-sharing report.

> In accordance with the terms of the Company Profit Sharing Plan (the Plan), the account of each participant in the Plan is maintained on a market value basis, except for shares of Company common stock which are maintained at average cost.
>
> However, the financial statements of the Trust reflect all of the Trust's assets at quoted market value. The unrealized appreciation or (depreciation) amounts in the participants' general and stock accounts section of the statement of trust assets and trust fund balances represent the cumulative adjustment on Company shares made to the Trust's records in order to reflect all of the Trust's assets at quoted market value.

11. Improve the following passage reprinted from William J. Gallagher, "The Technical Style: A Defense of Knowledge," *American Machinist*, March 17, 1966:

> It is believed that it is highly desirable to understand the

business of high vacuum equipment manufacturing in terms of the basic high vacuum component content of high vacuum systems. Obviously, if a company intent on entering the high vacuum equipment market wishes to do so on the basis of technological innovations in high vacuum technology as such, efforts must be related in some way to the production and/or measurement of high vacuum. On the other hand, it is perfectly feasible to base technological effort on a process which may require high vacuum for its proper operation. An analysis of the market tends to indicate that there are still a relatively few companies whose major technological thrust is in high vacuum technology as such and a great many others which have entered the market successfully by combining knowledge of high vacuum techniques and equipment with the requirements of affecting the end result. This is not as simple as it may sound because the broadline high vacuum equipment manufacturers, producing their own basic high vacuum components, also strive to remain in the forefront of process-related technology.

12. ***Orders to Oil Pricers:*** See how much you can clarify the following regulations.

    a. From section 150.354 of *Phase IV Oil Regulations*, Economic Stabilization Program, Cost of Living Council, Washington, D.C., August 17, 1973, pp. 8–9:

    (c) *Rule.*—

    (1) *General.*—Except as provided in subparagraphs (2) and (3) of this paragraph, no producer may charge a price higher than the ceiling price for the first sale of domestic crude petroleum.

    (2) *Special release rule*—Notwithstanding subparagraph (1) of this paragraph, a producer of new crude petroleum produced and sold from a property may in the month produced, beginning with the month of September 1973, or in any subsequent month, sell that new crude petroleum without respect to the ceiling price. However, if the amount of crude petroleum produced and sold in any month subsequent to the first month in which new crude petroleum was produced and sold, is less than the base production control level for that property for that month, any new crude petroleum produced from that property during any subsequent month may not be sold pursuant to this subparagraph until an amount of the new crude petroleum equal to the difference between the amount of

crude petroleum actually produced from that property during the earlier month and the base production control level for that property for the earlier month has been sold at or below its ceiling price.

b. From Part 150—Cost of Living Council, *Phase IV Price Regulations*, p. 24:

In computing base prices for a covered product other than a special product, a refiner may increase its May 15, 1973 selling price to each class of purchaser each month beginning with October 1973 by an amount to reflect the increased costs of imports and increased costs of domestic crude petroleum attributable to sales of covered products other than special products or sales of special products not otherwise allocated pursuant to subparagraph (1) (i) using the differential between the month of measurement and the month of May, 1973, provided that the amount of increased costs used in computing a base price is calculated by use of the general formula set forth in subparagraph (2) and provided that the amount of increased costs included in computing base prices of a particular covered product other than a special product must be equally applied to each class of purchaser. In apportioning the total amount of increased costs allocable to covered products other than special products, a refiner may apportion the total amount of increased costs to a particular covered product other than a special product at a particular level of distribution in whatever amount he deems appropriate.

13. ***Resolution on Recognition:*** The following letter was sent to employees of the "Eldnik Corp." (fictional name). It was printed on the president's letterhead.

All Eldnik Employees:

I am delighted to announce that we are establishing a major new recognition program in the company. It is called the "President's Circle" and it is specifically designed to recognize and reward non-sales people in every part of the company.

The President's Circle will form the third major part of a new set of recognition "Clubs" in which the Silver Circle and Golden Circle are specifically for the sales force.

The purpose of the President's Circle is to clearly recognize those people who demonstrate unusual dedication, commitment and contribution to our company goals. It is also to recognize the fact that those contributions will tend to be made with the kind of personal sacrifice that comes only with dedication . . . dedication to success.

Eldnik people who have been named to the President's Circle will be invited to join with their spouse in attending the President's Circle Conference. The conference will be held jointly with the Golden Circle Conference in the first quarter of each year. The next trip, incidentally, is planned for March and will be held at the Frenchman's Reef Hotel in the Virgin Islands.

In establishing these new recognition programs, we chose the "circle" as the theme to signify the unity we are achieving as a company. I am, personally, looking forward to the next conference of those people who represent the elite of our sales force as well as those who are the top people in all other parts of the company.

Any employee may nominate another employee for membership in the President's Circle. The nominations should be sent to my office with copies to the appropriate management for that nominee's department, up to and including the Vice President of that department.

We will, very shortly, be publishing a suggested format for nominations that will assist you in describing and writing about the qualifications that recommend a particular person to membership. Selection of people to membership in the President's Circle will be made by:

- The President
- The Vice President who manages the nominee's department
- At least three other Vice Presidents

Candidates may be nominated and selected at any time. During the course of a year, I expect approximately 20–30 members of the President's Circle will be announced.

Eldnik is a community of people. Every function and every job is important to all of us in growing and building the company. This important new program is to specifically recognize those people in the company who make us what we are.

And we are . . . ON THE MOVE!

Regards,
[president's signature]

Assume you are a trusted adviser to the president of "Eldnik Corp." He asks for your opinion on this letter. "Give any changes to me in writing," he says. What changes, if any, would you suggest?

14. ***Coming to Grips with Grievances:*** When the top management of a good-sized Midwestern corporation requested division managers to identify and summarize the various complaints of supervisors and employees, one division official sent the following memorandum to his boss. Reprinted by permission from John D. Glover and Ralph M. Hower, *The Administrator* (Homewood, Ill.: Richard D. Irwin, 1957), pp. 208–209:

To: Mr. Alben Bowles

From: Thomas Foley

The attached report is in answer to your request that we give you a list of the grievances together with our comments. You will notice that in most cases these grievances have not been ignored but we have had a very definite plan to eliminate them. I do not feel particularly proud of the progress that we have made; on the other hand, it has been a rather trying two years and certainly with help and material more available we should be able to make substantial progress on most of these grievances within the next year. Frankly, the number of grievances startled me a little bit when I wrote them out. I believe all this indicates the need for a real good grievance procedure, and I would like to make the following recommendations:

(1) That we immediately put into effect the tentative plan discussed in Chicago whereby meetings will be held in the divisions between the superintendent and the foremen and/or the men as the case may be. For example, in Iowa, I believe we could meet with the foremen and the men as we have so few foremen and the same is true in the Chesapeake Division. In other divisions, such as Pacific, Southwestern, and Northeastern, the meetings could best be held with just the foremen. However, I think every superintendent should be required to submit his recommendations as to the fre-

quency of the meetings and who should attend. These recommendations would then be reviewed and a definite schedule of dates would be issued by someone such as Mr. Roland. The dates should be staggered to permit someone such as Mr. Roland, or myself to attend, as I do not believe any of our superintendents, other than perhaps Fred Young of Pacific, are qualified to hold these meetings without having help or superivision from the Chicago Personnel Department.

I then feel that the schedule of the first meetings should cover the history of the company, Mr. Rand's talk, and all the information contained in Mr. Hodgson's talk on unions. At each of these meetings, a definite amount of time would be set aside to discuss grievances. This schedule would take up approximately three meetings and by that time perhaps we could follow through with the regular foremen training program.

I do not know what the letters will show that we receive from the supervisors and the superintendents but my guess is that it will show that we need considerable training to help our foremen recognize a grievance or a source of a potential grievance. For example, when I talked to Mr. Pepper he said that offhand he didn't know of a single grievance.

I would also like to suggest that the company announce through the superintendents that we are going to have two family parties a year and the company will pay the expenses, as I believe this will do a lot to create goodwill and there has certainly been a lot of confusion and misunderstanding on the matter in our department and it has certainly caused considerable ill will and while I have not listed it with the grievances it most certainly is an outstanding one. I feel that we should devise a new plan of a more permanent nature for handling grievances involving some of the following points that a man secures when he joins the Union:

(1) Ease in presenting
(2) Ease in getting around immediate boss
(3) Enjoys complete protection
(4) Is advised as to the final disposition and the reasons relating thereto
(5) Has complete access to progress all the way to top management as well as the fact that the top management have occasion to review the decision made on

> those grievances disposed of in the lower steps by virtue of the fact that all grievances are reduced to writing in the very first step.
>
> While the attached letter and report is the result of considerable thought and work, I do wish to point out that after all it was prepared in a matter of less than two days and every single item on every grievance has not been explained or brought to a final conclusion, however, I believe it is the type of thing to be of assistance to you and Mr. Hodgson at this time. You will notice there has been no complacency on our part regarding these matters but that in all cases we have not been able to bring the matters to final conclusions.

Rewrite this memorandum to make it clearer, more coherent, and more appropriate in any other ways you deem desirable.

Oh that my words were written!
Oh that they were inscribed in a book!
Oh that with an iron pen and lead
they were graven in the rock for ever!

The Book of *Job*, 19:23,24

There is a Southern proverb
—fine words butter no parsnips.

Sir Walter Scott

Chapter 10

Some Simple Rules For Using Charts and Diagrams

You may seek clarity in words alone, or you may seek it in words and visual exhibits. The use of visuals is becoming increasingly common in the writings of business, scientific, and professional people. Once confined mostly to printed brochures and formal reports, visuals now are seen in everyday letters and memoranda, thanks to photocopying machines that reproduce pen or pencil sketches as readily as typewritten matter.

Some communicators seem to have a terror of this medium, graphics, and of this strange skill, drawing and illustrating. The world of the professional illustrator and designer is indeed specialized, but charts and diagrams are appropriate for us amateurs, too, and it is a shame to overlook them when they are appropriate.

When should you use charts and diagrams in a written presentation? Use them, first, when you have a variety of quantifiable or relatable facts and figures to convey that the reader can grasp more readily and fully in visual form than in a textual explanation. Second, use charts and diagrams if you want to attract the reader's attention and focus his or her interest. If, let us say, you have a series of different sets of facts to present, and one set is of more importance than the others, you might be well advised to use charts and diagrams in explaining just that set. (Or, if you need to use visuals for all sets, you might use more of them, or more handsomely done ones, for the key set than for the others.) Third, charts and diagrams are often economical; they may enable you to present an idea or relationship in less space than you could in words, and they may enable the reader to grasp the point in less time.

Do *not* let the length of your written message influence the decision—a two-paragraph message and three sheets of diagrams are as appropriate as the opposite balance of written and visual material. Do not let the availability of a commercial artist affect your decision, at least if you are dealing with an ordinary memo, letter, or report—a neat, clear, but amateurishly drawn bar chart or pie chart is perfectly appropriate. In fact, a good many manuscripts submitted to the *Harvard Business Review* over the years have been enhanced by charts and diagrams drawn with amateur skill.

Now let us turn to some rules and principles for making your charts and diagrams helpful, effective, and appropriate.

USE APPROPRIATE CHARTING TECHNIQUES

No two types of chart serve quite the same purpose. Once you know what information and ideas you want to convey, take a few minutes to consider what type of chart best suits your need. There is no need for a no-fault attitude toward charting, blaming the mechanism if it distorts the information presented.

The best-known chart forms, along with commentaries on their use, are shown in Exhibit 1. Probably you will recognize most of them and need only a few minutes to make your choice, for you have been exposed to charts and diagrams like these since you were in grade school.

KEEP IT SIMPLE

One of the prime ribs of a good visual exhibit is simplicity. Because an important purpose is clarification, strip the idea or ideas to be conveyed down to their essentials. Don't let your chart or diagram look like a can of tapeworms feeding on each other.

But suppose there is no getting around the complicated nature of the relationships—that to strip the information down more would be to distort the idea. In such a case, use a series of charts, focusing first on the individual parts, then on the whole. According to The Chartmakers, Inc.:

> It is safer to assume that a management group can comprehend only one set of data at a time—yet the coordination of many factors is one of the advantages of visual reporting. The answer lies in making the clearest possible presentation of each set of factors and then combining them on a composite chart.[1]

AVOID ART FOR ART'S SAKE

Top-notch professional chartmakers often do superb jobs of illustrating charts and graphs shown in books and magazines. Usually the drawings and cartoons are restrained, and invariably they are rendered by expert hands with knowledge of contemporary trends in illustration.

[1]See Harriet Edmunds, C. M. LePeer, and H. A. Morse, "Visual Reporting to Management" in *Effective Marketing Action*, David W. Ewing, Ed. (New York: Harper & Row, 1958), p. 281.

Exhibit 1. Leading Chart Forms

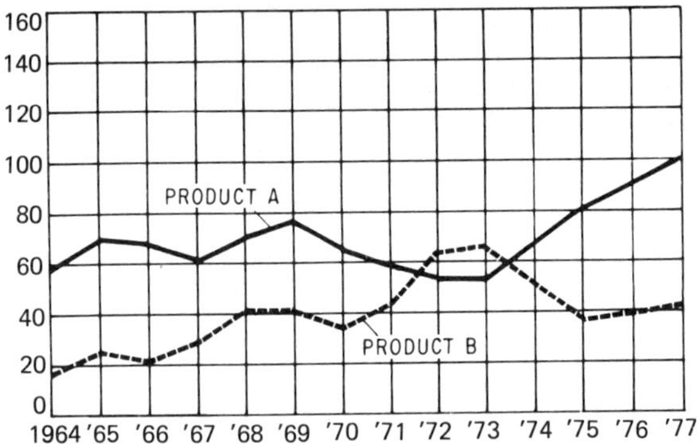

The *line graph* is probably the most frequently used of all visual reporting techniques. It is employed primarily to indicate a trend.

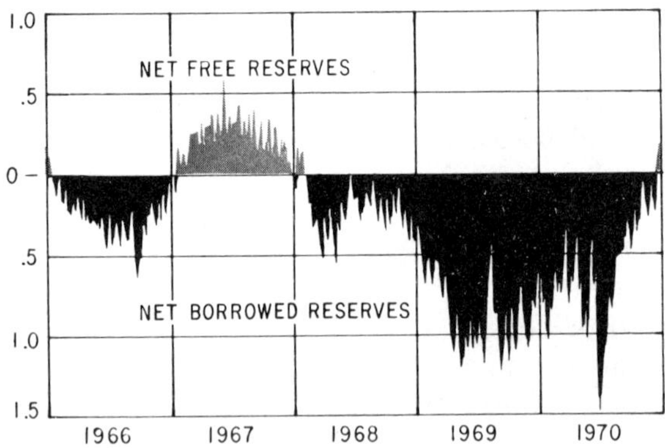

The *silhouette chart* is useful to accent plus or minus departures from a base, goal, or standard. In this illustration zero represents a state in which a banking system has neither free reserves nor borrowed reserves.

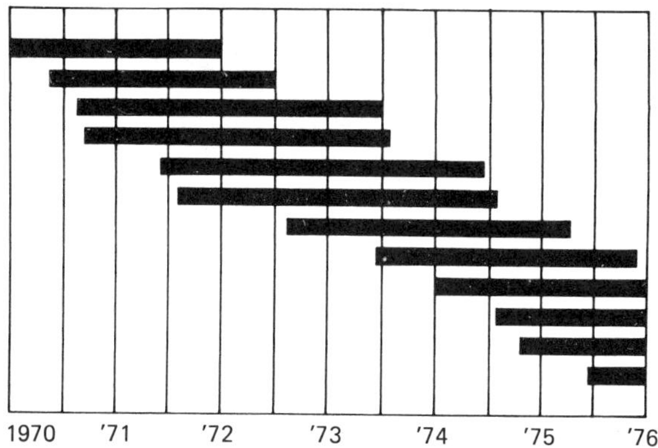

The *band* or *strata graph* can be used to show variations in time sequence.

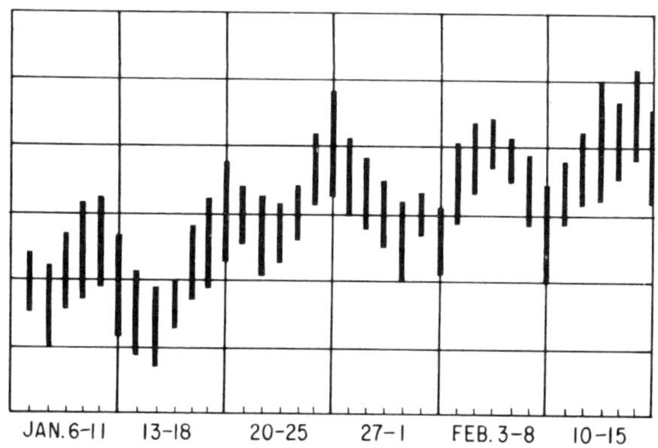

The *high-low graph* is a good way to portray variations within designated periods. The left-hand scale can be conventional or logarithmic.

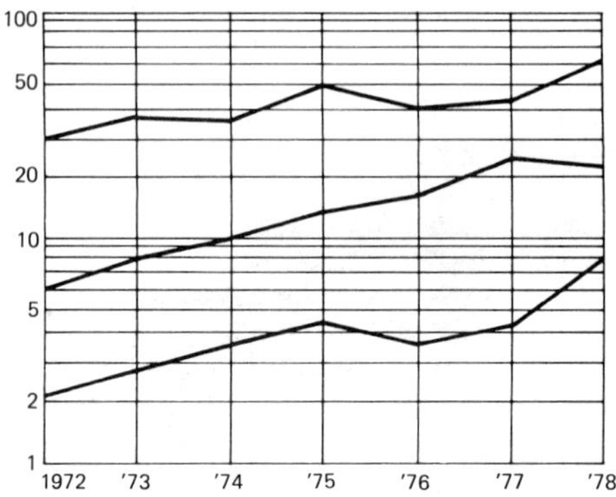

The *logarithmic graph* serves best to show rates of change rather than amounts of change.

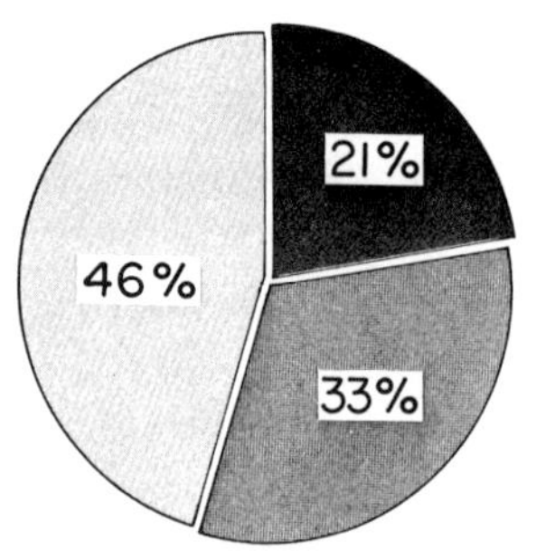

The *pie chart* is the most familiar form of area chart, another frequently used graphic form. The pie chart is used to represent component parts of a whole.

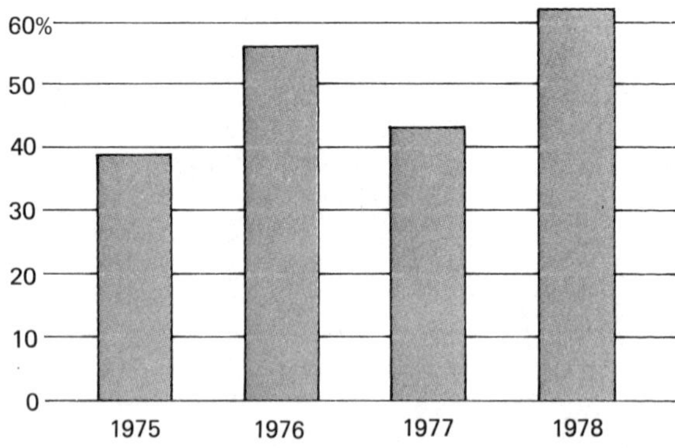

The *bar chart* runs a close second to the graph in popularity. This example is a simple bar chart. The bars can run vertically, as here, or horizontally, depending on the need.

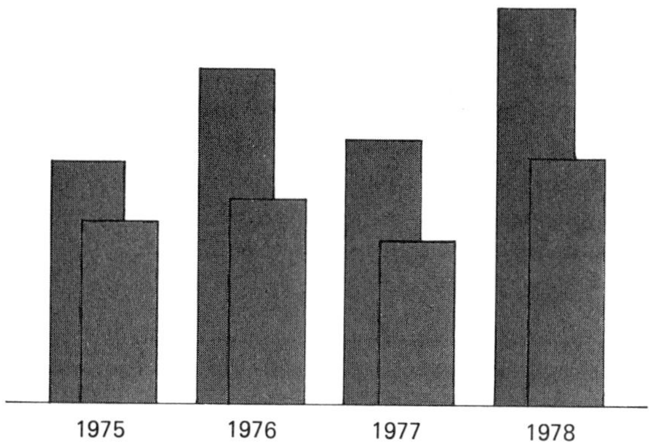

The *grouped* or *compound bar chart* is useful for contrasting two or more variables over a period of time (as here) or in different localities, functions, organizations, and so on.

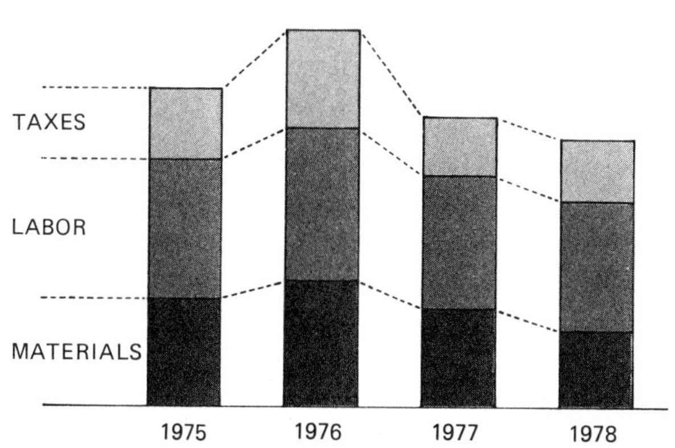

The *component* or *subdivided bar chart* provides the same information as a series of pie charts but in more manageable and compact form. The components of each bar can add up to 100% or to some absolute measure, such as sales volume, number of customers, or material costs.

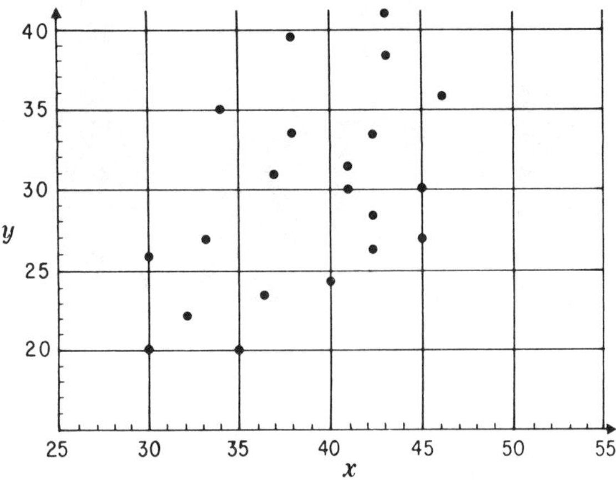

The *scatter diagram* is useful for showing the relationship (or lack of it) of two variables. This one shows a slight tendency for small and large values of x to be associated with small and large values of y.

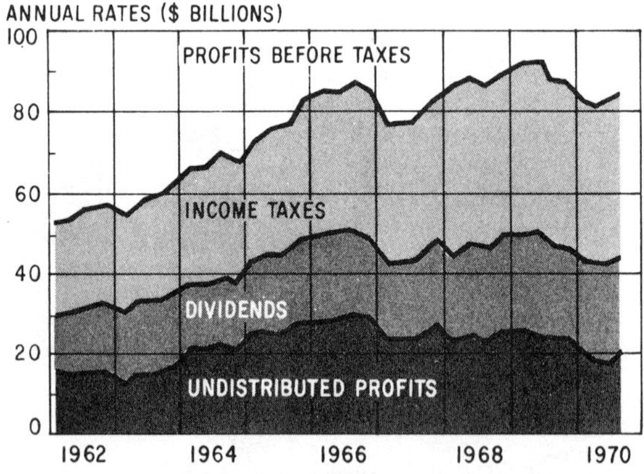

The *surface* or *stratum chart* shows trends in segments of a total amount. Note that only the bottom layer can be measured directly from the scale. Suggestion: because an irregular layer gives the illusion that others are moving up and down, too, put the most irregular layers on top, if that can be done logically.

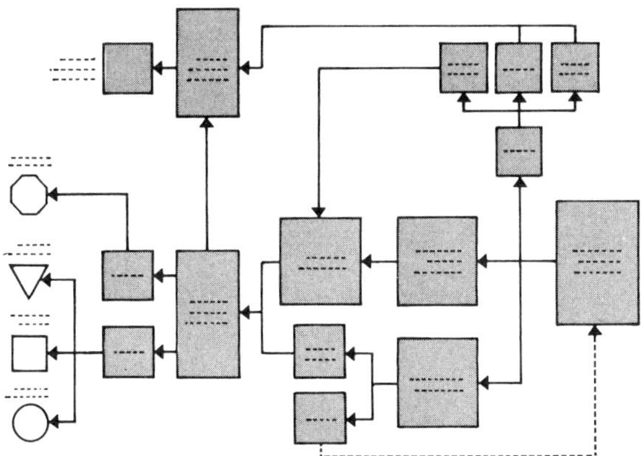

The *flow chart* is a favorite tool for portraying sequences in natural processes and organized operations, lines of command in organizations, time stages in development, and other subjects.

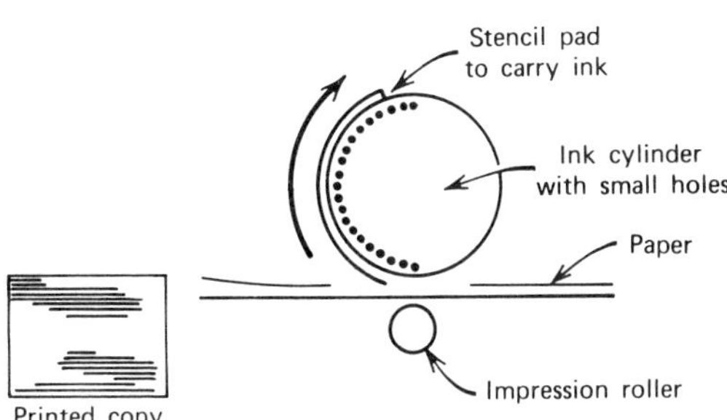

The *cross-sectional diagram* is useful for showing the operation or composition of a machine, material, or other object. This diagram, reproduced with permission from John B. Bennett, *Editing for Engineers* (New York: John Wiley, 1970), p. 122, shows the stencil process. It is a good example of clarity because it shows at a glance the essential relationships the reader wants to know, without complicating details.

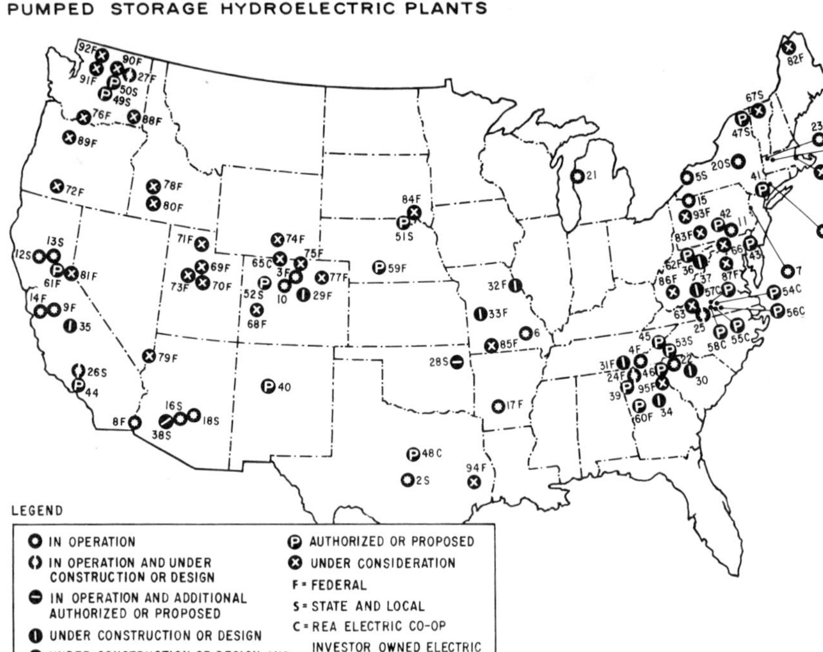

The *geographical* chart is simply a map, not necessarily drawn to scale, of operations, activities, resources, or other subjects of interest. It is one of the most common types of visual exhibits.

When we amateurs try to frost the cake this way, however—or have a colleague do it for us—the results are almost always deplorable. Baubles sit on bars, cartoonlike cars run up and down trend lines, a rising sales projection explodes into a corny sketch of a missile, stereotypes of bright or droopy faces hover like drunks near the bars of bar charts, little square-box factories squat puffing smoke in the background of area charts, and so on. The less resemblance business and professional communications bear to cartoon strips, the better.

Another temptation to which we amateurs often succumb is overdrawing the parts of a machine, process, cross-section of material, or other subject of a diagram.

Don't try to be as meticulous about shapes, appearances, relative proportions, and other such matters as, say, the art editors of *Scientific American* are. Fanciness is not necessary. Nor are you likely to succeed—chances are you will only muddy up the picture or waste time you should be investing in the substance of your communication or on some other problem.

USE APPROPRIATE PLOTTING SCALES

You can make a mediocre sales increase climb off the page like Jack on the beanstalk if you put the years close together on the horizontal axis and the sales marks far apart on the vertical axis. You can iron out vital differences in two contrasting trend lines by using logarithmic scales. You can temporarily conceal important changes going on among different variables by using pie charts instead of grouped bar charts.

All these things and others you *can* do with charts by manipulating the scales and diagrams—but don't. No matter how partisan your approach to a problem, use scales fairly and in the manner normally shown in books and magazines containing competent chartwork. Make your side of the case, if that is your mission, by the relationships you emphasize and the facts and ideas you can produce, not by manipulating mechanical media. Like bad and good money, funny charts tend to drive out good charts; besides, they can come back to haunt you someday.

REPORT ALL THE FACTS NEEDED TO SHOW A FAIR PICTURE

The emphasis here is on the word *fair*. If your chart emphasizes an increase in the value of your plant and much of that increase is due to inflation, you should show the effect of inflation. If your diagram shows power-line radiation measurements over a period of time and large-scale magnetospheric disturbances have an important effect on those measurements, your information on the disturbances also should be plotted.

USE SIMPLE, HELPFUL WORDING

The titles, labels, and captions accompanying your charts and graphs should be informative and as brief as possible. A verbose, jargony, pythonlike title at the top of a visual is far more conspicuous than it would be if coiled up somewhere in the text. Far better it is to choose a readable title that captures the essence of the chart than a long title full of qualifications; if necessary, you can always add the qualifications in the body of your document.

Best of all, see if you can devise a title that expresses the main message of the chart or graph. Such titles—often referred to as "narrative" or "statement" titles—are seen with increasing frequency in written communications. A senior researcher at Union Oil Company Research Center offers the following illustrations:[2]

Instead of	*You might write*
Selective plugging of stratified systems	Selective plugging can increase oil recovery from stratified systems
Pumpability of red-feather crude oil	Carbon dioxide increases the pumpability of red-feather crude oil

MAKING THE DATA AS READABLE AS POSSIBLE

If the chart or graph contains figures representing hundreds, thousands, millions, or billions of dollars, units, people, or some other item, be sure to write "Figures in thousands," or whatever, at the top, bottom, or sides of the drawing.

If abbreviations are used to denote lines, bars, or other

[2]Raymond A. Rogers, *How to Report Research & Development Findings to Management* (New York: Pilot Books, 1973), p. 9.

parts of the drawing, they should be spelled out, either in the body of the document or in a note beneath the chart.

If the drawing contains different components (as in some of the illustrative drawings in this chapter), you may be unable to label them clearly in the space available. In such a case you can use different textures for the bars, segments, or other parts—cross-hatching for one part, dots for another, solid black for another, and so on. In a "key" or "legend" beneath the drawing, show a small sample of each texture and, beside it, indicate what it stands for.

Sometimes it is desirable to add a brief explanation, usually beneath the chart, graph, or diagram, of what it purports to show. Such explanations should be short enough to read quickly while studying the drawing.

TIE THE CHART IN WITH YOUR WRITTEN PRESENTATION

Refer to the chart or diagram in the text of your document. Place it as close as possible to the section of the text where you discuss it. (Don't put it before the first mention in the text, however, for then readers don't understand yet why the chart is there.) By placing the chart near the place where it is mentioned, you can spare readers the annoyance of holding a thumb on page 11 while eyeing the drawing discussed at the bottom of page 3.

For technical writers in particular, L. L. Farkas offers the following sound advice in planning a report, academic paper, or article:

> In a technical paper you will often need sketches, drawings, tables or photographs to illustrate your text. Unless you plan for these you may end up with your paper completed minus the necessary illustrations. Examine the main points in your outline and decide where an illustration will help clarify the thought. You may want a sketch of a text set-up, a drawing or a photographic slide of equipment. At another point you may want to present a chart to discuss data obtained in an experiment. A drawing may be required to show construction. You may even want to show how you derived a particular formula. . . .

Once you have decided on the illustrations needed, you can make a separate illustration plan, or note the requirement beside the various points listed in your outline. The plan will act as a reminder that you must either do the work yourself or get someone else, like a presentation group, started so that you can have the illustrations ready with the paper. The notes in your outline remind you to refer to the illustrations as you write the paper. Some authors forget this. They add beautiful illustrations but they make absolutely no reference to them in their text. Thus, not only has the time spent producing illustrations been wasted but, worse, the help they could have provided to make the paper more interesting or convincing has been thrown away.[3]

LEARN FROM GOOD EXAMPLES

Although you probably have no desire to become an expert on visual exhibits, you may find it interesting to peruse magazines and books for good examples of bar charts, flow charts, and other types. For beautiful examples in the economic field it is hard to beat an annual booklet produced by the Research Department of Ebasco Services Incorporated (2 Rector Street, New York, N.Y.). Although many of these charts are done professionally in color and cannot be imitated by an amateur, they are instructive. The booklet, called simply *Business and Economic Charts,* is produced annually. *Scientific American* is a brilliant examplar of scientific charts, and in the corporate world *Harvard Business Review, Business Week,* and *Fortune* are prolific sources of good examples.

PROBLEMS AND CASES

1. From magazines or books, copy or photocopy charts that fail for each of the following reasons: (a) too much complication (b) too much "artiness" (c) poor explanations in captions and/or titles. In a paragraph of explanation for each, point out why the chart fails and what specifically might be done to correct the failure.

2. Examine some annual reports of corporations or other or-

[3] L. L. Farkas, "Writing Better Technical Papers," in W. Keats Sparrow and Donald H. Cunningham, *The Practical Craft: Readings for Business and Technical Writers* (Boston: Houghton Mifflin, 1978), p. 129.

ganizations for good examples of (a) a pie chart (b) a line graph (c) a grouped or compound bar chart (d) a compound or subdivided bar chart (e) a flow chart (f) an example of one other form of chart described in this chapter.

3. Samuel George Morton was a famous collector and authority on human skulls in the nineteenth century. He measured the "internal capacity" of a skull by filling it with white mustard seed or lead shot. He tabulated the following data on the internal capacity of the skulls of different Indian peoples he had studied (Stephan Jay Gould, "Morton's Ranking of Races by Cranial Capacity," *Science*, May 5, 1978, Table 2, p. 505):

People	Mean measured with seed	Mean for same skulls measured with shot
Peruvians	74.4	76.6
Mexicans	80.2	82.5
Seminole-Muskogee	88.3	93.5
Western Lenapé	84.3	87.3
Northern Algonquin-Lenapé	88.8	91.3
Natick	79.7	
Osage	84.3	86.3
Iroquois	91.5	
Ohio Caves	84.9	87.6
Mounds	81.7	83.2
Mean	83.8	86.0

In a neat pen or pencil sketch, show how you would put these data in chart form.

4. Five scientists studied the mechanism by which insulin produces its diverse effects on cells. As part of their study, they found various percentages of radioactivity recovered by Sephadex G-50 filtration from cell extracts obtained during association of iodine-125-labeled insulin with hepatocytes (P. Gordon et al., "Intracellular Translocation of Iodine-125-Labeled Insulin," *Science*, May 19, 1978, Table 1, p. 784). The three peak times shown are arbitrary designations. Labeling your chart "Percentage of Radioactivity Recovered," show the data in chart form in a neat pen or pencil rendition.

	Time of association at 37°C (minutes)					
Peak	2	5	10	20	30	60
I	4	7	4	7	9	15
II	80	68	81	72	72	70
III	4	10	5	8	3	6

5. A team of medics studied the effect on the blood pressure of six patients suffering from hypertension, of seven days of treatment with clonidine or α-methyldopa. They tabulated these data (R. K. Saran et al., *Science*, April 21, 1978, Table 2, p. 318):

	Blood pressure	
Patient	Before treatment	After treatment
1	185/115	140/100
2	210/135	160/105
3	190/120	175/100
4	195/120	170/105
5	220/125	165/110
6	170/105	145/95

See if you can show these data visually, rendering your sketch in pen or pencil.

6. You are the editor of a consumer magazine with a moderate budget for artwork. A writer has submitted an article you want to use on personal consumption expenditures. How would you ask the staff art director to show the data in the following paragraph in the article? Make a neat sketch and, if you think it will be helpful, use colored inks or pencils.

> Recreation expenditures are $72.59 billion. This compares with $16.89 billion for private education and research. What about religious and welfare activities? They are a shade under $14,000,000,000—at $13.77 billion. We come now to household utilities, where the figure is $50,720,000,000. Now, household operations are a staggering $160.15 bil. And food and tobacco even more staggering at $241.65 bil. As for foreign travel and related items, they come to a mouselike percentage of $4,240,000,000. (Compared, that is, with the total for the U.S.A., $1,093.95 billion.) Here are

some other figures: clothing, accessories, and jewelry, $89.27 billion; personal care, $15.28; housing, $167.92 bil; medical care expenses run at $106,400,000,000; and what might be called "personal business" items amount to a shade over 55½ billion dollars, or $55.65 billion, to be exact.

7. You are in charge of a report to financial executives on yields of public utility bonds. One contributor to your study has submitted the following material:

> Beginning in 1975, the yields began falling. In January 1975 the yield to maturity at market prices, expressed in percent, was 11.40% for Baa bonds, 10.25% for A+ bonds, 9.45 percent for Aa+ bonds, and 9.0% for Aaa+ bonds. Now, the latter stayed at their level until January of 1976, and Aa+ bonds actually rose to 9.48. But the A+ instruments fell to 10.1 percent, and the Baa+ bonds fell to 10.75. We come now to January of 1977, and the picture gets worse all around: for Baa+ bonds, 9.31%; for A+ instruments, 8.62; for Aa+ it's 8.43 and the yield is merely 8.23 for Aaa+ category. Here are the figures for September 1977, in the same order: 8.85 (Baa+), 8.46, 8.32, 8.07 (Aaa+). So we have a sobering picture of uniform tendency to decline in yield.

Fortunately, you have a budget for a consulting chartist. Show her how you want these data shown in chart form.

8. An important report you are responsible for contains the chart shown below. If you would have any changes made in it, show the revised form in a neat pen or pencil sketch for the printer to follow.

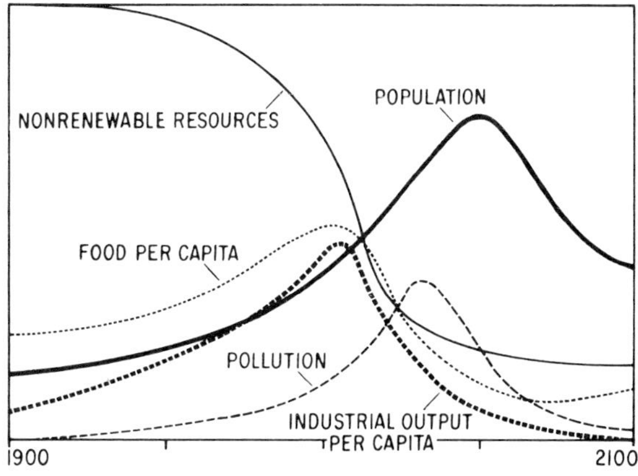

A lot of people
who don't say 'ain't,'
ain't eating.

Will Rogers

Will America be the death of English?

Edwin Newman

Chapter 11

Correctness

If the keys to persuasion are such qualities as appropriate sequence and intonation of facts and ideas; if quality of analysis depends largely on logic, the skillful weighting of information, and recognition of assumptions; if clarity is principally a matter of display, transition, and syntax—then why worry about details of correctness? Besides, if the content of your message is true and good, who cares about a few rough edges in grammar or syntax? In the words of the first prize winner of the "Legal Limericks" contest run by the *Harvard Law School Bulletin* in 1977:

> All alumni of old Harvard Law
> Are true gems, whether polished or raw;
> So why all this clamor
> About their poor grammar
> When their briefs is the finest I've saw?
>
> —Ellis Schein

For one thing, if your reports, memoranda, and letters are grammatically correct, you can save yourself from flak from those carping readers who know no other way to criticize your ideas. For another, incorrectness suggests to some readers that you do not think highly enough of them to bother with making a careful statement of your thoughts. Another reason is that errors are distracting; every time readers notice an error, their attention is interrupted, as if by a pesky mosquito or a telephone call.

Moreover, as we shall see, in numerous cases miscues in sentences reduce clarity. In fact, parts of this chapter are complementary to Chapter 9. Thus, though the bagatelle of correctness may seem to some to be nuisances to learn, they are useful. In the words of Alphonse Carr, "Some people are always grumbling that roses have thorns; I am thankful that thorns have roses."

Bear in mind, too, that unless you take pains to make your writing correct, you are going to form a habit of incorrectness. Practice makes imperfect (as well as perfect), and by practicing your errors in writing you may program them into your technique and style.

You do not need to know every last rule of correct English. Some of the details that English instructors, editors, and precisionists know are irrelevant to the communications of business, scientific, and professional people. Other rules, though still in textbooks, are outdated, for usage keeps changing, and no rule is fixed forever like a fly in amber. A few rules are of questionable value, their technical validity notwithstanding. Says Arthur D. Little's William J. Gallagher:

> Some of these "rules" are part of a "Never-never Land" remote from the practical world of technical, scientific, and business communication. "Never split an infinitive. Never begin a sentence with *and* or *but*. Never end a sentence with a preposition," read some of these "rules." With little logic to commend them, they are important only to misguided authors who look upon writing primarily as a matter of blind obedience to rules rather

> than a creative art in which the rules are used constructively in the transmission of ideas.[1]

The emphasis of this chapter is on (a) rules that may affect the results you hope to achieve in written communications and (b) bothersome errors often found in the writing of professionals, business people, and government officials in particular. This rundown is by no means comprehensive. Readers wishing to explore this area more thoroughly can turn to some fine expositions in other books. For example, John B. Bennett's *Editing for Engineers*[2] contains a short, expert selection of rules on grammar, punctuation, capitalization, and other aspects. H. J. Tichy's *Effective Writing*[3] contains many sections rich in examples and understanding of the ins and outs of correct writing, as does William J. Gallagher's *Report Writing for Management*.[4] And *A Manual of Style*[5] contains sections on punctuation, abbreviations, numbers, mathematical symbols, footnotes, and usage of special words, terms, and names which are hard to beat for succinctness and authoritativeness. This volume is useful especially for reports and documents that are to be published. *Elements of Style*[6], coming belatedly to be regarded as a kind of minor classic, offers some excellent guidance. These are just a few of the possibilities.

TO COSELL OR NOT TO COSELL

The popularity of Howard Cosell is driving some guardians of our language up the walls. "Despite the relative

[1]William J. Gallagher, *Report Writing for Management* (Reading, Mass., Addison-Wesley, 1969), p. 156.
[2]John B. Bennett, *Editing for Engineers* (New York, Wiley, 1970), pp. 85–114.
[3]H. J. Tichy, *Effective Writing* (New York, Wiley, 1966).
[4]Gallagher, *op. cit.*
[5]*A Manual of Style*, 12th ed. (Chicago, The University of Chicago Press, 1969).
[6]William S. Strunk and E. B. White, *Elements of Style* (New York: Macmillan, 1962).

paucity of scoring," Cosell says, commenting on a game. Or, "Let's continue on this point of this veritable plethora of field goals." A football team "procures a first down," and a mist drifts over the stadium "like a description in a Thomas Hardy novel." An analyst "applies true brilliance" to a problem. A gallery is left "numbstruck." A result "eventuates."

If you can imitate Cosell with style and flair, fine. Perhaps you can amuse your readers so skillfully that they pay more attention than usual and come back for more. Also, you're not really such a menace to the English language then because readers become aware of your miscues—they look for them and dote on them. But if you can't Cosell well, don't try it at all. Write as correctly as you can. If you see errors like the following, fix the sentences up before you send your report or memorandum out!

- The biology division's next step is to operationalize its objectives. [What's wrong with writing *to make its objectives operational*?]
- The governor has failed to make his programs motivational. [The consultant writing this meant the governor hadn't motivated people to support his programs.]
- There is a stampede in this firm for more horse-sense objectives. . . . [No comment]

Ralph F. Lewis, former editor and publisher of the *Harvard Business Review*, singles out the following common errors:[7]

- Substituting the adverb *hopefully* for *I hope*, as in "Hopefully, the dog went home." (That sentence gives Lewis a "mental image of the anticipatory grin on the dog's face.")
- Making verbs out of nouns when there is no need to do so;

[7]Ralph F. Lewis, "Letter from the Editor and Publisher," *Harvard Business Review*, May–June 1976, p. 1.

for instance, having one thing *impact* another thing, or deciding to *prioritize* an important activity.

Ed Kittrell, director of information for the American Academy of Pediatrics, nominates the following (among others) for expungement:[8]

> *Interface*—A rising star in the business lexicon. Everybody wants to have it, or thinks we need it. At first, the word itself looks simple enough; everybody knows what "inter" means, and what a "face" is. But put them together, and we get lost. Was it originally coined to describe what Eskimos do when they rub noses? It may be opposite of "outerface" or "intraface." I know from my Washington friends, however, that without effective interface, coupled with substantive (there's another story by itself) input, you cannot hope to have any definitive impact.
>
> *Feedback*—When I first heard this word, I thought it was actually two words, as in: "The horse had an upset stomach, and gave all his feed back." Then I asked some friends of mine who are hi-fi nuts, and they said it was a whining, high-pitched shriek caused by a malfunction of some sort. This seems to be closer to the mark, at least from the way I've heard some consumer relations executives describe the "feedback" they've been getting from their customers.
>
> *Spinoff*—A close cousin of "offshoot," which sounds vaguely menacing. But neither of these words seems to have an opposite: has any company's program ever had a successful "spinon" or "onshoot?" "Offshoot" is apparently not the same thing as a "shootout," which is what occurs when the "fallout" from an unsuccessful "spinoff" reaches members of your board of directors.

Personally, I have long since lost my ability to object to *feedback* and *spinoff* as nouns—authors throw them at us too often. But accepting them as verbs is another matter! Lines such as these (from manuscripts I have read) continue to cause an involuntary shudder: "In the months following, the computer unit feedbacked the data to man-

[8]Ed Kittrell, "Watch Out for the Verbal Briar Patch, Brer Rabbit," *IABC Journal*, No. 3, 1977, p. 8.

agement. . ." "After spinoffing the market research capability, the marketing director decided. . ."

A SHORT WO/MANUAL ON COMMONLY ASKED SEX QUESTIONS

Since the early 1970s, consciousness of sex discrimination in business, government, and the professions has advanced far enough that some traditional writing practices are no longer acceptable. Certainly we need not go to ridiculous extremes in eliminating discrimination, as some uncompromising and humorless reformers would have us do (see the heading above and the last rule in this section). On the other hand, the idea of sexual equality seems to dictate a fair number of changes. Since this aspect of writing is undergoing considerable change, any statement of the new rules must be tentative. With that qualification in mind, I offer the following.

1. **Be consistent in your manner of referring to males and females.** If you refer to men by their last names, refer to women by their last names, also. If you use only the first names of men, use only the first names of women. If you call the women *girls,* call the men *boys.* If you put *Mrs.* or *Ms.* before a woman's name, put *Mr.* before a man's name. Don't write a sentence such as, "The strongest objections to the findings have been made by Blodgett and Ellen Fales," or "Victor Hutchinson and Ms. Allison Kindle made corrections in the transcription." Don't write a sentence such as, "Henry Gumpert is a shrewd lawyer and his wife Ann is a striking brunette." McGraw-Hill Book Company, in a set of guidelines on this subject, suggests various alternatives for this sentence—for instance, "The Gumperts are an interesting couple. Henry is a shrewd lawyer and Ann is very active in community affairs."
2. **Do not describe characteristics of women that you would not describe if the people were men.** Referring to Maxwell as a *buxom blonde,* or to Esposito as a *grandmother of three*

is inappropriate if you would not think of calling Tamoshunas a *broad-shouldered guy* or Andrews a *grandfather of three.*

3. **Avoid patronizing references to women.** Such references are becoming as outmoded as the mandarin's three-inch fingernails. For instance, don't refer to *the fair sex* or *the weaker sex;* say *women.* Don't refer to a *lady lawyer;* just write lawyer. Don't write *authoress, poetess,* or *Jewess;* write *author, poet,* or *Jew.* Don't describe someone as a *career girl* or *career woman;* describe her as an *attorney* or a *secretary.* The term *housewife* is in disfavor; use *homemaker* instead. *Co-ed* is out; *student* is in. Diminutive forms such as *usherette* are being ushered out in favor of just *usher.* And, of course, *girls* instead of *women* is a solid no-no.

4. **Recognize that decision makers in most fields today are male and female.** A manager is no longer always *he,* nor is a government official, or a scientist, or a certified public accountant, or an architect. Similarly, nurses and secretaries are no longer always *she.*

   Therefore, do not blithely write sentences such as "Before commencing the tests, the engineer should test his equipment" and "As for the supervisor in the field, he should follow Directive B." Unless you know for a fact that every engineer referred to in the first case and every supervisor referred to in the second case is a male, such sentences are incorrect. Reword them in such ways as: "Before commencing the tests, the engineer should test his or her equipment," and "As for supervisors in the field, they should follow Directive B." The latter approach—that is, changing the subject to the plural form—has much to recommend it, for *his or her* usage can be awkward and unwieldly, especially if repeated often.

   There are two exceptions to this rule. First, the words *men* and *mankind,* in the Biblical sense of referring to men and women, are sometimes appropriate. For instance, it may be appropriate to write "All men are created equal" if you are tying your thoughts in with the ideal of our Declaration of Independence; again, it may be appropriate to write about "reverence for mankind" if your remarks are tied in with Biblical history. In each case you are adopting the usage of those famous documents, borrowing their tone and vintage.

In the absence of such justifications, it is better to play safe with such well-accepted terms as *people* instead of *men, humankind* instead of *mankind, human power* instead of *manpower*, and *artificial* instead of *man-made*.

Second, if there is no way to escape repeated references to male and female individuals as subjects or objects, and when using adjectives, it may be appropriate to write *he (or she), him (or her)*, or *his (or hers)* the first time such a reference is needed in a paragraph or series of related paragraphs, but to use only the male pronoun in subsequent references. The justification for this exception is simply economy and clarity; it avoids awkward repetition and wordiness, and at the same time it should be clear from the use of dual pronouns the first time around that the words *or she, or her*, or *or hers* are to be taken for granted. Remember, though, that the dual pronoun must be repeated every so often (as when commencing a new line of thought), else the reader cannot continue to assume that you are referring both to males and females.

5. **Use nondiscriminating occupational terms.** You can write *chairperson* instead of *chairman, leader* instead of *spokesman, fire fighter* instead of *fireman, business executive* instead of *businessman, sales person* instead of *salesman*, and so on. Don't write either *policeman* or *policewoman;* write *police officer*. A *congressman* is better referred to as a *member of Congress* or *representative*. (However, as the McGraw-Hill guides mention, if you are addressing a particular representative you can indicate the person's sex—for instance, *Congressman* Markey or *Congresswoman* Holzman.)
6. **Don't go to ridiculous extremes.** Those who seek to remake parts of the English language in the name of nondiscrimination, urging such monstrous terms as *s/he* instead of *she* and *he*, and *wo/manual* instead of *manual*, do not help the cause. A more moderate, more reasonable campaign would avoid producing some of the overreaction that has cursed constructive efforts to change usage, to say nothing of the ridicule. (For example, one wag claims that the next term we will have to learn is *person-person* instead of *mailman*.)

A delightful article on the outer limits of this debate comes from columnist Tom Wicker. It seems that Wicker raised some questions about nondiscriminatory usage in *The New York Times* in April 1978. The response from readers was greater than from any other column he had written. Accordingly, Wicker later reported some of the proposals—all apparently made quite sincerely—that he had received in the mail. They included the following:

- Write *hesh* for *he* or *she;* do away with *him* or *her* in favor of *him;* and substitute *hizer* for *his* and *her.*
- Use *thon* (a contraction derived from *that one*) to denote *he, she, it,* and *they;* that is, all singular and plural pronouns in the third person.
- Write *mowen* instead of *men* and/or *women.*
- A novelist reportedly was using the term *per,* presumably derived from the word *person,* instead of masculine and feminine pronouns like *he* or *she.* The letter-writer proposed universal adoption of this practice.
- A professor from the University of Texas proposed giving every English noun a gender by making all nouns feminine that begin with A to M, and all nouns masculine that begin with N to Z. However, Wicker noted, "This would require one to say that 'he cut her face while shaving,' which would be troublesome."[9]

A few of Wicker's respondents offered tongue-in-cheek comments (at least, we hope they were tongue-in-cheek). "Several readers pointed out that something should be done about hysterectomies and hernias," he notes.

One may also speculate about the impact of such rules on literature. For example, if Shakespeare were reborn and writing today, would he be debating whether to have Othello say, "Hesh that stirs next to carve for hizer own rage" or "Thon that stirs next . . ."?

UNORTHODOX SENTENCES

It is appropriate to begin sentences with such transitions as *and, but,* and *so,* as well as old standbys such as *how-*

[9]*The New York Times,* May 14, 1978.

ever, consequently, and *subsequently.* Also, sentences can end with prepositions. When you should and should not use such beginnings and endings depends on the amount of emphasis you want to give the transition or preposition, as well as on the need for variety of sentence style and any prejudices your readers may have. But none of these forms is good if overworked.

Sentences without subjects and verbs may be appropriate. A one- or two-word sentence ending with an exclamation point or question is the most common form—for instance, *Under what authority?* or *Indeed!* But question or exclamation marks are not necessary to justify fragmentary sentences. Henry Luce once wrote a memorandum to the staff of *Time* that began as follows (Luce's concern here was with economy of words, as it often was during the formative years of *Time*): "The other day a fairly interesting item was written in 50 lines. I got fussing with it. Fuss. Fuss. Fuss. I fussed for an hour. . . ."[10]

Fragmented sentences are useful to emphasize a point or impart a tone that might be lost in a traditional sentence structure. Accordingly, they are correct only if used sparingly. Make sure that most of your sentences contain a subject of thought and a predicate expressing something about that subject—what it is, what it does to something else, or what something else does to it. The traditional sentence is still the basic unit of all logical writing and thinking.

SENTENCE LENGTH

No sound rule exists concerning the maximum permissible length of sentences. However, the following observations are in order:

1. Although a sentence *can* run to 80 or 100 words (or even longer) and meet the test of grammatical correct-

[10]Robert T. Elson, *Time Inc.* (New York, Atheneum, 1968), p. 159.

ness, such length is hard to justify except in very unusual cases or if your name is William Faulkner or James Joyce. Readers become confused about the relationship of subjects, verbs, objects, clauses, and so forth.

2. Long compound sentences (sentences with self-sustaining subject-verb sequences joined by *and*) are rarely defensible. Thus

> **POOR:** Sufficient biomedical technology exists for our health care delivery, and so we should direct our efforts toward applying such technology efficiently, and the emphasis should be placed on more efficient organization and management of health care facilities.
>
> **BETTER:** Sufficient biomedical technology . . . efficiently. The emphasis . . . health care facilities. (*Or better still:* Since sufficient biomedical technology exists for health care delivery, we should direct our efforts . . .)

3. Highly complex sentences are increasingly difficult to justify as business and professional readers grow more demanding, even when the readers are scientific, engineering, and legal people. In this category fall turgescent sentences that contain long series of modifying phrases and clauses piled one on top of the other, like driblets of sand on a sand castle.

INFORMAL SPEECH PATTERNS

Even though written communications—even interoffice memoranda—should be clearer, better constructed, and more efficient than speech, they do not need to be formal. Often they are more expressive and effective if they borrow everyday speech patterns.

1. Colloquial and slang expressions may be quite appropriate in a letter, memorandum, or report.
2. Split infinitives are permissible *if* the sentence would seem stilted or unnatural otherwise. For example, *You must try*

to really believe me is a better sentence, if it enables your reader to "hear" your emphasis better, than the more formal and literary *You must try really to believe me*. Again, the author of a memorandum in the Watergate affair of 1972 justifiably used a split infinitive in his statement: "Intense pressure was applied on some of the defendants to falsely claim . . . that the Watergate operation was a C.I.A. operation."[11] The alternatives—*falsely to claim* and *to claim falsely*—would have been less natural in this statement.

3. The traditional textbook distinctions between (a) *shall* and *will* and (b) *should* and *would* no longer need to be observed except in unusual cases (e.g., legal documents). *Will* and *would* are seen freely in dual uses in good writing now, indicating both what the writer intends or wants to happen as well as statements or suppositions of what in fact may happen. This development is not surprising. The old distinctions were often perplexing for many people; even fastidious and scholarly writers were likely to confuse them. Accordingly, feel no compunctions about writing *I will look forward to hearing from you* instead of the once-correct *I shall look forward . . .*; or about writing *I would be happy to see you* instead of worrying if *I should be happy to see you* is what you really mean. (Of course, *should* is as correct as ever to express obligation or contingency, as in *I should have done that* or *Should you arrive in Chicago before I do. . . .*)

NONCONJOINING CONJUNCTIVES

Do not use such conjunctions as *and, but,* and *though* to link nonlinkable thoughts. Even when readers can see what you mean, the misleading link makes them hesitate momentarily or feel confused. This is why an editor friend of mine once said, "What drives me bananas more than anything else is the conjunction that doesn't conjoin." Here is an example of what he meant: "Donovan

[11]*The New York Times*, May 9, 1973.

was a good executive but she liked flexible working hours."

The second part of this sentence is irrelevant to the first. If the second part were *but she was never satisfied with herself* or *and she took advantage of such perquisites as flexible working hours* the sentence would make sense. As it stands, the words through *but* lead us to expect an exception, contrast, or extenuating circumstance that never materializes.

PARAGRAPHS

A paragraph is a way of grouping closely related sentences that deal with a thought or division of thought. The sole purpose of a paragraph is to make the reader's job easier by "packaging" the information and ideas conveyed.

There is no suitable rule for length of a paragraph. Where paragraphs break depends just as much on the thought and style as do changes in conversational tone and manner. In fact, one way to decide on paragraph breaks is to imagine yourself speaking the words to the reader. Where would you pause, raise or lower your voice, smile, or gesture? Wherever those places are, it is likely they should mark the beginnings of fresh paragraphs. These are the places where key sentences are likely to be found, that is, fresh statements of an idea, opinion, fact, or question that is amplified in one or more sentences that follow.

Another criterion is visual. When, for instance, an entire page (typed or printed) contains no paragraph breaks, some readers are repelled. A friend of mine calls such a paragraph a "paragiraffe."

A paragraph can consist of one sentence. The contrary notion that a paragraph should be a minimum of two sentences, of nine words, or of some minimum combination of sentences and words is nonsense. Indeed, a very short, one-sentence paragraph may be just what your message needs here or there to emphasize a point, a contrast, or a transitional thought. Statistically speaking, however, most good paragraphs range from 2 to 10 sentences.

CONSISTENCY OF TENSE

The times that things happen or exist should be consistent with one another in a sentence, paragraph, and passage. If you write that a complaint was filed yesterday because of dissatisfactions felt for some time prior, you must indicate that by your choice of tenses.

INCORRECT: Our office filed a complaint yesterday because of dissatisfactions that accumulated for several years.

CORRECT: Our office filed a complaint yesterday because of dissatisfactions that had been accumulating for several years.

Similarly, if you are describing what a person told you yesterday, report the thoughts or action described in a manner consistent with the time of telling.

INCORRECT: The customer said he is unhappy with our product. [How could he say yesterday something that he feels today?]

CORRECT: The customer said he was unhappy with our product.

INCORRECT: The customer said he was deceived by our salesman. [The implication is that the salesman was right there deceiving the customer, and that the customer knew it.]

CORRECT: The customer said he had been deceived by our salesman.

Most editors and teachers feel that it is correct to mix tenses when a situation described in the past obviously continues into the present, as in this example:

A study showed that 17 million Americans own alligators.

PARALLEL STRUCTURES

As indicated in Chapter 8, parallelism is helpful in many ways; it improves readability, economizes on words, and aids comprehension. Before using it for these purposes, however, you must make sure the facts and ideas involved can be set up as parallel thoughts. If they cannot, revise the structure. For example:

INCORRECT: The analysts found a discrepancy between actual and reported income, discovered irregularities in the handing of funds, forged signatures on checks were detected, and all this time the FBI kept the treasurer under surveillance.

IMPROVED: The analysts found a discrepancy between actual and reported income, discovered irregularities in the handling of funds, and detected forged signatures on checks. All this time the FBI was keeping the treasurer under surveillance.

MODIFYING CLAUSES

Attach a modifying clause to the subject or predicate it is meant to modify. (Whether it should go before or after the modified word depends on the emphasis, structure, and style of the sentence.) Do not separate the two by several words or more. If necessary, revise the modifying or modified words so this requirement can be met.

INCORRECT: Like any other cause of waste, we must eliminate duplicate computer facilities. [The *like*-clause obviously modifies duplicate computer facilities, not we.]

CORRECT: Like any other cause of waste, duplicate computer facilities must be eliminated.

INCORRECT: 10 milligrams of ascorbic acid were administered by the researcher to the animals in the control group, repeating the dosage every 24 hours. [It was not the control group that repeated the dosage but the researcher.]

CORRECT: Repeating the dosage every 24 hours, the researcher administered 10 milligrams of ascorbic acid to the animals in the control group. *Or:* The researcher administered 10 milligrams or ascorbic acid to the animals in the control group. He repeated the dosage every 24 hours.

INCORRECT: As a member of the inventory control group, my job has been to strike a satisfactory balance between costs and service. [How can my job be a member of the inventory control group? But that is what the sentence says.]

CORRECT: As a member of the inventory control group, I have sought to strike a satisfactory balance between costs and service.

In such cases, a helpful general rule is this: The person or thing described in the modifying clause should be the subject of the main part of the sentence.

INTIMATELY RELATED WORDS

The following rules will help you to avoid some of the most common and bothersome types of error in written communications.

1. **Keep the parts of a compound verb together unless there are strong advantages to be gained by separation.**

TROUBLESOME: We would, on the assumptions that you are willing to cooperate and will not be inconvenienced, prefer to delay a decision until next month.

IMPROVED: Assuming you are willing to cooperate and will not be inconvenienced, we would prefer to delay a decision until next month.

2. **If a verb is closely related to and is ordinarily phrased with its object or object, keep the two close together.**

TROUBLESOME: At noon on March 28 the judge instructed, after consultation behind closed doors with the attorneys for the plaintiff and the defendant, the jury to disregard the evidence in Titus's deposition.

IMPROVED: At noon on March 28, after consulting behind closed doors with the attorneys for the plaintiff and the defendant, the judge instructed the jury to disregard the evidence in Titus's deposition.

In a case like this, David Lambuth says, "The active force in a verb should pass readily over to its object."[12] The same can be said of some subject-verb connections. For instance, it is discombobulating to read, "The arrow, shiny-tipped, blue-shafted, and elaborately feathered, struck the defendant. . . ."

3. **Place pronouns so they refer unmistakably to their antecedents.**

INCORRECT: Just as Kindle began going over the data with Frawley, a message came for him. [Technically, this sentence is clear; the rule is that *him* must refer to *Frawley*. But not being able to take this rule for granted, the reader is forced to hesitate. Besides, the intended meaning may be just the opposite, as the next version, the author's revision, makes clear.]

IMPROVED: A message came for Kindle just as she began going over the data with Frawley.

4. **Place phrases introduced by relative pronouns—and short modifying phrases in general—as close as possible to their antecedents.**

More than other pronouns, the so-called relative pronouns, such as *who, whose, whom, which,* and *that,* have a chronic tendency to stick to whatever noun, verb, or dominant phrase is nearest them. Two- to four-word modifying phrases, especially those beginning with words such as *in, of, with,* and *for,* have a similar tendency. Therefore it is almost always helpful to put these mod-

[12]David Lambuth, *The Golden Book of Writing* (New York, Viking, 1964), p. 19.

ifiers immediately next to the word you intend them to modify.

INCORRECT: Janowsky intends to send you an explanation of the new control system which I hope you will find clear and satisfactory. [It is not the control system that will be clear and satisfactory—or is it?]

IMPROVED: Janowksy intends to send you an explanation, which I hope you will find clear and satisfactory, of the new control system. *Or:* Janowsky intends to explain the new control system to you. I hope you will find his explanation clear and satisfactory.

INCORRECT: Next week Muriel will give an analysis of stock-out costs in Conference Room B.

IMPROVED: Next week, in Conference Room B, Muriel will give an analysis of stock-out costs.

PRONOUN SUBJECTS OF CLAUSES

When a pronoun is the subject of a clause, it takes its case (i.e., whether it reads as a subject or object) from its role in the clause, not from its relationship with prior words in the sentence.

INCORRECT: Allison's long record of success will make it difficult for whomever follows her.

IMPROVED: Allison's long record of success will make it difficult for whoever follows her. [The pronoun *whoever* is the subject of the verb in the final clause.]

WHO VERSUS THAT VERSUS WHICH

Use the relative pronoun *who* only for people, not for inanimate things.

INCORRECT: There are few companies who pay so much attention to quality control.

CORRECT: There are few companies that pay so much attention to quality control.

Use *which* to introduce nonrestrictive modifying clauses, that is, clauses that are helpful to the meaning of the sentence but not indispensable to the meaning. (If you can cross the clause out without destroying the meaning of the sentence, consider the clause nonrestrictive.)

INCORRECT: After viewing the site, that was rocky and covered with shrubs, Banks returned to the conference table.

CORRECT: After viewing the site, which was rocky and covered with shrubs, Banks returned to the conference table.

If the modifying clause is restrictive, *that* is usually a better choice of relative pronoun than *which*. (Some authorities consider *that* mandatory in such a case.)

INCORRECT: Organisms differ in the proportion of rDNA, the DNA which is complementary to ribosmal RNA.

BETTER: Organisms differ in the proportion of rDNA, the DNA that is complementary to ribosmal RNA.

SUBJECTS AND VERBS

Statistically speaking, mismatched subjects and verbs probably account for more errors, in the writing of business and professional people, than any other problem does. At least, this is the impression I have gained from reading and working with many kinds of communications.

As every schoolchild learns, a verb should agree with its subject. A singular subject takes a singular verb; a plural subject takes a plural verb. But as every communicator in business, scientific, and professional life soons learns, the rule is not so easy to follow in practice. In fact, if you are typical, you are prone to not one but several types of errors. The rules following should rectify nine common mistakes.

1. **Use a singular verb for a collective noun (that is, the word for a group or organization) when the group is regarded as a unit.**

In United States business, government, and professional circles there in an ever-strengthening tendency to regard the collective noun as standing for a unit. By contrast, in England this tendency is not nearly so pronounced. For instance, the British say *Unilever are* instead of *Unilever is,* as United States writers say. In the United States, the following groups are always—or almost always—regarded as a unit taking a singular verb:

management
government
company, corporation, firm, enterprise
organization, group
department, bureau, level, division, agency
class
committee
sales force, production line, accounting staff
profession
jury
court, bench
hospital

Thus, United States practice is to write:

Management *intends* to attack *its* problems.
The third class of employees *poses* a different problem.
Glickman's division *has* to plan *its* operations.

One exception to this tendency is the word *number* when it refers to several things. You can regard it as singular or plural, depending on the way you think of it. Almost always this means using a plural verb with *a number*, and a singular verb with *the number:*

A large number of errors *are* to be expected.
The large number of errors *is* to be expected.

In the United States, the following nouns also take singular verbs, even though they are plural in form:

economics	ethics
statistics	news
dynamics	politics
mathematics	physics

A few collective nouns are erroneously regarded as units. A leading example is *data*. This noun takes the plural form of verbs, pronouns, and adjectives:

The data are here. They show an upturn in sales.

Subrule a: *When a verb denotes the singular or plural sense of the subject, keep the rest of the sentence consistent with it.*

INCORRECT: This group of claimants believes in their cause.
CORRECT: This group of claimants believes in its cause.

2. Use a singular verb for an indefinite pronoun.

The indefinite pronouns that seem to give the most trouble are: *anybody, anyone, everyone, everybody, everything, somebody, someone.* Accordingly, write:

Everybody who *comes* to Scott's meeting must bring *his (her)* own copy of the manual.

I will talk to anyone who *is* there, and I will tell *him (her)* exactly what the troubles are.

3. When using a plural number to indicate a sum or unit, keep the verb singular.

The following sentences are correct.

A hundred feet *is* all we have left.
Thirty percent *is* our commission.
Five years *is* the length of the program.
Half a million dollars *is* needed right away.

However, when the plural number refers explicitly to the subjects in question, it is more natural (and correct) to use a plural verb:

At least 49% of Eliza's samples *are* contaminated.
Five columns of Donna's figures *have* been lost.

4. Use either singular or plural verbs for the pronouns any *and* none *when the latter are subjects.*

Grammarians make distinctions as to when singular or plural verbs should be used, but the rules are delicate. Often the sense of *any* or *none* suggests what form of verb to use. For instance, it may seem more natural to write *none of the divisions is* rather than *none of the divisions are* simply because you probably are not thinking of two or more. On the other hand, it might seem natural to write *If any of you are going to the conference* because you are probably thinking that several may be going.

In any event, use your "ear" or feeling for the situation to decide.

5. Use a singular verb for a singular subject even if the subject is followed by a plural modifier or a plural predicate noun that gets major emphasis.

When a subject is followed by a modifier referring to several people or things, the sentence may sound like one calling for a plural verb. But this is one case in which your ear can be misleading. The following sentences are correct:

> A list of the employees requesting flexible working hours *is* in Jacobs' office.
> A summary of Blair's tests and findings *is* going in the mail.

Similarly, don't let an attention-getting predicate noun deceive you into using a plural verb if the subject is singular. Here again your ear can be misleading. It is correct to write:

> The result *is* many dollars of savings.
> The most significant addition *is* Pat's findings about corrosion and the test on colorfastness.

6. When the subject comes after the verb, continue to use a verb that agrees with the subject.

When you reverse the natural subject-verb order so that the verb comes first, words before the verb may suggest it should be singular or plural when the real subject is not. Ask yourself: What is the subject of this sentence? What is being or doing or being acted upon? The singular or plural nature of the subject determines whether the verb should be singular or plural. The following expressions are correct:

> Around the city *are* numerous superstores and warehouses.
> Behind the threats and blandishments *lies* an inferiority complex.

Subrule a: *Sentences beginning with* here *or* there *follow the general rule.* The tendency in speech is to lead off sentences with *Here is . . .* and *There is . . .* even though plural subjects follow the verb. But in writing, take care to make the verb agree with the subject:

> There *are* Ginny, Manny, and Ronnie in favor of the motion, and here *is* their reason.

7. **When two or more singular subjects are connected by** or, nor **or** but, **use a singular form of the verb.**

> Neither psychological testing nor increased recruiting *solves* the problem of medical school admissions.
> Either alcoholism or drug addiction *is* the scheduled topic of discussion at the September 12 meeting.
> Not only the Chase Manhattan Bank but also Irving Trust *plans* to be represented at Ryan's hearings.

8. **When one of two subjects connected by** or, nor, **or** but **is singular and the other plural, or when the subjects differ in person, make the verb agree with the nearer subject.**

> Not only the Chase Manhattan Bank but also Irving Trust and Chemical Bank *plan* to be represented at the Fales hearings.
> Vertically growing lateral branches or reerection of the main stem apex *shows* up in the majority of cases studied.
> Neither the Blodgett parents nor their daughter *is* aware of the consequences.

9. **Use a singular verb for a singular subject that is followed by such connectives as** in addition to, together with, along with, as well as, accompanied by, including, and not, **and** no less than.

You may not hear this rule followed consistently in speech, and sometimes the sense of it seems to be wrong, but you should observe it in all written communications. The following examples are correct:

> The treasurer no less than the controller *plays* an important role in Sarah's system.

The New Orleans plant as well as the East Texas factory *is* up for sale.
The reordering procedure along with the invoicing and accounting systems *has* to be revised.
The Mafia leader accompanied by his bodyguard *comes* regularly to Donovan's office.

Logically, this rule seems to be wrong. In all the cases above, the subject, as the reader visualizes it, is two or more people or things. Those who devised the rule many years ago probably would defend it as follows: One singular subject is what the writer must be thinking of, with the following clause (what the reader visualizes as the second subject) being parenthetical or added for purposes of comparison. Otherwise the writer would have linked the two "subjects" with the conjunction *and*. Such an explanation is only partially convincing. This rule may be ripe enough to fall in the next decade or two.

NO-WAY STATEMENTS

Jim Wohlford, baseball player with the Milwaukee Brewers, is reported to have observed, "Ninety percent of this game is half mental." Reporters relish lines like these, as do their readers—but managers and professionals should not laugh too loudly. Statements that, on their face, are just as illogical and implausible creep like poison ivy into many business and technical reports, where they make many a reader itch to throw the document aside. Here are just a few examples picked from a multitude:

- An alternative approach is to direct individual specialists to sell multiple products to the specific needs within a single market. (There is no way this action could occur. Can anyone sell a product to a need? Products have to be sold to individuals, groups, committees, agencies, and so on.)

- The probability of error in a hand-picked sample is greater than a random sample. (How can the probability of anything be greater than a random sample? Probably what the writer means is that the probability of error in a hand-picked sample is greater than that in a random sample.)
- Before we began long-range planning of our marketing programs, all we knew about it was talks at conventions. (How can something you know be talks at conventions? Your knowledge can be drawn from talks at conventions, or it can be the principles and insights imparted at conventions, but it can hardly be the talks themselves.)
- Because Mayor Miller has governed a well-to-do, white, Anglo-Saxon community, he has never come to grips with the realities of black power. (Now, it may be true that Mayor Miller has never come to grips with black power, but if so, the reason can't be that he has served in a well-to-do, white neighborhood. After all, some people who have lived in such neighborhoods are quite vocal and well-informed about black power. What the writer probably means is that because Mayor Miller has preoccupied himself with the problems of a well-to-do white community, he has failed to come to grips with the realities mentioned.)

PUNCTUATION

The rules of correct punctuation should give you little difficulty. If there is a problem here, it is seeing faulty punctuation so often in the memoranda, letters, and reports coming across your desk that you imitate it unconsciously. Here are a few points often missed.

Quotation Marks, When the quoted words of someone are followed by other words in the sentence, put a comma *inside* the quotation mark after the last word quoted.

> "Obsession with control is a destructive tendency," Millicent stated.

When a quotation ends the sentence, put a period *inside* the quotation mark at the end.

> The Japanese sales executive told Greyser, "I hope our equipment was not used in the bugging at Watergate."

Follow the same rules for titles of speeches or publications put in quotes:

> You will want to read "Planning at a Crossroads," discuss it, and summarize it for the Andrews Committee.
> I hope you will be able to attend Kay's lectures on "Phosphorus Dynamics in Lake Water."

(Annoying exceptions to this practice are the semicolon and colon, which go outside the quotation marks. But the rule seldom comes into play in the writing of business people, public officials, and other "doers"; editors and journalists are the ones who need to know it.)

Adjectives. When you use several adjectives before a noun, do not separate them with commas if they are short familiar words. Use commas only to help the clarity or emphasis of the phrase:

> This short clear response typifies a majority of the returns that Ken has received to date.
> Why do we spend billions of dollars on such a complicated, high-risk, long-term investment?

Contractions. Such common contractions as *it's, that's, they're,* and *she'll* are correct in the majority of written communications in business and the professions. Whether or not you choose to use them is a matter of personal preference.

Nouns in Series. When you write a series of nouns with *and* or *or* before the last one, insert a comma before the *and* or *or.*

> The location study covered labor, tax, freight, and communications costs, all in terms of 1972 prices.

Although this rule is not observed by all publishers, it is

valid and helpful. Professional magazines follow it frequently, and such authorities as David Lambuth support it. The reason is that the comma before the *and* helps the reader to see instantly that the last two adjectives are not joined. In the example cited, suppose the last comma in the series is omitted; *freight and communications costs* could then be read as one category, though it is not meant to be.

Amount of Punctuation. The tendency in contemporary business and professional writing, as in journalism, is to use commas less than in the early twentieth century or nineteenth century. As a general rule, commas are justified now only if they serve to avoid confusion or momentary misunderstanding. For instance, the punctuation following is generally approved now:

> The novel *The Godfather* was made into a movie in 1971.

Traditionally, commas would have been inserted before and after the title of Puzo's book, and that practice is still necessary for clarity in such cases as:

> You know, Jane, I think you exaggerate the danger.
> His talk, *On Top of the Mark,* came last in the program.

As for semicolons and colons, they still should be used in the common cases specified by textbooks. However, many good writers tend to use dashes more than in the past, often in place of semicolons and colons.

COMMONLY MISUSED WORDS, PHRASES, AND EXPRESSIONS

Here are some errant words and phrases that, though appearing frequently in business and professional communications, both oral and written, should be kept out of your writing. In the case of some phrases, typical word settings are used.

INCORRECT	*CORRECT*
different than	different from
these kind, those kind	this kind, that kind
try and come	try to come
a long ways	a long way
anywheres	anywhere
affect a change	effect a change
American government	U.S. (or United States) government
born in mind	borne in mind
sort (kind) of a problem	sort (kind) of problem
write like I do	write as I do
looks like sales were rising	looks as if sales were (are) rising
throw your hat in the ring	throw your hat up
throw up the sponge (towel)	throw in the sponge (towel)
apply on this problem	apply to this problem

THE MINUTIAE OF FORM

We have been considering the minutiae of writing in organizations and the professions. One by one, these minutiae are not momentous. Some of them are petty details, some are easily overlooked by readers, some won't even be noticed by many readers. Yet errors in correctness, taken together, are important. Like the dust and ice in Saturn's rings, accumulated errors are barriers, impediments, obstacles to penetration. As Saturn is obscured by its rings, so may a fine idea or piece of information be obscured by errors in syntax, structure, grammar, and punctuation. These errors become the grains of sand that obscure a reader's vision and impede understanding.

Edwin Newman, NBC's "house grammarian," sees the subject in larger terms:

The rules of language cannot be frozen and immutable; they will reflect what is happening in society whether we want them to or not. Moreover, just as libraries, which are storehouses of wisdom, are also storehouses of unwisdom, so will good English, being available to all, be enlisted in evil causes. Still, it remains true that since nothing is more important to a society than the language it uses—there would be no society without it—we would be better off if we spoke and wrote with exactness and grace, and if we preserved, rather than destroyed, the value of our language.[13]

PROBLEMS AND CASES

1. Notions about sexism in nonfiction writing are changing. If you could write the rules, what would you add to, subtract from, or change in the section on sexism in this chapter?
2. Without changing the substance of the memorandum from the "Aggressive Applicant" at the end of Chapter 6, edit Patton's writing for correctness.
3. Review the following copy, put out by Morgardshammar AB, a Swedish company, and make any corrections you think the company should have made.

> When the Granges Company decided to build a pelletizing plant at their iron mine at Grangesberg, Sweden, the concentrated lump ore with a certain amount of fines had to be ground to a finess, adequate for the pelletizing process chosen. The pelletizing plant using the Grangcold Pellet Process has a yearly output of 1.5 mill. metric tons of cold-bond pellets.
>
> In order to reduce the operation costs it was decided to apply autogenous grinding. Pilot tests showed that the character of the mill feed with a maximum size of 60 mm (2½″) gave a product of the desired finess and size distribution when treated in a full autogenous wet grinding mill, operating in closed circuit with hydrocyclones.
>
> The mill was ordered from Morgardshammar AB, who

[13]Edwin Newman, *Strictly Speaking* (New York: Bobbs-Merrill, 1974), p. 18.

could refer to several successful installations of the same kind in Sweden, at Kiruna, Laisvall and Atik.

4. If you had been given the following copy, which appeared in an article on project management, before it was sent to the printer, what revisions, if any, would you have made in it?

> At the moment, there are seven company projects under way. Five people reporting directly to me, with the exception of the secretary, are called "project leaders." One of these is accountable for three projects, another for two, and two part-time leaders are accountable for one project apiece. Each company project is split up into many small tasks, normally 50 to 200. Some are one-man tasks, but many require team action. In some instances, a task coordinator is accountable for getting the work done, for getting it done on time, and for reporting to the project leader. A man can be a coordinator of a task team and at the same time be a member of a task team coordinated by another man. There are 20 task coordinators at the moment.
>
> Most regular part-time members devote less than half their time to the project team. A functional manager makes up for their absence by rearranging job priorities and redistributing assignments within his department or division. Sometimes he gets temporary help from another part of the company.
>
> Up to now, nobody has turned down a team assignment, even though, when it comes to a full-time project member, this means taking on a temporary assignment with no assurance of returning to his old job. While he may have expectations of a promotion when the project is terminated, no promises are made and no assurances given that he will end up with a better—or even equal—position. The men are drawn to the assignments by the opportunity to develop their management skills and demonstrating what they can do.

5. In the fall of 1973 special prosecutor Archibald Cox sought the release of the now-famous White House tapes concerning the Watergate break-in. *The New York Times* printed several exchanges of correspondence between Cox and other principals in the struggle. The following

letter to Cox, dated October 19, 1973, came from Charles Alan Wright, a member of the President's legal staff. If you had been given the opportunity to edit this letter, how, if at all, would you have changed it?

Dear Archie:

This is in response to your letter of this date. It is my conclusion from that letter that further discussions between us seeking to resolve this matter by compromise would be futile, and that we will be forced to take the actions that the President deems appropriate in these circumstances. I do wish to clear up two points, however. . . .

I note these points only in the interest of historical accuracy, in the unhappy event that our correspondence should see the light of day. As I read your comments of the 18th and your letter of the 19th, the differences between us remain so great that no purpose would be served by further discussion of what I continue to think was a "very reasonable"—indeed an unprecedentedly generous—proposal that the Attorney General put to you in an effort, in the national interest, to resolve our disputes by mutual agreement at a time when the country would be particularly well served by such agreement.

Sincerely,

6. Edit the following copy, which was printed for customers by a flower retailer.

LUDWIG AMARYLLIS

Cultural Directions

POTTING & GROWING INSTRUCTIONS

You will have success with Ludwig Amaryllis if you follow a few simple rules.

Amaryllis can be potted from November until April. Use a fairly deep flower pot which is about an inch larger in circumference than the bulb, and place a small stone or similar object on the hole in the bottom of the pot. Plant the bulb about half its depth above the top of the soil. Place your amaryllis in a warm shaded place, preferably where it has gentle bottom heat (70–75°). Even temperature day and night will give the best results. Very little water should be given until the bud is formed.

Once the flower bud is well developed the pot could be placed in a cooler and lighter atmosphere (not direct sunlight). At this stage the roots can stand more moisture and regular watering is required.

When the amaryllis is in full bloom, cool night temperature (50°) will lengthen your flower's life.

HOW TO PRESERVE BULBS FOR THE FOLLOWING YEAR

After flowering, the bulb should be kept growing indoors by keeping the soil moist. Add a little plant food from time to time. When chance of frost outside is past take pot with plant and plunge this in the garden, preferably in semi-shade. Top of the pot should be about 2 inches below soil level. Dehydrated manure can be placed on top of the soil around the pot. This treatment will enable the bulb to regain strength and firmness which it has lost while producing flowers. Before any frost occurs possibly the latter part of September or early October, take the pot and the plant out of the soil. Store in a dry place about 65° and stop watering completely. The foliage will gradually turn yellow and when it has done so, you may cut off the foliage 2 inches above the top of the bulb. Leave the pot dry and undisturbed for a month or two and then repeat the potting and growing instructions mentioned above.

ADDITIONAL HINTS

An earthen pot is better when plunging the pot outside than using a plastic pot.

This bulb can be kept growing indoors if you have no place for planting outside. Just keep watering it and give it some plant food every few weeks. You may cut the foliage off the latter part of October—then follow the above instructions.

7. The following paragraphs are the beginning of a proposal for a study of the nature of corporate planning. Assume you are a good friend of the authors of the proposal and they have asked you to "fix it up" for them. If your changes are more than minor, write a fresh version of this material.

We believe that a functionally organised profit center will structure and operate its planning system in a manner which reflects its business environment, corporate objectives, strengths and weaknesses and its organizational structure.

We hypothesize that a relationship exists between characteristics of the business situation and elements of the Formal Planning system design. Specifically we feel that the situational factors will be reflected in the system output and that specific industries will organize in a particular manner. For example, one hypothesis would be that Integrated Capital Intensive companies would conduct planning at top management and staff level only, that contradiction and optimisation would be an important feature of the planning system and that the plan would be closely tied to budget setting, capital budgeting and performance evaluation.

We plan to examine hypotheses such as these through the correlation of business characteristics and system design characteristics. We have tried to describe the business and system through measures that are clearly divided between those for which a *quantitative* measure (or *objective*) such as profit/sales ratio, is appropriate or available and those for which a qualitative measure (or subjective or perceptive measure) is necessary.

Exhibit 1 represents a framework of the process of designing each element of an FPS subject to situational factors. The model is an adaption of operating model proposed by Gingold & Norton. [The exhibit is omitted]

8. The following letter, dated March 19, 1973, came to me from the head of a consulting firm in Washington, D.C. It is reprinted by permission of the author, Sol C. Bennett. The first publication he refers to had been issued by the *Harvard Business Review;* the second was a paper he had written and shown me earlier. If you had been shown the letter before it was typed up for mailing, would you have suggested any changes in it? Draft any revisions you would have offered.

Re: The Science of Selling
to the Government
'The Correct Answers'

Dear Sir:

Upon receiving one of your periodic circulars "Handling People", I am prompted in again writing you upon the subject reference. In that we have dwelled upon the unique status of 'The Correct Answers' it would be repetitious to review same.

Briefly though, to our knowledge no other article has ever been published upon this subject by one who has had the practical experience in selling to the U.S. Government as I have.

We therefore feel that it would be a major adjunct in your communications with your clientele interested in participation in U.S. Government business CONSTRUCTIVELY.

Sincerely yours,

9. The following paragraphs are the central portion of a small brochure, "Your Land, Your Jeep, and You," put out by American Motors Corporation in 1972. Written by Ed Zern, described as "an internationally-known outdoors writer and conservationist," the brochure was distributed to owners of the company's Jeeps, Jeep clubs, conservationists, government agency officials, and others who might have an interest in driving in ways that would not harm the land, flora, and fauna. The ellipses in the second paragraph are in the printed copy. If the company had asked for your advice on this copy, would you have suggested any changes, and if so, what?

A pioneer ecologist pointed out one time that although the earth is 25,000 miles around and weighs billions and trillions of tons, almost all the life-supporting elements are contained in a "skin" or thin layer of topsoil and vegetation that's less than a hundred feet thick anywhere on earth and, over much of the planet's surface, only a few inches thick, or nonexistent. Yet this incredibly thin "skin" of soil supports all the terrestial plant life which absorbs the sunlight which activates the formation of carbohydrates which feed the animals (including you and me) which convert the carbohydrates into protein which is the basic stuff of animal life (including yours and mine).

If a super-bulldozer should push off the earth's topsoil into the sea (where too much of it has already been lost through man-caused erosion), most land-animal life, including the human kind, would shortly disappear from the planet. By the same token, every time I damage the earth's soil-skin by ploughing where it shouldn't ploughed so that the final crop is a dust storm or by driving my Jeep where it shouldn't be driven so that I make ruts that grow into gullies or damage soil-holding, wildlife-supporting foliage or make permanent scars on the thin layer of soil in a high-country meadow, I reduce the capacity of the earth to support life . . . not by much, perhaps, but in a world where literally millions of people drive some kind of off-the-road vehicle, it adds up.

And in addition to damaging the earth's skin, I may injure another important value of the land: its naturalness and unspoiledness and wildness and beauty. Someday you may take your children or your grandchildren on a hiking trip or pack trip to a remote wilderness area, to show them how the land was before man came. If you find a landscape scarred by tire ruts, you'll be disappointed, and so will they. . . .

10. The following letter, reprinted from *America's Working Women*, compiled and edited by Rosalyn Baxandall, Linda Gordon, and Susan Reverby (New York: Vintage Books, 1976), pp. 373–374, is presented by the book's editors as "an example of the constant pressure that women apply to their unions. It also illustrates the many ways in which women's working lives can be made miserable by sexist foremen." The letter was undated, but it probably was written in 1973. If you had been asked to correct it, what would your revision look like?

OPEN LETTER TO LOCAL #1299

Dear Union Representatives:

In the past four months since Great Lakes Steel was FORCED to hire women, they have followed a policy of rampant discrimination. Many women, especially Black women, have been fired for no reason at all. Before a woman really gets into the department she is told that the foreman doesn't want women in his department at all, and from that point on she is picked on until they find some "cause" to fire her. She is also forced to lift twice as much as a man just to prove that she can do the job.

Examples:

#1. This one woman's husband was a weight lifter and she could also lift weights. She worked in the masonry department. She could carry two buckets when most of the men carried only one. She got fired because she was too short and they said it was unsafe for her.

#2. The foreman's always complimenting the women on how good they work, and then they get fired for "not being able to do the work." Women really don't have a chance to pick their jobs like many of the men do, even if they might have more seniority than some of the men. One foreman would give out all the jobs before starting time. When the women got there he would turn to them and say, "All I have left is. . . .!!"

There were two Black women working in the BOP #2, and although they had the most seniority in their department, a white woman was given a bid job, when the Black women didn't know about it. They were given the impression you couldn't bid on a job until you got your 35 days in.

#3. In one particular case two Black women were given the job of rod straightening and were told to do 15. When the foreman came around to check on them they had already done eight. The foreman told them to stop. So they didn't do anymore. The next day they were off. The following day when they were supposed to go back to work, they got calls telling them they were terminated.

#4. In another incident one woman was told by one foreman to do a certain job in general labor. Then another foreman came along and told her to do something else. She got fired by the first foreman for leaving her job. So either way you lose, because there are too many people telling you what to do.

These are just a few examples of some of the women who have been fired. After all don't think any woman would be working in a steel plant if she didn't have to work. Most women are the head of their household just like the men working there. They have the nerve to apply there in the first place; and most of them work harder than some of the men there just to prove that they can do the job.

We call on Local #1299 to do its best to get these women their jobs back. Although many of these women weren't allowed to keep their jobs long enough to get in the union, we're asking the union Reps to please fight for these jobs, regardless of your specific contract obligations.

A failure to fight against such open discrimination will hurt all union efforts. Please don't allow the company to continue such divide and conquer tactics between women and men, Black and white.

Must women lift twice as much as men in order to keep their jobs?

Waiting For Our Jobs,

Women Fired by Great Lakes Steel

11. Correct the following statements [cited in a paper for a writing course at the Marlboro Training Center, New England Telephone & Telegraph Co.] so that they say what you think the writers intended to say.

a. The guy was all over the road. I had to swerve a number of times before I hit him.

b. I had been driving my car for forty years when I fell asleep at the wheel and had the accident.

c. I was on my way to the doctors with rear end trouble when my universal joint gave way causing me to have an accident.

d. The indirect cause of this accident was a little guy in a small car with a big mouth.

12 Correct and improve the following statements:

a. The purpose of the present study was to determine whether the long-term administration of desipramine, a prototype of the tricyclic antidepressants, potentiates adrenergic nerve transmission by increasing the release of norepinephrine, and the investigation of the possible mediation of such increases in release by changes in the sensitivity of the presynaptic α receptor to norepinephrine. Rats were treated with desipramine (10 mg/kg, intraperitoneally) every 12 hours either for

1 day or for periods up to six weeks, being killed one-half day after the last injection.

b. The formation of nucleosome arcs and cylinders yields information not only on intranucleosomal movements but insight into internucleosmal interactions additionally is provided.

c. A company can add space by plant expansion on existing sites, by establishing new branch plants or plant relocation following a study.

d. A process plant strategy is less prevalent than the other strategies causing concern because of its expense and complexity.

13. Without concerning yourself now with coherence, take the "Kudos for King's Grant" case at the end of Chapter 8 and make any revisions necessary for correctness.

Style is the dress of thoughts.

Philip Dormer Stanhope
(Lord Chesterfield)

Let there be gall enough in the ink; though thou write with a goose-pen, no matter.

William Shakespeare

Chapter 12

Your Style: Rare, Medium, or Well-done?

Your writing style is the product of your knowledge, skill, values, and feelings. It is the output of countless subtle impulses and experiences in your mind that influence you to synthesize words in a certain way. Style is fickle, changeable, dynamic. It may have Dr. Jekyll and Mr. Hyde qualities, changing from document to document in response to heaven knows what mysterious moods and impulses. It may grow in a certain way without any conscious thought on your part. Or it may be adopted after due deliberation, cultivated, or learned.

You may combine two or more well-known styles, creating an interesting hybrid. Yet, under the scrutiny of experts, your style may reveal certain fingerprint-like characteristics which pervade all mutations and variations. The late Fritz J. Roethlisberger once spoke of human relations as "rare, medium, or well-done." An equally great range is possible for your writing style.

Some writing instructors, in an effort to encourage experimentation with different approaches, ask their students to imitate the styles of different well-known writers. For scientists, professionals, and business people, I think this is a mistake (though I applaud the motive). You cannot develop a sound style unless you feel comfortable with it. Feeling comfortable with it in turn depends on your feelings about your audience, how your audience thinks about you, the conditions that affect the "atmosphere" of communications, and, above all, yourself. Truly this is a case where, to use again Charles I. Gragg's felicitous observation, "Wisdom cannot be told."

For these reasons, regard questioningly any advice to use a particular style of writing, no matter how finely it "sings" when you see it in print. These days, short sentences and short-syllable words are the rage—the salted peanuts of many writing courses. Style is equated with freshness, zip, verve, earthiness, Erma Bombeck, Art Buchwald, Mike Royko, and Abraham Lincoln. Write two experts:

> Style is, first and foremost, the imprint of character upon action. A warship comes into port at speed, swings alongside the wharf with a flourish and all with a minimum of orders. In a matter of minutes she is secure, a gangway is down and a sentry is at the end of it. Watching the process, a knowledgeable onlooker will say: "That will be Captain Dashing—I can recognize his style." An announcement, a message, can and should convey a sense of character. . . . While precise and terse, it should go beyond precision and brevity.[1]

[1]C. Northcote Parkinson and Nigel Rowe, "Better Communication: Business's Best Defense," *The McKinsey Quarterly*, Winter 1978, p. 30.

Now, I am sure the authors quoted would be the last to urge all professional and business people to try to write like expert journalists. Yet the inference is clear here that the journalistic pole is what the writer's compass should point to.

And this, in my view, is where the mistake lies. If it is within your power, and if it is appropriate, given your audience and your relationship to it, to write a rollicking sentence like "Captain Carpenter rose up in his prime, put on his pistols, and went riding out" (John Crowe Ransom), well, beautiful! But a sentence like that often won't get results if you are writing for many important audiences in the Western world. If, let us say, you are writing a memorandum or report for scientists, far more appropriate it may be to write (as a biologist recently did): "Optical absorbance changes and electron spin resonance signals that occur under certain conditions suggest that the initial acceptor is a nonheme iron complex called bound ferrodozin." If you are writing about quantitative methods business executives can use, far more appropriate it may be to write (as a business school dean recently did): "Conjoint measurement is used when the decision maker seeks to predict an ordered arrangement of information from two or more variables."

"For life's not a paragraph/And death i think is no parenthesis," wrote Edward E. Cummings. One of the meanings here, I believe, is that in a world of feeling, intuition, and the subconscious there is no way that any form or structure or style of exposition can capture the reality of life or death. And so we must idolize no style, let no technique of presentation become an exclusive model. For purposes of communicating effectively, the biologist's sentence and the dean's sentence may rate equally with Ransom's line about Captain Carpenter, and if they do not, only the audience and the writer can make that negative judgment, not an expert from afar.

Everything that follows lies in the shadow of this one dominating principle, like the mountains around Mount

Rainier. Hence I state the ideas as questions. These questions are useful to ask of any style, and, since all styles are relative, they should help you to get the best results possible from whatever approach seems well-suited to the needs of your audience and you.

LET VERBS TRIUMPH OVER NOUNS?

While it is inappropriate to make all verbs brisk and dashing, or even active, it is rarely necessary to go to the other extreme and use verbs that are comatose. For instance, if the sentence you are staring at, as you review and revise a memorandum, reads like this:

> Changes in DNA conformation that were the product of increases in the spacing between neighboring base pairs were examined by a color computer film which was the product of the research team's effort.

you can change it to this (what actually appeared):

> The research team made a color computer film that examined changes in DNA conformation brought about by increasing the spacing between neighboring base pairs.

If the sentence in your first draft has the saturnine quality of this one:

> In the event that the gears manifest a tendency to stick, sound maintenance involves the necessity of cleaning them with an approved solvent.

you can change it to something like this (as the writer did):

> If the gears tend to stick, clean them with an approved solvent.

Unfortunately, a kind of pathological professionalism in fields like psychology, law, and engineering encourages us to write in the style of the first examples instead of the second. Speaking of sociologists in particular, Malcolm Cowley indicted the habits of the trade as follows (but his remarks apply equally to many other professions):

> The sociologist likes to reduce a transitive verb to an intransitive, so that he speaks of people's adapting, adjusting, transferring, relating, and identifying, with no more of a grammatical object than if they were coming or going. He seldom uses transitive verbs of action, like "break," "injure," "help," and "adore." Instead he uses verbs of relation, verbs which imply that one series of nouns and adjectives, used as the compound subject of a sentence, is larger or smaller than, dominant over, subordinate to, causative of, or resultant from another series of nouns and adjectives.
>
> Considering this degradation of the verb, I have wondered how one of Julius Caesar's boasts could be translated into Socspeak. What Caesar wrote was "*Veni, vidi, vici*"—only three words, all of them verbs. The English translation is in six words: "I came, I saw, I conquered," and three of the words are first person pronouns, which the sociologist is taught to avoid. I suspect that he would have to write: "Upon the advent of the investigator, his hegemony became minimally coextensive with the areal unit rendered visible by his successive displacement in space."
>
> The whole sad situation leads me to dream of a vast allegorical painting called "The Triumph of the Nouns." It would depict a chariot of victory drawn by the other conquered parts of speech—the adverbs and adjectives still robust, if yoked and harnessed; the prepositions bloated and pale; the conjunctions tortured; the pronouns reduced to sexless skeletons; the verbs dichotomized and feebly tottering—while behind them, arrogant, overfed, roseate, spilling over the triumphal car, would be the company of nouns in Roman togas and Greek chitons, adorned with laurel branches and flowering hegemonies.[2]

CLARIFY WHO DOES WHAT, OR WHAT DOES IN WHOM?

In diplomatic notes and negotiations we are sometimes ambiguous on purpose, but in almost all other writing

[2]Malcolm Cowley, "Sociological Habit Patterns in Linguistic Transmogrification," *Reporter*, September 20, 1956.

ambiguity should be avoided. One of the most common causes of ambiguity is a sentence that describes what happened or will happen, but leaves the action taker or cause in doubt. Such a sentence may, to use playwright Tom Stoppard's felicitous phrase, "make up in obscurity what it lacks in style."

For example, early in 1978, when mice appeared in and around President Jimmy Carter's office in the White House, presidential secretary Susan Clough told the General Services Administration. The GSA proceeded to mount a mammoth antimice campaign. When it finished, it sent the following memorandum to presidential assistant Hugh Carter:

> All traps were checked over the weekend throughout the East and West Wings. One trapped mouse was found on the grounds of the West Wing. No other activity was found. Some traps were rebaited as necessary.[3]

This dark, faceless, nameless, mysterious method of describing an action might be called the Cupid style, after the god of Greek mythology who married the beautiful Psyche but did not want her to behold him. Cupid gave his new bride the run of his palace, had the choicest foods brought to her, and visited her regularly at night. But he always came after dark and left before daybreak. When Psyche asked to see his face, he refused. "If you saw my face," he answered, "you might be afraid of me, or you might adore me, but I would rather you love me as a husband than adore me as a god. Only trust me—and love me."

In an age of popularity for detective novels, suspense films, and cloak-and-dagger operations in government, it is no wonder that the Cupid style attracts many writers—"gentlemen of the shade, minions of the moon," Shakespeare would call them. So we find ourselves having to solve for unknowns in everyday business communications in the same manner as when groping with a

[3]*Boston Globe*, March 12, 1978.

mathematical problem or "whodunnit." Consider these statements from reports:

- The cost of the equal-opportunity program was estimated incorrectly. (Who was the villain? He or she was still at large when the report ended.)
- In the next stage, when the powder was mixed with α-alumina of low surface area as an inert diluent, it was observed that the presence of the oxidic material could increase yields by a factor of two or more. (Who mixed the vital powder? Who observed the unusual result? Unlike Agatha Christie, this author never divulged the answers or relieved the suspense.)

Writers use the Cupid style most often when the subject or action taker would be *I* or *me*. Why? Some writers say the reason is modesty; they hesitate to call attention to themselves. Others explain they think it distracts the reader to interject an *I* or *me*. Sometimes, of course, writers do not want to identify the subject of the action for ulterior motives. The directors of the Watergate operation in 1972 preferred to say, "Surveillance measures were undertaken . . ." rather than, "We bugged the Democratic headquarters. . . ."

A variation of this style is to refer to oneself in the third person. "The writer cannot believe this finding," it is stated, instead of "I cannot believe this finding." Or, "The Chairman of the Finance Committee reported on February 27 that . . .," when the writer is the chairman and could have said *I*. Or, "One gains the impression from the evidence that the accused is guilty," when the writer means "*I* gain the impression. . . ."

H. J. Tichy has a charming anecdote about the Cupid style:

> A director of training asked me to confer with a foreign-born engineer who had learned English while working for two years in the United States. When I met the engineer, I apologized for my lateness.

"It is nothing," he replied courteously. "A cigarette was smoked and a book was read while waiting."

He was learning engineering English fast—not only the passive voice but the incorrect ellipsis that often accompanies it.

Later I asked another engineer and a chemist, "Can you improve the sentence *A cigarette was smoked and a book was read while waiting?*"

"No error can be seen," decided the engineer.

"No improvement can be made," said the chemist, studied my expression, and added, "by me."[4]

HARDER NOUNS AND CRISPER ADJECTIVES?

Often you can improve your style by "hardening" the nouns and "crisping" the adjectives. In general, a noun is hard when it is short and refers to a specific tangible thing. Also, Anglo-Saxon nouns generally are harder than nouns of French and Latin derivation—*ride* instead of *transportation, drink* instead of *potation, den* instead of *retreat.* The same principle holds for adjectives. *Good* is crispier than *beneficial, hot* is crispier than *intense, poor* is crispier than *insufficient.* Instructor David Lambuth says: "Writing too largely in abstract terms is one of the worst and most widespread of literary faults. It sounds learned; it saves the writer from having to use his eyes and ears; and it makes slovenly thinking possible because it does not require definiteness." Tell the reader, Lambuth advises, *"that the man gave a dollar to the tramp* rather than that he *indulged in an act of generosity."*[5]

Why don't we use more hard nouns and crispy adjectives and fewer soft, fuzzy, abstract nouns and adjectives? One reason is that in science, the professions, and management, the latter tend to be common. We learn to eat them for breakfast in training programs and schools. For

[4]H. J. Tichy, *Effective Writing* (New York: Wiley 1966), p. 192.

[5]David Lambuth and others, *The Golden Book of Writing* (New York: Viking 1964), pp. 32–33.

example, often there is no acceptable substitute for words like *organization* (words like *group* and *unit* won't do), *integration, absorption, conclusion,* and *synergism*. You simply can't write intelligibly about your subject in the style of John Steinbeck or Erma Bombeck.

But there is another reason—and this one gives us the leeway for improvement. William J. Gallagher explains as follows:

> The writer is constantly trying to reconcile two conflicting worlds: the world of reality outside his head and the world of ideas inside his head. The world outside consists of specific, tangible objects. The world inside his head is impalpable and nondimensional. For example, when a person views the panorama of a countryside ablaze with the colors of autumn, he identifies green meadows, rich brown farmland, yellow and red leaves, stretches of blue sky, and puffs of white clouds. In his mind, however, he strips away specificity and concreteness and labels the scene *beauty*, an abstraction.
>
> The distinction between the two worlds is important because the more a writer resorts to abstraction and generality, the less clear and precise is his writing and the more susceptible it is to misinterpretation.[6]

Abstract, wordy, jargony nouns and adjectives make it more difficult for your readers to concentrate on your message (even though they must work harder to understand your words). Unless your readers have strong incentives to figure out your meaning, they may grow cold and turn away. For this reason the wordy, jargony style might be called after Medusa, a once-beautiful girl who, in Greek mythology, was turned into a hideous figure after she angered the goddess Minerva. The goddess turned Medusa's yellow locks into hissing snakes and made her eyes so terrible that they changed spectators into stone. When the warrior Perseus succeeded in beheading Medusa, he used the head as a weapon, holding it up to his enemies and turning them into stone.

[6]William J. Gallagher, *Report Writing for Management* (Reading, Mass.: Addison-Wesley 1969), p. 11.

No matter how difficult your subject and how technical the terms you must use, you usually can avoid holding up a Medusa style to your readers. The secret is to work over your sentences until they say what you want as concretely as possible. Here are two examples of sentences that, though dealing with the most difficult concepts, are clear, hard, and expressive:

- From the absorption of a quantum of light, which takes about 10^{-15} second, to the growth of a field of beans, there are more than 20 orders of magnitude of time—a greater span than the age of the universe measured in years.[7]
- The cerebral cortical neuron of the cat shows a characteristic bursting firing pattern on injection of pentylenetetrazole.[8]

If you must use the Medusa style at all, save it for declarations of war, announcements of ethnic purges, sentences of lengthy imprisonment or execution, and hate letters.

TRIM OFF SOME FAT?

In addition to hardening the nouns and crisping the adjectives, often you can improve your style by getting rid of whole words, phrases, and sentences (whether hard or soft). Mark Twain once write to a schoolboy named Watt Bowser:

> Now, I have read your composition, and think it is a very creditable performance. I notice that you use plain, simple language, short words, and brief sentences. That is the way to write English . . . When you catch an adjective, kill it. No, I don't mean that utterly, but kill the most of them—then the rest will be valuable. They weaken when they are close together, they give strength when they are wide apart. An adjective habit, or a wordy, diffuse, or flowery habit, once fastened upon a person, is as hard to get rid of as any other vices.[9]

[7]William W. Parson, writing in *Science*, May 19, 1978, p. 756.
[8]Eiichi Sugaya and Minoru Onozuka, writing in *Science*, May 19, 1978, p. 799.
[9]Quoted by Mary Bromage in *Writing for Business* (Ann Arbor, Mich.: The University of Michigan Press, 1965), p. 138.

The business and professional world is notorious for its fatty language. It is dispiriting. We get in the habit of writing in the style of a letter from a credit company or a summons to appear in court. As writer Mary McCarthy once noted, we use words and phrases that seem to have been born in a briefcase, like the compendious ones we carry around. If the U.S. Treasury could take $1 for each unnecessary word and phrase used in our written communications during an average year, the national debt could be paid off.

See if you can make more frequent use of contractions. See if you can write *since* instead of *in view of the fact that*, *to* instead of *in order to*, *like* instead of *along the lines of*, *if* instead of *in the event of*. See if you have sentences like *It would be desirable for marketing managers to be present* which can be changed simply to *Marketing managers should be present*, or sentences like *This problem is one that must be watched carefully* that can be changed to *This problem must be watched carefully*.

See if you have phrases like *make an evaluation* that can be changed simply to *evaluate*, like *lead to the result of* that can be changed to *result in*, or like *come to the conclusion* that can be changed to *conclude*. See if you have word-polluting sentences like *Mr. Cook failed to properly appearance-maintain his car*[10] which can be boiled down to the real meaning, *Mr. Cook didn't wax his car*.

In one of his regular "Sunday Observer" columns for *The New York Times Magazine* Russell Baker did a spoof of fatty language that makes the point as well as exposition can:

> Utile.
>
> That was how Carruthers felt. Naturally, he worked for the Government. It is the nation's biggest employer of the utile. This is because one of its biggest jobs is utilizing. If you have a lot of utilizing to do, it is vital to have utile people on the payroll.
>
> One day Carruthers was utilizing busily when he noticed a capa-

[10] Attributed to General Motors Corp. by *The Wall Street Journal*, April 9, 1976.

> bility sitting in the corridor. Carruthers had just utilized the water cooler and was returning to his office to utilize the telephone, and he noticed the capability watching him. Carruthers did not like that.
>
> This, he realized, might very well be the Government's investigative capability checking to see if Carruthers had become redundant. It was time to engage in the decision-making process, but there were so many processes surrounding him—they were essential to the government process—that he made a mistake and wound up engaged in the political process.
>
> It was less harrowing than the legal process, and the other persons wandering about inside were friendly. "Can you direct me to the decision-making process?" Carruthers inquired. "Straight ahead until you pass the final boarding process of the flight to Cleveland, then sharp right," said the man.
>
> That was the kind of input Carruthers admired. It enabled a man to adopt a policy that could be implemented. Carruthers enjoyed implementing things, but especially policies. He immediately undertook the implementation process . . .[11]

As the poet Alexander Pope once wrote, "Words are like leaves; and where they most abound /Much fruit of sense beneath is rarely found."

SEASON AND COOK LESS?

"In one of the old Marx Brothers' movies," Ralph F. Lewis remembers, "Groucho's secretary came into his office and said, 'Messrs. Smith and Jones have been waiting in the outer office for over an hour and they are waxing wroth.' Groucho's reply was something like, 'Send Roth in and tell the other two bums to wait.'"[12]

Our business and professional communications are full of overseasoned, overcooked prose, most of it the result of trying too hard, of pretending to too much, or of imitating

[11]Russell Baker, "Minimizing Intelligibility," *The New York Times Magazine*, July 3, 1977.

[12]Ralph F. Lewis, "Letter from the Editor and Publisher," *Harvard Business Review*, May–June 1976, p. 1.

the wrong writers. If wordiness and redundancy (*periphrasis*, if you want a more technical word) are the only sad results, writer and reader both can feel lucky, for often the result is that plus ridiculousness. For example:

- The admissions director at Vassar College mentions exotic verbiage like the following in letters of recommendation for candidates: "She can be trusted to not only exploit college like a striphammer, but to replace every bit of topsoil—fertilized as well."[13] Was the writer penning these lines from the cab of a bulldozer?
- A person who had worked "in a veritable Bloomsbury of corporate memo writing," a company in the food industry, saved the following example from a memorandum by a motivational research director on consumer attitudes toward rice: "Rice suggests a strong female—young, healthy, blessed with great fertility. Respondents seem to subconsciously associate the behavior of rice while cooking with biological phenomenon. Rice gains life while it cooks. It expands and swells. It is as if little eggs were maturing fast, ready to burst into new life at any moment."[14]

If Jack the Ripper had sat at the feet of modern writers who habitually overseason and overcook, Sydney J. Harris muses that he might have produced an explanation like this for his crimes: "I regret that my sexual anomalies, stemming from a repression in childhood, led me to indiscreet violations of the persons of some ladies."[15] Damon Runyan injected such rhetoric into the conversations of the con men he wrote about in order to make his short stories humorous.

The pretentious writer reminds me of Icarus. In Greek mythology Icarus was the son of Daedalus. The father made wings for himself and his son out of feathers and

[13]Richard W. Moll, "College Admissions: A War of Words," *The Wall Street Journal*, July 7, 1978.
[14]Helen R. Stephenson, "Sexy Rice as a Conceptual Input," *The Wall Street Journal*, September 26, 1974.
[15]Sydney J. Harris, undated syndicated column.

light wooden frames, and together they flew to Sicily. Despite his father's warning not to fly too high, Icarus became intoxicated with the thrills of flight and soared up and up. The wax in his wings melted and he crashed to his death in the sea.

In the hands of an experienced writer, flowery prose and lofty feeling may come off well. In the hands of the average business person or professional, however, there is a danger that the wax between ideas will melt while the writer waxes.

Here are some suggestions for avoiding overseasoned writing:

1. Write your memorandum, letter, or report in the single, direct, everyday terms that (one hopes) you use in conversation.
2. Don't try too hard to avoid repetition. In overreacting to injunctions against tiresome repetition of a word, we sometimes go to the other extreme and make things even worse. A simple word like *house* becomes *abode, habitat, living quarters, building, domicile, place of habitation,* and so on—one after the other in a self-conscious, confusing succession in a short space. Far better it would be to let the word *house* get repeated several times and use just one or two synonyms. The late Charles W. Morton devised a label for the synonym craze that has stood the test of time. His label is "Elongated Yellow Fruit School of Writing." He explained: "It was around two decades ago, in the city room of the Boston *Evening Transcript,* that I first became aware of the elongated-yellow-fruit school of writing. The phrase turned up in a story . . . about some fugitive monkeys, and the efforts of police to capture them by using bananas as bait."[16]
3. Use clichés judiciously, for often they sound overly ripe in a business report or scientific paper. When reviewing your message before typing up a smooth version and sending it out, lop off anything that sounds like this: "In the wake of

[16]John Bartlett, *Familiar Quotations,* 14th ed. (Boston, Little, Brown, 1968), pp. 1045–1046.

the death of an underworld figure who came under fire from the mob, a reputed Mafia kingpin was struck down in a bowling alley." Or, as one friend of mine urges with a twinkle in his eye, "Avoid clichés like the plague."

4. Avoid clumsy suffixes. A suffix (i.e., syllables added at the ends of words to give them new meanings) like *-ness* in *gentleness* is fine, but a suffix like *-wise* tacked on to a noun that doesn't need it is an atrocity. Examples are "Clientwise we are in good shape" (from a lawyer's letter) and "Budgetwise we have a number of obstacles to overcome"(from a controller's report). Perhaps the point could be made best by stating the rule as follows: "Don't go off the deep end suffixwise . . ."
5. Don't switch your metaphors at midstream. If you begin a sentence with a metaphor about, say, animal life, don't end the sentence with a metaphor about the stars at night. In fact, it is usually advisable to wait until the next paragraph or later before switching to another metaphor. If you do not restrain yourself you may end up with a sentence like this (from a letter about the controversial removal of a college administrator): "Dean Gross stands in sharp contrast to the hand-wringing mollusk-type administrator who gains his sustenance from tilting with windmills."[17]

VARY THE STYLE MORE OFTEN?

Just as a baseball pitcher with a great fastball needs a change of pace to be as effective as possible, so a writer with one good style should try to mix it with a few others. In The *Pentagon Papers,* for example, we find some examples of "shirtsleeves English" mixed in with technical passages and "Pentagon English" to make the whole message more effective. Thus William P. Bundy, an accomplished writer, turns to such phrases as "tit-for-tat actions" and "unused dirty tricks" to vary his style in a very serious memorandum on military strategy; and George W. Ball changes the pace of an important memo-

[17]Editorial page, *The New York Times,* May 19, 1978.

randum to the President by using such phrases as "catcalls from the sidelines" and "pull the rug out from under us."[18]

In addition—and perhaps more useful still—try to vary the structure of your sentences so that they aren't monotonous. For instance, a simple statement such as "Employee turnover increased in 1973" can be written "In 1973, employee turnover increased," "Increases in employee turnover took place in 1973," "1973 was a year of increasing turnover among employees," and so on. Almost always, too, a series of long sentences can be interrupted by one or two short sentences, and vice versa.

Benjamin Franklin had Poor Richard say: "After three days, men grow weary of a wench, a guest, and rainy weather." The paradigm in writing is that after about three paragraphs readers grow weary of an unvarying style.

BE MORE PERSONAL AND COLLOQUIAL?

One of the most potent styles is one that mirrors some flair of the writer in personal conversation, some notable or memorable manner of presenting himself or herself. Although this style can misfire disastrously if used inappropriately (as in a letter that demands a more formal tone because of the subject matter, such as a death or a personal crisis), it is so powerful in the right circumstances that business and professional people should consider it.

Harold Ross, the famous founding editor of *The New Yorker*, was renowned for a kind of brassy, mischievous, exaggerating manner in personal dialogue. Some of his letters are marvelous examples of that style in print. For example, in 1936 *The New Yorker* scheduled a profile of *Time*. Written by Wolcott Gibbs, the piece was a parody. Ross let Henry Luce, *Time's* editor-in-chief, see the piece

[18]*The Pentagon Papers* (New York: Bantam, 1971), p. 297 and pp. 449, 451, and 454.

before publication. Luce protested that it should not run. Ross's reply contained passages like these:

> As Gibbs pointed out subsequently in a memo written to me: "Having chosen this parody form . . . the piece was bound to sound like *Time*, and you will go through a hell of a lot of copies of *Time* without finding anybody described in a way that would please his mother." I was astonished to realize the other night that you are apparently unconscious of the notorious reputation *Time* and *Fortune* have for crassness in description, for cruelty and scandal mongering and insult. I saw, frankly, but really in a not unfriendly spirit, that you are in a hell of a position to ask anything.[19]

Luce had written that he was disturbed by the description of his spacious apartment in the parody. Ross answered this complaint as follows:

> The now famous apartment was left at 15 rooms, and I trust to God that it has 15 rooms. Our earnest reporter-checker on this fact swears it is, itemized the rooms, and supplied us with a real estate announcement calling it a fifteen room apartment. He is a faithful lad and feels the whole thing deeply. He suspects you don't know about four servant's rooms and a servants' dining room, and points out that you are offering the place for rent as a fifteen-room apartment, a pretty state of affairs if it isn't true.[20]

A GLOSSARY OF EXPUNGIBLE WORDS AND PHRASES

The famous bloodsucking Transylvanian vampire dramatized by Bram Stoker in his immortal novel, *Dracula*, published 80 years ago (and now the basis for a popular play), was based on historical reports about Vlad Dracul, Prince of Wallachia, who ruled a Rumanian province in the fifteenth century. Vlad Dracul, known as "Vlad the Impaler," once frightened the soldiers of an invading Ottoman army near Targoviste out of their wits

[19]Harold Ross, letter to Henry Luce, dated November 23, 1936.
[20]*Ibid.*

by setting up a virtual forest of impaled Turks to greet them.

Reading some of the scientific, legal, business, governmental, and educational documents put out today, we may well wonder if Vlad the Impaler's spirit does not live on. As we commence reading the memorandum or report, we are greeted with a verbal forest of impaled words and phrases well-calculated to make us shudder and recoil from advancing further.

Why does such forbidding prose poison our daily writing so much? No one knows. By virtue of their humanity, if nothing else, writers might be expected to avoid toxic phrases as much as they can. Lawrence R. Klein of the University of Arizona writes:

> It is one of the mysteries of our times that the American educational system, which so effectively teaches matrix, algebra, music, symbolic logic, bookkeeping, physics, football, and French, fails so utterly at teaching students to write in their own language with lucidity if not with grace. The sins of the English teacher, especially at the junior and senior high school level, are egregious, and strain the powers of redemption.[21]

The glossary that follows contains several lists of words and phrases that, as the saying goes, would be much improved by death. The lists omit some words and phrases that logically should be included. The trouble is they have become so well impaled in the language that it is too late to expunge them.

If it is easier to describe the offensive word or phrase by an example, it is put in a typical phrase, and the improved version uses that phrase, too. Sometimes an alternative improvement is listed (after a slash). Often the suggested improvements are only examples; a different sentence might call for a slightly different substitute expression. For instance, *concerning* is given as the recom-

[21]Lawrence R. Klein, "The Doctoral Dissertation: Writing Without Fun or Profit?" *Proceedings of the 1978 Annual Spring Meeting, Industrial Relations Research Association* (Madison, Wis.: IRRA, 1978), p. 547.

mended substitute for *with reference to*, but in some sentences a substitute like *about* or *as for* would be more appropriate.

Word or phrase	*Example of improvement*
1. *Descriptions and specifications*	
9 *a.m. in the morning*	9 a.m.
a substantial segment of the population	many people
absolutely complete	complete
achieve purification	purify
adequate enough	adequate
any and all	any/any or all
at a price of $6	at $6
at the present writing	now
at this time	now
at your earliest convenience	as soon as you can
basic fundamentals	fundamentals
enclose my *check in the amount of*	enclose my check for
circle around	circle
circulate around	circulate
collect together	collect
connect up	connect
cost about $65.95	cost $65.95
descend down	descend
disappear from sight	disappear
during the year of 1978	during 1978
each and every one of us	each of us/all of us
early beginnings	beginnings
empty out	empty
end result	result
enclosed herein	enclosed
enter in the program	enter the program
exactly identical	identical
few (many) *in number*	few (many)
first and foremost	first
following after	after

give an estimate	estimate
have duly noted the contents of	have read
three hours *of time*	three hours
neat *in appearance*	neat
in close proximity	near
the glass is blue *in color*	the glass is blue
brief *in duration*	brief
in the initial instance	in the first place/first
eight *in number*	eight
circular *in shape*	circular
large *in size*, large-sized	large
in the not-too-distant future	soon
in the proximity of	near
in the state of Texas	in Texas
in this day and age	today/in this age
inside of	inside
is applicable	applies
it is often the case that	often
make an adjustment to	adjust
make an approximation of	approximate
make an examination of	examine
make an exception to	except
make mention of	mention
make out a list	list
make a study of	study
ten miles *distant from*	ten miles from
necessary requisite	requisite
never before in the past	never before
not of a high order of	not very
obtain an increase (decrease) in	raise (lower)/increase (decrease)
of considerable magnitude	large
of the order *of magnitude of*	about
one and the same	the same
outside of	outside
penetrate into	penetrate
protrude out	protrude
recur again	recur
reduce down	reduce
replying to yours of December 12	your letter of December 12
resultant effect	effect

resume again	resume
retreat back	retreat
ruination	ruin
shall appreciate your prompt compliance with	please do this as promptly as you can
single unit	unit
to the fullest possible extent	fully
throughout the entire week	throughout the week
to the northward (southward, etc.)	to the north (south, etc.)
until such time as you can	until you can

2. *Decisions, desires, actions, and reactions*

advance forward	advance
advance planning	planning
advance warning	warning
afford an opportunity	allow
analyses were made	analyze
anxious and eager	anxious/eager
are found to be in agreement	agree
are of the opinion that	believe that
ascertain the data	get the facts
attach together	attach
we *await your favor*	please let us know
beg to differ	disagree
beg to inform you	think you should know
carry on the work of developing	develop
bring *to a conclusion*	conclude/complete/finish
the contents of your letter have been duly noted	I have read
continue to remain	remain
cooperate together	cooperate
effectualize	make effectual/make effective
effectuate the policy	carry out the policy
enclosed herewith	enclosed
endorse on the back	endorse
for the purpose of providing	to provide
get an evaluation	evaluate
we *have shipped same*	we have shipped it

we *herewith hand you* our check	we enclose our check
hold in abeyance	wait
hope and trust	hope/trust
in accordance with your request	as you requested
in my opinion I think	I think/in my opinion
in the opinion of this writer	in my opinion
institute an improvement in	improve
interpose an objection	object
the main problem is *a matter of*	the main problem is
answer is *in the affirmative (negative)*	answer is yes (no)
is suggestive of	suggests
it has been brought to my attention	I have learned
it is deemed advisable that we	we think we should
it is incumbent on me	I must
it is our *conclusion as a result of* our investigation	our investigation leads us to believe
it would not be unreasonable to assume	I (we) assume
join together	join
kindly return	please return
make the acquaintance of	meet
make a decision to	decide to
melt down	melt
merge together	merge
minimize as far as possible	minimize
mutual cooperation	cooperation
my personal opinion	my opinion
permit me to say how delighted	I am delighted
permit me to take this opportunity	I want to
perform an analysis of	analyze
plan ahead	plan
present a conclusion	conclude
proceed to separate	separate
prolong the duration	prolong
state the point that	state that
still continue	continue
structure our *planning pursuant to your thinking*	make the plans you suggested
take cognizance of	note
take into consideration	consider
undertake a study of	study

3. *Reference and explanation*

abovementioned	this/these/that/those
accounted for by the fact that	caused by
add the point that	add that
along the lines of	like
am in receipt of	have
an example of this is the fact that	for example
are of the opinion that	think that/believe that
as per your request	as you requested
as to whether	whether
attached hereto	attached
attached please find	you will find attached
consensus of opinion	consensus
consequent results	results
due to the fact that	because
duly noted	noted
enclosed please find	you will find enclosed/I enclose
encounter difficulty in	find it hard to
equally as good as	as good as
exhibit a tendency to	tend to
finalize	complete/finish
final completion	completion
for the purpose of	for
for the reason that	since/because
give an indication of	indicate
give proof of	prove
give a weakness to	weaken
have at hand	have
hopeful optimism	optimism
I am in receipt of	I have
if at all possible	if possible
in accordance with our request	as we have requested
in favor of	for
in order to	to
institute an improvement in	improve
in the event that	if
in the matter of	about
in the normal course of our procedure	normally
in the same way as described	as described

involve the necessity of	require
is corrective of	corrects
is found to be	is
is indicative of	indicates
it appears that an oversight has occurred	apparently we have overlooked
it is incumbent on me	I must/I want
joint cooperation	cooperation
kindly return same	please return it
main essentials	essentials
modern methods of today	modern methods
more preferable	preferable
on account of the conditions described	because of these conditions
potential opportunity	opportunity
pursuant to your request	as you requested
reason is because	reason is that
recall back	recall
report back	report
surrounding circumstances	circumstances
taking this factor into consideration, it is apparent that	therefore/it seems that
this is to acknowledge receipt of	thank you for
to be cognizant of	to know/to understand
to summarize the above	in summary
total effect of	effect of
true facts	facts
ultimate end	end
very unique	unique
within the realm of possibility	possible
with reference to	concerning
with the result that	so that
with a view to seeing, finding out, etc.	to see, find out, etc.

PROBLEMS AND CASES

1. Review the Glossary of Expungible Words and Phrases. What words and phrases, if any, do you think should be added? What items might be deleted from the list?

2. Comment on the meaning of the quotation from Shakespeare on the title page of this chapter.
3. From an article, paper, or annual report, pick an example of the Cupid style and show what words and phrases make it qualify for that description.
4. From an article, paper, or annual report, pick an example of the Medusa style and comment on the words that put it in that style category.
5. Comic strips often satirize pompous, stuffy language. Write a short commentary, with examples, on a comic strip that makes fun of such language.
6. Discuss the limitations of Mark Twain's writing philosophy as explained in his letter to Matt Bowser.
7. Find a nonfiction book by a writer using markedly contrasting styles, and describe them with a couple of examples for each.
8. From the Problems and Cases sections of earlier chapters, find and discuss another example of the personal, colloquial style used by Harold Ross in his letter to Henry Luce.
9. See if you can rewrite the following passages in more readable English.
   a. From a memorandum written in reply to a friendly inquiry to a marketing manager on the progress of his company's latest food product, a stuffing mix (Quoted by Helen R. Stephenson, "Sexy Rice as a Conceptual Input," *The Wall Street Journal*, September 26, 1974):

      > Currently, we see no major demographical skews in concept acceptance. Inferentially, since the exclusive out-of-meat stuffing preparers (largely scratch-users) tend to be somewhat older, downscale, and from small families, our media can gain polarity by being skewed somewhat in the opposite direction.

   b. From a 1972 study by the Institute of Society, Ethics and the Life Sciences for the Federal Commission on Population Growth and the American Future (Quoted by Clive Lawrance in *The Christian Science Monitor*, February 19, 1972, p. 36):

The ultimate goal of a population policy should be human welfare. And not only such proximate goals as a reduction of population growth rates. The ethical acceptability of a population policy will be enhanced by its compatibility and consistency with policies designed to meet a broad range of other social needs. While this contention might, of course, be made concerning any major social policy, it has a special pertinence in population matters. Patterns of population growth and distribution have a pervasive impact, directly and indirectly, on the structure and quality of society. . . . If it is this perception which has given rise to the quest for an American population policy, it is no less apparent that any policy which results will make a difference in the lives of those affected by it.

c. From a paper on the governance of multinational companies:

Until now we have spoken of codetermination in multinational companies (MNCs) in general terms as institutionalized enfranchised representation of workers in decision-making bodies of the enterprise, without having actually identified the exact locus of the employee representation in question. In the following we shall now chalk out concrete conceptual alternatives as brought forward by various institutions for actually tieing up and implementing codetermination in MNCs. One can assume at this stage that even if these models of worker representation by themselves for some reason or the other do not materialize, they will, however, render conceptual assistance to the development of alternative proposals if and when codetermination in MNCs per se takes the political hurdle and gets ripe for practical implementation.

10. In a letter published in the June 10, 1977 issue of *Science*, R. Grantham argued that short sentences are a key to good writing, in particular, clarity. In the July 15 issue of *Science* the following letter appeared.

R. Grantham's letter on sentence length and obscurantism (10 June, p. 1154) exploded upon my mind as one of those simple but forceful hypotheses which bring the light of rationality to bear on areas once dark and murky. It is a brilliant deductive leap to suggest that clarity of writing is inversely proportional to the incidence of grammatical periods. Grantham has done a great service to the art of literary criticism: by one simple test it has been reduced to an exact science. He has done for the study of English what Lowry did for the study of biochemistry.

Some of my initial researches on books hitherto considered to be among the foremost in the English language are summarized in Table 1. Like Grantham, I have determined the average sentence length of the first 32 sentences in the listed books. It is encouraging to note that, with minor exceptions, the clarity and lack of obscurantism of *Science's* news writers exceeds that of some of the most highly regarded exponents of the art of English prose. Even Metz writes with only 83 percent of the obfuscation of George Eliot.

The strength of the method is its objectivity. Many of us had formerly thought that James's *The Golden Bowl* was rather an opaque text, but we can now see that in fact, it is 5 percent more readable than *Martin Chuzzlewit,* and a staggering 84 percent more clear than *Tristram Shandy,* which I had always mistakenly assumed was a rollicking, roistering, and readable book. The increased critical insight yielded by this test is clearly demonstrated by an examination of Faulkner's works. *Light in August* has the amazing average sentence length of only 19 words, beating even the best of *Science's* writers. Now we can see why he was the only author listed below to win the Nobel prize. He wrote the book in 1932. But see how decayed the older Faulkner became! Written in 1951, *Requiem for a Nun* at 116 words per sentence can hardly be considered literature at all.

The application of this tool extends beyond literature. As a

Table 1

Writer	Book	Words per sentence	
		Mean	Range
Faulkner	*Light in August*	19	3–85
Fitzgerald	*Tender is the Night*	33	7–68
James	*The Golden Bowl*	37	6–107
Dickens	*Martin Chuzzlewit*	39	5–112
Eliot	*Middlemarch*	42	10–86
Boswell	*Life of Johnson*	64	14–168
Sterne	*Tristram Shandy*	68	5–292
Faulkner	*Requiem for a Nun*	116	4–476

pharmacologist, I was pleased to discover that counting words was a specific remedy for insomnia. Indeed, I fell asleep between sentences 16 and 17 of Boswell. I am now engaged in research as to the optimum number of sentences that should be counted to obtain the most satisfying sleep. (The average sentence length of this letter is 19.5 words, range 6–53.)

RYAN J. HUXTABLE

Department of Pharmacology, College of Medicine, University of Arizona, Tucson 85721

What is Huxtable saying in this letter? Do you agree with him? Write a commentary on the letter.

11. ***The Rapturous Recommendations:*** The following recommendations for college applicants were printed in the April 7, 1978 issue of *The Wall Street Journal,* in an article by Richard W. Moll, director of admissions at Vassar College. (The names in the letters were changed to protect the identities of the applicants.) In the light of what you know about admissions offices, do you think these letters served their purpose well? If you had been advising the letter-writers, how, if at all, would you have suggested they revise their letters?

a. Perhaps the finest, most glowing, most representative example of Ann's total personality and personhood is the emotionally demanding, magnanimous, character-expanding type of volunteer service she has performed at the local hospital. But the sphere and scope of Ann's constructive, productive endeavors encompass yet much more than her consuming occupation with service.

b. An able, yet somewhat inscrutable product of intellectually oriented and academically distinguished parents, Monty has quietly and resolutely carved out an interesting act of scholarly interests and personal pursuits. . . . His reluctance to become his own advocate may cause him to get lost in the shuffle of your high-powered applicant pool. But secure in his own abilities and eager to expose himself to a wide variety of experiences, Monty is slowly coming to the conclusion that it is decidedly in the best interests of the entire community for him to heighten his profile. Thus his accomplishments at college will undoubtedly transcend his rather mediocre high school achievements.

12. ***Tutelage on TSO:*** The following passage appears in an important report on computer facilities to the top management of a large corporation. Assume the clock is turned back and you are in charge of the report. What changes, if any, would you make in the presentation of this section? Although you don't know all the top executives individually, you know they are familiar in a general way with computer jargon, but they lack expert knowledge of the subject.

> What is TSO? TSO is an abbreviation for "Time-Sharing Option," a real-time software package designed and marketed by IBM that has been available for over six years. It belongs to a branch of data processing usually referred to as "interactive computing" or "interactive programming." Interactive programming is a process or mode of operation whereby a programmer sits at a terminal (usually a CRT, but hard copy is also used, and desirable in certain instances) and keys program source codes (or other data) directly into a computer. The program controlling this process (i.e., TSO) handles all of the mechanics of line numbering and textual maintenance such as insertions and deletions, and formatting. The computer can then be directed to compile the program immediately and pass error messages right back to the programmer at the terminal. This process can even be done on a line by line basis for certain languages and processors.
>
> Test data and other information can also be entered in this fashion and used to execute the program in an "on-line" mode with results being sent back to the programmer at the terminal. The overall effect is to make the turnaround time considerably shorter than when operating in the batch mode. Variations on the above process are possible and being used in some installations. For example, after editing and correction of a program "on-line" using TSO, it would be routed to a background partition for a compilation, a technique particularly useful for lone listings.
>
> The TSO package is a control program with its own set of instructions. In addition to a number of control instructions the package is also rich in instructions useful for source data manipulation and basic text editing. The TSO

system also supports compiles for the major programming languages.

13. ***Admission about Army Accidents:*** The following report appeared in the *Washington Post* and *Boston Globe* on April 14, 1978.

> WASHINGTON—Five Fort Carson, Colo., soldiers were killed during a recent 11-day period in training deaths ranging from tear gas asphyxiation to being run over by a tank.
>
> A Fort Carson spokesman conceded yesterday that the number of deaths for 1978 is unusually high but denied there is any pattern indicating the training practices are to blame.
>
> But the Army is still investigating the first of the accidents, the asphyxiation death, and said yesterday that disciplinary action "against individuals is under consideration."
>
> Pvt. Edward Sanders, 20, of Sussex, N.J., died from tear gas apparently inhaled in quantity while he was in a tent during a training exercise at Fort Carson on Feb. 13.
>
> Sanders' artillery unit of the 4th Infantry Division based at Carson had neither oxygen nor an ambulance on hand. He was placed in a jeep and taken to the base hospital where he was pronounced dead on arrival. . . .
>
> In a written statement last night Maj. Gen. John F. Forrest, commanding general at Fort Carson and the 4th Infantry Division, called the training deaths "an aberration of what had been an improving safety record."
>
> He stated, "Subsequent to this series of unfortunate training-related deaths we have received expert help. Our safety regulations and procedures have been examined and found to be in accordance with existing regulations and procedures within the Army. Analysis of our program reveals that safety awareness at the individual level has not yet permeated the command, and that continued emphasis is necessary." . . .

If you had been General Forrest, would you have been content with this written statement? If not, offer a revised version of it.

14. ***Rationale for a Rightabout:*** A decertification election (an election to show whether a majority of a company's

employees want to get rid of the union) was held in a company in which the rank-and-file were getting restless with the union's leadership. Before the election, management decided to stay out of the argument and let employees make up their minds on their own. In a written statement to employees explaining its position management said: "The Company believes that the best position in this decertification case will be to remain strictly neutral and let the employees decide the issue for themselves, in order to avoid any charges of 'maneuvering' by management." The election was won by the union.

However, employees became disenchanted again with the union, and a second decertification election was scheduled. (For more details on this case, see William E. Fullmer, "When Employees Want to Oust Their Union," *Harvard Business Review*, March–April 1978, p. 166.) After debating whether to become involved, top executives decided this time to enter the fray. In a written statement to all managers and supervisors, top management explained its position as follows:

> Finally, management aloofness may result from a belief that neutrality during an election will bring friendlier relations with a union if that union wins the election. Aside from the defeatist nature of this view, there is no indication that a union would believe other than that the employer is an easy touch, and hike its contract demands accordingly when bargaining begins. Unions (and employees) respect a hardnosed, forthright, and honest management, and there is usually basic dishonesty in a management pose that it really does not care one way or the other about unions.
>
> An attitude of aloofness, an unwillingness by management to participate in the infighting, is the great loser. This fatal, fatuous posture is promoted by the NLRB, and it is often adopted by the employer who dreads the legal entanglements that mistakes in a campaign can cause.
>
> Aloofness may also be practiced in the belief that the man will respect the management the more, and therefore vote down the union. A more likely result is that this attitude will be read by the men as disinterest, leaving them free to maintain their allegiance to the company and vote on a basis of a coexisting allegiance to the union. A worker may

> thus be led to recognize no conflict in holding both a loyalty to company and a loyalty to union. Management, by making its wishes forcefully known, will bring a clear-cut test of allegiance rather than a loss by default.

Assume the above statement has not been released yet. Anxious for the best advice possible, the chief executive naturally turns to you for counsel. Would you answer that the statement looks fine and should be distributed as is? Would you revise it—and, if so, how?

15. ***An Embattled Black:*** The letter that begins below, reprinted from Jim Bishop, *The Days of Martin Luther King, Jr.* (New York: G. P. Putnam's Sons, 1971), p. 291, was written from a prison cell in Birmingham, Alabama, during the black demonstrations of 1955. The writer, Martin Luther King, Jr., was responding to a highly publicized plea, signed by eight leading white churchmen, to stop the demonstrations. In their open letter the clergymen had urged King's activists to press their cause in the courts and in negotiations with local officials, not on the streets. "We appeal," they had concluded, "to both our white and Negro citizens to observe the principles of law and order and common sense."

    The first four paragraphs of the black leader's letter are reproduced below. Assume you were a trusted friend of King's and had been asked to review the letter before mailing. Would you have advised changes? Because of visitor limitations, you have to put your thoughts pro or con in a brief note to him.

> My Dear Fellow Clergymen:
>
> While confined here in the Birmingham jail, I came across your recent statement calling my present activities "unwise and untimely." Seldom do I pause to answer criticism of my work and ideas. If I sought to answer all the criticisms that cross my desk, my secretaries would have little time for anything other than such correspondence in the course of the day, and I would have no time for constructive work. But since I feel that you are men of genuine good will and that your criticisms are sincerely set forth, I want to try to answer your statement in what I hope will be patient and reasonable terms.

I think I should indicate why I am here in Birmingham, since you have been influenced by the view which argues against "outsiders coming in." I have the honor of serving as president of the Southern Christian Leadership Conference, an organization operating in every southern state, with headquarters in Atlanta, Georgia. We have some eighty-five affiliated organizations across the South, and one of them is the Alabama Christian Movement for Civil Rights. Frequently, we share staff, educational and financial resources with our affiliates. Several months ago, the affiliate here in Birmingham asked us to be on call to engage in a nonviolent direct-action program if such were deemed necessary. We readily consented, and when the hour came we lived up to our promise. So I, along with several members of my staff, am here because I was invited here. I am here because I have organizational ties here.

But more basically, I am in Birmingham because injustice is here. Just as the prophets of the Eighth Century B.C. left their villages and carried their "thus saith the Lord" far beyond the boundaries of their home towns, and just as the Apostle Paul left his village of Tarsus and carried the gospel of Jesus Christ to the far corners of the Greco-Roman world, so am I compelled to carry the gospel of freedom beyond my own home town. Like Paul, I must constantly respond to the Macedonian call for aid.

Moreover, I am cognizant of the interrelatedness of all communities and states. I cannot sit idly by in Atlanta and not be concerned about what happens in Birmingham. Injustice anywhere is a threat to justice everywhere. We are caught in an inescapable network of mutuality, tied in a single garment of destiny. Whatever affects one directly, affects all indirectly. Never again can we afford to live with the narrow, provincial "outside agitator" idea. Anyone who lives inside the United States can never be considered an outsider anywhere within its bounds.

PART FOUR

WRITERS AND EDITORS

All writers know that on some golden mornings
they are touched by the wand—
are on intimate terms with poetry
and cosmic truth. I have
experienced these moments myself.
Their lesson is simple: It's total illusion.

John Kenneth Galbraith

I have never thought of myself
as a good writer. Anyone who wants reassurance
of that should read one of my first drafts.
But I'm one of the world's great rewriters.

James A. Michener

Chapter 13

Writing for Publication

Managers, professionals, and scientists send many thousands of manuscripts every year to professional journals, trade magazines, general magazines, and sometimes book publishers. Their motives range from public relations and personal vanity to the simple desire to present strong convictions and significant information to people who are in a position to act on the ideas.

What is the procedure for offering a manuscript for publication? What "tips" are useful in writing the manuscript? These are the questions to be considered in this chapter. Let us focus on magazine articles, since they are a more common endeavor than books. And let us assume that you can meet such needs as clarity, coherence, and efficient organization—all very important matters to editors, and all discussed in previous chapters.

If you are thinking of writing for a magazine, thumb through some back copies of the publication and get a feel for its editorial approach. This step seems almost too elementary to be worth stating, yet I doubt there's a veteran editor in America who wouldn't stress it. At or near the top of the list of editors' favorite complaints about authors is unfamiliarity with the publication.

A few years ago some reporters asked the new National Open Golf Champion, Lou Graham, about his approach to the course. They expected him to mention some fine points of his game. Instead he answered that he played his shots with the main aim simply of hitting the fairway or putting the ball on the green—"getting it on the dance floor," he said. Similarly, before you ever shoot a manuscript at an editor, find out what's "right" for that magazine or group of magazines so that, whatever else are the merits or shortcomings of your piece, it will at least be seen as a serious candidate, as being "on the dance floor."

For some successful article writers, this is the initial step. For others, it is a step taken after the shape of an article or book has formed in their minds, or perhaps after the manuscript has been partly drafted.

What audience or audiences do the editors seem interested in serving? This is the first question to ask. Some trade journals are aimed at people in certain industries, but a magazine like *Harvard Business Review* generally avoids "one-industry" articles. Some magazines address themselves to specialists and professionals; others, like *Scientific American* and *Human Interest*, to a fairly broad segment of the public.

What is the prevailing "tone" of the articles or books? For example, some editors like to challenge, to prod, to provoke. Others appear to want most to reassure readers; like Shah Dev, the young monarch crowned in Nepal in 1955, their motto is: "I will be popular like the raindrop. I will be friendly like the sun."

Are the articles and books highly technical, or do they eschew technicality? At one extreme are specialized journals that seem to welcome almost a pathological degree of specialization in their pages; at the other extreme is *Reader's Digest.* And what about the level of detail? Some editors show a penchant for pulling wings off gnats; others favor broad brush strokes.

Does the editorial staff show any interest in humor? *Harper's* and *Country Journal* do; *New England Journal of Medicine* doesn't. What about articles that express feeling, intuition, hunches, personal experience? Or is almost everything published an exercise in objectification—in linear, reductionist, rational, quantitative, inductive thought—what writer Hazel Henderson calls "the whole Cartesian trip"?

Do the editors emphasize articles that instruct, that offer readers specific steps and guidelines for solving problems and meeting needs? This is an especially important question. Generally speaking, *Harvard Business Review, Reader's Digest, Psychology Today,* and a variety of other magazines know they are read (among other things) for practical guidance. On the other hand, *Science, Scientific American, Saturday Review,* and many other prestigious journals are read more for their truths, facts, findings, and perceptions than for whether this information helps the reader solve a problem.

Do the editors like material that is newsy, that ties in with events or personalities currently being reported in the media? If so, they may not be interested in your article even though it may offer timeless insights or solve problems never before solved. *The New York Times Magazine* is an example.

Are there mechanical features of the magazine that may be useful to you? Some journals have regular features concentrating on certain kinds of subjects, or emphasizing a change of pace from the writing style of most other articles. Some always publish abstracts at the beginnings of articles—if you submit to one of these, don't fail to include an abstract at the start of your piece. Some magazines like to put odd or special bits of information in "boxes." If you're submitting to one of these, this device could be the solution you're looking for in arranging a certain set of facts that don't fit anywhere else.

Who writes for the magazine or book publisher? Glancing through by-lines, you may find that a certain group is heavily favored—academicians, lawyers, scientists, or professional journalists. If you don't belong to this group, you may have two strikes against you before you even mail your manuscript. If you do belong, sleep well.

I emphasize questions like these because there is a popular illusion that a magazine's readers are the audience to satisfy. Favorite advice to an author is: "When you sit down at your typewriter, imagine a typical reader of that magazine in front of you." This is sound counsel, of course, but it is simple-minded. You write really for two audiences, not one. The first is the editorial staff. This audience you *have* to please or you get no further. Moreover, its pleasure is measurable—simple yes or no votes in the editorial offices. The second audience, the magazine readers, should be pleased if possible, but neither you nor the editors may ever know for sure if you succeeded. The satisfaction obtained by a far-flung readership is difficult to measure.

A magazine's audience can be satisfied in many ways. It is the editors who decide how the magazine seeks this satisfaction. Their decision is subjective. It is based on personal values as well as factual information. If the editors feel comfortable with their approach and can make enough money with it for the publisher, that is all that counts.

Over the years I have talked hundreds of times with authors who were absolutely convinced that their rejected articles had important things to say to my audience, that is, to the *Harvard Business Review* audience. They might have been quite right. Nevertheless, the editorial group I belong to has always had a certain concept of *how* it wanted to help business leaders. It has had convictions about which needs *in particular* of this important audience it is best able to meet. And so we, too, were confident that our decision was correct. The unhappy author was asking: "Will it play in Peoria?" and the answer might well have been, "Yes." The editors were asking a more complicated question: "Is it what readers in Peoria look for in *HBR*?" and their answer was, "No."

THE WRITE WAY TO START

A wise way to begin is with an outline or "prospectus" in which you describe the major points and ideas of the article you intend to write. For most magazines it is unimportant whether you follow the outlining style you were taught in high school and college or simply give the editors a bird's-eye view in a letter. But keep the prospectus short, whatever its form, and concentrate on the substance of your proposed message, not the topics. A topical outline is next to worthless for most editors.

For samples of several recent outlines that met the need for the magazine I know best, *Harvard Business Review*, see Exhibit I. Judging from conversations with the editors of numerous other magazines, specialized and unspecialized, I believe that these samples would do the job for most publications.

Exhibit I. Examples of Article Proposals

A. *Letter from Partner in Accounting Firm*

Dear Dave:

As I'm sure you're aware, most of the professions, including accounting, have recently changed, or are currently in the process of changing, their ethics codes to permit advertising, competitive bidding, and solicitation of clients (and of other firms' personnel). At the same time, there is clearly going to be much greater disclosure—in the financial reports of their clients, at annual stockholder meetings, and (in many cases) through self-disclosure—of fees paid for professional services to, and revenues earned by, professional service firms. All of this, in my view, adds up to a very different, and much more competitive, market for professional services than has existed in the past. That, of course, is a very large subject, but the particular aspect to which I'd like to address my own attention is what kinds of change we can expect to see in the way professional firms market their services. In short, my focus would be primarily on the how-to aspects of "Marketing Professional Services in a More Competitive Environment." While such an article would obviously be oriented most directly toward the interests of readers who are themselves professionals (accountants, attorneys, consultants, engineers, et al.), I suspect such readers comprise more than an insignificant proportion of your subscribers—and I also suspect that your many other readers who use the services of such professionals will find the article of more than casual interest.

Do you already have anything in the works along these lines? If not, would you like me to write an article on this subject for you?

As ever,

B. *Letter from Executive in Public Relations Firm (client names disguised)*

Dear Mr. Ewing:

Here's an unusual article opportunity.

Careerists and some appointees in the U.S. government relate more to the ivory tower than to the real world. That few in key government posts have business backgrounds is increasingly evident.

Proof of this and what to do about it is contained in a straight-from-the-shoulder article by former Ford White House executive B. W. Wing, who is now with our client, Kindle & Banks, Inc., worldwide executive recruiting consultants.

Convincing evidence is given for ascribing lawyers, academics, careerists, and the rich to the ivory tower.

Why are they sought for key government posts? Mr. Wing says because they are easy to reach, mobile, fairly free of conflict-of-interest problems and can afford taking the positions. Recruiting among other groups is tedious and not well underwritten by the

White House or other agencies. Also post-Watergate attitudes put terrific pressure on for microscopic scrutiny at confirmation hearings.

What is the solution to the need for broader-based, business-oriented intelligence in the government? There really is no solution, concludes Mr. Wing. He says learn to live with the status quo (it will probably get worse), help the government understand you, and participate in cooperative lobbying efforts with others in your industry.

The article can be available for review and/or modification to the interests of a business and general audience . . . maybe to your readers?

Please let me know if you want a follow-up.

Sincerely,
Thomas D. Hopps
Vice President

C. *Outline Submitted by Expert on Pensions (Brief cover letter omitted)*

What Reported Pension Numbers Really Mean

I. Introduction
   A. Problems reported in financial press dealing with future charges to income, cash flow difficulties, etc
   B. Impact of ERISA on financing of benefits and highlighting of unfunded obligations
   C. Uncertainty for management in evaluating future impact on the company and comparison to others in its industry
   D. Why management needs to have a broad understanding of pension numbers:
      - To make knowledgeable decisions on plan modifications in light of overall corporate objectives
      - To respond to questions posed by stockholders, financial analysts
      - To negotiate from a position of strength with union representatives
      - To understand the often major impact of pension liabilities in corporate acquisitions

E. Here's the real story—where others have gone wrong, and you can go right

II. Actuarial Methods
   A. What are they
      1. Technique for budgeting the cost of future benefits to time periods
      2. Budgeting cash disbursements requires assumptions about future events and conditions
   B. Description of alternative methods
   C. Illustration of impact of alternative methods on cost and liability numbers
      1. Sensitivity analysis to changes in actuarial and economic factor
      2. Criteria for evaluating alternatives

III. Accounting Principles
   A. Historical perspective of APB Opinion No. 8
      1. Conflicting views on recognition of past-service costs
      2. Compromise and tentative nature of the opinion
   B. Prescriptions for corporate pension accounting
      1. Relies on actuarial methods
      2. Establishes broad guidelines for judging minimum and maximum annual expense provisions
      3. Requires systematic and rational method and consistent application of methods and techniques chosen
      4. Rejects liability concept
      5. Disclosure provisions

IV. What everyone wants to know about pension reporting but has been afraid to ask
   A. What is the future impact of pension liabilities on cash flow and earnings? Consideration must be given to:
      1. Funding policy
      2. Extent of asset accumulation
      3. Future economic conditions
      4. Potential for plan amendments
   B. How can one compare pension costs and liabilities between two or more companies?
      1. Impossibility of direct comparisons
      2. Methods of approximation must consider:
         a. Effect of interest rate
         b. Significance of vested benefits
         c. Adjusting for alternative funding methods

   C. Why is there a different liability reported in:
      1. Annual report to stockholders vs.
      2. Form 10K vs.
      3. Form 5500 (financial statements vs. Schedule B)?
V. What may be coming in the near future
   A. Establishing rules by FASB for plan reporting
      1. Exposure draft of 4/77
      2. Conflict between accountants and actuaries
      3. Coordination of FASB efforts with DOL statutory reporting mandate
   B. Narrowing of alternatives by FASB for employer accounting and reporting
   C. Contingent employer liability insurance
      1. Requirement of ERISA
      2. PBGC problems of implementation
VI. General conclusion and summary
   A. Many fears of future impact on companies are unfounded
   B. While some analysis can be performed, publicly available data is not sufficient to permit exacting comparisons and conclusions
   C. Reporting standards will increase amount and quality of disclosure in the foreseeable future

Some magazines, especially general magazines with large audiences, such as *Atlantic*, *Harper's*, *Saturday Review*, *The New York Times Magazine*, and *Reader's Digest*, prefer an additional step: a draft of the opening pages of your proposed article. If so, append this copy to the outline. Sometimes my associates and I like to see such material, too, and I am faintly amused when the author objects on some such ground as "But in a few pages you won't be able to see what I'm driving at" or "I don't know that I have the proper perspective to write the opening pages now." Such holding back reminds me of a legendary incident at the battle of Chicamaugua during the Civil War, when a general who had ordered a charge cried to one of his brigade commanders, "Why have you halted? Move forward, sir, at once!" And the brigade commander replied, "I am persuaded, sir, that any further display of valor by my troops will bring them into collision with the enemy."

Sometimes a speech may serve as your "prospectus." It may come close in tone and content to the article you want to write, even though the details are different.

In the letter containing your prospectus—or in a short letter attached to the outline or précis—tell the editors who you are or what research you have done for the article. Often this has an important bearing on the credibility of your opinions and conclusions.

From your prospectus the editor wants to learn—and learn quickly—the answers to several questions:

- Are the proposal subject and approach relevant and interesting to this publication's audience as I think of it?
- Does this writer know what he or she is writing about? As Wendell Barry once observed: "What gets my interest is the sense that a writer is speaking honestly and fully of what he knows well."
- Is this writer proposing to offer mostly opinions or facts and findings or a combination of the two? Factual information, if it is fresh, is almost always of interest to magazine editors; opinions, as we have seen, may or may not be interesting, depending on the circumstances. The editor may want to counsel you on this question.
- Will the manuscript be easy or difficult to edit? If the outline itself is garbled, poorly arranged, and overly long, the editor's reaction may be: "We've got enough troubles without adding this one" (though he or she probably won't tell you that). If the outline is succinct and readable, it is a beckoning invitation to continue. In addition, the editor will be looking for any clues as to whether you will be a pleasure or a pain to work with. Many editors have a nose for arrogance and pomposity like a preacher's for sin and fried chicken. Telltale clues may be in the letter—for instance, a demanding or overly assertive tone—as well as in the wording of the proposed ideas; ominous omens may even be in the let-

terhead, as when it contains officious rosters of names, cute slogans, or pompous logos.

What about calling editors to get their opinions on your article ideas? Sometimes it is a good idea—but not nearly so good as many would-be writers think. Generally speaking, it is easier for an editor to react to something in writing than to an oral message. The reason is simple: editors trade in the written word, not the spoken word. What is more, most editors, especially the good ones, are busy and always short of time; from the standpoint of time management, it is easier for them to appraise a written proposal than a spoken one.

If you have a question that is settled easier by phone than by mail, call the magazine and ask for an editor to help you—or call one in particular if you know the name. But be sure to get to the point quickly and succinctly—nothing is better calculated to make an editor groan inwardly than opening with "Have you got a few minutes to chat?" Don't waste your time by trying to con him or her with soft talk, testimonials to your importance, and so on—it does no good when what counts is what you can deliver in writing. Most editors I know are as hypersensitive to con artists as any foundation executive is (and, like the latter, don't know who their friends are until they leave their jobs).

Should you try to lunch with an editor to discuss an article idea? As a general rule, it is best to suggest a lunch talk *after* the editor has shown interest in your proposal. However, there are some obvious exceptions—personal friendship, for example, or a project of unusual interest and importance that you have been working on.

Once you have sent an article proposal or manuscript to an editor, *stay off his or her back!* One of the best ways to irritate the people you are trying to sell is to badger them with phone calls—"I sent my manuscript yesterday. Have you got it yet?" "What do you think of the article I sent you two weeks ago?" "I'll be near your office next

Thursday and would like to drop by and talk to you about the article proposal I sent you." It is quite true that editors are slow, often inexcusably slow, I can say from experience—but it doesn't help much to pester them about it.

Submit to one magazine at a time. Only in the most unusual cases are you justified in sending the same proposal or manuscript to different publications simultaneously (and, if you feel you must do that, tell them so). You can't run with the hare and hunt with the hounds, at least, not if the editors catch you doing it.

When your article is prepared, be sure to double-space the typing and to leave reasonable margins. Also, make a reasonable effort to comply with any obvious style practices of the publication, such as frequent headings, a beginning abstract, a summary at the end, minimal or lengthy footnotes, and so on. For detailed expositions of the finer points of this subject, consult an authoritative book such as *A Guide to Writing and Publishing in the Social and Behavioral Sciences.*[1]

After uncounted discussions with other editors about article proposals and manuscripts, I have no doubt whatsoever that a neat, carefully prepared manuscript gives the author a psychological advantage as well as a practical one, viz., ease of reading. If you are a top dog in your field and the editors know it, you may be able to get away with a dog-eared manuscript (frequent crossings-out, hard-to-read handwritten inserts, poor photocopies, etc.), but it's poor practice for the rest of us.

THE MAIN ASSAULT

Having conducted the early probes and scouting approaches and gained, we hope, some promise of success,

[1]Carolyn J. Mullins, *A Guide to Writing and Publishing in the Social and Behavioral Sciences* (New York: Wiley, 1977).

you are now ready to launch the invasion. The following guides may help you carry out the assault successfully.

Time management. Set off some blocks of time for the writing—two or three hours each, clear of phone calls, visitors, and other routine interruptions. When the appointed times come, don't postpone the effort for lack of inspiration. Galbraith's observation on the title page of this chapter says it all. If the words don't come or the notes don't hang together, sit and ponder them anyway—if necessary, through the entire block of time you've set aside.

Alcohol. I know a couple of writers who seem to work better with a drink at the elbow, but such people are almost as rare as Swiss admirals. Good writing rarely is done in the coils of rapture, alcoholic or otherwise. If such counsel seems suspect to you because it comes from a timid drinker—the chastity of the castrated—consider the following opinion, which comes from one who appreciates a martini as well as the next person:

> Nothing is so pleasant [as alcohol at writing time]. Nothing is so important for giving the writer a sense of confidence in himself. And nothing so impairs the product. . . .
>
> We are all desperately afraid of sounding like Carry Nation. I must take the risk. Any writer who wants to do his best against a deadline should stick to Coca-Cola. If he doesn't have a deadline, he can risk Seven-Up.[2]

Humor. Indispensable advice comes again from Galbraith's essay:

> Reluctantly, but from a long and terrible experience, I would urge all my young writers to avoid all attempts at humor. It does greatly lighten one's task. I've often wondered who made it impolite to laugh at one's own jokes; it is one of the major enjoyments of life. And that is the point. Humor is an intensely personal, largely internal thing. What pleases some, including the source, does not please others. One laughs; another says, "Well, I cer-

[2]John Kenneth Galbraith, "Writing, Typing & Economics," *The Atlantic*, March 1978, p. 104.

tainly see nothing funny about that." And the second opinion has just as much standing as the first, maybe more. Where humor is concerned, there are no standards—no one can say what is good or bad, although you can be sure that everyone will. Only a very foolish man will use a form of language that is wholly uncertain in its effect.[3]

When the right author and subject come together at the right time with the right editor, however, humor is both delightful and powerful. Certainly the magazine I work for is not known for its humor, yet I can vouch for the fact that when an appropriately humorous piece does come in, the editors rejoice. Thus it might be said that humor is somewhat like brain surgery, in that when it succeeds it is spectacular, but when it fails it is hideous.

Preaching. In a memorandum for members of McKinsey & Company, the management consulting firm, Roland Mann, editorial director, offers this counsel:

> Try not to preach. Don't, for example, try to tell readers how they *must* manage a business. Instead, tell them how others have benefited from the use of the approach, and let them draw their own conclusions. More than advice, they will welcome information on how other organizations have dealt with a particular problem . . .[4]

Mann's counsel is sound for most professional journals and technical magazines. It applies as well to an article for *Scientific American* as to an article for *MBA* or *Sloan Management Review.*

Facts versus generalizations: Galbraith writes:

> Nothing is so hard to come by as a new and interesting fact. Nothing is so easy on the feet as a generalization. I now pick up magazines and read through them looking for articles that are rich with facts; I do not care much what they are. Richly evocative and deeply percipient theory I avoid. It leaves me cold unless I am the author of it. My advice to all young writers is to stick to research and reporting with only a minimum of interpretation. And especially this is my advice to all older writers, particularly

[3]*Ibid*, pp. 104–105.
[4]Reprinted in *Harvard Business Review*'s memorandum for prospective authors (1977). Available on request.

to columnists. As the feet give out, they seek to have the mind take their place.[5]

Opening. A century and a half ago, in the days when chauvinism was taken for granted, litterateur Leigh Hunt wrote: "It has been said of ladies when they write their letters, that they put their minds in their postscripts—let out the real objects of their writing, as if it were a second thought, or a thing comparatively indifferent." How many potentially useful articles, written by both men and women, are rejected out of hand because the authors don't "let out the real objects of their writing" until they get so far along that what they say appears almost like a postscript!

Your opening paragraph, even in a farily long manuscript, should catch readers' attention. It should also start readers thinking about what you most want to tell them. Fortunately, it can do both things at once if you begin with some interesting facts, examples, questions, or statements that deal with the main ideas or findings of the text that follows. Recognizing the importance of such an opening, some accomplished writers don't write their opening page—or, at least, don't write it carefully and with any finality—until they have completed the main sections of their manuscript.

The first line on the first page of text of *African Genesis* reads: "Not in innocence, and not in Asia, was mankind born."[6] In these ten words the author, Robert Ardrey, stated the central thesis of a 357-page book—that human beings did not originate, as popularly supposed in 1961, in Asia (but in Africa), and that human aggression was not acquired from experience but born in the genes. Only anthropologists can judge the soundness of Ardrey's arguments, but anyone can see what a superb start the author makes.

Bear in mind you do not have a captive audience in

[5]Galbraith, *op. cit.*, p. 104.
[6]Robert Ardrey, *African Genesis* (New York: Atheneum, 1961), p. 9.

publishing. To put yourself in the position of the editors, consider how you glance through a copy of, say, *Harper's* or *Time*. You thumb through the pages; in a matter of seconds or minutes your eye checks out the opening lines of an article that arrests your attention; if the article doesn't prove itself immediately, you may leaf your way to the next article. Now, editors may not be quite so ruthless, but this sort of appraisal comes closer to the reality than the bucolic image many authors seem to hold of an editor sipping their typed words to the last as if they were fine wine.

One would think that *Science* is a magazine that could, if any magazine could, get away with leisurely openings for its articles. Its audience is, after all, professional; its authors are usually professionals; and the editors have won a reputation for not letting readers down. Yet articles in this journal are likely to open with lines that strike swiftly at the heart of what the authors have to say. For example:

- The rivalry between Roger Guillemin and Andrew Schally in pursuit of the brain's hormones spans a period of at least 21 years.[7] (The rest of the article focuses on the nature and effects of the rivalry).
- Songs of the African Pygmies tend to be repetitious, to have short phrases, and to be sung in counterpoint. Similar song styles are found among some groups that are geographically isolated from the Pygmies, such as the Northern California Indians . . .[8] (The rest of the report spins out research findings linking singing style to social structure.)

Revision. The secret of most good writing lies in revision. Michener's statement on the title page of this chapter comes as close to reflecting the secret of successful nonfiction writers as any statement I know.

[7]Nicholas Wade, "Guillemin and Schally: A Race Spurred by Rivalry," *Science*, May 5, 1978, p. 510.
[8]"Singing Styles and Human Cultures: How Are They Related?" *Science*, April 21, 1978.

Authors sometimes tell me: "But if I rewrite my paper, it will lose its spark and freshness." I like to remind them of something Galbraith once said while reflecting on the many books and articles he had written. It was his conviction that it was not until the third or fourth rewriting, in some cases, that his best writing had gained the spontaneity that editors and readers like so much.

The two things the public never should see made are sausages and good writing. In both cases it would be horrified if it saw the product at the earlier stages. A couple of years ago—I have lost the date of the item—the Sunday book review section of *The New York Times* ran a list of favorite bad lines collected by a magazine editor. (For example: "She stood beside her handsome husband as he ate the rare prime rib she had prepared, stroking his wavy brown hair." "Bernie's virginity fell before Katrina like wheat before a hailstorm." And "During their lunch of Quiche Lorraine and Welsh Rabbit, Brian asked, 'Ms. Connolly, is there a Mr. Connolly?' ") For weeks afterward editors could be heard laughing about some of the examples. And yet I wonder if any successful author can honestly say that early drafts of his or her own manuscripts have not carried equally bad examples or [perish the thought] worse ones. However, no editor ever saw these verbal monstrosities because they were killed in revision and rewriting.

Delivery. Don't mail your manuscript to the publisher until you have completed *all* the changes that you may wish to make. A pet peeve of many editors in the manuscript that, like efforts to beat the mark at a ski-jumping contest, is followed by a succession of efforts to better it—versions containing amendments, pages with corrections, and letters offering alternative wordings.

Editorial directions. If the editors like parts of your manuscript but feel that some parts must be reworked before it can be accepted, follow their instructions as closely as you can. Unless you have compelling reasons for doing otherwise, don't dismiss any of the reactions and suggestions given—and, at the other extreme, don't launch out on your own and rewrite other portions of the manuscript. Editors eat for breakfast manuscripts that have been revised without regard for the staff's instructions.

Here are some wise observations from a veteran newspaper editor, teacher, and literary judge:

> You can trust your editor in the role of word surgeon who ties syllables with surgical knots so the thoughts cannot slip away. That's part of the shared labor between writer and editor. But sometimes the editor can only point out passages where passages are not passages. In the margin or in a cover note words appear: "It doesn't hang together."
>
> The reason may be found in one of several traps. It could be departure from the outline or the natural arrangement of the subject matter. Or it could be fouled in the beginnings or endings of difficult sentences or paragraphs. Or it could be in the selection of words, or the omission or insertion of direct quotations.[9]

Editing. If your manuscript is accepted, chances are that the editors will send you an edited version or proofs later on. Unless the editing distorts your message and introduces inaccuracies, accept it and mark it approved and return it promptly. Don't re-edit; don't try to do a better editing job than your editor did. Even if you believe passionately that he or she is wrong, accept the assumptions about what length is right, what tone is appropriate, what style is best.

Rejection. "If at first you don't succeed," someone has said, "you're about average." The majority of articles written for publication are never published, and yours, despite its merit, and despite all the time you put into it, may join the unhappy roll. If this happens, you are free, of course, to curse the editorial diadem and explain its egregious misjudgment to your friends. But don't resubmit your article and urge the staff to try again. And don't bother writing the editorial culprit a letter pointing out

[9]Paul S. Swenson, "Keys to Good Writing," *Matrix*, Fall 1977, p. 7.

his or her errors and urging the magazine to take another look (or bring in a referee). You'll have only a little more luck than unhappy baseball players do when arguing with the umpire about called third strikes.

If you're sure the manuscript is worthy of publication, send it on to another publisher. Judging from my own experience, a fair number of articles published in magazines are rejected by one or more editorial staffs before they find permanent homes.

The hazards of writing for publication are as terrifying as ever, yet it can be said that living conditions for writers generally have improved. Reflecting on his days as a journalist on Grub Street in London in the 1740s, Samuel Johnson recalled his colorful poet friend, Samuel Boyce, who was chronically on the verge of starvation. To raise money to stay alive while writing a book, Boyce would pawn the first few pages after drafting them, then retrieve them by pawning the next few pages, and so on. A time came when Boyce had pawned everything he owned, including his clothes and bed sheets. Writing for magazines in this predicament, Boyce "sat up in bed with the blanket wrapt around him through which he had cut a hole large enough to admit his arm, and placing the paper upon his knee, scribbled in the best manner he could."[10]

Today a writer who is harried and unsuccessful may also write in bed, but the chances are good that his or her hunger is for publication, not food and warmth. Pillows and hot water bottles cushion the back and knees, a tray of coffee and Danish rolls stands nearby, and a half dozen credit cards are within easy reach.

PROBLEMS AND CASES

1. A colleague shows you the outline below. She has excellent credentials for writing on the subject. "I want to send it to one of the leading health care or computer journals,"

[10]Quoted by W. Jackson Bate in *Samuel Johnson* (New York: Harcourt Brace Jovanovich, 1977), p. 211.

she says, mentioning several specific candidates. "Is this the right way to start?" Write a memorandum to her with your reactions and any suggestions.

I. Survey of data processing in hospitals
   A. General findings
   B. Example: Atkins Community Hospital

II. Brief history
   A. Early introduction of computers in hospitals and health organizations
   B. Developments in the late 1960s

III. Computer applications
   A. Accounting and finance
      1. Billing
      2. Payroll
      3. Inventory
      4. Purchasing
   B. Medical diagnosis
      1. Patient history analysis
      2. Case analysis

IV. Problems and limitations
   A. Expense
   B. Service and maintenance
   C. "Computer error"
   D. Resistance to change

V. Conclusion

2. The following paragraphs are the beginning of an article by an expert on ecology and public works planning. The article will be submitted to a journal that has indicated interest in seeing the manuscript. Assume that the manuscript is in first draft form and the writer has asked you to edit and revise the paragraphs shown, if you think any further work is advisable.

TROUBLES AT TOCKS ISLAND

Major environmental decisions have a way of getting stuck and staying stuck. The discussions about whether to undertake substantial transformations of natural areas—to bring about new power plants, dams, airports, pipelines, deep water ports—have several pathologies in common. A cluster of detailed technical analyses accompanies the formulation of the program and its initial rush onto the stage;

the proponents of the project imply, and generally believe, that all one could reasonably have expected has been done, both to justify the program and to anticipate its pitfalls. As after a carefully planned transplant, the reaction of rejection is slow in coming but grows relentlessly. The analyses are shown to be incomplete, and new analyses starting from different premises are eventually produced by those who wish to stop the program. But, contrary to what one might naively expect, the existence of disparate analyses does not help appreciably to resolve the debate.

The failure of technical studies to assist in the resolution of environmental controversies is part of a larger pattern of failures of discourse in problems that put major societal values at stake. Discussions of goals, of visions of the future, are enormously inhibited. Privately, goals will be talked about readily, as one discovers in even the most casual encounter with any of the participants. But the public debate is cloaked in a formality that excludes a large part of what people most care about.

The land use debate I have most pondered, and the source of most of my generalizations, is the debate over whether to build a major rock-fill dam on the Delaware River at Tocks Island, thereby creating a 37-mile long lake along the New Jersey-Pennsylvania border. The dam was proposed by the Corps of Engineers and was authorized by Congress in 1962. Although land has been acquired, and the National Park Service has arrived on the scene to administer the Delaware Water Gap National Recreation Area that is intended to surround the lake, construction has not yet begun. It may never begin.

I happen to hope that the dam will not be built. Building the dam, it seems to me, would buttress an attitude of impudence toward our natural resources. Not building the dam, on the other hand, would stimulate the development of alternate technologies, intrinsically more respectful of nature, which are ever more urgently needed. Of all the arguments for and against the dam, this need to stimulate a reorientation of our technology is for me the single most compelling one.

If the Tocks Island dam is built, nuclear power plants will follow. Next, factories, warehouses, power lines, and roads will rise up around the nuclear plants. But if the dam is not built, many promising ideas about how we should adjust to the limits of nature—for instance, water recycling, flood plain zoning, and staggered work weeks—will at last get a serious hearing. As one leading conservationist told me, "We've got to learn to accommodate to nature sometime. Why not start here and now, while there is still some room to maneuver?"

3. Assume that the following letter and outline were shown to you before mailing by the author. As the letter indicates, a magazine is interested in seeing the proposal, but the writer also tells you that the editors are "fussy" about new material for publication in this area; the magazine's competitors have run articles on the topic, and they don't want to come out with a "second best" or "warmed over" article. Write a memo to the writer explaining your reactions and offering any recommendations you think would be helpful.

a. *The letter*

Dear Mr. Kindall:

Last spring we talked about my preparing an article for your publication on "Stress and the Black Executive." I have finally got around to thinking through the article and preparing a proposal, which is enclosed.

As I see it, the purpose of the article will be to help corporate policy makers (who are mostly white) anticipate problems that come up as organizations become more integrated, to alert them to causes and symptoms of stress in their new black executives, and to give them suggestions as to what to do to minimize stress and maximize the contributions of the black managers.

I hope this is the sort of thing you're looking for. Please let me know your reactions to this outline and give me some idea as to deadline.

Sincerely,

b. *The outline*

STRESS AND THE BLACK EXECUTIVE

I. Introduction

As black managers slowly make their way up the corporate

ladder, they join white managers in facing the challenges of the business world. In the process of doing this, they are experiencing new forms of success and new forms of stress.

—Definition of stress: an emotional state that occurs in situations where no adequate response is perceived.

—Every manager faces stress, and much has been written about executive stress and how to counteract it. But *black* executives, new to the higher echelons of organizations that have been formed according to white norms, are subject to extra dimensions of stress.

—White managers are largely unaware of what black executives are having to cope with and unsure what role they should play in managing black executive stress. As a result, often they face problems of turnover, low productivity, and tension that could be avoided.

II. Causes and symptoms of stress
—The black/white interface, relatively new in higher management circles, raises some new issues and causes new manifestations of stress.

—Concerns of black managers today, as revealed in discussions I have had with more than 800 of them.

—Interpersonal situations that cause stress.

—Symptoms of stress.

—Why career development needs of blacks are different from those of whites.

III. Why the white response to black stress is usually dysfunctional.

IV. Eight steps to avoiding or alleviating stress in the black executive.

4. Study each of the following article proposals, put yourself in the authors' shoes as well as you can, and, if you think desirable, revise or rewrite the proposals. If you think any items of information should be added, indicate specifically what they should be.

Each letter is dated and typed on the letterhead of the writer's organization. All names are changed to conceal the identity of the writers and editors. In each case, assume that the subject proposed is "in the ballpark" of interest to the editor and publication to whom the letter is sent.

a. *Dear Ms. Edwards:*

Would you be interested in an article concerning the evaluation of entrepreneurial capabilities?

This article would deal with the psychology of the entrepreneur in having the business, organizational and sustaining traits to run an "entrepreneurial" business(up to $5 million to $7 million in sales). I consider entrepreneurism to be a state of being which doesn't always last a lifetime. Much like the star athlete who bows out after only a few years, many individuals lose the entrepreneurial interest after several years or become managerial prone.

The article would address points such as

—Some successful entrepreneurs are only successful with a business of a size appropriate to the entrepreneur's capabilities. That is, some entrepreneurs can only handle a business with no more than 10–15 employees, others can handle a business with an employment up to 50 or so, but no more.

—When an entrepreneurial business is acquired, with the same entrepreneur at the helm, he may not be the one to take it to its next stage of growth.

—Entrepreneurism is a state of being. With certain significant events in one's life (as wealth, marriage, divorce), the entrepreneur's state changes.

—An individual (or a team of individuals) interested in running their division as a separate business by buying it out from its corporate parent may not have the traits to run the new company if it will be of the size to consider it entrepreneurial.

I look forward to hearing from you.

Sincerely yours,

b. *Dear Ms. Mather,*

As we discussed on the phone in late November, I am submitting for your consideration an idea for an article under the signature of C. H. Weld, President of Kindle and Millicent, specialists in recruitment advertising.

Mr. Weld believes that most corporations overlook a potential goldmine of good will and enhanced corporate image because they fail to recognize that many publics, in addition to the job seeking public, see and react to recruitment ads. Such companies do not perceive help wanted advertising as part of their communications effort, while such ads can serve as eloquent representatives.

Why is this important to your magazine's readers? Simply because indirect communication—"over the shoulder" communications—is a highly credible and influential voice about the true nature and objectives of a firm. Psychologists have shown, and good salesmen have always known, that a message is accepted as more believable when it is not seen as part of a selling effort.

More important, because those who are "listening in" are exactly the audience the chief executive aims to influence—investors, customers current and prospective, and employees on staff. Mr. Weld argues that it is possible to impact all these audiences through carefully planned recruitment ads while, at the same time, improving communications with potential employees.

We're convinced that this is not a story for a narrow-interest publication. The advantage of viewing recruitment advertising as part of the communications armamentarium flow far beyond the personnel department. For this reason, the chief executive officer is the only person who can provide the leadership necessary for a re-evaluation of recruitment ads with an eye toward gaining more than the immediate objective of the personnel function.

The article will show examples of how some companies use recruitment advertising to serve non-personnel ends as well. It will include backup statistics to illustrate the number and type of readers for recruitment ads; present corporate expenditures for such advertising; and, if you think them appropriate, samples of good and poor ads.

I am eager to talk with you about how we can bring this important idea to print. You can reach C. H. Weld at (405) 808-8532. Or me at (405) 808-5794.

Sincerely,

c. *Dear Irving:*

Nearly seven years ago, you published my article on welfare control. In complete honesty, your editing of the piece has always struck me as more important to its usefulness than our drafting it. The fact that individual executives still approach me about it and about management of specific programs of their organizations, such as controlling drug abuse, is a continuing compliment to the job we did, however the weighting of credit lies in fact.

Six months after publication of the piece, I took a new job in this much smaller organization, a national voluntary health agency concerned since 1951 with control of VD and since 1967 with drug abuse, both relatively unglamorous to prestige leadership, but both so bad now that such leaders are beginning to notice them. Consequently, it may soon be possible to convert this small scientifically and medically oriented group of consultants to a voluntary health impact in the usual sense—preserving excellence but adding clout. Except for saying that it is one helluva lot different to manage an organization instead of telling others how they should manage one, I shall skip the hurdles of transformation and get on with the purpose of this inquiry.

The staff and consultants of my organization are writing a set of guidelines for the development of comprehensive community programs to control drug abuse. These are timely and sound, exceeding any such exposition of working concepts in the field. They are needed in top echelons of leadership, lay and professional, if hysterical proliferation of community programs, largely wasteful and useless, is to be replaced by soundly comprehensive and coordinated community programs. Even the best known approaches will not be enough, but they will be a great improvement, will begin to provide baseline data, and will have a capacity to encourage and benefit from needed research.

At present, we are developing the guidelines as an inhouse program. My opening inquiry to you is based on a few simple assumptions and not so simple questions. The two assumptions are:

> that drug abuse is here to stay in considerable magnitude and variety; and
>
> that little which is constructive will be done about it, regardless of political speeches and government expenditures, until the top leadership of business and industry becomes actively and productively involved.

A recent "information paper" of the Ford Foundation, which is resulting in formation of The National Drug Abuse

Council supported by a syndicate of foundations besides Ford, bears out these assumptions and underlines the timeliness of our guidelines.

Before getting into the questions, take my word for this much about the guidelines, subject to your complete verification if the idea finally seems worth it. They are not a do-it-yourself manual. But neither are they scholarly treatises. They are for the use of engineers rather than physicists, shall we say. Their implementation requires the best of interdisciplinary work that can be pulled into focus, yet they take into account the usable knowledge available in the present state of the art.

The basic questions are:

> Should these guidelines be recast and published, generically, granted the quality which I attribute to them, by a journal recognized by top business management and technical people, with appropriate credit to our organization, but not as its particular and, therefore, limited program?

If the answer to the above question is 51% positive, offering us a reason for an exploratory conference, could and would you consider publishing our material for the benefit of the professionals of many disciplines and corporate leaders as good corporate citizens of major communities across the land?

Sincerely,

PART FIVE

CONCLUSION

It is not the hand
but the understanding of a man
that may be said to write.

Miguel de Cervantes

I like the way you write memoranda
—crisp, to the point and concise.
Work-think-work-think hard. . . .
I depend on you.

Lyndon B. Johnson
(to Walter Heller, December 1963)

Chapter **14**

The Writer's Wheel

The job of the writer who wishes to influence readers with information and ideas might be compared to a wagon wheel. The writer's message is like the hub of the wheel, and the different qualities of written communication are like the spokes (see Exhibit I). The message doesn't travel unless the wheel turns, and the wheel doesn't turn unless it is sound.

The wagon wheel of old might be four or five feet in diameter. A steel rim covered the wooden perimeter. Between the hub and the perimeter were set hardwood spokes that might be up to two inches thick. The hub also was made of hardwood, of the best stock that could be found. So long as all the spokes were in good condition, nothing serious was likely to go wrong, since damage to the rim or to the steel bearing sleeve in the hub or to the axle could be repaired. But once a spoke let loose or rotted, there was real trouble. Other spokes would then

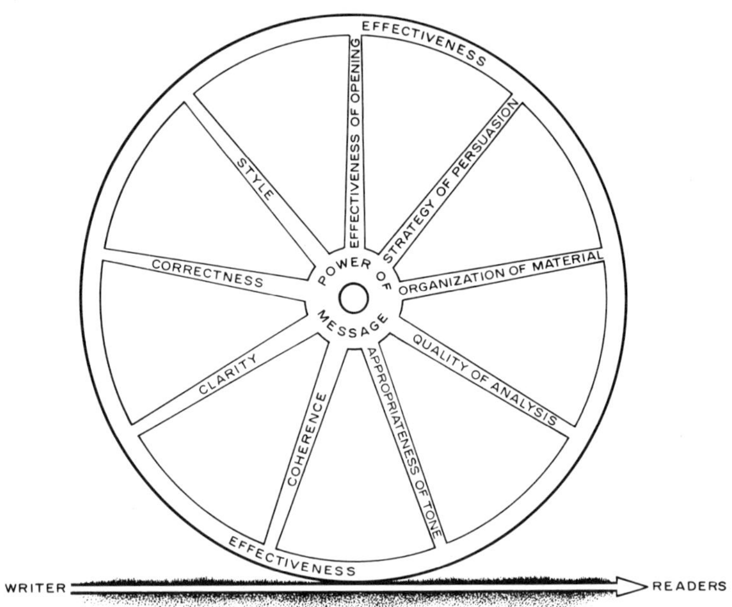

loosen where they joined the hub. The wheel couldn't be trusted to take the load. My friend Jack Zoerheide, who remembers working on wagons in his youth, says the wheel was discarded not because the outer rim wouldn't carry the load but because of the weakness in the spokes and the hub—*any weakness anywhere was translated to the hub.*

Similarly, any weakness in the spokes of the writer's wheel translates to the hub, the message. When that happens, the other spokes are liable to weaken. The wheel won't carry the load anymore. The message doesn't move from the writer's mind to the reader's.

THE SPOKES AND THE HUB: A SUMMARY

To see how this happens, let us look back at some of the main points in Chapters 3 to 12. These are the chapters that describe the spokes of the writer's wheel.

Helpful Beginning

A beginning that points to or "previews" the main findings, recommendations, or ideas to follow is important for two reasons. It increases the depth of readership, that is, it arrests attention and whets interest. Also, it increases the quality of readership. Knowing what to look for, readers can proceed more intelligently to read the rest of the report, letter, or memorandum.

"Go wrong at the beginning and nothing afterwards will go right," C. Northcote Parkinson once observed. He might have stretched the point a little but not outrageously. You need a helpful beginning to keep the other spokes from loosening early in the ride. Don't lead off with some notes about the history of the national health insurance debate, if that history is not your main purpose in writing; state that compulsory health insurance is going to encourage hypochondriacs to monopolize doctors' time (or whatever else is your main theme).

Appropriate Persuasion Strategy

Appraise the attitudes and desires of your readers. Try to look at yourself as your readers may do. Think for a moment about your relationship with your readers. Then and only then decide how to play the cards in your hand—which facts and arguments first, what points last. Then and only then decide whether to use bushels of facts or pint boxes, lots of technicality or practically none, "testimonials" or just your own opinions or perhaps no opinions whatever.

Sizing up the writer-reader situation in writing is as important as sizing up the buyer-seller situation in marketing, the lawyer-judge situation in a court pleading, or the doctor-client situation in a medical case. "Devise, wit; write, pen" said Shakespeare—the devising comes before the drafting.

Weakness in this spoke of the writer's wheel can play havoc with the other spokes. Often it spells the difference between readers looking at the information you give them sympathetically or with hostility.

Effective Organization

Whether your report or memorandum is long or short, technical or nontechnical, personal or impersonal, you need to help your readers to see how the thoughts relate to one another. Consciousness itself means awareness of relationships. Facts should be grouped logically. First points should be separated from second points. Changes in direction or emphasis should be indicated, just as sharp curves and hazards in a road are indicated by signs.

If you want your letter or report to be what people call "readable," begin by organizing your facts and ideas logically and helpfully. Once your readers see these things in relationship, the other efforts you make can pay off, too.

What might be called "mechanical aids"—headings, for instance—can be quite helpful. So are transitional sentences and paragraphs. And, for many professionals, managers, scientists, and officials, nothing can take the place of an outline in planning the written presentation.

Convincing Analysis

If you are trying to make a new point or prove a fresh conclusion by facts and ideas, you must reason with your material, using it—as you would tools in a home workshop—with awareness of its strengths and limitations. "Loaded" words can be dangerous; concealed assumptions can backfire; misleading inferences can damage your credibility; irrelevant quotes and facts can be confusing; unreasonable brevity or length can be distracting. Put your finger on the key problems and their main dimensions; specify their causes; outline alternative ways of coping with them; argue most for the solution you consider best; if action must be taken, specify who should take it.

For scientists, professional people, and a fast-growing multitude of managers in business and government, this spoke of the writer's wheel deserves a great deal of attention. Unless you win the confidence and respect of readers for your treatment of evidence, it does you little good to work on achieving such other qualities as style, correctness, and a good opening.

Appropriate Tone

Your readers "hear" the words and phrases of your letter or report. The sounds may be comforting or abrasive, harmonious or dissonant, lively or dull—just as clearly as with a musical score. Examine the writer-reader situation in much the same way that you did in planning a convincing strategy for your paper (that quality is, in fact, an extension of this one). Choose words that will be heard in the way you intend—friendly or challenging, respectful or taunting, sympathetic or unsympathetic, warm or cold, and so on.

"Apt words have power to suage the tumors of a troubled mind," John Milton wrote. This spoke of the wheel can have a reinforcing, firming effect on the others if you give it some thought and attention.

Coherence

See that the opening sentence of your paragraph indicates plainly what the rest of the paragraph is about; see that the opening paragraph in a long series fulfills a similar purpose. Use pronouns and demonstrative adjectives to keep the viewpoint clear in a paragraph. Use conjunctions and transitions to clarify relationships between people and things; use parallelism to give emphasis to facts and ideas; use "echo words," too, for that purpose.

If the sentences within paragraphs seem to flow together instead of eddying and crossing one another (and if, in the case of long reports, the paragraphs within sections also flow together), you will make it far easier for readers to appreciate the sense of your views and information. This spoke performs much the same function as proper organization of facts and ideas does, only at a finer level of detail.

Clarity

You can gain clarity by simple devices, such as enumerating ideas that are sequential and inserting headings and subheadings. You also can gain clarity by working over the words and phrases in your document. Are there unnecessarily abstract or long words? Is there a logic in the sense of the words? Are the subjects and verbs reasonably close together? Do the pronouns have clear antecedents? Are modifying words and phrases placed so as to be connected readily with the words described?

"In these long sentences rich in involved parentheses, like a box of boxes within one another, and padded out like roast geese stuffed with apples, it is really the memory that is chiefly taxed," Arthur Schopenhauer, the nineteenth century philosopher, once wrote. Lack of clarity puts a strain on all other spokes in the writer's wheel.

To some extent, lack of clarity is unavoidable. The English language itself is full of ambiguities. However, in the great majority of cases much of the problem can be avoided; all that is needed is a little more thought by the writer, a little more consideration for the reader's problem.

If you use charts and diagrams, acquaint yourself at least briefly with the different types and functions of charts. They may be extraordinarily effective in making your message more powerful. Also, they can save you and your readers time.

Correctness

Correct usage is important not only because it enables you to be more precise but also because it provides reassurance to readers that you regard them highly enough to take time with the "little points" of usage. Since so many readers have been taught to look for errors in grammar and usage, they may take sadistic glee in faulting you for lapses. Sometimes, in fact, such lapses provide them with the easy rationalization they want for repudiating some of the substance of your letter or report. Hence this spoke can weaken almost any of the other spokes. It can cast doubt over the most carefully worked out organization, or even over the most painstaking efforts to make the strategy and tone of a message appropriate.

Since the early 1970s, sexism has become taboo in the writing of business, scientific, and other professional people. Although the fine points of these prohibitions are not clear yet, the guiding principles are apparent and relatively easy to follow.

Effective Style

"Style is the dress of thoughts," remarked Lord Chesterfield. Your style should reflect you—the way you talk, the way you think, the way you look at situations. Also, your style should reflect something of your regard for your relationships with your readers. If you want to whet their interest in your material, if you want to relieve some of their burden of assaying your letter or report, there may be much you can do by putting life in the verbs and nouns used, getting rid of jargon and verbal undergrowth, and adding color and vitality and personal interest.

Strength in this spoke can do a great deal for the durability of the wheel. Some thoughtful observers feel that style may even have a contagious effect, throwing a whole letter or report in a more auspicious light for readers, so that they seek merit in it, want to ponder it, and are glad to take time with it.

Of course, style is particularly important in writing for publication. For editors whose judgments are partly subjective, style may be the subtle but critical difference between, as the advertisements say, brand *X* and brand *Y*.

In sum, visualizing the writer's job in terms of a wheel has two major values.

First, it emphasizes the relationships between the various qualities and requirements—the often subtle interdependencies of the spokes. The qualities do not exist in compartments, where each can be treated separately like patients in hospital rooms. Instead, they are a blend, a whole.

Second, the wheel shows the need for a situational approach. Every message, every hub, is different in size and makeup from other messages. It is different because of its intended readership and timing as well as because of its makeup of facts and opinions. And every writer's wheel is slightly different in size from other wheels. Therefore each message must have its spokes made up and set to fit it. Though the wheel may benefit from your knowledge of how spokes are set in other hubs and wheels, it cannot take other spokes ready-made.

GETTING THE WHEEL TURNING

How is good writing written in business, government, science, and the professions?

Peter Drucker asserts that, for any written communication requiring extended concentration by the author, writing time should be consolidated. He states:

> To write a report may, for instance, require six or eight hours, at least for the first draft. It is pointless to give seven hours to the task by spending fifteen minutes a day for three weeks. All one has at the end is blank paper with some doodles on it. But if one can lock the door, disconnect the telephone, and sit down to wrestle with the report for five or six hours without interruption, one has a good chance to come up with what I call a 'zero draft'—the one before the first draft. From then on, one can indeed work in fairly small installments, can rewrite, correct and edit section by section, paragraph by paragraph, sentence by sentence.[1]

[1]Peter F. Drucker, *The Effective Executive* (New York, Harper & Row, 1967), p. 29.

Before and after you draft or dictate an important message, including one of the scope just described, you may want to draw on the help of your colleagues or other people in the organization. Doing this *beforehand* pays the largest dividends. It is relatively easy to take apart and reorganize a set of notes or an outline. It may be agonizing to do that to a finished draft.

Whom should you talk to? If practical, consult with the person or some of the people who want the report, letter, or memorandum. What are they looking for? What facts or questions do they consider most important? What thoughts do they have about the distribution of copies of the document? If it is not practical to get guidance from prospective readers, your associates may be helpful. Naturally, if portions of the message deal with matters about which you are uncertain, it is wise to check out your questions with those who have more perfect information.

Another good stage at which to seek help from associates comes after you finish a preliminary, rough, or "zero" draft. (If you learn then that major overhauling is necessary, the task is more painful than at the rough-note stage—but much less so than after a smooth draft is done.) A senior research executive at Union Oil Company offers this advice to researchers:

> The place to start searching for feedback is your own laboratory. Ask the co-workers to check your outline and your first draft. They have participated in the work you are reporting, and their viewpoints will be different from yours. The aspects of the project that interest them will probably be quite different from the ones that interest you. They may, therefore, be able to show how you can improve the balance of your presentation. They may even be able to point out features of the work that you have entirely overlooked.
>
> Next, try one or two of your professional colleagues who are working on different but related problems. Some of your most valuable feedback will come from these associates. They have interests and background somewhat different from yours. The value of comments from such people is universally recognized. . . .

> Finally, it is nothing less than essential to get some early reactions from your supervisor. Not only will his viewpoint be different from yours, but also he may know more than you do about the viewpoints of some of the other management men who will be receiving your report. Moreover, if your report is to be sent to people outside the Research Department, your supervisor must approve it and therefore share the responsibility for it.
>
> For this special reason, his ideas about it must be considered with special care. You should consult with him early in the game.[2]

Besides helping you on questions of accuracy, balance, and viewpoint, associates may point out biases of which you are unaware. This does not necessarily mean you must revise your presentation—you may want to stick with that bias to the end. But it does mean you can indicate in writing that you are *aware* of the bias.

Project reports, involving a team of contributors, are a special case. J. C. Mathes and Dwight W. Stevenson estimate that 20% to 30% of the total time required by a technical project goes to pulling the elements of the final report together. Any proportion of budgeted time less than 20%, they say, is almost certain to be inadequate. They urge that, in planning the project—from refinement of methodologies and the study of physical and technical constraints to the integration of the findings and recommendations—a realistic amount of time be scheduled for the writing. This block of time should be laid out on the same schedule as other blocks of required time are set aside. They write:

> When you receive an assignment or voluntarily undertake a technical investigation, first schedule adequate time for both the investigation and the report. If you fail to schedule adequate time for the whole project, you will almost certainly end up stealing from report writing time to complete the investigation. Yet in terms of your function in the organizational system, the report writing time is instrumentally your most important time. One consulting engineer stresses the importance of this—and at the

[2]Raymond A. Rogers, *How to Report Research and Development Findings to Management* (New York, Pilot Books, 1973), p. 26.

> same time indicates how difficult it is to schedule realistically. He says, "I usually allow about three days to write a report at the end of a thirty day consulting assignment. For a ninety day assignment I might allow a week. It is never enough. I always end up coming to the office after dinner and on weekends to get the report out on time. And I end up paying my secretary overtime to get the typing done. You would think that after eight years as a consultant, I would finally learn how long it takes to knock out the report, but I still haven't. I have never sent out a report that I thought was really finished."[3]

What about editorial specialists and consultants? In general, the answer depends on what stage of writing you are in. Particularly in the early stages, where the decisions involve whether to write, what points to emphasize at the beginning, what strategy of persuasion to follow, and how to organize the main ideas and arguments, you should use editorial aides who have analytical skills. You should *not* try to delegate decisions to them. Instead, use them in the manner some executives use management consultants, that is, to help formulate and think through the problem, which in this case is a communication problem. But when you reach the late stages in the writing, especially questions of correctness, clarity, and coherence, you can delegate more. In addition to counsel of the question-raising, problem-formulating variety, if you want it, you can profitably turn over to trusted aides the responsibility for parts of the copy itself. They may not work out the details just as you would, but they should be able to see what needs to be done and do it well.

THE SHORTEST WAY HOME

A writer's wheel, like a wagon wheel or a bicycle wheel, is strong when every spoke is fitted and tapered to the common rim. You can no more succeed by borrowing

[3]J. C. Mathes and Dwight W. Stevenson, *Designing Technical Reports* (Indianapolis: Bobbs-Merrill, 1976), p. 191.

assorted spokes from other people's wheels than can the maker of a wagon wheel. The wagon maker may collect the finest spokes around—a polished hickory spoke from this wagon, a bright new steel spoke from that—but he won't be able to make a serviceable wheel out of them because they were designed to fit rims of different perimeters and hubs of different thicknesses. Similarly, your writing wheel cannot be made up of assorted spokes from this writing technique and that. You cannot make a serviceable wheel by applying different people's writing formulas to a problem that did not exist until your current need to put information in writing.

You will find a teacher here who says the secret of good writing is short sentences and words of few syllables—"shirtsleeves" English. You will find a teacher there who says the secret is logical thought patterns, so logical they can be diagrammed like geometry on a blackboard. You will find a person here who says the key is "power words," that is, words with certain dynamic qualities. You will find a person there who says the key is transitions and connectives. You will hear this authority claim the solution is Anglo-Saxon words. You will hear that authority claim the solution is "psychology." You will hear this expert assert the answer is well-placed vignettes, quotes, names, examples. You will hear that expert assert the answer is coherence and format.

They are all right—up to a point. Individually, each of these people's techniques is a good spoke. Each has served well in many a writer's wheel. But they won't necessarily work in *your* writer's wheel. You can't force someone else's spokes into your rim and hub. Some of the Apostle Paul's letters to the Corinthians were beautiful writing wheels, but they would have been ruined if the concepts of, say, good reportorial writing had been forced into them. In the *Pentagon Papers* there are some superb examples of reportorial and analytical writing that would have been ruined if the concepts of good "shirtsleeves writing" had been forced into them.

In fact, even when the same people are writing for the same type of audience on the same subject, attempts to take proved solutions off the shelf may prove ludicrous. John A. Walter, a veteran observer, writes:

> The organizational flaw that I have most often observed is that of too heavy dependence on traditional or stereotyped patterns. Writers tend to organize the report, proposal, article, or whatever they are working on almost exactly like the last one, without regard to the suitability of this organizational plan for the current presentation. Let me mention one illustration of this. While I was working for one company, I examined dozens of proposals, all set up with the following main divisions: Introduction, Items and Services to be Supplied, Technical Approach, and Conclusions. There is nothing intrinsically wrong with this pattern—if it fits the circumstances. But often it did not. For instance, some of these proposals were for study contracts, and there were no items or specific services (other than to conduct the study and report) to be supplied. Moreover, the terminal section entitled Conclusions did not represent conclusions, but merely a hollow-sounding affirmation that the company would perform to the utter and complete satisfaction of the client.[4]

Now, all this may seem obvious when stated as a principle. Almost any discerning reader knows it. Thoughtful writers know it. Yet the situational approach to writing is rarely described. It is practiced—but it is not often taught.

Why is this so? The answer may lie in prejudices and unpleasant associations about rote writing that we picked up in school. We like to feel that we have "graduated" from that rote in adult life. We don't want to wrestle with it anymore. We want to skirt around it, if we can. We yearn for an alchemist's stone. We lust for a nonfattening hot fudge sundae. Like Peter Pan, we'll face anything except reality.

My proposition is that the situational approach is more natural, more interesting, more fun to play with by far

[4]John A. Walter, "Industrial Communication," address to the Society of Technical Writers and Publishers (Society for Technical Communication), 1969; reprinted in *STWP Proceedings*, 1969, pp. S-57–S-58.

than the simpler, more mechanistic approaches. If we could begin learning it earlier, we would never get sick of it. In tailoring writing to the requirements of a particular problem, in blending techniques so they work together, there are prospects of reward—in the doing as well as in the achieving—that are impossible in rote writing. Consider other vocations and professions. Subjects like medicine, architecture, and marketing are fascinating to practice because of the never-ending variety of problems, diagnoses, adaptations, compromises, improvising, innovations. For an architect, all the fun would go out if every house had to be designed like a ranch house; for a surgeon, all the fun would leave if every appendectomy were identical. In writing, much of the fun goes out where every sentence must be manufactured to a certain word- and syllable-length limit, or if every report must follow a prescribed outline, or if every article must begin with two short examples and be based on "you words."

In business, government, and the professions, an effective writer is not like a drill press worker in an auto body plant, performing repetitive motions all day. A good writer is more like an architect or a physician or a sales manager at work. Indeed, as frequently noted, the good writer may *be* that architect, physician, or sales executive, approaching the writing task in much the same way that he or she customarily approaches the tasks of design, medicine, and marketing—that is, with style and strategy, with analysis and design, rather than with little mental squirts, as if through the ticker tape of the mind.

Several hundred pages ago we noted General Liddell Hart's maxim that in strategy the longest way around may be the shortest way home. In business, science, and the professions, writing is a strategy. It has a purpose, costs, tradeoffs, rewards. Between what is best for the whole and "suboptimizing" for the parts there is an enormous difference. Turning the wheel all the way around and fitting every spoke is the best way to assure success.

PROBLEMS AND CASES

The following assignments are designed to bring into play a combination of writing needs, to challenge a variety of writing skills. As you do these assignments, bear in mind that when one spoke in the writer's wheel is loose, a couple of others are likely to become weak, too.

1. ***Plea for a Pension:*** Because of your many efforts to help people whose civil liberties have been infringed, including employees in business and government, you put aside a little time each week to counsel individuals who want your help. One day you find yourself listening to the case of Nathan Ammer, a graying, soft-spoken 64-year-old engineer. For nine years he had been a project manager for Winchester Corp., a large and well-known manufacturer of electronic equipment. He shows you a variety of documents—letters of commendation, citations, professional journal articles, and so forth—indicating his accomplishments. However, he says that one year before his pension would have vested, he was assigned to a boss who took a strong personal dislike to him and managed to manuever him out of the company.

   After half a year of unemployment, Ammer found another job as project engineer in an agency of the Defense Department. Although he had to take a reduction in salary, he has been happily employed in the agency for several years.

   Ammer explains to you that he will reach retirement age in another year. Because of some severe and unexpected medical expenses as well as a decline in his health, he realizes that he is poorly prepared financially for retirement. If he could get the pension he would have become eligible to receive from Winchester Corp.—or just nine-tenths of that pension—his difficulties would be eased considerably.

   By chance you have a friend in Winchester's research division. You call him that evening and ask him to make a confidential check on Ammer's case. In a few days he phones back. "It didn't take me long to find out about it," your friend reports. "Ammer's boss was widely hated. He was accused of being a sadist and a psychotic. The word is that he fired Ammer because Ammer stood up to him one time and disagreed with him on a technical solution." You learn also that Ammer's boss died of a heart attack two years ago.

You are impressed with the equities on Ammer's side. In addition, you happen to know that Roy Oliver, the chief executive of Winchester, is a veteran executive with a strong sense of ethics. You do not know Oliver personally but you have seen his name often in the newspapers.

Ammer is writing a letter to Oliver asking for a review of his case and, if possible, a hearing so that he can argue his eligibility for a pension. You would like to help him. You feel that if you wrote a letter to Oliver on Ammer's behalf, it might help assure that he receives a fair hearing. On the other hand, you are an outsider, you don't know Oliver or any of his close lieutenants, and you have no way of confirming further the information Ammer and your friend have given you. You realize also that Oliver is a terribly busy man.

Can you draft a letter to Oliver that may help Ammer, yet leave you feeling that you have not pried improperly into another company's affairs?

2. With the "Fired-Up Females" letter at the end of Chapter 11 edited for correctness, turn to it now and make further revisions to improve its effectiveness.

3. ***Valuable Vendors:*** The following problem, "Case of the Valuable Vendors," appeared in the September–October 1978 issue of *Harvard Business Review*, beginning at page 40. The case was written by Eliza C. Collins, the article by Mary P. Rowe. After you have read the case, assume that you are a consultant hired by Sam, the division manager. You are to give Sam a memorandum stating (a) your thoughts about the situation (b) what you think Sam should do. "Keep it on one side of a page," Sam has told you.

Harry Fenway is one of the best computer salesmen on the eastern seaboard. He sells equipment for Data-Run Corporation, one of the largest computer manufacturers in the world. His sales record is impressive. The company, which has lagged in recent years because of growing competition, is just ready to test-market a minicomputer model with which it hopes to recapture its share of the market. The company expects big things of Harry for this project launch; to top management he is nearly indispensable.

Gwen Barrett is an up-and-coming junior salesperson whom the company hired in a trainee program specifically to increase the number of women employees in sales. The computer industry has historically been a good employer of women, especially in systems analysis. Lately, Data-Run headquarters had decided there should be more women in sales and had made it a high-priority development program for division managers. One of the main reasons for this emphasis, aside from EEO goals, is that recently more women have been found in buyer positions in companies acquiring new computer equipment; Gwen has really hit it off with one such buyer already.

One hot, steamy day, Gwen asked to see the division manager, Sam Finch. She and Harry had just returned from a sales trip to a large manufacturing company in Connecticut, United Chemicals, Inc., where they signed a contract they had been trying to get for months. It was a great coup; Finch, very pleased, thinks "they obviously work well together." When Gwen asked to see him, Finch got ready to welcome a happy worker. What greeted him was an unhappy woman.

Harry, Gwen says, is the worst kind of macho, male chauvinist pig. His symptoms, she reports, are offensive: he berates his wife; he makes too many inquiries into her (Gwen's) personal life; in front of senior men they meet on the trip, he acts as if she were his property; he is patronizing; he tells dirty jokes to other men in her presence; and he interrupts her when she talks. Twice he has failed to introduce her to people they met.

Gwen complains that she'd tried to stay reasonable and calm about it and had overlooked Harry's behavior because he was such a good salesman and she felt she could learn about the business from him. But, she tells Finch indignantly, she feels alternately invisible and like a showpiece. Up to now, she had accepted the situation, but on this last trip she overheard a UCI buyer asking Harry why on earth Data-Run would send out a woman. Gwen hoped Harry would mention her *magna cum laude* as a math major and her excellent sales record. Instead, she heard Harry insinuating to this buyer that he had been sleeping with her. That did it. She insists that she would not work with Harry again. She wants to be transferred.

Sam Finch listens to Gwen and then asks Harry to come in, telling Gwen he'll see her later. Much to Sam's surprise, Harry does not get defensive at all. In fact, he is astounded that Gwen has asked for a transfer. He thinks she's overreacting to a few one-liners that maybe were a little blue. But, he says, she's a big girl and if she's going to play in the big leagues, she's going to have to take it like a man. Harry laughs. He thinks Gwen is a really sweet kid and brightens things up a lot, but he wouldn't worry if he were Sam. He advises Sam just to talk her up, and she'll come around.

Sam talks to Gwen again. No way, she says; Harry is a dyed-in-the-wool MCP and it just isn't worth it to hang around. She can find a job elsewhere, there's no problem with that. The computer industry is wide open for someone with her capabilities and training; she has had a number of job offers already. Sam tries more persuasion. She responds that he doesn't really understand either, does he? It's not only she, she adds, the women buyers don't think Harry's patter is so great either; she's talked with a number of them and they, too, find Harry offensive.

In fact, Gwen says to Sam, she bets that in the future Harry's sales record will not be as great as it has been in the past. And it's just possible that the minicomputer test launch could be affected. Think it over, Sam, she says, and let me know how it comes out. I'm flexible, but some things just aren't worth it.

4. In their book, *Technical Report Writing* (New York: Wiley, 1977), James W. Souther and Myron L. White of the University of Washington offer the following opinions and suggestions (p. 86):

> In reality, aren't some of the kinds of writing we produce quite adequate even if they are "quick and dirty"? Some of the things we write must, of course, possess as high a quality as we can provide.
>
> Many of the kinds of writing that we do, however, belong somewhere between these two extremes. It would be help-

> ful if technical and scientific writers and their supervisors would discuss the degree of quality required for the different kinds of writing that the staff must produce. Definition of quality standards would do much to clarify the writing task, both for the writer and for the reviewing supervisor.
>
> Writing is varied. A memo to the shop, an order for parts from the storeroom, a memo to the personnel department requesting a technician, an article for a learned journal, or an environmental impact statement to come under the scrutiny of a concerned public—all require a different degree of polish and quality. Certainly each of these kinds of writing exists in an environment of its own. Because the use requirements vary in each environment, we suggest that the quality of writing might also vary.
>
> We are not suggesting, of course, that writing can be unclear, ambiguous, distorted, or sloppy. What we are suggesting is that the time and effort writers and their reviewing supervisors put into seeking the most effective way of stating an idea should not be the same for all kinds of writing. We would place the various kinds of writing performed by the staff in any organization at different points along the improvement curve so that we could establish standards for quality that are related realistically to the different writing situations.

Suppose your boss has become interested in this idea and asks you for a critical evaluation of it in writing. "One side of one page," he tells you.

5. ***Pugnacious Presidents:*** Will Madden is the president of Virginia Padding, Inc., a subsidiary of a larger corporation, Patio Time, Inc. Madden is angry that Dave Cooper, head of the parent corporation, wants him to be less independent and more cooperative with the parent corporation. Over the telephone Cooper has urged Madden to merge Virginia Padding with the parent and take on a fifth director representing the parent.

   At present Virginia Padding is only 50% owned by the parent. Therefore, Madden would have to sell all or part of his interest in Virginia Padding to make the merger possible. Madden is an old friend of Cooper's. Also, he knows that the close relationship between the subsidiary and parent is beneficial. However, he has made Virginia Padding prosperous and he relishes his power and independence.

Madden drafts the following letter, reprinted from Kenneth J. Hatten, "Case of the Pugnacious Presidents," *Harvard Business Review*, January–February 1978, p. 34, to Cooper:

> Dear Dave,
>
> I haven't been able to dismiss our last conversation from my mind. I have to tell you what I feel.
>
> First, there is no need for a fifth director. Originally, our fifth director was your man, Ned Bryant, but our agreement clearly spelled out that either Bryant would resign or a sixth director from Virginia would be chosen when Patio Time, Inc. was paid back its original investment. The choice was not necessary because Bryant resigned from your company and Virginia Padding. The original debt was repaid within a year. Now suddenly, when Virginia is financially independent you make a request like this. We owe you $21,400. Every invoice older than October 1 is being paid today. Last year we bought merchandise worth $392,000 from you. Also, I promised you that I would not extend our payments beyond 60 days next season when you explained that Patio Time Inc. could not finance it. Furthermore, Patio Time has not had to "execute guarantees" for us. It isn't necessary now.
>
> Why are you pressuring me to merge with Patio Time? I hate to come right out and say 'no' because I feel we will be driven apart. Yet, I do not share your opinion of how great the combination of the two companies might be. Nor do I see how this union you're proposing can be better for me. I enjoy what I am doing so much and business here is so promising that I do not want to risk changing things. Whether you agree with me or not, those are my feelings.
>
> You have been pressuring me for months. Don't try to convince me to sell out my interest in Virginia and merge. I won't do it. I don't know what more I can tell you other than I want our relationship to continue as it has for the past four years. Virginia isn't failing. Can't you see we are succeeding totally?

The last guy in the world I want on the opposite side of the fence is you. But all of our recent exchanges have been loaded with, "Do this, or else." You never call without mentioning how naive I am—that I have no "Sechel"—that's no compliment. The whole essence of your conversation has been loaded with veiled threats. In your office, your marketing manager said that if it were necessary to open an Eastern plant, you would do it, and compete with me. You heard him. You didn't contradict him.

What do you want out of me? I will be happy to continue on our present basis for as long as we find it profitable. I don't want any other basis.

Best Regards,

You are a close associate of Will Madden. When he asks for your help on the letter, would you revise it for him? If so, offer a draft incorporating your changes.

6. ***The Assertive Applicant:*** After working six months in the Textile Corporation of America (TEXCORP) as a marketing analyst, John Mitchell decided to ask for a promotion. TEXCORP was a family-owned textile company with headquarters in New York City and plants in Massachusetts, North Carolina, and South Carolina. Mitchell was 27, married, the father of one child, a business school graduate, and a one-time college football star. He wrote the following letter to his boss, Andrew Thompson, vice-president of sales for one division. He anticipated that the chief executive of the company, William Abbott, would see the letter after Thompson read it. A portion of the letter not important to our purposes here is deleted. This problem is extracted from "Textile Corporation of America," a case in Jay W. Lorsch and Paul R. Lawrence, Eds., *Managing Group and Intergroup Relations* (Homewood, Ill., Richard D. Irwin, 1972), pp. 136–137.

Dear Andy,

I hope this note will help you understand my as yet unresolved anxieties concerning my future here in TEXCORP. I am putting this in writing to save your time and to facilitate any further discussions. Let me try and describe my perspective.

First, I see a lot of work to be done at all levels of the organization. Much of this work is a matter of analysis (data collection, organization, setting priorities, etc.). Systems must be set up, studies made, programs established and monitored, etc.

Second, I see a limited number of people with the background and training to accomplish all of the analytical work that has to be done.

Third, I see myself and my own selfish goals. I have spent all of my lengthy (four year) business career doing analytical staff work. I have developed a certain facility for this kind of work. But it no longer offers the challenge I desire. I want to assume more complete responsibilities. I want to be a boss. I want to be able to look back and say, "Look, I did that . . . that's my success." When I spoke to you earlier, I hoped you might have a line position for me in your division. I have been told—and I am forced to agree—that I lack the experience to be a line manager in Sales or in Manufacturing. Those are the only two lines at the divisional level.

Given what I see around me, I conclude that from the organization's point of view, I should be in a position where I could move freely about; conduct market studies in the divisions, assist Engineering in plant relocation studies, help establish systems and procedures, etc. (As William would say, "For Chrissake, John, we have so much to do, let's just do it!") I would need some source and position of authority that everyone saw as "legitimate" so that cooperation would be maximized. I guess my present status and title of "Assistant to the President" seems best suited to these organizational needs.

From a personal point of view, however, this role is less than ideal. . . . I would like to be in the position of Vice President of Administrative Services. Here I would have the challenge of line responsibility and the opportunity to test myself. (Although I still wouldn't have the kind of "line" challenge and satisfaction you have when you sell a good fabric order, or a plant manager has when he reads the bottom line of his P&L statement.) In charge of administration I would still have both the time and the authority to conduct the needed analytical studies and services. I would be available to all departments—both informally and formally. In this position I would also be able to involve myself in those kinds of administrative tasks that do not require twenty years of experience in the textile business.

Before you laugh at my conceit, let me explain why I think it's a reasonable gamble from the organization's point of view. We all agreed some time ago that the job should be created. We knew that systems were needed and that a man was needed to supervise these tasks as well as Purchasing and Credit (neither of which involve close or imaginative supervision). Bill Berkeley can handle the job, and I've heard his name mentioned. But he has said "No" to both of us privately, and I doubt anyone will change his mind.

"NOW WAIT A MINUTE!! You really want me to say you can be VP of Administrative Services?!?" Yes, I'm only 27 (But, just think! I'll be 28 in June!) Yes, I just started shaving last year. Yes, only six months in textiles . . . only six months in this company. I realize William is the man to talk to in the end. It's his ball game. But with your understanding and support, my feelings, expectations, and anxieties can be more carefully presented to him. Anyway, I've got enough guts to think I can do a better job there than anyone else we've got. And I don't think it's the kind of position that a new man would be able to take over. I'd be the lowest paid VP in the city, and that'll help our budgets.

I'd like to speak with you about this note and try to cover the 100 other questions that arise from my cocky, impertinent ambition before approaching William.

If and when you show this to William, remind him he once told me to stick around because "the way we are, there are plenty of opportunities to learn." Remind him he said that, and then ask him how he learned to catch a football.

John

If John Mitchell possessed your understanding and skill in written communications, would he have written the letter in this way? Write revisions of any paragraphs that would have been different.

7. ***Misery at the Met:*** Rudolf Bing, for many years the manager of the Metropolitan Opera in New York, was bothered perennially by "the truly unceasing clamor of the bankers," that is, the trustees who thought he was spending too much money. In the interests of compromise he "cooked with water a little bit," as he and his fellows put it, in planning productions, but it was always clear that he valued economy less than the trustees did. In the spring of 1952 he wrote a long letter to Lowell Wadmond, one of the trustees. The major portions of the letter are reproduced below, with permission from Rudolf Bing, *5,000 Nights at the Opera* (Garden City, N.Y.: Doubleday 1972), pp. 328–329.

> An opera organization can be run on an expensive level or on a cheap level. I am trying to run the Metropolitan Opera, deliberately and with conviction, on the expensive level. However, on either level operations can be conducted extravagantly or economically. I also believe that I am conducting our affairs on their expensive level in an economic manner. I also believe, however, that important members of the Board consider the fact that our operations are on an expensive level already as extravagant. That, I think, is the basic point of difference. Therefore, however important an addition to the budget of $30,000 or so may be, this would not solve the basic question of approach to the whole problem of the level on which the Metropolitan Opera's management should be conducted. . . .
>
> One of the main points at issue between some members of the Board and myself is the question of new productions and the large expense involved in such new productions. Naturally, it is the way of least resistance to say "let us cut new productions" and thereby of course save all the money involved which, indeed, may balance our budget . . .
>
> The enormous success accorded to our new productions and the almost exaggerated interest suddenly shown in the Metropolitan Opera, both nationally and internationally, speak pretty clearly that changes were overdue and are welcomed even though individuals may disapprove of individual measures, which is only natural . . . [Yet] I still have the impression that some members of the Board seem

> to think that the new productions are more or less a private fancy of mine and that in particular I wanted these vehicles to show off my own ability for what it may be worth. These members of the Board do not seem to recognize that I do not look upon these productions as my special toys but as the basic artistic necessity to revitalize the Metropolitan and to make it what it once was and what it should be—the world's leading opera house. I hope I may feel that the beginning of my efforts in that respect have at least shown that I am on the right way.
>
> Now, Mr. Sloan very rightly has taken up my statement at a recent committee meeting that I don't think that $50,000 per production is an adequate figure . . . The whole difference arises from—if I may be forgiven for saying it—what is in my view a wrong approach to the budget. It is unrealistic to say "here are $150,000, and now go ahead and make three productions." The only realistic way is to ask what three new productions will cost and then provide the funds accordingly. I am greatly distressed that in this year's budget the $200,000 figure originally provided for new productions will appear considerably overspent; but again it is not a question of having spent recklessly, carelessly or extravagantly. If you only had the time I could prove to you in innumerable cases where and how we have cut expenses and saved money but—and this brings me to the first part of my letter—we are of course operating on an expensive level and this is the basic question. I have come here under the impression that I was supposed to manage the world's leading opera house in the world's capital within the world's most important country. This is not only a privilege but it is a great responsibility with many obligations. These obligations as I see them, and I admit this frankly, are in the first place artistic. The Metropolitan Opera will be judged by future critics on its artistic merits and not on deficits or profits.

How, if at all, might the letter have been different if you had been in Bing's shoes? Write out the paragraphs that would be changed.

8. ***Managerial Mordancy:*** Write an improved version of the following memorandum. Assume that all division managers in the corporation (see the chart on page 426) are roughly equal in status.

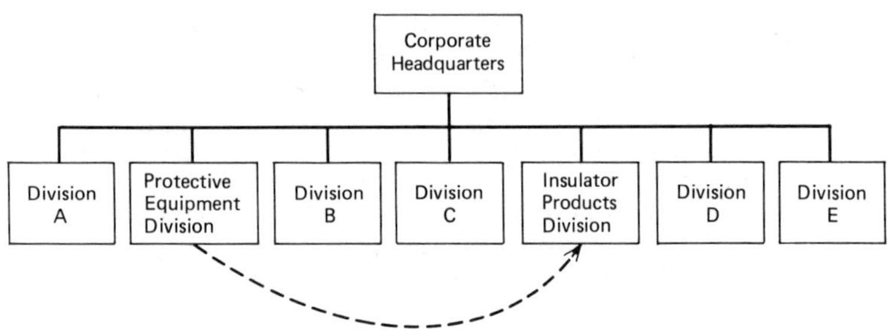

May 21

FROM: Manager of Protective Equipment Division

TO: Manager of Insulator Products Division

As one of your largest internal divisional customers, I want to call your personal attention to the poor delivery performance of your Muskegon Plant on high voltage porcelains. This is causing severe customer problems for our department with both internal and external organizational customers as well as utilities. I know I don't have to emphasize the critical nature of dealing with divisional customers.

At this point I want you to be aware of the fact that your performance in April and May has been abominable. You really only made 55% of the promised units against the April schedule. The balance was received too late to do anything in the way of assembly. Saleswise, this cost my division over $87,000 in billing in the month of April and many, many phone calls and literally hundreds of hours in delivery extensions and expediting with the resulting promises missed to our customers.

What is particularly hard to understand is that you enjoy such a good reputation in your bushing business on service to corporate divisional customers and you treat us so poorly on arrester housings. I know that your department can use the additional billing this year. I also want you to know that you have already lost business from us because of this performance. We cannot tolerate a loss in billings of an estimated $110,000 in the months of March and April. I would like to have you come over and meet personally with me and tell me what you are going to do to meet June and July schedules.

9. ***Epistle from an Editor:*** Despite some evidence to the contrary, editors are human. Therefore their writings can be reviewed critically, too. An editor wrote the following letter to an author (whose name has been changed) who had submitted an article proposal and possessed good credentials for writing a journal article on the subject mentioned.

> Dear Dr. Alemap:
>
> I am in receipt of your letter of July 11.
>
> I am of the opinion that the subject of your proposed article on tumor therapy would be suitable for our audience, but I encounter some difficulty in respect to the elements of your approach. It exhibits a tendency to rely on subjective opinion, and I find also that the emphasis is arbitrary. For the purpose of attracting our readers, you would do well to strive for a more balanced presentation.
>
> Consequently, while I am willing to read your article when it is completed, I am unable to commit our board of editors in advance to your article.
>
> On the assumption that you will proceed on these terms, please notify my office as to when we may expect the completed article.
>
> Very Sincerely Yours,

See if you can improve this letter by revising it. Assume that the journal's editorial policy was to encourage the submission of articles by authorities like Dr. Alemap.

10. ***Missions of MTMTS:*** The third quarter progress report for fiscal year 1972 of the Military Traffic Management and Terminal Service (MTMTS) was sent to the Assistant Secretary of Defense with a covering letter from Major General Clarence J. Lang. The progress report began with a "Special Report" entitled "Conserving Defense Transportation Dollars." The first half of this report, including a boxed-off insert, is reproduced below.

The MTMTS Technical Regulatory Review Group protects the interests of the Department of Defense against the publication of rates and charges that adversely affect military traffic and instigates litigation before regulatory bodies or courts when unlawful rates and charges are discovered.

Picture a $400,000,000 DOD freight transportation bill representing the cost of two million CONUS shipments with the cost of each shipment developed from carrier tariffs. Visualize a file of 8,500 tariffs and Section 22 tenders which prescribe rates, charges, and rules numbering literally in the trillions. Add thousands of changes in rates, charges, and rules occurring daily and you have the problem faced by the MTMTS Technical Regulatory Review Group in assuring that transportation charges are fair and reasonable to the Department of Defense (DOD) as well as compensatory to the carriers.

Conserving the Defense transportation dollar starts with reviewing carrier docket rate proposals for adverse impact in the form of increased transportation charges. Action against increased charges takes the form of protests to individual carriers or carrier bureaus against proposals detrimental to DOD interests, petitions to Federal regulatory bodies for relief from carrier published supplements, and appeals against adverse decisions. When required, technical information is developed to support complaints and litigation. A clear understanding of the meaning of review, protest, petition, appeal and complaint actions and their relationships with dockets, published supplements, and decisions is essential to a fuller appreciation of the efforts of the four man Technical Regulatory Review Group.

The Group is alerted to potentially detrimental situations by reviewing carrier dockets; by keeping a vigilant eye on published supplements announcing rate changes within 30 days; by cases referred by the General Accounting Office, by DOD and its various elements; and by situations arising from unsuccessful negotiations. As with an iceberg, the visible actions of the Group to protect the Government's interest are only a fraction of the total mass of documents which form the foundation on which every case is won or lost. . . .

The normal rate case starts with a proposed change submitted by a carrier or carrier bureau in the form of a docket;

however, changes may also be proposed by shippers. During calendar year 1971, approximately 225,000 rate proposals or docket items were initiated by carriers and shippers. The Review Group completed a cursory review of approximately 175,000 items and selected 3,517 items for detailed analysis. Selection was based on priority of interest with top priority given, in order, to those involving Section 22 rates, rules, and charges; commercial tariff changes affecting DOD traffic; and, lastly, commercial tariff charges having only an indirect bearing on the Department of Defense.

The detailed analyses of 3,517 items resulted in the filing of 160 protests with the carrier bureaus. Basically, the initiation of a protest reflected the determination that the proposed change had an adverse impact on the DOD. . . .

Action	Against	By	To	Purpose
Review	Docket Rate	MTMTS	Carrier / Carrier	Accept /Reject
Protest	Docket Rate	MTMTS	Bureau	Withdrawal / Amendment
Petition	Published Supplement	MTMTS	ICC	Suspension and Investigation
Appeal	ICC Decision	MTMTS	ICC	Reconsideration
Complaint	Established Rate	MTMTS	ICC	Stop Alleged Violations

If you had been given this portion of the report in rough draft form to revise as you saw fit, what would your revised copy look like?

11. ***Assault on the AMA:*** In 1961 two rival vaccines for polio, the Salk (killed vaccine injected by needle) and Sabin (live vaccine taken orally) were competing for approval by the American Medical Association. When Dr. Jonas Salk learned that the House of Delegates of the AMA had decided to report in favor of the Sabin concept, he wrote a long and angry letter to the heads of the AMA. "Of course

I was mad," Salk told his biographer, Richard Carter. "And of course I fought back. I did so knowing very well that my motives would be misconstrued. People would think that Salk was defending himself against Sabin, or defending his 'product' against Sabin's. But a scientific principle was at stake." Portions of Salk's letter are reproduced below, from Richard Carter, *Breakthrough: the Saga of Jonas Salk* (New York: Trident, 1966), pp. 375–379.

> The physicians of this country and the public are interested in the control of polio. They are less concerned with whether this is accomplished by a killed-virus vaccine or a live-virus vaccine; and in this they are joined by the writer of this communication. The people are interested in a vaccine that is safe, effective, and available. Their own experience makes them aware of the fact that polio has been sharply reduced by the killed-virus vaccination procedure that has been practiced in the United States. Factual evidence substantiates the view that failure to use the vaccine which has been available for six years in the United States has prevented the earlier eradication of polio in this country. They understand that this is related to, if not wholly caused by, social and economic factors which, in turn, are related to a deeper social problem . . .
>
> No issue is taken with the House of Delegates or its councils or committees for their desire to approve the use of a live-virus vaccine for polio. Nor is issue taken with their desire to apply mass vaccination procedures for the use of live-virus vaccines. Issue is taken for failure to acknowledge scientific facts and for recommending action based upon a medical dogma that can no longer be maintained in the light of scientific evidence and of experience in practice. Issue is taken for failure to acknowledge the degree of individual and community protection that has resulted from killed-virus vaccination and for failure to acknowledge evidence for durability of immunity. All of this opens to question the justification for the conclusions reached with respect to the action of the House of Delegates in a matter that concerns the health of the nation. The House of Delegates is establishing a precedent in endorsing medications or biologicals still in the stage of development and in recommending to physicians which medications they should and should not use. . . . Responsibility for the

> awkwardness with which the country has proceeded in the past several years toward the control of polio cannot be ascribed to the vaccine that has been available but must rest with all those who have the authority and the power to influence and to administer preventive measures that are available but who place questions of procedure above purpose and goals.
>
> It is superfluous to say that the sincerity of the AMA's desire to bring about the end of polio as soon as possible is not questioned, but their sincerity would be conveyed and expressed more convincingly if they were to declare war on polio to the finish under AMA leadership, starting now, and with whatever vaccine preparations are available to be applied by mass vaccination techniques. While this might imply a tacit admission that this should have been done sooner, it would be more acceptable than to make it appear that the proper vaccine for effective immunization is not yet available.

Suppose Dr. Salk had asked you, while this letter was still in rough draft, to "fix it up." Offer a revision to him.

Fine writing is next to fine doing,
the top thing in the world.

John Keats

Appendix

To illustrate the range of issues that writing instructors and students should expect to be raised when one of the cases in this book is discussed in class, let us consider "Mrs. Beard's Bombshell" at the end of Chapter 2.

As some readers will recall, Beard's memorandum was one of the big news stories of the early 1970s. Within three weeks of columnist Jack Anderson's exposé, "the furor created by the memorandum had generated a series of charges, countercharges, denials, counter-denials, evidence and 'newly found' counter-evidence, some of which was extremely bizarre in nature. It became a sort of high-stakes game of 'can you top this?' "[1]

But in considering the wisdom of Beard's decision to

[1]Arthur I. Blaustein and Geoffrey Faux, *The Star-Spangled Hustle* (Garden City, N.Y., Doubleday, 1972), p. 235.

send the memo, it is unfair to judge in the light of hindsight. No decision maker has this luxury. So let us put ourselves in Mrs. Beard's place on June 25, 1971. How might we have thought about the question then, knowing only what she knew? How much weight to attach to the pros and cons is a question readers must decide for themselves, but considerations like the following should be part of any careful appraisal.

In favor of sending the memo are the following arguments:

1. If Mrs. Beard really wants to impress Mr. Merriam (the addressee), perhaps she can shock him more by putting it in writing than by a telephone call.
2. Perhaps she has tried to reach Mr. Merriam by phone but could not get through to him.
3. She may have almost absolute confidence in the delivery system of ITT. (Remember, we do not know for sure, even now, that this memorandum was actually sent; it is what Jack Anderson's informants *claim* was sent.)
4. Mrs. Beard may fear that her telephone is being tapped, or, at least, that this possibility is greater than that of interception in the company mail system.

Arguments against sending the memo are:

1. Several times in the memorandum Mrs. Beard stresses her understanding that none of this highly sensitive business is to be aired in any way. Then why add to the risk by putting it all down on paper? This is for a personal face-to-face meeting somewhere out of reach of anyone's ear or interception device!
2. "We all know Hal and his big mouth!" Mrs. Beard writes. Remember that Hal is the chief executive of ITT. Is it wise to say something like this in such a way that there is *any* risk of its being heard or seen by someone else? A politically wise person like Mrs. Beard should know that wisdom in secret projects like this calls for anticipating the worst that may happen (that is, interception), and using tactics to avoid that risk.

3. "Please destroy this, huh?" Mrs. Beard asks at the end. Isn't this a concession that she really shouldn't be saying this in writing? After all, Mr. Merriam isn't thousands of miles away. He's head of the ITT office right in Washington!

The Beard memorandum can be discussed from standpoints other than Chapter 2. For instance, does it start well enough? Depending on your assumptions about the closeness between writer and reader and how recently they have been thrashing out these problems, you could argue that the start is appropriate or inappropriate. Again, is the material in the memorandum organized as clearly as it should be? There is a tendency for "sprawl" here, though again the conversational nature of the memo may excuse some of it. What about the tone? The last two paragraphs are interesting in this connection.

What about correctness? Even allowing generously for the informal, offhand nature of the memo, some opportunities for editing are present. The word "commitment" is misspelled several times. (This error, by the way, might be one way to check on the authenticity of the document. Did Beard habitually misspell the word in her other unedited writing?) Writing "400 thousand" instead of $400,000 or $400 thousand is awkward. At the end of the third sentence in the first paragraph, "including me" is left dangling out of place at the end of the sentence; it might better be inserted after the words "anyone" or "office" (thus: "under no circumstances would anyone in this office, including me, discuss with anyone . . .").

It might be interesting also to discuss the memorandum from the standpoint of style. Personally, I rather like the offhand, somewhat satirical, tête-a-tête style. However, some wise writers and instructors I know would surely argue against it.

Finally, consider the memorandum in terms of the writer's wheel, as described in Chapter 14. For instance, if you take a liberal, generous position on the question of style, you will take a rather loose attitude toward correctness. Thus you might be expected to pay no attention to some lapses in punctuation, such as the comma dividing the last sentence of the first paragraph instead of using a period or semicolon as a divider. On the other hand, if you take a strict position, arguing that anything worth writing, even an offhand memo, is worth writing carefully, then you would logically argue in favor of improving the punctuation in that sentence and in several others, in favor of deleting the adjective "very" in front of "thoroughly" in the second sentence of the first paragraph (how can something be done more thoroughly than just thoroughly?), and other changes.

Index